PAUL
AND THE SALVATION
OF MANKIND

PAUL
AND THE SALVATION
OF MANKIND

JOHANNES MUNCK

SCM PRESS LTD

Translated by Frank Clarke from the German
Paulus und die Heilsgeschichte
Universitetsforlaget, Aarhus and Ejnar Munksgaard,
Copenhagen, 1954

550707
H

334 01229 5
First published in English 1959
by SCM Press Ltd
56 Bloomsbury Street, London WC1
Second impression 1977

Translation © SCM Press Ltd 1959

Printed in Great Britain by
Fletcher & Son Ltd, Norwich

JENS NØRREGAARD
IN MEMORIAM

CONTENTS

PREFACE

The studies of Paul that are presented here began by chance, and in a way the investigation pursued its own course from one point to another, so that the book wrote itself and gave its author endless trouble to write it as it ought to be written. From an investigation limited to the apostle's call, the way led on to Paul's apostleship and the most important problems relating to it; and it gradually became necessary to deal with practically all the essential problems within the scope of Pauline studies and of primitive Christianity. The work has therefore extended over a longer period than was originally expected. Indeed, a number of questions must be postponed to a later publication (which I announced earlier) dealing with the apostolate in the New Testament.

It is not possible here to thank all those who have helped me in many different ways during my work on this book. I remember with gratitude that the theological faculty in Lund (1948), Studiorum Novi Testamenti Societas (1950), and the theological faculty in Oslo (1951), by invitations to lecture, gave me the opportunity of presenting single sections of the book in their provisional form, and of discussing them with colleagues. Besides the above-mentioned separate investigation of the apostle's call, originally published in an abbreviated form in the *Nørregaard Festschrift*, 1947, and later in *ST* 1, 1948, pp. 131–45, under the title 'La vocation de l'Apôtre Paul', one of the Lund lectures has appeared in *ST* 3, 1950, pp. 96–110, as 'Paul, the Apostles, and the Twelve'; and the Oxford lecture has appeared in *JTS*, n.s. 2, 1951, pp. 3–16, as 'Israel and the Gentiles in the New Testament'. Also my treatise *Petrus und Paulus in der Offenbarung Johannis* (Publications de la Société des Sciences et des Lettres d'Aarhus, Série de Théologie, I, 1950), and the article 'Discours d'adieu dans le Nouveau Testament et dans la littérature biblique' in *Aux Sources de la Tradition Chrétienne, Mélanges offerts à M. Maurice Goguel*, 1950, pp. 155–70, originated as investigations that were necessary as preliminary work on this book. My thanks are also due to participants in my seminar, whose co-operation has prompted and furthered my own reflections. The fruitful joint work in the Collegium Biblicum has also been of great importance for my studies.

But I wish very specially to express my thanks to the man to whose memory this book is dedicated. When I was quite a young student, I was taught in his seminar at Copenhagen, and there I learnt scholarly method by working on patristic texts. It was there that my love of research was first aroused as a necessary preliminary to the years of study on which this book is based. Jens Nørregaard was not only the great teacher, the centre of vigorous growth; he was also the man whom the University of Copenhagen chose as its Rector during the German occupation. During the worst of the Terror he was the fearless representative of Danish civilization and humanity at its best. It was my privilege to be in close and intimate co-operation with him during those difficult years. I had asked to be allowed to dedicate this book to him. Today it is sad not to be able to hear his criticism, which was always friendly but unsparing. Now I must content myself, instead, with dedicating this book to the memory of a great teacher and a faithful friend.

At the last revision my friend Professor Bent Noack, Th.D., read and criticized the MS., and thereby greatly helped both author and readers. I offer him my hearty thanks for doing so. For the translated biblical quotations I have used the Zürich Bible,[1] but where it seemed to me necessary, I have changed the text without comment. The MS. was being translated from April to November 1953, and the whole book was set up in type before the end of the year. From the New Year to Whitsuntide 1954 I was travelling in Palestine and the Near East, and I was therefore unable to take account of the literature of 1953 and 1954.

I must again express my thanks to my wife.

JOHANNES MUNCK

[1] In the English translation the Revised Standard Version has been used, with occasional modifications by the author. (Translator's note.)

I

THE CALL

WHEN Paul was on his way to Damascus to extend the persecution of the Christians by the Jews into that city, he was stopped short by a revelation. Christ spoke to him and called him, and the zealous Pharisee and tireless persecutor was baptized in the church of Damascus, and then went out to take the Gospel to the Gentiles. That is how the Acts of the Apostles, and Paul himself, described the turning-point of his life. It is a meeting between the risen Christ and his passionate opponent, through which the latter is forced from the path that he has hitherto followed, and is set on the way along which his new Master is leading him.

Scholars have been reluctant to confirm this account, as they thought that such a complete change of course could not be effected so suddenly and without preparation, and that there must have been something in Paul's earlier life which predisposed him towards it, some previous history that could explain the meeting with Christ near Damascus. The attempted explanations are numerous, and vary greatly in value. Some have sought this predisposition in the Jewish religion, whose piety based on the Law is supposed to have been a terrible burden to the young Pharisee. Others have pointed to Paul's intensive preoccupation with Christianity and his continual contact with Jesus' disciples, by which the persecutor was impressed and attracted. And lastly, an attempt has been made to find the preparation for Damascus in the religiosity of Hellenism.[1]

What these attempts have in common is that they are really working on suppositions without documentary support. A former period regarded Rom. 7.7 ff. as an autobiographical section, and saw the antecedent of Paul's conversion in his realization that the fulfilling of the Law was impossible. That view has been generally abandoned; but there will still be many who see in Paul's struggle with the Law during his life as a Jew the antecedent of the Damascus experience.[2] It is

[1]These and other explanations appear in E. Pfaff: *Die Bekehrung des h. Paulus in der Exegese des 20. Jahrhunderts* (Rome, 1942), a work through which some idea can be obtained of a number of articles and extracts not available in northern libraries.
[2]So Deissmann, *St Paul*, ET 1912, p. 122. Kümmel, in *Römer 7 und die Bekehrung des Paulus* (UNT 17), 1929, produced ample evidence to refute the exposition of Rom.

11

reasonable to suppose that Paul's contact with Christianity set the scene for his activities as a persecutor, but we do not know the extent of that contact, nor in particular its effect on him. Nor do we know much about Paul's attitude to Hellenism before Damascus.[1]

7.7 ff. as a description of Paul's earlier life as a Jew. Later, in contrast to Nygren's interpretation in his *Commentary on Romans*, ET 1952, pp. 277 ff., Lyder Brun defended the autobiographical view of Rom. 7.7 ff. in an article, 'Rm. 7.7–25 ennu engang', *SEA* 12 (Lindblom Festschrift), 1947, pp. 67–84. As an example of these interpretations of Rom. 7.7 ff. as representing Paul's earlier life, we may quote Deissmann, *loc. cit.*: 'The conversion of the persecutor to the follower, and of the apostle of the Pharisees to the apostle of Christ, was a sudden one. But it was no magical transformation; it was psychologically prepared for, both negatively and positively. Negatively, by the experiences which the soul of the young Pharisee, in its passionate hunger for righteousness, had had under the yoke of the Law. We hear the echo of his groanings even twenty or thirty years afterwards in the letters of the convert: like a curse there had come upon him the awful discovery that even for the most earnest conscience, in fact especially for the most earnest conscience, it is impossible really to keep the whole Law. Positively the conversion was no doubt prepared for on the one hand by the prophetic inwardness of the old revelation acting on Paul the Jew, and on the other hand by a relatively close familiarity with genuine tradition about Jesus and the effects that Jesus was able to produce in the persons of the confessors of Jesus whom Paul persecuted.' Again, Dibelius writes on Phil. 3.7: 'To the disillusioned Pharisee, the gospel of Freedom from the Law was salvation from his most dire distress.'

While modern research at first thus regards Paul's conversion as an ideal experience of the Law's oppressive weight and of liberation by the Gospel (although Phil. 3.7 shows that Paul did not come to Christ out of despair under the Law, but that Christ showed him the way to break with the Law), psychology gradually becomes more and more prominent; and as this science progresses, ideas and expressions change. As an example, we may mention here G. J. Inglis, 'The Problem of St Paul's Conversion', *Expository Times* 40, 1928–9, pp. 227–31. With regard to this drift to the psychological, I should like to quote a passage by Loisy from his article 'La Conversion de Paul et la Naissance du Christianisme', *Revue d'Histoire et de Littérature Religieuses* 5, 1914, pp. 289 f.: 'The account of his conversion, assuming that it is historical, has none of the features of a psychological study; it is sheer miracle, and we are not told what led up to it.'

[1]Thus Hans Böhlig's investigation, *Die Geisteskultur von Tarsos im augusteischen Zeitalter mit Berücksichtigung der paulinischen Schriften* (Forschungen zur Religion und Literatur des Alten und Neuen Testaments, n. F. 2), 1913, is on the whole an unprofitable excursion. Quite apart from the questionable method of proceeding from the assumption that Paul's environment must have influenced him (Albert Schweitzer deals sharply but suitably with that particular bias when he says in *Paul and his Interpreters*, ET 1912, p. 87: 'The greater probability, however, is on the side of the assumption of exclusiveness. Although he lived in the middle of Hellenism, it is possible that Paul absorbed no more of it than a Catholic parish priest of the twentieth century does of the critical theology, and knew no more about it than an Evangelical pastor knows of theosophy. The decision lies solely with his works'), Böhlig has first to reconstruct the society that is supposed to have influenced Paul in Tarsus; and both in this reconstruction and in showing parallels in Paul's letters he is very uncritical. When Böhlig wrote his book, he had to point out that there was no information about excavations in Tarsus. Since then there have been excavations at Gözlü Kule in the south-west corner of modern Tarsus, under which is situated the greater part of ancient Tarsus; in the meantime there has appeared *Excavations at Gözlü Kule, Tarsus*, Vol. I, Text, The Hellenistic and Roman Periods, with the companion Vol. I, Plates, Princeton, 1950, edited by Hetty Goldman, who conducted the excavations. While it will be realized that a solution of the problems raised by Böhlig can scarcely be provided by the excavation of parts of a poor suburb of ancient Tarsus, the fact is worth mentioning that the statuettes of religious

Moreover, these attempts to explain events as they are described in the New Testament, by a series of psychological and other circumstances of which we know nothing certain, have had an unfavourable influence on the treatment of the texts. People have lost interest in the dramatic occurrence at Damascus and the brief but decisive conversation with Christ, and have instead become engrossed in the spiritual anguish that Paul experienced—or rather, is supposed to have experienced—about which, in fact, we have no information.

Here we will try to take from the narrative of the Damascus experience some salient features that may contribute to its understanding.

I

First it must be stressed that the texts agree that there is no previous history about it. The Damascus experience comes without any preparation.

In this connexion there is no difference between Gal. 1.13–17 and Acts 9.1–19a, 22.3–16, and 26.4–18. In the three accounts from Acts, and in Paul's own account of his conversion and call to the apostleship, it is stressed that there is indeed a previous history, but quite a different one from what is usually found in recent research. Paul is described as a Jew and a persecutor, and directly afterwards there follows the account of the sudden meeting with Christ.

In Acts 9.1 ff. the description of Paul as a Jew is lacking, but on the other hand his zeal in persecuting the Christians is stressed: ἔτι ἐμπνέων ἀπειλῆς καὶ φόνου εἰς τοὺς μαθητὰς τοῦ Κυρίου, as is the authority, obtained at his urgent request from the High Priest, to continue the persecution in Damascus. In 22.4 f. we are told that Paul persecuted the Christians ἄχρι θανάτου (corresponding to φόνου in 9.1), but we are not told that the mission to Damascus was at his instigation. The most impressive account of Paul as a persecutor is found in 26.9–11, where details are given, whereas in v. 12[1] the mission to Damascus is only mentioned in passing. In Gal. 1.13 this side of his earlier life is mentioned only quite briefly.[2]

---

interest that were found there are more of a Greek, and less of an oriental kind, than might have been supposed from Böhlig's description of Tarsus. No trace of Jewish inhabitants was found, and the Christian graves that were found are not from the time of the mission.

[1] On the other hand its connexion with the rest of the story is brought out more clearly in v. 11: περισσῶς τε ἐμμαινόμενος αὐτοῖς ἐδίωκον ἕως καὶ εἰς τὰς ἔξω πόλεις.

[2] In certain details there is a close correspondence between Acts 9.1 f. and 22.4 f. The two passages have in common τῆς ὁδοῦ (τὴν ὁδὸν) and ἄνδρας τε καὶ γυναῖκας, δεδεμένους ἀγάγῃ (ἄξων). 22.5 makes the letters to Damascus come, not from the High Priest (9.1 f.), but from ὁ ἀρχιερεὺς καὶ πᾶν τὸ πρεσβυτέριον, while according

In the accounts of Paul as a Jew there are greater differences. As already mentioned, no such account appears in Acts 9; but in 22.3 he refers to Tarsus as his native place, and to his further studies under Gamaliel in Jerusalem, and says[1] that he is πεπαιδευμένος κατὰ ἀκρίβειαν τοῦ πατρῴου νόμου . . . , after which he goes on with the words ζηλωτὴς ὑπάρχων τοῦ Θεοῦ καθὼς πάντες ὑμεῖς ἐστε σήμερον (like the roaring sea of people in front, who a moment before had been trying to lynch him) to speak of his persecution of the Christians. In 26.4–8 Paul gives a more precise description of the Jewish period of his life before Damascus. Both here and in Gal. 1.13 there is an indication that he is relating what everyone knows. The latter passage indicates that the Galatian churches knew of his past; and it is therefore probable that the story of his call was part of the Christian education of his churches. According to Acts 26 the story of his Jewish past was well known to all the Jews; and the part of it that was well known to them was the fact that Paul had been a Pharisee. In his own account in the letter to the Galatians, it is emphasized how he stood out from his contemporaries[2] and was particularly zealous for the traditions of the fathers.[3]

---

to 26.10 Paul generally obtained his authority from the chief priests (παρὰ τῶν ἀρχιερέων ἐξουσίαν λαβών . . .), and in v. 12 he is going to Damascus μετ' ἐξουσίας καὶ ἐπιτροπῆς τῆς τῶν ἀρχιερέων. Chs. 9, 22, and 26 have only a few expressions in common, but φυλακὰς (φυλακαῖς) occurs in 22.4 and 26.10. There is no point of contact with the account in Gal. 1.13, apart from the use of the verbs διώκω and πορθέω (Gal. 1.13) which corresponds to ὁ πορθήσας in Acts 9.21 (cf. Lake and Cadbury *ad loc.*, and O. Linton: 'The Third Aspect. A Neglected Point of View. A Study in Galatians 1–2 and Acts 9 and 15', *ST* 3, 1950, p. 81). It is interesting that the four accounts use different terms to denote Christians: Acts 9.1, τοὺς μαθητὰς τοῦ Κυρίου; 22.5, τοὺς ἀδελφούς; 26.10, τῶν ἁγίων; Gal. 1.13, τὴν ἐκκλησίαν τοῦ Θεοῦ (as in other passages, where Paul describes himself as a persecutor: I Cor. 15.9; Phil. 3.6 where ἐκκλησία is used alone).

[1]On 22.3 see W. C. van Unnik, *Tarsus of Jerusalem, De Stad van Paulus' Jeugd,* met een appendix over: 'het gebruik van τρέφω en verwante woorden in verband met de opvoeding', *Mededel. d. K. Nederl. Ak. van Wetenschappen, Afd. Letterk. N.R., Deel* 15, No. 5, Amsterdam, 1952.

[2]In spite of all the differences, there is a certain parallel in the use of ὑπέρ and the note struck in Test. Joseph 18.4: καὶ ὡραιότητα ἔδωκέ μοι ὑπὲρ ὡραίους Ἰσραήλ.

[3]In Acts 26 those traditions are named, while in 22.3 the Law of the fathers is mentioned; the word ζηλωτής occurs both in Acts 22.3 and in Gal. 1.14. A parallel to the latter passage is in Josephus, *Ant.* XX.2.5, § 41: ζηλοῦν τὰ πάτρια τῶν Ἰουδαίων, where, however, the expression is used in the more comprehensive sense of belonging to the Jewish religion. We see another example of Paul's earlier history in Phil. 3.5 f.: κατὰ νόμον Φαρισαῖος, κατὰ ζῆλος διώκων τὴν ἐκκλησίαν, κατὰ δικαιοσύνην τὴν ἐν νόμῳ γενόμενος ἄμεμπτος. Here we have in the second part of the sentence Paul as a persecutor (cf. Gal. 1.13), and in the third the Jewish period of Paul's life, with expressions which are not the same as those in Acts 22.3 and Gal. 1.14, but which fit quite well into the rest of the letter to the Philippians. The first part might be grouped with the other details in v. 5; but it is joined to the two other parts in v. 6 by the twice repeated κατά (cf. Dibelius on this passage, p. 88). This first part, the only passage in which Paul uses the word Φαρισαῖος, reminds one of the description of Paul as a Pharisee in Acts 26.5–8. Acts 26.4 might serve here as a parallel to the third part of the sentence, κατὰ δικαιοσύνην τὴν ἐν νόμῳ γενόμενος ἄμεμπτος, and

Both these facts—his position in the Jewish community and his opposition to and persecution of Christianity—lead singly and jointly to the conclusion that he went to Damascus not only without any preparation for Christ, but as one who was to quite a special degree proof against the Gospel.

The narrative of the Damascus experience itself also assumes the most diverse forms. Only the brief exchanges between Christ and Paul at the beginning of the vision are given in exactly the same words in the three accounts in Acts. They are the well-known words: 'Saul, Saul, why do you persecute me?' 'Who are you, Lord?' 'I am Jesus[1] whom you are persecuting.' In the introductory verses there is again a closer connexion between 9.3 and 22.6 than between these two texts and 26.12–14.

Besides the many details into which it is not necessary to enter here,[2] there is one essential difference between the accounts in Acts. What happens according to 9.1 ff. and 22.6 ff. is simply that Paul is stopped short and ordered by Christ to go to Damascus, where he is to hear what he has to do. After that 9.10 ff. tells how Ananias, a disciple in Damascus, receives in a vision the command to go to Paul; and when he refuses on the ground of the latter's reputation as a ruthless persecutor (this again emphasizes the fact that we must regard him, in his previous history, as showing no inclination to Christianity), there come the words explaining Paul's vision, which are not repeated in the conversation that follows between Ananias and Paul. We must, however, assume that such repetition is implied (cf. 9. 6).[3] 22.12 ff. does not relate the childlike and intimate conversation that Ananias had with the glorified Christ; but Ananias goes straight to where Paul is, and

---

to Acts 22.3 and Gal. 1.14; then we should have the same three parts in the speech before King Agrippa as here in Phil. 3.5 f. It is probable, however, that 26.4 is only the introduction to the description of Paul as a Pharisee in 26.5–8, and that this third part of the sentence in Phil. 3.5 f. does not appear in Acts 26, or in Acts 9. When we meet in Phil. 3.5 f. the two often mentioned characteristics of Paul's life before Damascus, in connexion with the facts which, according to Acts, the hearing in Jerusalem particularly stresses, viz., that he has been, and indeed still is, a Pharisee, and that the accusation concerns one of the doctrines of the Pharisees (Acts 23.6; cf. 26.5–8, 19–23), it can well be supposed that the imprisonment reported in Philippians is the Roman imprisonment that followed the prosecution in Jerusalem and Caesarea.

[1] Acts 22.8 adds: 'of Nazareth'.
[2] An exception should be made regarding περὶ μεσημβρίαν in Acts 22.6. Lake and Cadbury remark, p. 280, that the statement as to the time (ἡμέρας μέσης) is also found in 26.13, but not in ch. 9; and they add that Deut. 28.28 f. with the reference to blindness in broad daylight (LXX μεσημβρίας) may possibly have something to do with the insertion of this detail here.
[3] We must also assume that Paul is baptized (Acts 22.16); but after Ananias' invitation in this verse the narrative proceeds at once to Paul's experience in the temple at Jerusalem.

explains the vision to him in words that must be supplemented by the experience that follows directly afterwards in the temple at Jerusalem (22.17–21), where Christ speaks to Paul and sends him to the Gentiles. Acts 26.12 ff. differs from the other accounts in that the experience begins and ends near Damascus; no further scene is added, and Ananias does not appear. It is Christ who gives the explanation in words that come immediately after the pronouncement, ἐγώ εἰμι Ἰησοῦς ὃν σὺ διώκεις, which is common to all the accounts.

Finally, the account in Galatians is not a real parallel on this point, as it does not bring in any of the details which have so far occupied us; on the other hand it is made important by Paul's explanatory words, which soon prove to be very significant as a parallel to the accounts in Acts.

A hypothesis put forward by Kirsopp Lake about the value of the four accounts deserves serious consideration, as it is based on careful observation of the texts and shrewd reflections on their interpretation.[1] Lake is not unduly concerned about the differences that critics so often regard as vital; but he stresses the fact that in 9.6 and 22.10 Paul receives from Jesus the command to go to Damascus, where he will be told what he is to do, whereas in 26.16 ff. he receives with the vision the call to be an apostle. In Lake's view, these differences, which have just been alluded to, are to be regarded seriously if we take into account Paul's statements in Galatians. Then we see that the difference did not arise merely through a natural abbreviation of the narrative. Paul himself says in Galatians that he is an apostle, not from men *(ἀπ' ἀνθρώπων)* nor through man *(δι' ἀνθρώπου,* Gal. 1.1), and in Gal. 1.11 f. he asserts that he had not received from man *(παρὰ ἀνθρώπου)* the gospel that he preached, and that he had not been taught it, but that it had come to him through a revelation of Jesus Christ. And in vv. 15 f. Paul says: As it pleased God 'to reveal his Son to me, in order that I might preach him among the Gentiles, I did not confer with flesh and blood, nor did I go up to Jerusalem to those who were apostles before me, but I went away into Arabia . . .'

In no circumstances, Lake thinks, can these statements agree with the story that Paul did not receive his call direct from Jesus, who only told him to go to Damascus to receive further instructions, and that these were given him by a man named Ananias. If Paul wanted to contradict the narrative in Acts, he could have chosen no better expressions than those that he actually did use when he asserts that he is an apostle 'not from men nor through man'. Or can his assertion that he 'did not confer with flesh and blood' really be more flatly denied

[1] *Beginnings* 5, pp. 188–91.

than by the story that both his baptism and the information that he was to be a witness came to him through Ananias?

Lake thinks that Luke had access to three sources, all of which gave him an account of the experience at Damascus. The first source is Paul himself, the second is the tradition of the church in Jerusalem, and the third is the tradition handed down in the church at Antioch.

It is possible that the story about Ananias was generally known in Jerusalem, and was intended to emphasize that Paul, in spite of all his protests, was an apostle only 'from men' and 'through man'. The narrative in chapter 26, where Ananias is not mentioned, can be brought into line with Paul's own account in the letter to the Galatians. Acts 9 and 22 may possibly be combinations, originating in the church at Antioch, of accounts from Paul and from Jerusalem. But there is no reason to suppose that Ananias is a fictitious character. It is possible that a man of that name made friends with Paul when the latter found himself in Damascus profoundly shaken and half blind, and that Jewish Christians imagined that he acquired more influence over Paul than the latter admitted.

There is, however, a difference between the accounts of Ananias in Acts 9 and 22. In ch. 9 he talks like a Hellenistic Christian of the same type as Luke. He is sent by the Lord, by Jesus, and offers Paul baptism in words that show that baptism and receiving the Holy Spirit go together. The case is otherwise in ch. 22, where Ananias talks like a Jewish Christian of the most primitive type. He is sent by 'the God of our fathers', and Jesus is described neither as 'the Lord' nor as 'the Messiah', but as 'the Just One'.[1] Baptism signifies only cleansing from sins, and the Holy Spirit is not mentioned. It is most probable that ch. 22 is the source, and that ch. 9 is a Hellenized adaptation by Luke. Ananias probably was as he is described in ch. 22; he befriended Paul, and possibly healed him; and so, in spite of Paul's protest, he became known in Jerusalem as the one who had converted him. In ch. 26 Luke left Ananias out of the story, either because he knew that Paul regarded him as of no importance, or because he felt that he was superfluous in a speech before King Agrippa. So the narratives of Paul's conversion in Acts are probably forms of the version that was current in Jerusalem, and give a less full account of it, as Paul himself wished.

This ingenious attempt to balance against each other the four accounts and their variations comes from Paul's claim that his apostleship originated from above, not from men. The text in Galatians formerly

[1]On this see Lake and Cadbury's interesting argument, p. 83, regarding Acts 7.52.

led to the assumption that Paul built up his own gospel from his experience at Damascus, and people were inclined to take his words literally when he says in I Cor. 11.23 that he had received the account of the institution of the Lord's Supper 'from the Lord'. But there is hardly any ground for that; even Paul's words in Galatians must not be interpreted literally. He always proceeds from the assertion that his call as an apostle, and the gospel that he preaches, are from God and not from men; but it can scarcely be doubted that he was baptized in Damascus.[1] A human mediation of this kind, bringing to him baptism and the tradition of the Christian Church, does not prejudice his assertion that both his call and his way of presenting the Gospel were from God and not from men. There is nothing to prevent Ananias from having been an intermediary, when it was a case of supplementing the direct conversation between Christ and Paul.[2]

But it must be added here that what is said in Galatians is not about Damascus and the church there, but only about Jerusalem. It was here that Paul—so his opponents asserted—had received his gospel; and he rejects the assertion, recounting the few occasions that made it possible for him to have any contact with the 'pillars' in Jerusalem—first the short visit three years after the call at Damascus, and then

[1]It might seem natural to write here, 'but it can scarcely be doubted that he was baptized and probably received some preparation for baptism in Damascus' (as I wrote in my manuscript of 1946, which was printed only in an abbreviated form—see Preface). But on working through Acts again, I decided to delete the reference to a preparation for baptism. In Acts, as in the rest of the New Testament, there seems to have been no hesitation about baptizing. In a way that is remarkably casual compared with the modern formal ceremony, one baptizes and goes on one's way. That is what happens with the Ethiopian treasurer (Acts 8.26–40), with Cornelius the centurion (10), with Paul (9.18 and 22.16; see p. 15, note 3), and with the jailer at Philippi (16.25 ff.). The last example is very significant: at midnight, while Paul and Silas were praying and singing hymns, all the prison doors were opened by an earthquake. Paul prevented the jailer from doing himself any harm, and he and Silas preached the word of the Lord to him and to all who were in his house. The jailer washed their wounds, and was baptized at once with all his household. He took them into his house then and there, gave them a meal, and rejoiced with all his household that he had come to believe in God. At daybreak Paul and Silas left the prison and Philippi too. Now it may be that this and the other narratives in Acts were told in such a way as to bring out only their main features, and that what took place over a longer period was condensed into only a few hours. But baptism is put at the beginning of the Christian life—so early, in fact, that no lengthy teaching and examining of the candidate under the more normal conditions of daily life can have been demanded. In contrast to this, see the *Acts of Paul and Thecla*, where Paul says to Thecla (ch. 25), μακροθύμησον, καὶ λήψῃ τὸ ὕδωρ, and after she has administered baptism to herself (ch. 34), she explains to Paul (ch. 40), Ἔλαβον τὸ λουτρόν, Παῦλε· ὁ γὰρ σοὶ συνεργήσας εἰς τὸ εὐαγγέλιον κάμοὶ συνήργησεν εἰς τὸ λούσασθαι . . . .

[2]As we shall see later, Acts 22.14 f. presupposes that Christ has spoken to Paul about his call, although we are not told so in the account of the vision itself. According to 9.11 f., after the experience at Damascus Paul had a vision in which he saw Ananias, who came in and healed him by the laying on of hands. It is difficult to see how the story of Ananias can have satisfied the Jerusalem church, which regarded Paul as an apostle called by men.

fourteen years later the meeting at which he received the assent of the leaders in Jerusalem. Moreover, his dependence on the 'pillars' is refuted by his vigorous encounter with Peter in Antioch, where Peter was rebuked by Paul himself.[1] If Lake were right in thinking that the narrative of Paul's conversion, with Ananias taking a leading part, was a Jerusalem tradition, this narrative would necessarily—according to the usual view of the history of primitive Christianity—have reached the Galatian church; but we have no rejection of this tradition in the letter. The remarks in Galatians that according to Lake are directed against Acts 9 and 22, are really aimed at the accusation that Paul had his apostleship from the 'pillars' in Jerusalem, and at nothing else.

But it is also important that the explanatory words—the words that interpret the occurrence near Damascus and indicate the uniqueness of the call—are not essentially different in the account that is supposed by Lake to be nearest to the Jerusalem version. We read in ch. 22 that Paul is to be a witness for Christ to all men of what he has seen and heard; and in the following narrative about the experience in Jerusalem, Christ speaks directly to him and sends him to the Gentiles. Obviously no distinction is made between the words that Christ speaks through Ananias and those that he speaks directly to Paul.[2] And we should certainly expect that a Jerusalem version—always on the usual assumption of a marked contrast between Paul and the earliest disciples— wanted, by means of the explanatory words, to minimize Paul's apostleship, so that his lower standing and his dependence on the 'pillars' in Jerusalem should stand out clearly.

Finally, we must not ignore the fact that two of the three accounts in Acts are extracts from speeches—ch. 22 from Paul's speech to the excited mob in front of the steps to the Antonia fortress in Jerusalem, after the Jews had just been trying to lynch him in the temple, and ch. 26 from the speech before King Agrippa and the governor Festus in the latter's palace at Caesarea. Lake has already pointed out that for literary reasons the author of Acts did not mention Ananias in Paul's speech before King Agrippa. In the same way it could be shown that Ananias' words in ch. 22 were given a more Jewish turn in view of Paul's Jewish audience—a matter about which Luke must have been clear, and which also finds expression in the Jewish character of the preliminary history in vv. 3–5. Indeed we see how, by avoiding in detail the expressions that occur in the parallel accounts of the Damascus

[1]See below, pp. 91–129.
[2]In Acts 9.10 ff. Ananias is simply a messenger for Christ, whereas in 22.14 f. he simply indicated what God intended by sending the experience, and he does not, as in ch. 9, add anything to it. See W. L. Knox, *The Acts of the Apostles*, 1948, p. 27 n. 1.

experience, Paul succeeds in keeping his audience quiet till in v. 21 he mentions his mission to the Gentiles. The only account that is not contained in a speech and therefore did not undergo any adaptation, either because it was a speech or because of the audience, is contained in 9.1 ff. It is characteristic of this account that the story of Ananias takes up nearly twice as much space as the account of the experience itself.[1]

For these reasons it is in my opinion not possible to agree with Kirsopp Lake's hypothesis; but we will look at the explanatory words more closely, and then make a few remarks about the mutual relation of the four accounts.

II

But before we examine these explanatory words in their proper connexion, there is one point to be dealt with. Whereas up to now material has been put together to prove that, according to the texts, the experience came to Paul without any preparation, we shall try in what follows to show that when he met Christ and the call, he was confronted by something inevitable. There is in the Damascus experience an element of compulsion that can be understood only on the assumption that Paul was not prepared for it.

In Acts 26.14 Christ says to Paul (in Aramaic), 'Saul, Saul, why do you persecute me? σκληρόν σοι πρὸς κέντρα λακτίζειν.' It has long been known that this last sentence is a proverb to which there are parallels in Greek literature.[2] As the words are spoken in Aramaic, it has been thought that there must be a similar proverb in that language, but no confirmation of this has been found in Jewish literature.

A more difficult question is what the words mean in their context here. It has been supposed that they refer to Paul's past, and denote the resistance that he has hitherto shown to the inward pull towards Christianity, a resistance that he now has to abandon.[3] Thus we got the previous history, explaining the sudden conversion: Paul, it was supposed, had long tried to resist the attracting force emanating from

---

[1]Lake thinks that we have in ch. 22 an abbreviation of the original, so that the account in ch. 9, while it is a Hellenized version, comes nearer to the original as regards completeness.

[2]Smend has tried, in 'Untersuchungen zu den Acta-Darstellungen von der Bekehrung des Paulus', ΑΓΓΕΛΟΣ I, 1925, pp. 34–45 (esp. pp. 36 f. and 41–43), to prove that the sentence is a direct quotation from Euripides' *Bacchae* 795; but Kümmel (*Römer 7 und die Bekehrung des Paulus*, pp. 155–7) is certainly right when he says that the only certain conclusion is that the author of Acts took over a frequently used Greek proverb. See further, p. 21 n. 2.

[3]Thus Wendt on this passage, also his article, 'Die Hauptquelle der Apostelgeschichte', *ZNW* 24, 1925, p. 304, and Heitmüller, 'Die Bekehrung des Paulus', *ZTK* 27, 1917, p. 144.

Christ, and had rushed with redoubled energy into the struggle against his followers; but now all that had been imprisoned in his soul was released, and at one stroke he became Christ's servant.

The difficulty of such a view is that the words appear in an account that rejects the existence of a previous history of this kind. We have to try to interpret the proverb so that it fits into the context, and understand it as something referring to the future, not to anything that happened before the Damascus experience—from now on it will hurt you to kick against the goads,[1] i.e., from now on you will have no discharge from the service that I, Christ, have now laid on you.[2]

[1]Thus too Windisch in 'Die Christusepiphanie vor Damascus', *ZNW* 31, 1932, p. 13 n. 1, and Zahn, *Die Apostelgeschichte des Lukas* II, p. 802.

[2]In the stress laid on the parallel, Euripides, *Bacchae* 795, where the god tells the mortal not to persecute him any more, but to bow down before him (thus Smend, *op. cit.*, pp. 36 f., and Windisch, *op. cit.*, pp. 9–14), it has been overlooked that the proverb is used there in a way that its content does not justify. It speaks of the folly of resisting what is inevitable; and its application, even in more ancient times, shows that it has this meaning, and does not express a rather special idea as do Dionysus's words in the *Bacchae*. It is quite certain that we have a similar meaning in Aeschylus, *Prometheus* 323, where the proverb is a counsel, given by Oceanus to Prometheus, not to kick against the goads, i.e., not to rebel against Zeus, who can make his lot harder than it already is. On this Smend writes on p. 37, 'The use of the proverb in Aeschylus' *Prometheus* (v. 322) comes still closer to that of the text in the Acts narrative because it is there spoken by the god himself.' As to this, however, it may be remarked that it is an already existing proverb that is put into the mouth of a god, just because it is gods who appear in the tragedies. In modern speech the biblical phrase about not kicking against the goads has again become a proverb; but the special point in its application to Paul has not become part of its content. The two other passages where the proverb is used in more ancient times are intended to express the view that one must not rebel against what is inevitable. At the end of the second Pythian Ode, v. 95, Pindar addresses envious people who do not realize that one must not fight against the gods who have in their hands the bestowal of high honours. He is of the opinion that one must bear one's yoke with good courage, instead of kicking against the goads. In Aeschylus, *Agamemnon* 1624, Aegisthus warns the chorus, which is threatening that he will be execrated by the court because of his murder of Agamemnon, of the reprisals that he will carry out against the citizens; and he suggests that they had better not kick against the goads. (Smend, on p. 37, takes a different but probably incorrect view.)

In the later use of the proverb, where Smend thinks the meaning has been weakened in comparison with these older examples, we have the same meaning—to cease rebelling against what is inevitable, what is one's destiny. This is clear: see Terence, *Phormio* 77 f.; cf. Plautus, *Truculentius* 768; and Ammianus Marcellinus, 18.5.1. Libanius used the proverb in his *Vita*, § 47 (ed. R. Foerster, Teubner I, 1903, p. 107); and he is content to write in a letter (429 = W 1190, Teubner X, 1921, p. 417), 'τὸ δὲ μὴ πρὸς κέντρα', which shows the proverb's great popularity.

Smend stresses the two passages (Euripides, *Bacchae* 795, and Aeschylus' *Prometheus* 323) where the god demands that all further resistance be given up, and in Euripides, even Dionysus summons his chief opponent and pursuer not to resist any more. These passages may be rightly quoted as close parallels, if the line of thought in Acts were concerned with the god who warned his chief opponent not to continue the hopeless conflict of mortals against gods. But there is a great difference between the human presumption that leads to disaster in the Greek tragedy, and the biblical atmosphere that characterizes the accounts of the apostle's call. It is a pity that Smend was not familiar with W. Nestle's 'Anklänge an Euripides in der Apostelgeschichte' (*Philologus* 59, 1900, pp. 46–57), as it is the best article on this question, and one in which abundant material has been given and great care taken not to go too far with the conclusions that could be drawn from the points of

This interpretation is confirmed by another passage, viz., I Cor. 9.15–18, which has surprisingly played no part in the discussion of the Damascus experience. In I Cor. 9 Paul speaks of his right to be supported in the same way as are the other apostles, the Lord's brothers and Cephas. After producing formal proof of this common right, he adds that he renounces it, that in fact he would rather die than be supported by the churches. The explanation is that, as a preacher of the Gospel, he has a different position from these others: ἐὰν γὰρ εὐαγγελίζωμαι, οὐκ ἔστιν μοι καύχημα· ἀνάγκη γάρ μοι ἐπίκειται· οὐαὶ γάρ μοί ἐστιν ἐὰν μὴ εὐαγγελίσωμαι. εἰ γὰρ ἑκὼν τοῦτο πράσσω, μισθὸν ἔχω· εἰ δὲ ἄκων οἰκονομίαν πεπίστευμαι, τίς οὖν μού ἐστιν ὁ μισθός; [1] The unique position that Paul claims for himself arises from the compulsion brought by the Damascus experience. The compulsion was for him only, not for the others—ἀνάγκη γάρ μοι ἐπίκει ται.

One other text may perhaps tell us something about the compulsion that Christ exercised on Paul at Damascus. That is Phil. 3.12, in which Paul says, 'Not that I have already obtained this or am already perfect; but I press on to make it my own, because Jesus Christ has made me

---

contact that he believes he has found. Smend could have found another passage here where the proverb is used—a fragment from Euripides' *Peliades* (cf. Nestle, *op. cit.*, p. 51): πρὸς κέντρα μὴ λάκτιζε τοῖς κρατοῦσί σου (fr. 607 in Nauck's ed., Teubner III, p. 164). From an inscription found in the valley of the upper Meander, Zahn (*Die Apostelgeschichte*, p. 801 n. 23) quotes another example, which was published by A. H. Smith and W. M. Ramsay in the *Journal of Hellenic Studies* 8, 1887, p. 261. It concerns a stone with γνῶμαι μονόστιχοι inscribed on its four sides. On one side there is, *inter alia*, Λακτίζεις πρὸς κέντρα, πρὸ [ς ἀ]ντία κύματα μοχθεῖς. If Smend (*op. cit.*, p. 41) and Windisch (*op. cit.*, p. 13 with n. 3) want to find in the plural form κέντρα, which was necessary in the verse form of the tragedy, but does not fit well into Acts, a proof of the dependence of Acts on Euripides' *Bacchae*, it is enough to point out that in the Greek examples only the passage from Pindar has the singular.

Nestle, in his article just quoted, has set out carefully (pp. 48–50) the instances of the use of θεομάχοι, θεομαχέω in Acts and in Greek literature, so as to point out the probability that the author of Acts knows Euripides; and here Windisch follows him (*op. cit.*, pp. 10–13). The use of θεομάχος in Acts 5.39 can hardly be held to prove that the author of Acts knew the *Bacchae*, as this adjective and the corresponding verb are not used quite as rarely as Nestle assumes; see Arndt and Gingrich, and Liddell and Scott s.v. A positive answer to the question whether Euripides' *Bacchae* can be in the narrower sense a 'source' of Acts is given by Otto Weinreich in *Genethliakon Wilhelm Schmidt* (Tübinger Beiträge zur Altertumswissenschaft, Heft 5), 1929, pp. 332–41. See further L. Schmid in *TWNT* III, 664–7, and Dibelius, 'The Speeches in Acts and Ancient Historiography', in *Studies in the Acts of the Apostles*, ET 1956, pp. 187–91.

[1]This punctuation must be preferred to that used by Nestle, who puts the full stop after πεπίστευμαι. In dealing with Acts 26.17 Zahn has referred to I Cor. 9.17, and so has Koch on II Cor. 11.8 f. (p. 397 n. 1). Zahn also points out that Paul draws a comparison between a preacher of the Gospel and an ox treading out the grain and ploughing (I Cor. 9.8–10 and I Tim. 5.18), and that this striking image results from the first words that he heard from Jesus' mouth (Zahn, *op. cit.*, p. 803). This, however, is not convincing, even if we have in I Cor. 9 another reference to the Damascus experience—as we shall see later (p. 34).

his own.' The whole section, vv. 7 ff., or single passages, have been made to refer to the Damascus experience, e.g., ἥγημαι in v. 7,[1] ἐζημιώθην in v. 8,[2] and ἔλαβον[3] and κατελήμφθην in v. 12.[4] And indeed, the most obvious explanation is that in this passage Paul is thinking of Damascus; and the question is then whether κατελήμφθην ὑπὸ Χριστοῦ 'Ιησοῦ means being overpowered, which expresses something similar to what we found in Acts 26 and I Cor. 9.

The commentators have regarded the expression in various ways. Franke makes it refer directly to the Damascus experience (p. 192): 'The force of the expression, however, is not derived merely from the context, but is a measure of the energy that was in the apostle's experience of salvation; he could say, like the prophet (Jer. 20.7), "Thou art stronger than I, and thou hast prevailed." '

The others do not enter into a more detailed explanation; but while Franke thinks that the understood object of the verbs ἔλαβον and καταλάβω in v. 12 is τὴν ἐξανάστασιν τὴν ἐκ νεκρῶν, Haupt and Ewald are against completing the sentence with an object, on the ground that Paul thought of the verbs intransitively because he wanted to emphasize their force as verbs. Lohmeyer too thinks that the verbs have no object. Any object may be chosen to complete the sentence, but it should be either ἐξανάστασιν ἐκ νεκρῶν or, as the end of v. 12 suggests, Christ. This has been taken up by Dibelius and developed as follows: 'κατελήμφθην ὑπὸ Χριστοῦ 'Ιησοῦ corresponds to καταλάβω, and therefore καταλάβω must be completed by the corresponding personal object, Jesus Christ. And the same must be done with ἔλαβον of which καταλάβω is only an emphatic form.'

We still have to consider Paul's remarkable expression, κατελήμφθην ὑπὸ Χριστοῦ 'Ιησοῦ, in which καταλαμβάνω must mean to seize or overpower. And here it is difficult to think of anything except the forcible seizure of Paul by someone stronger, who would not let him go again.[5]

---

[1]Thus A. H. Franke, E. Haupt (in the 7th edition), Lohmeyer and Dibelius; Ewald rejects this view, but it is supported by Kümmel, *Römer 7 und die Bekehrung des Paulus*, pp. 146 f.

[2]Thus Franke and J. B. Lightfoot; Ewald rejects this view, and the other commentaries mentioned above do not make the passage refer to the Damascus experience.

[3]Thus Haupt, Lightfoot, and Lohmeyer (perhaps from Damascus).

[4]Franke, Haupt, Lohmeyer (presumably), Lightfoot, and Dibelius (in the 1st edition, 1911).

[5]It has been claimed that a further proof of the sudden and violent nature of the Damascus experience is found in the word ἔκτρωμα, which Paul uses about himself in I Cor. 15.8. This interpretation, however, must be rejected: see Fridrichsen, 'Paulus abortivus, Zu I Kor. 15.8', *Symbolae philologicae O. A. Danielsson*, Uppsala, 1932, pp. 82 f.; and see Windisch's criticism of Fridrichsen's interpretation in *Paulus und Christus*, 1934, p. 144 n. 1. See now my article, 'Paulus tamquam abortivus (I Cor. 15.8)' in *New Testament Essays*, Studies in memory of T. W. Manson, ed. A. J. B. Higgins, 1959, pp. 180–93.

But this inescapable character of the revelation and call by Christ at Damascus fits in exactly with the unpreparedness to which we have referred above. Christ's revelation is not the final phase or the necessary result of Paul's inner development; on the contrary, the texts show Christ meeting Paul as his opponent, and forcing him into obedience to him and into the service of the Gentiles.

III

If the Damascus experience, as it is told in Galatians and Acts, was not only unprepared but inevitable, so that the modern psychological explanations that are supposed to elucidate the long preparation contradict the texts, which know nothing of any such previous history, our task is not to explain why the way of the psychological explanations takes us no further. Nor, we must add, would it do so, even if better psychological explanations were found than those that have hitherto been produced.

The reason for this is that the account of Damascus is not a piece of ingenuous narration, in which the modern researcher, with his superior knowledge, can put things in their proper places. We have four versions of an account that gives a quite definite picture of the apostle's call. It is quite certain that the picture does not set out the detailed occurrences before and in Damascus; but the more closely we approach what is essential in the account, namely its nature and meaning, the greater becomes the agreement. That will be seen as we now turn to the explanatory words with which Paul speaks of the occurrence in Galatians, and which, in the account in Acts, Christ speaks either directly to Paul (ch. 26), or through Ananias (ch. 22), or to Ananias (ch. 9). These explanatory words in the three accounts in Acts and in Galatians are just as varied as the remarks about Paul's earlier Jewish life, and they are rarely identical.[1] If, however, we examine the texts more closely, we do find important points of agreement.

If we begin with Paul's own words in Gal. 1.15: ὅτε δὲ εὐδόκησεν ὁ ἀφορίσας με ἐκ κοιλίας μητρός μου καὶ καλέσας διὰ τῆς χάριτος αὐτοῦ ἀποκαλύψαι τὸν υἱὸν αὐτοῦ ἐν ἐμοί, ἵνα εὐαγγελίζωμαι αὐτὸν ἐν τοῖς ἔθνεσιν . . . , we have here, besides the brief mention of the actual revelation of Christ and the call to be an apostle to the Gentiles, a characterization of God as the one 'who had set me apart before I was born, and had called me through his grace.'

The words might read as if we had here before us the previous history for which so many have searched—that is, if they expressed a con-

[1] μάρτυς κτλ. in 22.15 and 26.16; cf. 22.18 (μαρτυρίαν).

tinuity in his life, which was in fact marked by a break that sharply separated what happened before Damascus from what happened after it. In that case Paul would have realized afterwards that he was in God's hand in spite of everything, even in the years before the break, when he was a Jewish theologian and a persecutor of the Christians. But it is hardly likely that Paul would mention this in a context whose polemical intention was to prove that he had received his gospel direct from Christ, and nothing at all from men, and where all the stress is laid on the break that has been caused in his life by the direct revelation of Christ. The words must therefore be regarded in a different way, so that election and call point in advance to the moment when God revealed Christ to him on the road to Damascus.[1] This interpretation is probable, because the expressions originate in two calls to Old Testament prophets.

The expression ἐκ κοιλίας μητρός μου is found in several passages in the LXX; e.g., Samson says (Judg. 16.17), 'For I have been a Nazarite to God from my mother's womb.' The two passages in Psalms may also be mentioned: 21.10 f. (EVV 22.9 f.) and 70 (71). 6, where the uninterrupted connexion with God from birth on is stressed. In Deutero-Isaiah the expression occurs in a few passages about the people, and in one important passage about the calling of God's servant. This passage reads (49.1–6):

> Listen to me, O coastlands,
>   and hearken, you peoples from afar.
> The Lord called me from the womb,
>   from the body of my mother he named my name.
> He made my mouth like a sharp sword,
>   in the shadow of his hand he hid me;
> he made me a polished arrow,
>   in his quiver he hid me away.
> And he said to me, 'You are my servant,
>   Israel, in whom I will be glorified.'
> But I said, 'I have laboured in vain,
>   I have spent my strength for nothing and vanity;
> yet surely my right is with the Lord,
>   and my recompense with my God.'
> And now the Lord says,
>   who formed me from the womb to be his servant,
> to bring Jacob back to him,
>   and that Israel might be gathered to him,
> for I am honoured in the eyes of the Lord,
>   and my God has become my strength—

[1]Goguel, *Les Premiers Temps de l'Église*, 1949, p. 98: 'By this act of power, God put into effect the plans which he had made for Paul from his mother's womb (Gal. 1.15).'

he says:
'It is too light a thing that you should be my servant
to raise up the tribes of Jacob
and to restore the preserved of Israel;
I will give you as a light to the nations,
that my salvation may reach to the end of the earth.'

We have here, both in v. 1: ἐκ κοιλίας μητρός μου ἐκάλεσεν τὸ ὄνομά μου, and in v. 5: Κύριος ὁ πλάσας με ἐκ κοιλίας δοῦλον ἑαυτῷ, the idea of God's election and call 'from the womb'. These two ideas are, in fact, linked in the text with the call to be a light to the Gentiles, and this fits in well with Paul's next sentence (Gal. 1.16): ἵνα εὐαγγελίζωμαι αὐτὸν ἐν τοῖς ἔθνεσιν.

Another text may be quoted, in which the parallelism lies not in the expressions, but simply in the train of thought. It refers to Jeremiah's call as prophet (Jer. 1.4 f.):

Now the word of the Lord came to me saying,
'Before I formed you in the womb I knew you,
and before you were born I consecrated you;
I appointed you a prophet to the nations.'

In the translation used here, 'nations' means the same as Gentiles, so that Jeremiah too is called from the womb to be a prophet to the Gentiles. But what follows in v. 10 shows that the office is to combine prophecy with politics, and is not, as it is conceived in Gal. 1.15 f., to be concerned merely with proclaiming.[1]

When Paul applies these biblical expressions to his own call, he must be thinking, not only that he thereby illustrates God's call to him personally, but that that call is the same as it was in the case of Jeremiah and Deutero-Isaiah, a renewal of God's will for the salvation of the Gentiles, giving him a place in the history of salvation in line with those Old Testament figures.[2]

But it is not only Paul who uses about the Damascus experience these characteristic words from the calling of the Old Testament prophets; the accounts in Acts allude to the same texts, and it is interesting here that they remind one of those texts, but not of the same expressions in them. There seems to have existed a tradition of applying to Paul those Old Testament texts about a call; but taken in detail they were

[1]This distinction is important. Lohmeyer makes no clear separation when he writes on Matt. 28.16–20, 'But the fact that they proclaim and that they teach the nations means that these eleven are in the same category as Jeremiah' ('Mir ist gegeben alle Gewalt!', *In memoriam Ernst Lohmeyer*, 1951, p. 39).

[2]In *Der zweite Korintherbrief*, p. 303, Windisch rightly points out that Paul, in his formal assertion of the authority that the Lord has given him εἰς οἰκοδομὴν καὶ οὐκ εἰς καθαίρεσιν (II Cor. 10.8 and 13.10), is alluding to Jer. 1.10: ἰδοὺ κατέστακά σε σήμερον ἐπὶ ἔθνη καὶ βασιλείας ἐκριζοῦν καὶ κατασκάπτειν καὶ ἀπολλύειν καὶ ἀνοικοδομεῖν καὶ καταφυτεύειν.

not applied in the same way.[1] Between the three accounts, moreover, there are parallels that appear only on closer examination.

The account that is nearest to Paul's own words is that in Acts 26.12–18, where Christ says that he has revealed himself to Paul 'to appoint you to serve and bear witness to the things in which you have seen me and to those in which I will appear to you.' Then follows the remarkable sentence, ἐξαιρούμενός σε ἐκ τοῦ λαοῦ καὶ ἐκ τῶν ἐθνῶν. Here both meanings of ἐξαιρέω are possible—to single out or select, and to save or deliver; and several commentators prefer the latter interpretation,[2] as in their opinion Jer. 1.8, with its μὴ φοβηθῇς ἀπὸ προσώπου αὐτῶν, ὅτι μετὰ σοῦ ἐγώ εἰμι τοῦ ἐξαιρεῖσθαί σε, λέγει Κύριος, has influenced the text.[3] In Nestle's version the next words, εἰς οὓς (sc. τὰ ἔθνη) ἐγὼ ἀποστέλλω σε, are printed in heavy type, and Jer. 1.7 (πρὸς πάντας, οὓς ἐὰν ἐξαποστείλω σε) is quoted. Since presumably Jer. 1.8 (as mentioned above) has influenced the text, we may also assume a connexion with Jer. 1.7. The next words, 'to open their eyes', are used by Deutero-Isaiah in the expression 'to open the eyes that are blind', referring to the conversion of the Gentiles to Yahweh; thus 42.6 f., cf. 61.1 LXX: κηρύξαι . . . τυφλοῖς ἀνάβλεψιν.[4] 42.7 speaks of καθημένους ἐν σκότει, and v. 16 reads, ποιήσω αὐτοῖς τὸ σκότος εἰς φῶς.[5]

[1] In Acts 18.9 the Lord says to Paul, μὴ φοβοῦ, ἀλλὰ λάλει καὶ μὴ σιωπήσῃς, διότι ἐγώ εἰμι μετὰ σοῦ κτλ. This is an allusion to Jer. 1.8: μὴ φοβηθῇς ἀπὸ προσώπου αὐτῶν, ὅτι μετὰ σοῦ ἐγώ εἰμι κτλ., cf. vv. 6 f. with reference to λαλεῖν. It is hardly likely that the writer is thinking of Isa. 41.10, as is thought by Nestle, and by Cerfaux in 'Saint Paul et le "Serviteur de Dieu" d'Isaïe', *StAns* 27–28, 1951, p. 353. And the *Epistula Apostolorum* 31 (42) describes Paul as 'a wall that does not collapse' (in C. Schmidt and I. Wajnberg, *Gespräche Jesu mit seinen Jüngern nach der Auferstehung*, TU 43, 1919, p. 98); cf. Jer. 1.18.

[2] Thus Wendt and Zahn. Preuschen translates 'to deliver' ('erretten').

[3] We have a parallel—and a fulfilment of Christ's words—in Claudius Lysias' letter, Acts 23.27.

[4] 'A light to the nations' also appears in Isa. 49.6 and 51.4 ('. . . peoples') as well as in 42.6. About the interpretation of these texts at that time, see Billerbeck II, 139, 156. Regarding the Isaiah Targum, see P. Seidelin, 'Der 'Ebed Jahwe und die Messiasgestalt im Jesajatargum', *ZNW* 35, 1936, pp. 194–231. In Acts 13.47, Isa. 49.6 is quoted with direct reference to Paul: 'For so the Lord has commanded us, saying, "I have set you to be a light for the Gentiles, that you may bring salvation to the uttermost parts of the earth."' Cerfaux assumes (*op. cit.*, *passim*) that Paul is to continue the work of Christ, the Servant of God, for the Gentiles; and of course this is correct, but it is hardly an exhaustive interpretation of the application of these texts from Isaiah to Paul. In Nestle's edition of the New Testament and in Cerfaux' article (*op. cit.*, pp. 361 f.) there is supposed to be a connexion between Phil. 2.16 (εἰς κενὸν ἐκοπίασα) and Isa. 49.4. But this expression is a general one in the LXX (Job 2.9; 20.18; 39.16; Isa. 65.23; Jer. 28 [EVV 51]. 58), so that the connexion with Isa. 49.4 is not quite certain. If the correct interpretation of Phil. 2.16–18 is that given below (p. 50), the connexion with Isa 49.4 is probable.

[5] Acts 26 also uses Ezek. 2.1 (cf. 2.2; 3.24; [and 37.10]) in v. 16: στῆθι ἐπὶ τοὺς πόδας σου. When the vision connected with the call has thrown Ezekiel to the ground (1.28), the Lord says to him, 'Son of man, stand upon your feet, and I will speak with you.' And the Spirit sets Ezekiel on his feet (2.1 f.), whereupon the call comes in 2.3 ff. Something similar takes place in 3.22 ff. and in Dan. 8.17 ff. In II (4) Esd. 6.13, 17 Esdras is commanded, 'Stand up upon thy feet' before the

In Acts 9 the explanatory words are in vv. 15 f. (cf. v. 17): 'But the Lord said to him [Ananias], "Go, for he is a chosen instrument of mine to carry my name before the Gentiles and kings and the sons of Israel; for I will show him how much he must suffer for the sake of my name." ' There are no Old Testament parallels to the expression σκεῦος ἐκλογῆς in v. 15.[1] On the other hand Wendt, writing about the words βαστάσαι τὸ ὄνομά μου ἐνώπιον [τῶν] ἐθνῶν τε καὶ βασιλέων υἱῶν τε Ἰσραήλ in v. 15, has referred to Jer. 1.10 LXX, ἰδοὺ κατέστακά σε σήμερον ἐπὶ ἔθνη καὶ βασιλείας. V. 16 says briefly, without further explanation, 'For I will show him how much he must suffer for the sake of my name.' There is a parallel in 26.17, as ἐξαιρούμενος κτλ. assumes that Paul will be persecuted as a preacher of the Gospel, but that Christ will save him from the attacks of the Jews and Gentiles.

Acts 22.14 f. contains the least informative of the explanatory words: 'And he [Ananias] said, "The God of our fathers appointed you to know his will, to see the Just One and to hear a voice from his mouth; for you will be a witness for him to all men of what you have seen and heard." ' προχειρίζω has a different meaning here from that in 26.16, where it meant that Christ revealed himself to Paul to appoint him a servant and witness. In 22.14 the verb refers to an anterior choice that Paul might know God's will, and it forms a parallel to Gal. 1.15.[2] Paul had been chosen to hear what God's will towards him was, as he now heard it at Damascus. From this it may be supposed that during the vision something was said to Paul that has not been reported. If regard is had to the parallelism with the other accounts, God's will must mean God's will towards Paul, and signify the same thing as 'to see the Just One and to hear a voice from his mouth', so that the text assumes here that Christ announced to Paul his will towards him, and therefore said something corresponding to his call to him in 26.16–18. The expression 'all men' is used here in v. 15 instead of the more detailed 'Gentiles and kings and the sons of Israel' in 9.15.

---

revelation takes place, because there is to be a mighty voice and an earthquake. Both in Daniel and in II (4) Esdras the revelation deals with the last days, and is to enlighten or comfort the recipient, whereas Ezekiel receives a call to go to the Israelites, who are a stubborn people. The use of the expression from Ezek. 2.1 in Acts 26.16 with the following εἰς τοῦτο γὰρ ὤφθην σοι κτλ. scarcely expresses the well-known characteristic of visions, that before the revelation or call comes the divine Being frees the mortal from his fear of what is happening; it means here, as Wendt says, 'Get ready to go', in fact, as the following sentence explains, 'to go out as an ἀπόστολος of the Lord' (v. 17).

[1] On this expression see Windisch, *Paulus und Christus*, p. 138.
[2] Lake and Cadbury (p. 280) point out the use of a similar expression in Rom. 2.18 and Col. 1.9, supposing that we have to do here with a Jewish expression in general use, but they have not found it dealt with in literature. See also Lohmeyer's commentary on Colossians, p. 32 n. 7; cf. n. 6.

As may be seen, there is a marked agreement between the four accounts, now in one detail, now in another; and three of them, Gal. 1.15 and Acts 26.16–18 and 9.15 f., refer to Old Testament passages from 'Ebed Jahweh texts and the story of Jeremiah's call. Paul thought that those texts from the prophets expressed his own call; and the three accounts in Acts are in part closely connected with each other, and in part—this concerns two of them—also stamped with the call of Jeremiah and the thoughts of Deutero-Isaiah on the call of the Servant of God in respect of the Gentiles. It is justifiable to assume that the accounts in Acts go back to Paul, as they show a close connexion with the description in Galatians, not only in the narration of the previous history, but also in the explanatory words. It is the apostle himself who shaped the story of his conversion and call as the churches were to hear it. As we saw, he was unprepared for it, and it was inescapable; but these features also characterize the calling of the Old Testament prophets. They have no previous history—the prophet and the call appear at the same time, and that is the starting-point of everything that happens. It is quite strange to hear from the prophet in Amos 7.14 f., 'I am no prophet, nor a prophet's son; but I am a herdsman, and a dresser of sycamore trees, and the Lord took me from following the flock, and the Lord said to me, "Go, prophesy to my people Israel." '[1] Elsewhere it begins with the call, and there is nothing from which the prophet is 'taken'—see Isa. 6, Jer. 1.4–10, and Ezek. 1–2.8. What distinguishes these calls from that of Paul is that with the latter the call is not to one who is an adherent and probably a blank page, but to an opponent who is a terrible enemy of Christ and his Church. We have parallels in the Old Testament to the compelling power exerted by the divine call. We read in Amos 3.8, 'The lion has roared; who will not fear? The Lord God has spoken; who can but prophesy?' And in Jer. 20.7–9 we read,

> O Lord, thou hast deceived me,
>   and I was deceived;
> thou art stronger than I,
>   and thou hast prevailed.
> I have become a laughingstock all the day;
>   everyone mocks me.
> For whenever I speak, I cry out,
>   I shout, 'Violence and destruction!'
> For the word of the Lord has become for me
>   a reproach and derision all day long.
> If I say, 'I will not mention him,
>   or speak any more in his name,'

[1] See further Engnell's exposition in *Profetismens ursprung och uppkomst* (Religion och Bibel 8), 1949, pp. 15 f.

there is in my heart as it were a burning fire
shut up in my bones,
and I am weary with holding it in,
and I cannot.

In other passages from the prophet, too, we see God's compelling power over him, shutting him out from ordinary human life (16.1–4), and causing him to complain bitterly of existing at all (chs. 14–15).[1]

It would help towards a better understanding of Paul's conversion and call, and of the connexion with the Old Testament prophets whose existence we have just established, if there were accounts of contemporary experiences. Isaiah, Jeremiah and Deutero-Isaiah are so far from Paul in time that he is not likely to have had an experience of exactly the same kind. Rather was his call identified with that of the prophets as interpreted in his time. But in fact, the age of Paul had no prophets, and we do not know of anyone among the Jews who was called by God to be a priest or a scribe.[2]

[1] In *TWNT* I, pp. 438–43 (ET, *Apostleship*, Bible Key Words, 1952, pp. 53–62), Rengstorf claims that in the consciousness of his mission Paul is linking himself with Jeremiah. In *Paulus und Christus*, pp. 150 f., Windisch has represented both Paul and Jesus as figures of the Jeremiah type. More cautiously Lohmeyer has characterized Paul as a prophet and a prophetic apostle (*Grundlagen paulinischer Theologie*, 1929, pp. 200 f.). Against Rengstorf's view Cerfaux writes pertinently ('Saint Paul et le "Serviteur de Dieu" ', p. 358 n. 3): 'Rengstorf's line of argument is not convincing. The fact that modern writers can compare the psychology of St Paul with that of Jeremiah matters little.'

There is another call that must be regarded as a parallel to the Damascus experience, although it is not as close to it as are the calls mentioned above. It is Moses' call in Ex. 3.1–4.17. There is the burning bush (in broad daylight), but what is more important is that Moses' call is a mission, which will soon take him to Pharaoh, the King of Egypt (3.10): καὶ νῦν δεῦρο ἀποστείλω σε πρὸς Φαραὼ βασιλέα ᾿Αιγύπτου, cf. Acts 9.15.

[2] Smend ('Acta-Darstellungen von der Bekehrung des Paulus', pp. 34 f.) has pointed to divine interference in the lives of the most dissimilar men in Hellenistic times; in Galen, *De Libris Propriis* (Kühn 19, p. 19), a command by the god Aesculapius causes Galen to reverse a decision; in his *De Methodo Medendi* IX (Kühn 10, p. 609), his father is led by a vision in a dream to study medical science; and in Tacitus, *Annals* XI.21, a man of humble rank, through meeting a supernatural female who prophesies that he will become a proconsul in Africa, receives the courage to take up a career in the government service. To these examples others might be added, e.g., Xenophon's dream that snatched him from despair at the plight of the Greek army and induced him to take over its command (*Anabasis* III, 1.11 f.); cf. Josephus' vision in a dream, described in *Vita* 42, §§ 208 f. See also A. Wikenhauser, 'Die Traumgesichte des Neuen Testaments in religionsgeschichtlicher Sicht' in *Antike und Christentum*, Ergänzungsband I, Pisciculi, 1933, pp. 320–33. But this material from Hellenism can throw no light on Paul's call. Galen, *De methodo medendi* IX (Kühn 10, p. 609): προτραπέντος ἐπὶ τὴν τῆς ἰατρικῆς ἄσκησιν, reminds us of the protreptic discourse and the *protrepticus* literature, whose task is simply to stimulate interest in philosophy, medical science, and other branches of knowledge. (See P. Hartlich, 'De exhortationum a Graecis Romanisque scriptarum historia et indole', *Leipziger Studien z. class. Philol.*, Vol. II, Leipzig, 1889, pp. 207–336; T. C. Burgess, 'Epideictic Literature' in *Studies in Classical Philology*, the University of Chicago, Vol. III, 3, Chicago, 1902, pp. 229 ff.). Here it is the admired teacher, not a god or a dream from above, whose words kindle the enthusiasm for study (Origen in Gregory Thaumaturgus, *Panegyricus* 6), or for a higher life (Lucian, *Nigrinus*).

Ludin Jansen, who has claimed to find in the Old Testament Apocrypha and Pseudepigrapha living witnesses for the religious life of later Jewish times, thought that he could demonstrate that three scenes describing calls in the Ethiopic Book of Enoch could be shown on closer examination to be calls to prophecy.[1] The third of these, chs. 12 f., cannot properly be held to belong to them, and is not considered here.[2] The second scene is, according to Jansen, in ch. 60; but even this scene is not a call to prophecy; the heavens tremble, and the innumerable hosts of angels are thrilled with emotion.[3] That makes Enoch (or Noah) shake with fear and fall to the ground, but Michael sends an angel who raises him to his feet, whereupon Michael expresses surprise at his terror. God, he says, has hitherto shown nothing but mercy, and even on the day of judgment none but sinners will be punished. Then he names two monsters, Leviathan and Behemoth, who will play their part on the day of judgment; and another angel shows various secret things—thunder and lightning, winds and fountains.

The third scene, in 14.8–16.4, is a different matter; Enoch is carried away into heaven in a vision. There he enters a house built of crystal, but he trembles with fear and falls to the ground. Then he sees another house of indescribable splendour, where there is the throne of the 'great Majesty', whom no angel in the unnumbered hosts that surround it can approach. Then the Lord calls to Enoch to come and hear his word. An angel raises him to his feet and takes him before the throne. Here God rebukes the angels who went down to the earth and united with the daughters of men. From their union there came the evil spirits. Now comes the last judgment, and Enoch has to go to the fallen angels and say to them, 'You will have no peace!'

The scene in 14.8 ff. is in Jansen's view closely connected with Ezekiel's vision in Ezek. 1–2.[4] There is more to be said for the definite pattern that Jansen claims to find in Ezekiel and also in the Book of Enoch:

1. The meeting with the bright light: Enoch 14.17–21, Ezek. 1.26–28;

[1] *Die Henochgestalt*, Oslo, 1939, pp. 114–17.
[2] It is not God, but angels, who commission Enoch to carry a message. Any call in the Old Testament sense is out of the question.
[3] The text mentions the Ancient of Days, who is on his throne surrounded by angels; but he has no significance at all in the context.
[4] Thus Ezek. 1.4 is parallel to Enoch 14.9; 1.13 to 14.11; 1.13 ff. to 14.10 ff.; 1.22 to 14.9. Between all these there is only very slight agreement or none at all. 1.26 f. is supposed to be parallel with 14.18 ff., but this passage in Enoch has nothing in common with that in Ezekiel, though probably with Dan. 7.9 ff. Ezekiel falls to the ground, 1.28, cf. Enoch 14.14, 24. But it is common to all visions and revelations that the man collapses before the divine Person, and also that God raises man up again by his Spirit (Ezek. 2.2; cf. 2.1) or by an angel, Enoch 14.24 f.; and then the man is addressed by God, Ezek. 1.28; 2.1 ff.; cf. Enoch 14.24.

this feature is not in Isa. 6 or Jer. 1.[1] Cf. Dan. 7.9 f., Enoch 71.2, 5 f.

2. The sight of the Lord on the throne: Enoch 14.18–20, Ezek. 1.26–28, Isa. 6.1; this feature is not in Jer. 1. Cf. Dan. 7.9 f., Enoch 71.10.

3. Man falls to the ground: Enoch 14.13 f. (cf. 24), Ezek. 1.28; in Isa. 6.5 this is expressed by Isaiah's words, and in Jer. 1.6 by Jeremiah's words; cf. Dan. 8.17, Enoch 71.2, 11.

4. Man is raised to his feet: Enoch 14.24 f., Ezek. 2.1 f.; in Isa. 6.6 f. this is expressed by the cleansing with the burning coal, and in Jer. 1.7 f. by the Lord's answer about Jeremiah's youth. Cf. Dan. 8.18, Enoch 71.3, 14a.

5. The call to prophecy: Enoch 15–16, Ezek. 2.3 ff., Isa. 6.8 ff., Jer. 1.9 f.; cf. Enoch 71.14–16.[2]

This vision in the Book of Enoch, and the pattern set out by Ludin Jansen in relation to it, help one to understand the narrative of the Damascus experience. The first, third, and fourth points in the pattern are found in all three accounts in Acts.[3] In ch. 26 the fifth point is simultaneous with the other three, whereas in chs. 9 and 22 it comes later (though here it is assumed that Christ had already called Paul before Damascus—see p. 28). The second point in the pattern is not in any of the three accounts in Acts. The vision in the Book of Enoch depends not only on Ezek. 1–2, but also to a considerable degree on Dan. 7.9 ff., and is only an imitation of Old Testament models. Further, the vision contains a very detailed description of what Enoch saw in heaven—a description that takes up nearly as much space as the uncommonly comprehensive message that is given to him. Compared with this, it is characteristic of the accounts of the Damascus experience that we do not learn at all what Paul saw, or, as we shall see later, how Paul saw Christ.

We can also make a comparison with the vision of Christ in Rev. 1.9–20, where Christ reveals himself to John and tells him to write down what he sees. Here too there is a detailed description of the vision, much more comprehensive than the words of the voice (v. 11) and the words of Christ (vv. 17–20)—words which we find both before and after

[1]Enoch 70–71, which Ludin Jansen does not deal with till later on, pp. 124 ff., are added here. On this text see E. Sjöberg, *Der Menschensohn im äthiopischen Henochbuch*, 1946, pp. 147–89. Levi's vision, Test. Levi 2.5–5.7, might also be mentioned; but there is no similarity with the biblical visions, as this vision is merely an apotheosis of the priesthood, in which the distance between God and men is forgotten.

[2]On this cf. Pfister's article 'Epiphanie' in Pauly-Wissowa, Suppl. IV, 1924, §§ 38–50, col. 314–21.

[3]Points 1, 3, and 4 are quite general, where a heavenly being reveals himself to a man. Point 4 corresponds to the 'Fear not' that the heavenly being says to the man who is terrified at the blaze of heavenly light.

the description of Christ who is walking in the midst of the seven lampstands. Here too we see, as we saw above, the bright light (the seven lampstands and Christ's resplendent appearance, vv. 12 f.); the beholder falls to the ground as if dead, but is touched by Christ and is told not to be afraid (v. 17), whereupon he receives the command to write the Book of Revelation (v. 19). The revelation of the heavenly Christ (vv. 13 ff.) corresponds here to the Lord's appearance on the throne.[1] The account of this vision has been formalized, as is shown by its connexion with the following letters to the churches, the individual features of the picture of Christ in the vision being used at the beginnings of the letters.

If we wish to indicate briefly the essential differences between the scene from the Book of Enoch, the vision of Christ in John's Revelation, and the accounts of the Damascus experience, we can take it that the first scene is purely literary, and is an echo of scenes in the canonical Old Testament. The details of the vision in Revelation are also strongly reminiscent of the Old Testament, but this does not entirely explain the vision. In the accounts of the Damascus call the Old Testament allusions are weaker. None of its features can be explained by pursuing its origin back to the Old Testament; but Old Testament forms are introduced as parts of the narrative, which serve at the same time to interpret the occurrence. They put Paul's experience on the same plane as the experiences that made the great Old Testament figures connecting links in God's plan of salvation.

IV

Even if we assume that the narrative of the Damascus experience is like the accounts of calls in the Old Testament, there is one point where uncertainty prevails, and on which we have already touched in our remarks about the simultaneous accounts of calls. Whereas Isaiah sees God sitting on the throne between seraphim, and Jeremiah hears God's voice but has no vision in conjunction with the words, the three accounts in Acts do not greatly enlighten us about what Paul saw.[2] A light from heaven shines about him, and he falls to the ground and then hears Christ's voice; but in Acts 9.7 we are told that Paul's companions heard the voice but saw no one ($\mu\eta\delta\acute{e}\nu\alpha$), from which we must infer a contrast between them and Paul. And Christ's words in 26.16, 'for I

---

[1] We therefore get the following pattern for Rev. 1.9–20, corresponding to the pattern mentioned above (pp. 31 f.): 1: 1.12–16. 2: 1.12–16. 3: 1.17. 4: 1.17. 5: 1.19.

[2] That is why many older expositors have assumed that Paul did not see the figure of Christ; see Pfaff's brief review, *Die Bekehrung des h. Paulus in der Exegese des 20. Jahrhunderts*, pp. 147 f. More recently a number of scholars seem to have felt that there is no problem of any kind here.

have appeared to you for this purpose,' imply that Paul has seen him. The same expression is used by Ananias in 9.17: 'the Lord Jesus who appeared to you on the road by which you came.' In 22.14 it is said clearly that God has chosen Paul 'to know his will, to see the Just One and to hear a voice from his mouth'; and it is added that this took place because Paul is to be God's witness to all men 'of what you have seen and heard', while the verses that describe the event itself repeat Christ's words verbatim; but, as we have seen, they are quite vague about what Paul saw.

Thus it is certain that the writer of Acts supposes that Paul saw Christ, although in narrating the revelation itself he avoids saying so. But it is clear from various passages in Paul's letters that he himself affirms that he saw Christ at Damascus. In Gal. 1.16 it pleased God 'to reveal his Son to me', and in I Cor. 9.1 we read, 'Am I not an apostle? Have I not seen Jesus our Lord?' See further I Cor. 15.8, where the Damascus experience is grouped with the manifestations of Christ after the Resurrection. Support has also been claimed from II Cor. 4.6: 'For it is the God who said, "Let light shine out of darkness," who has shone in our hearts to give the light of the knowledge of the glory of God in the face of Christ;' but there is hardly any reason to relate these words to the Damascus experience.[1] On the other hand, Phil. 3.12 may be quoted if the interpretation suggested above (pp. 22 f.) is approved.

But if it is clear that Paul saw Christ at Damascus, according to his own words as well as the accounts in Acts, it needs to be explained why the latter do not say so directly. It must first be pointed out that when Paul mentions the experience, he simply says that he saw Christ, without going into it in more detail. That is true of the passages mentioned above; and of these the closest to the accounts in Acts is Gal. 1.15. The writer of Acts also says that Paul saw Christ, but he does not mention this in his actual description, which merely speaks of a light from above. In this too there is close agreement between Paul's own presentation and the accounts in Acts.

Paul saw Christ at Damascus, but beyond that we learn nothing. How he saw Christ he does not relate, and that is very characteristic of him. Formerly people were inclined to see in his letters the open-hearted revelations of a man whom we therefore know better than we know any other man of ancient times. But Paul's letters are not intimate letters, but are in the category of pastoral letters. And the man himself is not one of those who are continually turning their life inside out and are never tired of talking about themselves. On the contrary, he is very reserved in giving any information about his own religious life. When

[1]Thus Koch *ad loc.*, and Kümmel, *Römer 7 und die Bekehrung des Paulus*, p. 147.

the dispute about his apostleship or the instruction of the churches makes it necessary, he will go into a subject that he would otherwise not touch. But as a rule there are only brief allusions, and they are not specially illuminating.

It is the same with Paul's visions and revelations. What do we really learn about them? We know various instances from Acts. In Troas the Macedonian appeared to him in a vision, and asked him to come over and help (16.9). In 18.9 f. the Lord speaks to Paul and puts courage into him during his stay in Corinth. It is not clear from this passage whether Paul simply heard Christ's voice without seeing him. On the other hand, in his experience in the temple at Jerusalem (22.17–21), where, according to this version of the Damascus narrative, he was first called to preach to the Gentiles, he heard and saw Christ as at Damascus. In 23.11 Christ reveals himself to Paul during the imprisonment in Jerusalem ('The following night the Lord stood by him'), and promises that he shall bear witness for him in Rome, as he has done in Jerusalem. And in 27.23 f. it is natural to assume that Paul saw, as well as heard, the angel in the vision at night.

From Paul himself we learn much less. In Gal. 2.1 f., as it is necessary for his line of argument, he mentions a revelation as the reason for his second visit to Jerusalem; and in his passionate self-defence in II Cor. 11–12 he also tells (12.1 ff.) of visions and revelations, but what he says about them is so veiled that this section has been thought to refer to someone else. Vv. 2–4 speak of being 'caught up to the third heaven' and 'caught up into Paradise', but they do not tell us what he saw. We are told, however, that he heard 'things that cannot be told, which man may not utter'. There is really not much that we learn when Paul, 'speaking the truth', boasts of his visions and revelations.[1]

In other words, the uncertainty as to how Paul saw Christ, according to the accounts in Acts, might be taken as evidence of the close connexion between these accounts and Paul's own presentation of the facts.

---

[1] One remark that slipped out about his religious life (I Cor. 14.18 f.) must indeed be regarded as illuminating. Paul speaks in tongues more than all the Corinthians, but in church he would rather speak five words with his mind than ten thousand words in a tongue. Did the Corinthians know, before Paul wrote those words, that he had the gift of tongues? He was probably one of those who spoke to themselves and to God, as he himself says later (v. 28).

2

THE APOSTLE TO THE GENTILES

IF God's calling of Paul near Damascus has been narrated, both by
himself and by others, like that of one of the Old Testament figures
in God's plan of salvation, we are thereby faced with a problem.
Does that view of Paul and his apostleship stand alone, or
do other texts too regard him as a decisive factor in this plan? In
modern Pauline research we are not accustomed to think of him in all
seriousness as having had a unique type of call, but rather to discuss
what place he occupies in relation to the twelve, and whether he had
not sometimes too much to say about this. But it will now be our task
to look for similar statements about Paul in his letters, and possibly in
Acts. As in the treatment of the call, what the apostle himself says must
be considered first; and other people's evidence can be used only after
it has been tested as to how far it agrees with the former.

It will not be possible in this chapter to take account of all the texts
that might be mentioned; but in the remaining chapters it will be our
task to be constantly citing new passages, and to see them in their
proper context. Otherwise their presentation would suffer from repetitions, and the whole book would have to be summarized in this chapter,
with an expansion of the summary in those that follow. It therefore
seems to me better to deal here with individual but important texts
that show us Paul's call as apostle for the salvation of the Gentiles,
and in this way to confirm our belief that we have rediscovered Paul's
own view of his apostleship. It will then be possible in what follows
to consider, in the light of what we have seen, the traditional lines of
Pauline research.

I

The first text to deal with in this connexion is II Thess. 2.6 f., which
has gained new importance from Cullmann's exposition in an article[1]
that has been of significance for the studies presented here. In II Thess. 2
Paul tells the church in Thessalonica that the day of the Lord is not
directly at hand, because Antichrist and the great rebellion have not
yet become a reality. It is true that the forces of Antichrist are already

[1]'Le caractère eschatologique du devoir missionnaire et de la conscience apostolique
de S. Paul. Étude sur le κατέχον (—ων) de II Thess. 2.6–7', *RHPR* 16, 1936, pp. 210–45.

at work in the world, but they are still being restrained by 'what is restraining him' or 'him who now restrains it'. This power which is restraining Antichrist, and which is referred to sometimes in the neuter and sometimes in the masculine, has long been regarded as the Roman state (neuter) and as the person of the emperor (masculine). Both this interpretation and the one that Cullmann presents in the above-mentioned article go back to patristic times.[1]

Cullmann first decides that κατέχειν can mean both 'to hold back (retenir)' and 'to postpone, delay (retarder)', and that the neuter κατέχον and masculine κατέχων in our text must mean the same. This delaying power cannot be the Roman state; it is out of the question that a Christian of the first century can have taken such a positive attitude towards imperial Rome, which was held in Christian apocalyptic thought to be the incarnation of Antichrist. Besides this 'historical' exposition, Dibelius' 'mythological' interpretation is rejected, according to which at the beginning of the world a monster was overcome and bound by the deity. At the end of the ages, this monster is to be freed and take part in the last fight.[2]

Cullmann starts from the Jewish calculations of the time for the coming of the Messianic age, while Paul seems to depend on the tradition that had been formed concerning the previous signs.[3] But in the

[1]Cullmann's exposition is found in Theodoret of Cyrrhus (*PG* 82, 665A); cf. Theodore of Mopsuestia (*PG* 66, 936A). The other view of the Roman state goes back to Tertullian, who stresses the intercession for the emperor and the Roman state, because '*vim maximam universo orbi imminentem ipsamque clausulam saeculi acerbitates horrendas comminantem Romani imperii commeatu scimus retardari*' (*Apologeticum* 32.1, *CSEL* 69, p. 81); cf. *De carnis resurrectione* 24 (*CSEL* 47, p. 60): *Quis, nisi Romanus status, cujus abscessio in decem reges dispersa antichristi superducet?* How far Tertullian is from the early Christians' view of the eschatological events and the longing for them to come to pass, is shown clearly by the next sentence from the *Apologeticum: Itaque nolumus experiri et, dum precamur differri, Romanae diuturnitati favemus.*

[2]Cullmann, *op. cit.*, pp. 215–17.

[3]But we have no material by which to determine the nature of any such possible dependence. Cullmann goes on to write at once (p. 217): 'Consequently, if the apostle speaks of an obstacle which is "now" holding back the coming of Antichrist and thus delaying the inauguration of the Messianic era, it is more than likely that he is alluding here to a *new* premessianic act, about which he has certainly already spoken to the Thessalonians, since they are supposed to know about it, but *which has not been directly forecast in the usual scheme of Jewish apocalyptic.*' This interpretation of ἄρτι in II Thess. 2.7 is unlikely, as the contrast with ἄρτι in v. 7 must be ἐν τῷ αὐτοῦ καιρῷ in v. 6 and the future manifestation of Antichrist in vv. 8 f. We can regard νῦν in v. 6 in the same way as ἄρτι and as belonging to τὸ κατέχον (so Dibelius *ad loc.*), but it may also be regarded as belonging to οἴδατε in view of the readers' knowledge now in contrast to the time of the mission (ἔτι ὢν πρὸς ὑμᾶς, v. 5). Such a distinction between the time of the mission and 'now' might rest on the distinction mentioned in I Cor. 2–3 between the first proclamation and the later imparting of wisdom. See pp. 154–57 and 159 f. If this view is right, it supports Cullmann's interpretation of II Thess. 2 (but not his interpretation of ἄρτι in v. 7), as in that case Paul let the church at Thessalonica share in 'wisdom' at a later time than the mission, giving it special information, which had not been mentioned in the mission-preaching, about God's plan of salvation.

usual Christian view, what preceded the coming of the Messiah was to be the preaching of the Gospel, whereas with Paul it was to be the preaching of the Gospel to the Gentiles. But we know from Mark 13.10 (and the parallel passage in Matt. 24.14) that the Gospel must first be preached to the Gentiles before the end can come: 'And the gospel must first be preached to all nations.' But if τὸ κατέχον means the preaching of the Gospel to the Gentiles, who is ὁ κατέχων? It cannot be God who is meant,[1] but only an instrument that God uses. It is in fact to disappear. ὁ κατέχων must be he whose task it is to carry out what is in τὸ κατέχον. It must be Paul, the apostle to the Gentiles, who is described as ὁ κατέχων.

The idea that the mission had any place in eschatological events was quite foreign to Jewry. But Jewish speculations as to the time of the coming of the Messianic age had set out from the seventy weeks mentioned in Dan. 9.24 ff. and the half week mentioned in 9.27, which are identified in Dan. 12.7 and 12.11 with the three and a half times and again with 1,290 days. Other Jews, who saw that the end still did not come, although it ought to have done so according to this apocalyptic arithmetic, drew the conclusion that something was delaying the coming of the Messianic time. They asked, מִי מְעַכֵּב, 'What is holding back?'

And the answer was: Israel must first be converted; before that happens the Messianic age cannot begin. We therefore find in Jewish literature an expression corresponding exactly to τὸ κατέχον. The verb κατέχειν can be regarded as an exact translation of עכב. Like κατέχειν this Aramaic verb means both 'to hold back, restrain' and 'to delay'.[2]

If it were the Jews themselves who were responsible for delaying the Messianic time, eschatology would be more a matter of human morality than a question of God's mighty deeds. Among the Jews, therefore, opposition to this view began to be voiced, and it was asserted that, on the contrary, what was delaying the coming of the Messiah was the time appointed by God.

The interpretation put forward by Cullmann is in line with the Jewish view that the conversion has to take place before the Messiah can come. But as the emphasis is on the possibility of the conversion that God will offer to men through the preaching of the Gospel immediately before the end,[3] the coming of the kingdom of God depends on God, and not simply on men. Thus τὸ κατέχον in II Thess. 2.6

---

[1]This was the opinion of Theodoret, Theodore of Mopsuestia, and others.
[2]Cullmann refers on pp. 224 f. to Billerbeck's evidence.
[3]We may here add to Cullmann's article a reference to the ideas in Paul's Areopagus speech (Acts 17.30 f.): . . . ὁ Θεὸς τὰ νῦν ἀπαγγέλλει τοῖς ἀνθρώποις πάντας πανταχοῦ μετανοεῖν, καθότι ἔστησεν ἡμέραν ἐν ᾗ μέλλει κρίνειν τὴν οἰκουμένην ἐν δικαιοσύνῃ . . . .

corresponds to the Jewish מְעַכֵּב which demands the conversion of the Jews before the beginning of the Messianic time. Among Christians the new incentive of preaching is added to the Jewish incentive of conversion. While the Jews already had in the Law instruction about conversion, a proclamation of the Gospel is necessary for conversion to Christianity; and as soon as Christianity leaves the Jewish sphere, it is natural for it to express this eschatological theme by the preaching of the Gospel to the Gentiles.

Now in Judaism too, preaching is regarded as an eschatological call to conversion in the tradition of the return of Elijah in the Last Days (Mal. 3.1; Ecclus. 48.10 f.). We find in the New Testament this idea about the coming of Elijah: Matt. 11.14; 17.10; Luke 1.17; John 1.21; cf. Rev. 11.3.[1] This tradition is important in understanding τὸ κατέχον in II Thess. 2, because it shows us not only that preaching was a part of the Jewish expectation, but that it involved at the same time—as in II Thess. 2—the personification of this proclamation of the Messiah's coming in a prophet who is his precursor.[2] In these two conceptions in Jewish thought—that the end cannot come before Israel has been converted, and that Elijah must first return and preach in preparation for the coming of the Messiah—we have the Jewish antecedents of the Christian idea that the preaching of the Gospel among the Gentiles will delay for the time being the coming of Antichrist and the events that will follow it.

Now II Thess. 2.6 f. does not stand alone. In Mark 13.10, Matt. 24.14, and various other passages, we find the same idea of the preaching of the Gospel among the Gentiles as the necessary presupposition for the coming of the Messiah. We refer to Rev. 6.1–8, where the rider on the white horse is a personification of the victorious march of the Gospel through the world before the coming of the apocalyptic plagues; and also to Acts 1.6 ff., where Jesus refuses to make any kind of calculation about the last days; but, as v. 8 shows, the kingdom is not to be established at once, as the disciples first have to spread the Gospel over the world. The same holds good for Mark 16.14 according to the manuscript W. In Matt. 28.19 f. the disciples are to preach to the Gentiles, and the Lord will be with them till the end of the age. This promise is of no indefinite kind, but relates to the period of time that is to precede the end, and during which the Gentiles are to be preached to. In Acts 10.42 Peter emphasizes that the message of Jesus as the eschatological judge must first be preached, before the end can come. In Acts 3.19 ff. we hear in Peter's speech the same summons to repentance,

---

[1]On this see my treatise, *Petrus und Paulus in der Offenbarung Johannis*, 1950.
[2]*Ibid.*, pp. 13–16.

so that the Lord may send the eschatological times that we know in Jewish eschatology.[1]

Although this idea that preaching was a sign that was to precede the Messianic age is not confined to Paul, it takes a particularly central place with him. That is made very clear in Rom. 9–11, where the need for preaching is plainly stated in 10.14 (cf. δεῖ in Mark 13.10). When Paul wrote the letter to the Romans, the Jews were not willing to accept the Gospel; and salvation was therefore no longer the exclusive privilege of Israel after the flesh. It does not depend on Israel whether the Gentiles may partake of the blessedness of the kingdom of God, as Jewish apocalyptic doctrine taught. On the contrary, according to Rom. 9–11 the Gentiles are to be the means by which the Jews participate in salvation. The Gentiles occupy the place of Israel after the Spirit, and inherit all the promises that have been made about the chosen people.[2] The old Jewish question: What is delaying the coming of the Messianic age? is formulated more precisely by Paul: What has become of God's promises to Israel? The answer is: The Gospel must first be preached to the Gentiles (Mark 13.10), but Paul lays the stress on the word 'Gentiles' (p. 236): 'As regards the eschatological task which must be fulfilled before the end, it follows that, for St Paul, it is no longer the preaching of the Gospel in general, but more precisely the preaching to the Gentiles.'[3]

The salvation of 'Israel' depends on the Gentiles, and to a decisive degree on the possibility that God offers them of being converted. Preaching to the Gentiles occupies a clear chronological place in God's plan of salvation. And even if the term κατέχον does not appear in that weighty presentation in Rom. 11, the idea about what is delaying the plan of salvation is clearly expressed there.

The significance that the apostle attaches to this idea is made clear by the special nature of his call. It cannot be sufficiently stressed that

[1]God's μαχροθυμία in II Peter 3.9, 15 has to do with the idea of the time of the preaching that precedes the judgment.

[2]As I have already shown in my article 'Israel and the Gentiles in the New Testament', *JTS*, n. s. 2, 1951, pp. 3–16, it is difficult to reproduce the line of thought of Rom. 9–11 without assuming the negative attitude of the later Gentile Church towards the Jews. What is noteworthy in Paul's standpoint is that Israel after the flesh is still covered by God's promises.

[3]Cullmann refers to this passage on p. 236 n. 1, which ends with the words: 'The eschatological plan remains as it was fixed by the Messianic promises, for, according to him, God was not bound by these promises to a racial group, but to Israel according to "the Spirit".' On this passage and note, it may be said that Paul is deeply grieved about the preaching to Israel, and takes comfort from the thought that it will be effected by preaching to the Gentiles; for although he is the apostle to the Gentiles, he has the salvation of his own people very much at heart, as is shown particularly in Rom. 11. In Rom. 9–11 Paul speaks of the salvation, not of a spiritual Israel, but of Israel after the flesh, and of God's plan for its deliverance.

with Paul it is not a matter of a call to apostleship in general, but of a clearly defined apostleship in relation to the Gentiles.[1] His personal call coincides with an objective eschatological necessity, namely God's plan that the Gospel is to be preached to the Gentiles before the end of the age. It is therefore very important that in the chapter in which he reveals to the Romans the mystery of the divine plan, he reminds them of his own service as apostle to the Gentiles (Rom. 11.13). In Col. 1.22–29 (cf. Eph. 3.6 ff.) Paul stresses in the same way the close connexion between his personal service and the plan of God's grace, which concerns this mystery in the Gentile world (τὸ μυστήριον τοῦτο ἐν τοῖς ἔθνεσιν). Because he knows that he is the instrument of an eschatological plan that comes from God, he relies on revelations when it is a matter of getting to know its smallest details. He himself relates (Gal. 2.2) that he went up to Jerusalem in consequence of a revelation; and Acts is certainly right in telling how the Holy Spirit prevents him from going to certain places in Asia Minor and preaching there (Acts 16.6 f.; cf. 20.22).

The call of the other apostles too has an eschatological character, as they are to prepare the way for the coming of the Messianic age; but in Paul's case the apostolic consciousness reaches a greater intensity than in the case of any other apostle or any Old Testament prophet. In a way he is called to play the part of prophetic herald in the sense of Jewish apocalyptic thought. When he describes himself in II Thess. 2 as ὁ κατέχων, it is quite in keeping with what he says in the other letters, according to which he is associated in person with God's plan for the salvation of the Gentiles. This is what produces his dual attitude— that he boasts, and that he expresses his weakness in the exercise of his commission (Rom. 15.17 ff.; II Cor. 10.8; I Cor. 9.16).

The fact that Paul regards himself as the one on whom the arrival of the Messianic age depends is therefore not as remarkable as it at first seems. The expression ἐκ μέσου γίγνεσθαι (II Thess. 2.7) need not mean 'to be forcibly removed', but simply means 'to disappear', and may refer to the apostle's death. This will coincide with the conclusion of the preaching among the Gentiles, and will specify the appointed time for the manifestation of Antichrist and the beginning of the Messianic age.[2] The context in II Thess. 2 also supports Cullmann's

---

[1]This question whether there is a separate apostleship will be dealt with later in a book on apostleship in the New Testament. For the present see pp. 46 f.

[2]In a way Albert Schweitzer's thesis that Paul expected to be taken up into heaven, in the same way as Enoch, Elijah, and Baruch, after his death (*The Mysticism of Paul the Apostle*, ET 1931, p. 136) may find confirmation in II Thess. 2.6 f., as Cullmann interprets this text. Such an expectation corresponds to the apostolic consciousness that makes Paul regard his own death as a decisive eschatological date (Cullmann, p. 243).

interpretation. The verses that follow the passage about 'what is restraining' show that the Gospel must be preached before the manifestation of Antichrist, those who have not received the love of truth, by which they may be saved, allowing themselves tỏ be seduced by him (2.9–11). This text requires, so to speak, a mention of the preaching that precedes it, and it would almost be necessary to assume this, if we had not the reference to 'what is restraining', namely the preaching of the Gospel to the Gentiles. The arguments that follow in the letter are also in keeping with the new exposition of ch. 2.6 f.

This exposition—and with it Cullmann ends his article—shows, when taken in conjunction with the texts quoted from the remaining letters, that Paul's apostolic consciousness in its eschatological form stands in the centre of his personality and theology in quite a different way from that usually supposed.

II

This extraordinarily valuable article has not only provided a fresh, and in my opinion correct, exposition of II Thess. 2.6 f., but it has also taken account of a number of texts which we shall examine in the following pages, and has thrown new light on them. The first text that we shall examine is Rom. 11, which Cullmann seems to me to have treated rather inadequately.

In Rom. 9–11 Paul describes the destiny of Israel after the flesh in relation to God's plan of salvation as a whole. In ch. 9 he shows that the Jew cannot claim salvation, for it is God who has the sovereignty over salvation and perdition; and God has in fact chosen for himself the Gentiles and a remnant of Israel. In 9.30–10.21 he shows how the Gentiles, but not the Jews, received salvation, because the Jews would not take God's way to it, but sought out their own. And in ch. 11, which is now to be considered, he asks whether Israel's refusal of salvation by faith involves the rejection of Israel. The answer is No. There remains a chosen remnant of Israel, and it was not God's will that the Jews should fall. Their fall led to the salvation of the Gentiles, and God's plan is that the fullness of the Gentiles shall in the future lead the way to the salvation of all Israel. For the way of God's salvation is: disobedience, and afterwards compassion; and in that way God will save everyone.

In these chapters Paul speaks, not of individuals, but of nations.[1] Abraham and Isaac, Edom and Pharaoh are nations. God chooses one nation and rejects another. In his time he has chosen Israel and hardened

---

[1]M. Dibelius and W. G. Kümmel, *Paul*, ET 1953, p. 34, are mistaken in thinking that in Rom. 9.15 the mercy is shown to individuals.

Egypt, and in Paul's day Israel was impenitent, while only a remnant was chosen. But in this connexion, when only nations are concerned, and where at last the acute crisis in the history of salvation is being worked out in relation to the two categories, Israel and the Gentiles, one individual, Paul, is taking part as though it were a matter of course. In 9.1–5 he says that, like Moses, he would willingly sacrifice himself for Israel's benefit; and in 11.13 f. he says, 'Now I am speaking to you Gentiles. Inasmuch then as I am an apostle to the Gentiles, I magnify my ministry in order to make my fellow Jews jealous, and thus save some of them.' 'For,' he goes on in v. 15, 'if their rejection means the reconciliation of the world, what will their acceptance mean but life from the dead?' This context shows that the salvation of the Gentiles and of Israel are inseparable. The Jews' 'No' to Christ and to the apostles' preaching causes salvation to come to the Gentiles. But that is not the only result that God brings forth from the Jews' 'No'. The salvation of the Gentiles is in its turn to exercise a positive effect on impenitent Israel, provoking her to emulation or jealousy *(ζῆλος); and* thus the fullness of the Gentiles will be the sign for the salvation of all Israel.

In this picture of the last events before the return of Christ—it should be added, with regard to the usual exegetical treatment of Rom. 9–11, that these events are to take place in the immediate future (we cannot indeed say in Paul's lifetime, as the apostle, according to Cullmann's interpretation of II Thess. 2, will no longer be there when the fullness of the Gentiles is accomplished)—Paul is not only the one who knows what God's plan is and can tell of it, but the one by whose action this fullness is to be brought about. What has been accomplished —that great numbers of the Gentiles are accepting salvation—is already arousing the jealousy of the Jews, with the result that some of them are being saved (11.13 f.). And before long the fullness of the Gentiles will bring this jealousy to its culmination and make all Israel receive salvation (11.25 f.). The apostle is certainly the apostle to the Gentiles, as he himself says (11.13); but his work in the mission to them is at the same time indirectly missionary work to Israel. In this way our text says the same as what Cullmann saw in II Thess. 2.6 f., namely that Paul's work is more important than that of all the apostles who went to the Jews and were turned away by that impenitent nation (Rom. 10.16–21). Where their work failed, the way of salvation provided by God for Israel will become a reality through Paul's work for the Gentiles. This also means that the apostle's work is more important than that of all the figures in Old Testament redemptive history, because he has been appointed by God to fill the key position in the last great drama of salvation.

It is not possible here to carry out a minute exegesis of this important text,[1] and we have to content ourselves with throwing some light on the essential points in Paul's apostleship and the earliest history of primitive Christianity.

1. The salvation of the Gentiles and of Israel are inseparable. What has so far happened after the coming of Jesus is that the Jews have rejected him and refused to accept from the missionaries who were sent out the proclamation of salvation through faith (9.30–10.21). The result of this unbelief by the Jews has been that the Gospel is now being preached to the Gentiles (11.11). As long as Rom. 9–11 is regarded as an isolated point of view peculiar to Paul, out of touch with the main line of Christian thought, it is difficult to understand the separate parts of the whole. But if we regard the questions that Paul answers, and the problems that he takes up and discusses, as burning questions among Christians of Jewish as well as of Gentile origin, the line of thought becomes clearer,[2] and the difference between Paul's standpoint and other Christian solutions of the same problems stands out more sharply. We may regard 11.11 in the following way: when the Jews rejected Jesus, their Messiah, had God willed their ever-growing sin, their impenitence? Paul denies it. God turned their sin to good ends, first for the Gentiles, and then for themselves. The question that Paul asks here is hardly his own, but rather a burning problem of the time. If we compare this with his warnings in vv. 17 f., and especially in v. 19, to the Gentile Christians, it is easy to suppose that this was their point of view. It was assumed that the Jews' present impenitence was a part of their final attitude, so that salvation was now open only to the Gentiles. But Paul is able to show that the salvation of the Gentiles and of Israel are not two isolated and mutually exclusive dimensions. On the contrary, the salvation of the Gentiles became God's plan when Israel sinned, and this plan will have its repercussions so that Israel too will be saved. God decrees that Israel's disobedience to God's Messiah shall be a means for the salvation of the Gentiles, and thereby at the same time for the salvation of Israel. That can be seen in the answer in v. 11: 'Through their trespass salvation has come to the Gentiles, so as to make Israel jealous.'

2. Paul denies in 11.11 that the Jews' fall was according to the divine plan: ἵνα πέσωσιν. Instead of that, the divine plan is εἰς τὸ παραζηλῶσαι

[1]My book, *Christus und Israel*, 1956, offers an exegetical examination of Rom. 9–11.

[2]It is remarkable that in other letters Paul cannot put such a question as 'Am I not an apostle?' (I Cor. 9.1) without the expositors' assuming that other people doubted his apostleship. But in the letter to the Romans everything that he says is supposed to be a systematic presentation with no connexion with his everyday life and his missionary work.

αὐτούς. παραζηλῶσαι has already appeared in the quotation from Deut. 32.21 in 10.19, where the passage served as proof that Israel had understood the apostles' preaching quite well. God intends to make the Jews jealous of a foolish nation, the Gentiles (who have therefore been able to understand this preaching by the apostles). Paul uses Moses' song in Deut. 32.1 ff. several times in his letters.[1] It is natural that Moses' sharp indictment of Israel occupies Paul's thoughts, and he too realizes that the doom will be averted. But of course he could not approve of the Jewish nationalist view that the doom that Israel had deserved would be transferred to the nation's enemies. The verse that speaks of Israel's jealousy of the Gentiles apparently carries great weight with Paul when it reappears here, to lay emphasis, not on the 'foolish nation', as when it was quoted in 10.19, but on the fact that Israel will be provoked to jealousy against the Gentiles. The following verses show that this 'provoking to jealousy' indicates the practical missionary method towards Israel. While there are Gentile Christians who think that Israel's fall means Israel's end, Paul insists that Israel's central place in the history of salvation will be clearly shown at the last. On the one hand, Israel's 'No' leads to salvation, and on the other, her later 'Yes' will mark a decisive turning-point. Paul's observations are therefore directed to his own time, to counter a misconception by the Gentile Christians, and his arguments about ζῆλος were therefore very pertinent to his own time.

What was Paul's conception of the way leading from the Jews' jealousy to their salvation? It is clear that Israel could feel no jealousy towards the Gentiles as long as she did not count on their attaining salvation. But as soon as the Jew can see and realize that the Gentiles are attaining what was promised to Israel, the possibility of jealousy exists, because what was promised to Israel was falling to the 'foolish nation' (10.19), and not to the Jews, for whom it had been destined.

Through this jealousy of the Jews towards the Gentiles, Paul will be able to save τινὰς ἐξ αὐτῶν. It has been assumed that the apostle showed a certain modesty[2] in expecting the salvation of *all* Israel through God's mighty intervention. Now τινές means in itself not a small number, but simply an indefinite number. And it is clear from the way in which τινές is used with regard to Israel's unbelief, that it is not in the least necessary to think of a small number in this connexion. In 11.17 we read εἰ δέ τινες τῶν κλάδων ἐξεκλάσθησαν, and earlier, in 3.3,

---

[1]Deut. 32.5 is used in Phil. 2.15; v. 17 in I Cor. 10.20; v. 21 in Rom. 10.19 and 11.11; another passage from v. 21 in I Cor. 10.22 (this use of Moses' song in I Cor. 10.20 and 10.22 throws light on Paul's account of Israel in the desert in vv. 1 ff.); v. 35 in Rom. 12.19; v. 43 in Rom. 15.10.
[2]Thus B. Weiss and E. Kühl.

εἰ ἠπίστησάν τινες. In these passages Paul is undoubtedly thinking how overwhelmingly unbelieving Israel has been, and that most Jews have been broken off the cultivated olive-tree. τινές reminds us of the οὐ πάντες which is applied to the Jews in 9.6 and 10.16. It must not be supposed, because of this cautious and almost veiled way of speaking about Israel's unbelief and stumbling, that τινές refers here to quite a small number of Jews who, in contrast to the many, attain salvation. There would then be a decisive difference between the present time, of the apostle's labours, and a time to come, that of God's intervention for the salvation of all Israel.

There are two possibilities. One is that the apostle's mission to the Gentiles denotes a preparation for God's future intervention for Israel's salvation. Although the conversion of the Gentiles has not yet been accomplished, Paul already sees the coming events in Israel as a consequence of his work among the Gentiles (παραζηλώσω and σώσω, 11.14, cf. v. 11). A certain number of the nation will be saved, even before all Israel attains salvation. The other possibility is that the apostle's mission to the Gentiles is itself the way in which God is intervening for Israel's salvation. The apostle does not feel excluded from this future, although he will not live to see it, as his work will be at an end when the fullness of the Gentiles is attained. In both these cases τινές means a great number of the chosen people; and the coming time with the salvation of all Israel is not an entirely new phase in the history of salvation, but follows from the jealousy that the apostle regards as the decisive means of breaking down Israel's hardness of heart, and of changing the destiny of the nation.

It is important that the text is able to show the unique nature of Paul's apostleship. We can agree with Zahn that ἐφ' ὅσον shows that Paul's apostleship has a special task in his preaching to the Gentiles. It appeals, as do the efforts of the other apostles, to the whole of mankind, and therefore does not exclude the work that directly concerns Israel. Or we can take it that Paul was solely a missionary to the Gentiles,[1] and that he is arguing here in the text that his mission to the Gentiles is an important task in relation to Israel. The presumption is, however, that Israel will not be obedient to the Gospel, but that God can reach the Jews with his salvation by a roundabout way, namely by way of the Gentiles, through the ζῆλος that the Gentiles' acceptance of the Gospel arouses among the Jews. But even then it is not necessary to insist on the expression 'apostle to the Gentiles' in such a way as to

---

[1] The treatment of Paul's apostleship will be carried further and deeper in the book that I have in prospect on apostleship in the New Testament. At present see pp. 40–42 (Cullmann's views) and pp. 119–22.

mean that Paul could not imagine himself appealing to the Jews. But while Peter and other apostles continued to appeal to Israel in spite of her hardness of heart, Paul received the task of preaching the Gospel to the Gentiles. And in respect of the salvation of the Jews this task is not simply a roundabout way, but is foreseen by God as the shortest way (Deut. 32.21) to turn the Jews from their unbelief and lead them through jealousy to salvation.

3. What is to bring about the salvation of all Israel is 'the fullness of the Gentiles', τὸ πλήρωμα τῶν ἐθνῶν. In 11.25 f. Paul reveals a 'mystery', namely that Israel's hardness of heart is limited, not only in extent (Rom. 11.1–10) but also in time, as it is to last only till τὸ πλήρωμα τῶν ἐθνῶν εἰσέλθῃ, and then all Israel will be saved. The last words in v. 25 cause difficulties. By εἰσέλθῃ one usually understands the entering into the community of salvation (Weiss) or into the kingdom of God (Maier).[1] Sanday and Headlam write that the word was used almost technically about the entry into God's kingdom or 'the Divine glory of life', and point to Matt. 7.21; 18.8, and Mark 9.43–47; and because of this technical use it came to be given the same meaning when used absolutely (Matt. 7.13; 23.13; Luke 13.24).[2] That is correct, but it must be observed that this usage is found more often in Matthew and Mark, less often in Luke, once only in John's Gospel (3.5) and in Acts (14.22), nowhere (unless it is here) in Paul, and in a number of passages such as εἰσέρχεσθαι εἰς τὴν κατάπαυσίν μου in Heb. 3.11–4.11. We are therefore not dealing with such a general usage that we can at once let Paul apply εἰσέρχεσθαι here in an absolute sense, understanding εἰς τὴν βασιλείαν τοῦ Θεοῦ. It is better here to take it in the weaker meaning of 'to come, enter' (see Arndt and Gingrich s.v. 1 and Liddell and Scott s.v.), and to translate 'until the fullness of the Gentiles come in'. The question here is whether it is correct to translate the subject of εἰσέρχεσθαι, viz. τὸ πλήρωμα τῶν ἐθνῶν, as 'the full completed number, the complement of the Gentiles', as Sanday and Headlam do. Sanday and Headlam think that, just as τὸ πλήρωμα αὐτῶν in v. 12 denotes the Jewish people as a whole, τὸ πλήρωμα τῶν ἐθνῶν must denote here the full number of the Gentiles. As evidence they refer to Baruch's Apocalypse 23.5: 'But now the number already mentioned is being completed, and thus the creature lives no longer. For my spirit creates the living, and the world below receives the dead,' and II (4) Esd. 2.40 f.: '*Recipe, Sion, numerum tuum, et conclude candidatos tuos, qui legem Domini compleverunt. Filiorum tuorum, quos optabas, plenus est numerus. Roga imperium*

---

[1] F. W. Maier: *Israel in der Heilsgeschichte nach Römer 9–11* (Biblische Zeitfragen XII, 11/12), 1929.
[2] Cf. Arndt and Gingrich, s.v. 2.

Domini, ut sanctificetur populus tuus, qui vocatus est ab initio.' It should be noted that the 'number' mentioned in both texts, must be in Greek not πλήρωμα but ἀριθμός. In Rev. 7.4 we hear of the number of the sealed; but we do not hear anywhere in the New Testament a figure quoted as a *numerus clausus*. There is therefore no reason at all to apply that meaning to the text here when we read τὸ πλήρωμα τῶν ἐθνῶν. If we consider Rom. 11.12, it becomes clear that its τὸ πλήρωμα αὐτῶν is of the greatest importance for understanding τὸ πλήρωμα τῶν ἐθνῶν in v. 25. If the Jews' stumbling means riches for the world—Paul uses other expressions and chooses ἥττημα, probably to prepare the πλήρωμα that follows—if indeed their present insufficiency means riches for the Gentiles, how much more will the 'fullness' of the Jews mean for the world and the Gentiles. The insufficiency of the Jews does not involve the πλήρωμα of the Gentiles, but it means riches for them. That is the stage that the Gentiles have at present reached, while their πλήρωμα is still in the future, marking the appointed time that will turn Israel's destiny.

If we compare these two passages with the use of πληρόω (πληροφορέω) in Rom. 15.19: πεπληρωκέναι τὸ εὐαγγέλιον τοῦ Χριστοῦ, cf. vv. 15 f.; Col. 1.25: πληρῶσαι τὸν λόγον τοῦ Θεοῦ, cf. vv. 26 ff.; II Tim. 4.17: ἵνα δι' ἐμοῦ τὸ κήρυγμα πληροφορηθῇ καὶ ἀκούσωσιν πάντα τὰ ἔθνη, we see how in three contexts πληρόω (πληροφορέω) is used of the completion of the spreading of the Gospel among the Gentiles (see Rom. 15.15 f.; Col. 1.26 ff.); and for that reason τὸ πλήρωμα τῶν ἐθνῶν may be the pregnant expression 'the fullness of the Gentiles'. How are we to think of this 'fullness of the Gentiles'? As we tried to show above, it is not likely to refer to a definite number that is to be reached. That would imply that Paul teaches a mechanical kind of predestination, whereas he always regards divine choice as an act by whose visible and manifest results it can be recognized; and in Paul's view God by his free grace took Israel into his care, afterwards making the disobedient nation hard-hearted, and again taking it into his care before the end of the world. That line of thought presupposes a plan of salvation, a living God who acts in human history, and to whom no abstract philosophical theory of predestination can be applied. But 'the fullness of the Gentiles' may refer to an aim that consists, not in the saving of a given number of people, but in the hearing of the Gospel by the Gentile world as a whole—in a representative form certainly;[1] that means that it consists both in the preaching of the Gospel to them, and in their hearing and believing it.[2] This fullness, which in the Synoptic Gospels

[1]See my article 'Israel and the Gentiles in the New Testament', *JTS*, n.s. 2, 1951, pp. 7–9.
[2]Lietzmann paraphrases τὸ πλήρωμα αὐτῶν (the Jews) in 11.12 by 'the complete conversion of Israel'.

(Matt. 24.14; Mark 13.10) precedes the last phase of eschatological events and the manifestation of Antichrist, is here conceived as what precedes the final salvation of the Jews.[1]

Thus Paul, as the apostle to the Gentiles, becomes the central figure in the story of salvation. While the apostles who were sent to Israel had to say at last, 'Lord, who has believed what he has heard from us?' (Rom. 10.16), the Gentiles accept the Gospel when Paul preaches; and this testimony to God's saving work will kindle the Jews' indignation and bring them as well as the Gentiles into obedience to God. The fullness of the Gentiles, which is Paul's aim, is the decisive turning-point in redemptive history. With that there begins the salvation of Israel and the coming of Antichrist, and through it the coming of Christ for judgment and salvation, and so the end of the world.

III

Another text in Romans is also capable of throwing light on the position that Paul takes up with regard to the history of salvation, not, as in chs. 9–11, in relation to Israel and the Gentiles, but as in II Thess. 2 simply in relation to his work of achieving the 'fullness of the Gentiles'. In Rom. 15.14 ff. the apostle turns to the church in Rome and explains what his attitude in the letter to the Romans is to that church, and what the significance of his anticipated visit is in relation to his call and his activity as the apostle to the Gentiles.

Paul points out that the arguments in the letter are not addressed to a church lacking strength and maturity, but that it is his apostleship to the Gentiles that justifies him in the exhortations that the letter contains. διὰ τὴν χάριν τὴν δοθεῖσάν μοι ἀπὸ τοῦ Θεοῦ in v. 15 reminds us of 1.5: δι' οὗ ἐλάβομεν χάριν καὶ ἀποστολήν and 12.3: λέγω γὰρ διὰ τῆς χάριτος τῆς δοθείσης μοι.[2] He then adds that that grace is given him by God so that he may be λειτουργὸν Χριστοῦ Ἰησοῦ εἰς τὰ ἔθνη. λειτουργός refers

---

[1] As Paul has the idea, according to II Thess. 2.6 f., that the preaching of the Gospel to the Gentiles will bring in, after its conclusion, the coming of Antichrist, the question must be asked how Paul came to connect in his mind the conversion of the Jews with the coming of Antichrist. The patristic and medieval expositors of the Revelation suppose a relation between the two events (see my *Petrus und Paulus* etc., pp. 89 ff.), but in Paul's case the material seems too scanty for us to be able to give a definite answer.

[2] This expression is also used in I Cor. 3.10 with regard to Paul's apostleship to the Gentiles: κατὰ τὴν χάριν τοῦ Θεοῦ τὴν δοθεῖσάν μοι, where Paul speaks of the founding of the church—a parallel to v. 20 in the passage we are considering. We also read of the apostleship in I Cor. 15.10: χάριτι δὲ Θεοῦ εἰμι ὅ εἰμι, καὶ ἡ χάρις αὐτοῦ ἡ εἰς ἐμὲ οὐ κενὴ ἐγενήθη ... οὐκ ἐγὼ δὲ ἀλλὰ ἡ χάρις τοῦ Θεοῦ σὺν ἐμοί; and in Gal. 2.9: γνόντες τὴν χάριν τὴν δοθεῖσάν μοι. Cf. Eph. 3.8: ἐμοὶ τῷ ἐλαχιστοτέρῳ πάντων ἁγίων ἐδόθη ἡ χάρις αὕτη.

here, as the context shows, to priestly service,[1] which is performed for
the Gentiles by Paul in his capacity as priest for God's Gospel
(ἱερουργοῦντα κτλ.). The object of that service is that the Gentiles'
offering may be acceptable, being sanctified by the Holy Spirit. It is
usual to make this remark by Paul refer to work that has already been
achieved; in that case the Gentiles, converted and sanctified by God's
Spirit, would be the offering that Paul as the priest of Jesus Christ has
brought to God, having kindled their faith by preaching the Gospel.[2]
But it is not in this text alone that Paul speaks of the Gentiles' offering.
It is true that he does not use the word προσφορά anywhere else (it
occurs in Eph. 5.2); but we have the picture of the offering again in
Phil. 2.17, where Paul as the sacrificing priest presents the Gentiles'
faith as a sacrificial gift, and at the same time pours his own blood
over it.[3]

The transition from Rom. 15.16 to v. 17 has caused the expositors
no difficulty. The assertion in v. 17, for example, is regarded as a
limitation: as a priest Paul has glory only in Christ and only towards
God (Lagrange). Or, as often happens elsewhere, controversy is brought
into an uncontroversial passage if, with Sanday and Headlam, we think
that Paul is defending his apostolic authority which has been asserted
in v. 15. With regard to Lagrange it must be objected that the great
emphasis placed in vv. 15 f. on Paul's having received his apostleship from
God, and on his being Jesus Christ's priest performing a priest's service for
God's Gospel, makes it unlikely that the words ἐν Χριστῷ Ἰησοῦ τὰ πρὸς
τὸν Θεόν are the new element in v. 17, limiting what has just been said.
The only thing that is new in v. 17 is (τὴν) καύχησιν, the glory arising
from his apostleship,[4] and v. 17 (not 16) is continued in v. 19b, after

---

[1]Zahn and A. Schlatter think that λειτουργός denotes the holder of a public
office. Paul does everything to spread the Gospel, and takes no payment for his work.
This view is rightly rejected by Kühl and M.-J. Lagrange.

[2]Thus B. Weiss, C. H. Dodd and Lagrange, who, however, deny that it is a
question here of baptism; Paul has not pursued the comparison.

[3]There is much dispute in the commentaries about this passage. Does θυσία
mean the victim, or the act of sacrificing (in addition to λειτουργία)? Is it Paul or
the Philippians who sacrifice? Paul might be regarded here as in Rom. 15.16 (in
spite of M. R. Vincent, *Philippians*) as a sacrificing priest, and (with Lohmeyer) as
a drink-offering and priest at the same time, so that the meaning of this passage is,
as Sass has suggested (*Apostelamt und Kirche*, 1939, p. 90): 'If death occurs "at the
sacrifice" or "during the sacrificial ceremony", then the faith of the Philippians or
the faith of all nations must be the sacrificial gift that is presented. Then Paul would
see in the act of sacrifice the moment when (according to II Cor. 11.2) he has to
present the Church of all nations to the Lord. Now it might be just possible that he
was having to give up his life at that very moment, that it was now, so to speak,
being poured out as a drink-offering over the victim, and so giving it the last and
highest consecration.' Again in II Tim. 4.6, during the prosecution in Rome, Paul
uses σπένδομαι about his death. On these passages about sacrifice cf. O. Schmitz:
Die Opferanschauung des späteren Judentums etc., 1910, pp. 231–5.

[4]Cf. O. Moe *ad loc.*

Paul has first declared negatively in vv. 18–19a that he will not boast of the καύχησις belonging to any other person; and this gives him the occasion to name the gifts that are bestowed on him for carrying out his work as apostle.

Thus the context becomes clear: Paul explains to the church in Rome that he is justified in speaking to them as he has spoken, because he is the apostle to the Gentiles,[1] but that for the time being he has finished his task only in the east, and that he is making it a point of honour to preach the Gospel where Christ's name has not yet been heard. That is why he has not yet been to Rome, and why, in spite of his longing to preach there, his future visit must be limited with a view to his preaching in mission fields that have not yet been visited. It is therefore natural to assume with Sass (see above, p. 50 n. 3) that the Gentiles' offering is still a future event which will crown Paul's work among the Gentiles. In such a case ἡ προσφορὰ τῶν ἐθνῶν of Rom. 15.16 is the same event as τὸ πλήρωμα τῶν ἐθνῶν of 11.25, and is identical with the ὑπακοὴ ἐθνῶν of 15.18.

It is not the only place where we hear of the Gentiles' obedience. In Rom. 1.5, as quoted above, Paul speaks of Christ, δι' οὗ ἐλάβομεν χάριν καὶ ἀποστολὴν εἰς ὑπακοὴν πίστεως ἐν πᾶσιν τοῖς ἔθνεσιν, in which he certainly includes the Roman church of Gentile Christians, just as in 16.26 he speaks of the mystery that was made known εἰς ὑπακοὴν πίστεως εἰς πάντα τὰ ἔθνη.[2] Of course, a beginning has already been made with the Gentiles' obedience; but it is important that their complete obedience has not yet been achieved, and that in what follows, Paul shows how far it has gone.[3]

The continuation of 15.17 in v. 19b shows how far Paul has performed the task that, according to v. 16, his call to apostleship had laid

---

[1]It will be shown later (see pp. 201, 204–7) that the church in Rome is a church of Gentile Christians.

[2]Rom. 16.25–27 is not authentic. See T. W. Manson, 'St Paul's Letter to the Romans—and Others', *BJRL* 31, 1948, p. 10; and R. Schumacher, *Die beiden letzten Kapitel des Römerbriefes* (Neutestamentliche Abhandlungen XIV, 4), 1929, pp. 116–24 (favouring authenticity).

[3]Another text in Phil. 4.18, πεπλήρωμαι δεξάμενος παρὰ 'Επαφροδίτου τὰ παρ' ὑμῶν, ὀσμὴν εὐωδίας, θυσίαν δεκτήν, εὐάρεστον τῷ Θεῷ, might suggest another view of Rom. 15.16, viz., of the Gentiles' gift to the church in Jerusalem—a gift that is described, not indeed as προσφορά or θυσία, but as λειτουργία; II Cor. 9.12: ἡ διακονία τῆς λειτουργίας ταύτης (cf. λειτουργῆσαι in Rom. 15.27, which, however, need not be regarded as priestly service). But this is evidence only of this one parallel, whereas we may infer from the context in Rom. 15 that Paul does not directly mention the Gentile churches' collection for Jerusalem before v. 25, although that collection can hardly be without importance for the effectiveness of his work among Gentiles and Jews, as we shall see later (pp. 287–308). The application to the collection of these terms, which are taken from the priestly and sacrificial service, is a sign of its central importance for his apostleship. The gift of the churches is a fragrant and acceptable offering, because it testifies that the final eschatological stage, the Gentiles' great offering, or the fullness of the Gentiles, is now approaching.

on him. He has preached Christ's Gospel to a region stretching in an arc from Jerusalem to Illyricum.[1] Here he has finished; he has no more 'room' in the east. There remains for him the west, namely Spain and, we may suppose, Gaul and Britain. It is clear from v. 18 that others besides Paul have worked among the Gentiles, but also that he alone is the priest who is to prepare the Gentiles' offering, and that what the others achieved is not to be compared with what he can claim for his work (cf. I Cor. 15.10). In vv. 20 f. he says that his choice of the mission field in the west, and the limits that are put to his visit to Rome, show that he feels in honour bound to preach Christ's name where it has not been heard, so that he will not build on another man's foundation.[2]

Paul's service is concerned with all the Gentiles; but so far he has finished it only in the east, though in the east he has, in fact, finished it. It has sometimes caused surprise that he can claim to have finished it in the east, and the surprise is justified from the point of view of modern missionary ideas, which do not regard missionary work as finished till all have become church members by baptism. Several expositors try to rationalize Paul's assertion by pointing to his preaching in the large centres, from which Christianity could be spread abroad;[3] but the real explanation is that he thinks in nations.[4] Althaus writes about 15.19: 'The nations stand as a whole before God and his judgment. They are whole entities. If the word has come to a people in its last generation, even to only a few of its members, that means that all are reached, and that the whole nation is responsible. That is the most that the apostle had tried to achieve. Therefore he has now finished in the east.' And Wrede expresses it as follows: 'If the name of Christ were only preached

---

[1]These two geographical names can be taken inclusively or exclusively. If κύκλῳ is translated as 'surrounding region', the passage becomes stronger evidence of Paul's work among the Jews in Judaea before he worked as the apostle to the Gentiles (cf. Acts 26.20). Thus B. Weiss, who makes Paul's preaching begin in Judaea and Syria, not in Arabia. The patristic expositors seem to regard the word as implying that the apostle preached God's word all over the many countries lying between Jerusalem and Illyricum, not simply along the shortest route (Chrysostom, *PG* 60, 656; Theodoret, *PG* 82, 213B; and Oecumenius, *PG* 118, 621D).

[2]Cerfaux writes in 'Saint Paul et le "Serviteur de Dieu" d'Isaïe', *StAns* 27–28, 1951, p. 362: 'Paul would have understood, as he read the great passage about the Servant with the guidance of the Holy Spirit, that these prophetic words applied to his own mission, and that, as a result, he must present the Christian message to those who had not yet heard it. If we allow this starting point, we shall interpret φιλοτιμούμενον in v. 20, not of a point of honour (Lagrange), but of a fixed purpose (a frequent meaning of φιλοτιμέομαι), which would be made more definite under the influence of the sacred text. We should thus exclude the probably anachronistic idea that Paul was sensitive in an extreme degree to a mere point of honour.' In Lagrange's exposition, which is rejected by Cerfaux, we have an excellent example of the secularization of Paul, which is to be resisted if we are to understand him historically.

[3]Thus Sanday and Headlam on 15.21, and Lagrange and Kühl on 15.19. Cf. Goguel, *Les Premiers Temps de l'Église*, p. 102.

[4]Thus Wrede, *Paul*, ET 1907, pp. 47 ff.; Lietzmann and Althaus on 15.19.

in every province, then the whole world . . . would have heard the gospel' (p. 48).

That is correct, but it needs adding to, so that we may not understand vv. 18 f. in the way that Jülicher does: 'A tremendous exaggeration, in view of the exertions of Christianity, century after century, to establish itself there—an exaggeration difficult to understand except from the apostle, to whom the world seemed rather small, who in his excited hope of the approaching end of the world could not hurry fast enough from one country to another, so as at least to have made an opportunity for Christ to be known, who finally (cf. 11.15 ff.) came to think, among "all the peoples" to whom salvation was to be preached, not of individuals, but of the nations as a whole. It was enough for him that the word of the Cross had been proclaimed, for example, among the Galatians, Achaians, Macedonians, Illyrians, and Asians; then the Galatians, Achaians, etc. could not complain on the day of judgment that they had been neglected. He was not a man made for working out small details—no one can be so made who believes himself called to accomplish gigantic tasks in so short a time.'

We will deal at once with this unjust judgment about Paul. First we must adduce support for the assertion that he thinks in nations, and for this we can turn to our text's nearest parallel, the treatment of the mission to Jews—Rom. 10.14–21, which speaks of the apostles who were sent to Israel (ἀποσταλῶσιν in v. 15) and of their complete failure: 'Lord, who has believed what he has heard from us?' The question whether the Gospel has been preached to the Jews Paul answers affirmatively, quoting Ps. 19.4: 'Their voice has gone out to all the earth, and their words to the end of the earth.' Here most commentaries follow Sanday and Headlam, who say, 'As a matter of fact the Gospel had not been preached everywhere. . . . But all that St Paul means to imply is that it is universal in its character.'[1] If we regard the words from Ps. 19 as scriptural evidence (although there is no introductory formula), and take the words of the quotation literally, they mean that the apostles who were sent to the Jews have now finished their work. If they too, like Paul in the east, have not been everywhere or preached the Gospel to every individual Jew, yet their task in respect of the whole of Israel has been completed. Those parts of Israel to which they have preached stand for the whole, for the Jewish people; and Paul can therefore go on to assert (10.21 and ch. 11) that Israel is unbelieving and hardened.[2]

---

[1]Thus Zahn and Lagrange, whereas Weiss and Maier, *Israel in der Heilsgeschichte* etc., regard what is quoted as an actual citation of Scripture.
[2]See my article, 'Israel and the Gentiles' etc., pp. 7–9.

While therefore it is true that Paul thinks in nations, we are justified in asserting with Kühl about 15.19, 'Moreover v. 22 shows clearly that in this very point Paul's judgment was not in the least superficial or frivolous.' From the letters of the third missionary journey, at the end of which the letter to the Romans and the words that are dealt with here were written, we clearly get the impression that the apostle had been checked in the east. The struggle for the Galatians, and especially the struggle for the church at Corinth, claimed the apostle's time and thought while he was staying at Ephesus, and cut across his great plan of ending that journey with a splendid gift from the Gentile churches to the poor in the church at Jerusalem. The struggle to keep those churches in the faith of Christ prevented him from going further on his way westward to complete the preaching of the Gospel to all the Gentiles. The apostles who were sent to the Jews seem indeed to have already finished, but Paul does not seem to have done so if, like them, he had only a negative report to make. He has not reached the stage of being able to leave the east till he has won back the church at Corinth —we are not told what happened to the Galatian churches[1]—and only then does he go to Jerusalem before the journey that he had planned to Spain.

In this solicitude for his churches, in the (approximately) two and three years that he spent in Corinth and Ephesus respectively (according to Acts 18.11, 18 and 19.8, 10, 21 f.), and in the embittered struggle with the church at Corinth, where he does not give way, but yet spurns honour and dignity if only he can win it back to fellowship with Christ, so that these communities may not be shut off from Christ for ever—in all this we see a man who takes great trouble to achieve his aim, and who displays an admirable carefulness in his work. The tents that Paul stitched during his missionary work in various towns were certainly no second-rate work, whatever the urgency of spreading the Gospel to the ends of the earth. The same care has long since been noticed by many researchers in his treatment of individual people: fellow-workers, individual Christian brothers and sisters; and this willingness to take trouble for the individual goes hand in hand with the work for God's plan of salvation, a plan demanding continual exertion and sacrifice. We need not be surprised in Paul's case at the trouble taken by the eschatological messenger over individuals and details while he travels the way appointed by God. We find the same thing in the picture of Jesus in the Gospels.

In vv. 20 f. Paul adds that his aim in the exercise of his apostleship

---

[1]On this see below, pp. 291–97.

is to preach the Gospel where Christ has not been named; that is in accordance with Isa. 52.15.[1]

Because of this great work in the east[2] he has often been prevented from going to Rome (cf. Rom. 1.13); but now, as he no longer has 'room' in the east, he will yield to his ardent wish of long standing and visit the Roman church on his journey to Spain. He hopes to see it on the way and get support from it for his coming work in the west.[3]

This visit, however, is not to take place just yet, as Paul must first go to Jerusalem in the service of the saints there. For the churches in Macedonia and Achaia have made a collection for the poor who are among the saints in Jerusalem.[4] But the journey to Spain, and with it the visit to Rome, will follow as a sequel to his visit to Jerusalem. The apostle asks the church for its intercession for a successful journey to Jerusalem, as regards the Jews and also the church in Judaea.[5]

If II Thess. 2 showed us the apostle as the man to whom the mission to the Gentiles was entrusted till this hindrance to Christ's return had been successfully ended, Rom. 9–11 gave us an insight into the connexion between the mission to the Jews and the mission to the Gentiles, and showed us Paul's work as the decisive factor in redemptive history. The text last discussed, Rom. 15.14 ff., is again concerned, in the verses dealt with, only with the mission to the Gentiles; but it shows Paul's method of work, his results, and his next objectives.

IV

The three texts that have been dealt with hitherto narrate Paul's apostleship as a call to eschatological labours within God's plan of salvation. They resemble each other in being entirely uncontroversial. Paul stands as the apostle of the Gentiles alone among the Gentiles, and when his work is finished, all Israel will be saved, Antichrist will manifest himself and have the sovereignty till Christ comes for judgment and salvation. In texts that will be dealt with later, Paul is compelled to compare himself with people whom the church at Corinth thought of putting on an equality with himself (see pp. 175–87).

What point have we now reached in this chapter? From a few uncontroversial texts we have worked out a view of Paul different from the

---

[1]Here too people (e.g., Jülicher and Lietzmann) have tried to see in Paul's words a criticism of the Judaizers. This is rightly denied by Althaus.
[2]διό refers back to v. 19 (Lietzmann and Lagrange).
[3]Thus Dodd, whereas it is denied by Sanday and Headlam.
[4]On this passage about the collection, see pp. 287–97.
[5]Other letters too ask towards the end for the intercession of the church; e.g., Col. 4.3; I Thess. 5.25; II Thess. 3.1. Cf. Eph. 6.19 and Heb. 13.18 f.

usua! one in recent Pauline research. Here we speak with a certain reserve about uncontroversial texts written by Paul. The tendency to find controversy everywhere in his letters is so marked that even his most innocent remarks are interpreted as controversial. Everywhere the Judaizers of Jerusalem are compelling him to defend himself against poisonous accusations—that is the usual view.[1] I therefore understand here by uncontroversial passages those texts that are not usually regarded as controversial, and whose content actually is in all probability uncontroversial.

In working out this new understanding of Paul I have not yet used the controversial texts—those passages that are regarded as controversial in Pauline research taken as a whole. Of course, controversial texts can be used to determine the characteristics of a historical person; they may define his standpoint in relation to other people, show his psychological reactions, and so on; but as sources they cannot have the value of uncontroversial texts; and this is especially so when we know nothing through other channels about those other people in relation to whom one's attitude has to be defined. Where, as in Paul's case, that is not possible, those other people must first be reconstructed from texts that must be regarded, not as objective evidence, but as unrestrained controversy, where the readers knew what the matter was and understood every allusion quite clearly. Thus an exposition of Paul that is based essentially on his encounters with his opponents in his letters becomes unsafe in its methods and can never produce certain or even probable conclusions. The right method must therefore be to proceed from the uncontroversial texts, and after that to try to find out whether the picture that they draw of the eschatological messenger is consistent with the controversial texts, which as a rule led to quite a different view of Paul. If those texts are not mutually consistent, the controversial texts must give precedence to the uncontroversial ones.

Several researchers have already tried to base their understanding of Paul on (among other things) some of the features that we adduced from the uncontroversial texts, which we mentioned above (p. 30 n. 1). A book that is particularly interesting is Windisch's *Paulus und Christus*.[2] It has a wealth of useful observations and interesting details. Among other things it anticipated various points in my article 'La vocation de l'apôtre Paul', but I did not know the book then. Windisch's problem

---

[1]"Thus the apostle Paul seems to be permanently armed for battle; and any of his writings in which he meets us in any other form must be suspect in advance.' H. Schmidt and J. Haussleiter, 'F. C. Baur' in *Realencyklopädie für protestantische Theologie und Kirche*[3] II, 1897, p. 475. 29–31.

[2]*Paulus und Christus. Ein biblisch—religionsgeschichtlicher Vergleich* UNT (24), 1934.

is important, but his thesis of Paul's likeness to Christ cannot be maintained in the way that he has done it.[1] In this, as often elsewhere, Windisch is not able to differentiate clearly between different things, and so does not succeed in convincing the reader, in spite of his mass of material and his excellent analysis of details.

As already mentioned (p. 30 n. 1), Rengstorf assumed (*Apostleship*, pp. 53–62) that Paul is directly linked with Jeremiah in the consciousness of his mission. And Windisch (pp. 150 f.) described both Paul and Jesus as figures of the Jeremiah type in the New Testament, whereas Lohmeyer more cautiously characterizes Paul as a prophet, a prophetic apostle.[2]

These and other attempts to classify Paul[3] are hardly as valuable as has been supposed. Of course, any comparison that such classification by types involves is of some importance in understanding the subject. But classification by types may easily lead to misunderstandings. After all, the things that are arranged in pigeon-holes are more important than the pigeon-holes themselves. But once they have been put into a pigeon-hole and ticketed, it is difficult to get a clear view of them. There is no better proof of this than Pauline research.

It is natural to arrange by types the phenomena of daily life and those that are bound to recur. But we are at once treading on dangerous ground if we try to do this, as Windisch and Rengstorf have tried, with Jesus and Paul or with Paul and Jeremiah. Just as it is reasonable in ordinary life to deal with special things in a special way, so in the sphere of knowledge too it is best to leave what is unique untrammelled by categories that are useful for relationships that recur or for the kind of person who is frequently met with.

If we think of Paul's relation to the figures of Old Testament redemptive history, there are no grounds for giving him any pre-eminent connexion with any one of them. For instance, he can express the wish (Rom. 9.3) to sacrifice himself like Moses for Israel, or he can compare himself with Elijah (Rom. 11.2 f.)—though in the latter case with the essential difference that Paul does not turn to God against Israel. But it is still more important that Paul's reason for comparing himself with these great Old Testament figures is not that he thinks he can do so

[1]It is therefore clear at once that Cerfaux is right, as opposed to Windisch, when he thinks in 'Saint Paul et le "Serviteur de Dieu" ', *StAns* 27–28, pp. 351–65, that Paul is chosen to perform the service of God's servant—that is, Christ's service in Jesus' steps—in relation to the Gentiles. Windisch thinks on the contrary that Paul himself is God's servant, greater than Jesus, because he is sent to all nations, whereas Jesus was sent only to Israel (Windisch pp. 143–50).

[2]*Grundlagen paulinischer Theologie*, 1929, pp. 200 ff.

[3]Cf. R. Otto, *The Kingdom of God and the Son of Man*, ET 1938, pp. 333 ff. ('The Kingdom of God and the Charisma').

without presumption. For Paul his own time and therefore his own task
is of greater importance than those figures of the Old Covenant. He has
in fact seen it as the 'Old Covenant' in the light of Christ and his
Church, because now is the time of fulfilment. We should therefore not,
with Windisch (p. 151) speak of prototypes, but only of characteristics
of Old Testament figures used to express the new and higher reality.

V

That this is true emerges from a closer consideration of II Cor.
3.7–18, where Moses' service is compared with Paul's far higher service.
Windisch in his commentary has called this passage a Christian midrash,
and thought it could quite well be taken out without injury to the co-
herence of the letter.[1] From that he infers, as he is clearly entitled to,
that it contains no allusions to Judaizers. Christianity and Judaism,
not Paulinism and the views of the Judaizers, are the great contrasts
(p. 112). But, as 3.1–6 and 4.1–6 show, the passage lying in between is
a part of Paul's argumentation, and Judaism and Christianity appear
personified in the figures of Moses and Paul respectively. It comes
without surprise that as far as the Gentiles are concerned the apostle to
the Gentiles embodies Christianity—that is as obvious as Moses'
embodiment of Judaism. As we shall see later, Paul is not contending
against Judaizing in II Corinthians, and in chs. 1–9 he is concerned only
with the church, and not with the opponents who have arrived from
elsewhere (see pp. 171–87).

While there is here no lack of clarity, there are many obscure passages
in 3.7–18. At first the argument is clear: if Moses' service was glorious,
Paul's service which was so much higher (Spirit instead of letter, stability
instead of destruction, justification instead of condemnation) will attain
much greater glory. It is often asserted that this glory is not a future one
($\check{\epsilon}\sigma\tau\alpha\iota$ in v. 8 is said to be logical future, and $\epsilon\lambda\pi\iota\delta\alpha\;\check{\epsilon}\chi o\nu\tau\epsilon\varsigma$ in v. 12 is
not purely future; thus Lietzmann and Koch, whereas Windisch ends
with a *non liquet*); and it may be pointed out that v. 9 has the present
form $\pi\epsilon\rho\iota\sigma\sigma\epsilon\acute{\upsilon}\epsilon\iota$, and that $\delta\acute{o}\xi\alpha$ in v. 18 is an inward glory which Christians make their own here and now. But the way in which the passage
speaks of Israel's past and present obduracy and coming salvation is
against this view. Paul's view here, as in Rom. 11, is that the Israelites
are now impenitent, but that this condition will not be the final one.

---

[1]These exaggerated words (on p. 112) are, however, corrected by H. Windisch himself on p. 131: 'Yet it appears clearly from 3.4–6 as well as from 4.1–6 that the digression
is caused by Paul's apologia.' It becomes still clearer by the remark interwoven in the
'midrash' in 3.12.

This emerges clearly from the expressions ἄχρι γὰρ τῆς σήμερον ἡμέρας in v. 14, ἕως σήμερον in v. 15, and ἡνίκα κτλ. in v. 16 (taken from Ex. 34.34).

If we can proceed from the assumption that the passage is extraneous matter, which underwent only a partial change when it was incorporated in the letter, much remaining unchanged, then the passage originally deals with Paul and Israel, Paul being the servant of the spiritual principle, and Moses of the literal principle. And if the service of the literal principle was associated with glory, as the Scripture shows (Ex. 34.29–35) that is still truer of the service of the spiritual principle to which Paul was called. This hope of a coming glory, which characterizes Paul's service, gives him boldness, so that he has no need at all for such devices as Moses used when he covered his face, to conceal from the Israelites that the glory faded. But they disregarded it and hardened their hearts, so that even today the veil remains, and it will not be removed till they are converted to the Lord (this holds good for Israel as a whole, not for individual Jews). As the Lord is the spiritual principle,[1] freedom will rule where the Lord's Spirit holds sway. That will be the case when every Jew, now without a veil, sees the glory of the Lord as a result of Israel's salvation in the last days, being transformed by that sight to ever greater glory.

The use of the present tense in vv. 9 and 18 is against this view, and in the same way we cannot help being surprised to meet in II Corinthians so clear a line of thought and such a comparatively logical presentation of a picture. But this could be explained by assuming that Paul had worked out earlier in another connexion this line of thought that Christianity has a greater glory than Judaism, but that in the future Israel will be freed from her stubbornness and will achieve the same glory as the Gentiles. If the comparison between Paul and Moses in v. 12 leads to Paul's saying that he needs no such devices as Moses did, that may well rest on the connexion in II Corinthians with the description of Paul's irreproachable mode of life.

It has also been claimed that the last verses, 17 f., relate to Christians in general and in the present world, not to the salvation of the Jews and their glory at the end of the world. But that leads to difficulties which the commentators do not seem to have realized. If vv. 17 f. are so regarded, then the use of δόξα in II Cor. 3.17 f. forms an exception to the usage

---

[1]Thus Koch, who rightly denies that Christ is identified in v. 17 with the Holy Spirit. Paul goes back here to the contrast between γράμμα and πνεῦμα in vv. 6–8. Just as he might have said, 'Moses is the letter', so he says here, 'The Lord is the Spirit'. Paul thereby declares which of the two principles Christ represents and therefore with which one he himself is in a certain sense united. The working of the Spirit is really the working of Christ.

in the rest of the New Testament (G. Kittel in *TWNT* II, pp. 254 f.; Kittel argues that the reference is to the present world).[1] It is a different matter if the last verses too are given an eschatological sense; in that case δόξα throughout the section refers to a reality that will not appear till the end of the world. And since elsewhere δόξα means for Paul something which man will not share till the end of the world (*TWNT* II, pp. 253–5), it is natural not to regard II Cor. 3.17 f. as an exception, but to relate this section in its entirety to Israel's true glory at the end of the world, by which the glory of Paul's service will be made manifest, in contrast to Moses' short-lived glory which has been a hindrance (a veil) to faith up to our own time.

This interpretation is also supported by a consideration of the context in II Corinthians. Did Paul intend at this particular point and in the existing situation of his readers to emphasize their glory? It is extremely unlikely. In I Cor. 4.8–13 we see that the Corinthians are already feeling well filled and rich and like kings and therefore in possession of the eschatological δόξα, and how Paul contrasts them with the despised and suffering apostles. And in II Corinthians Paul continues his description of the true apostle as one who has failed in the eyes of the world and of whom no one can be proud. Whenever Paul has anything positive to say about him, it is evident that he does so with reserve. Only the false apostle extols the values to which this world pays homage.

Apart from these reflections about principles, other considerations about the use of δόξα may be adduced as an argument for the eschatological view. It has already been mentioned that the word is generally used about a heavenly or a future eschatological glory.[2] With II Cor. 3.12, ἔχοντες οὖν τοιαύτην ἐλπίδα . . . we may compare Rom. 5.2, καυχώμεθα ἐπ' ἐλπίδι τῆς δόξης τοῦ Θεοῦ, and Col. 1.27, Χριστὸς ἐν ὑμῖν, ἡ ἐλπὶς τῆς δόξης. And with II Cor. 3.17, οὗ δὲ τὸ πνεῦμα Κυρίου, ἐλευθερία, we may compare Rom. 8.21, εἰς τὴν ἐλευθερίαν τῆς δόξης τῶν τέκνων τοῦ Θεοῦ. And to II Cor. 3.18 and the picture of the veil that is succeeded by uninterrupted vision, we can find a parallel in the other picture in I Cor. 13.12 in the words βλέπομεν γὰρ ἄρτι δι' ἐσόπτρου ἐν αἰνίγματι, τότε δὲ πρόσωπον πρὸς πρόσωπον.

Now whether one is convinced by these arguments or holds to the usual view of II Cor. 3.7–18, it is clear in either case that Moses and

---

[1] So does J. Schneider, *Doxa* (Neutestamentliche Forschungen III, 3), 1932, pp. 96–99, who assumes that Paul is speaking here of the 'culmination of his vision of Christ'; and H. Kittel, *Die Herrlichkeit Gottes* (BZNW 16), 1934, pp. 202–7, who thinks that the passage speaks of the δόξα of the state of justification.

[2] In this sense in Rom. 2.10; 8.18; 9.23 twice; II Cor. 4.17, as well as here; Col. 3.4; I Thess. 2.12; II Thess. 2.14; cf. II Tim. 2.10.

Paul are compared here with each other.[1] The service of the former cannot in any way be matched in glory with the service of the latter. Of Paul's many new and startling utterances, this is perhaps the most surprising. The greatest man in the history of Israel is put beneath the travelling tentmaker, a man who is at the same time contending for the church at Corinth, so that it may submit to him.

No stronger proof can be produced that as a figure in redemptive history in the age of the Messiah Paul far surpasses even the greatest of the great figures of Israel.

VI

It is natural to add to this comparison of Paul and Moses a further comparison, namely one between Paul and Peter. With this comparison we can fittingly leave the texts that are now under discussion and go on to discuss the controversial Pauline texts.

In Gal. 2.1–10 Paul, as part of his controversy with the Judaizers in the Galatian churches, mentions a few significant points about a meeting in Jerusalem. Gal. 1–2 will be dealt with in detail later in ch. 4; here we would expound only 2.7 f., so as to understand Paul's view of his own and Peter's apostleship. This is the only place where Paul speaks of the apostleship of another person who above all, like himself, was called.[2]

The two verses are introduced as follows: 'But on the contrary, when they' (viz. those of repute) 'saw that I had been entrusted with the gospel to the uncircumcised, just as Peter had been entrusted with the gospel to the circumcised (for he who worked through Peter for the mission to the circumcised worked through me also for the Gentiles) . . . ', and they go on to state that James, Cephas, and John on the one side and Paul and Barnabas on the other had shaken hands on the agreement that the latter were to go to the Gentiles and the former to the circumcised.

The noteworthy use of 'Peter' and 'Cephas' in the text[3] does not seem to be explicable along exegetical lines, and this change from one name to the other must be left as a problem of textual criticism, while we regard v. 7 as Paul's report on what took place at the meeting, and v. 8 as an explanation formulated in his own way.[4] The two verses say just

---

[1]In *Petrus und Paulus* etc., p. 119, I have expressed myself against a Moses-Christ typology in II Cor. 3 (in contrast to Joachim Jeremias in *TWNT* IV, pp. 873 f.).

[2]'Paul, the Apostles, and the Twelve', *ST* 3, p. 108.

[3]'Peter' is used by Paul only here in Gal. 2.7 f. Zahn thinks that he uses 'Peter' with the Judaizers in mind.

[4]Thus too Lietzmann: 'An incidental remark.'

about the same thing, but the explanation in v. 8 is given with the help
of the word 'apostle', ἀποστολή being used of Peter's preaching of the
Gospel to the Jews. In this way the comparison and parallel between
the two is expressed more strongly in v. 8 than in v. 7. This text has
caused many people to express their surprise that Paul ventures to
compare himself here with Peter, the first of the apostles. But coming
from the uncontroversial texts to Gal. 2.8, we see in the verse a great
concession by Paul. He has received a call that can only with difficulty
be compared with the call of any other person or be put on the same
level with it. But what we know of his apostleship helps us to understand his words—he admits that Peter can be compared with him; as
he himself has the eschatological call to the Gentiles, so Peter has it to
Israel. We know from Rom. 9–11 that even for Paul the apostleship in
relation to Israel is the more important, thanks to the special position
of the chosen people; but the results of the mission show that the
apostles who were sent to the Jews have so far achieved nothing except
the hardening of Israel. The mission to the Gentiles will therefore prove
to be the more important one, because its completion will usher in the
salvation of all Israel.

There are details in the text that throw still more light on Peter's and
his own apostleship. He mentions in 2.9 that James, Cephas, and John
were regarded in Jerusalem as pillars. If Peter was regarded as a pillar,
he cannot at the same time have been regarded as the rock on which
Christ builds his Church. We see too that several pillars—at any rate the
three named—are carrying the Church, and no distinction is made
between them. The order too—James, Cephas, and John—suggests that
Peter did not occupy a special position among them. We may infer
from this that on his visits to Jerusalem, at any rate on his second visit,
Paul found in Jerusalem an order of precedence not in accordance with
Jesus' words to Peter in Matt. 16.18. Now it is peculiar that in his comparison in v. 8 Paul gives the three leaders a different valuation from
that which he found in Jerusalem. He has long since lost sight of
Barnabas (v. 1) and Titus (v. 3), and at the critical moment 'those of
repute' and the 'pillars' disappear.[1] After citing the relative position of
Peter and himself according to the Jerusalem meeting, he puts Peter and
Paul in contrast to each other in his own formulation.[2] This might be
connected with the fact that it is a question here of the apostleship, to

---

[1]'Those of repute' and the 'pillars' are regarded as the same persons by F. Sieffert
and M.-J. Lagrange. Zahn and H. Schlier make the 'pillars' a smaller circle within
'those of repute'.

[2]Of course the words in both verses are Paul's own, and the assertion that the
last verse gives his own formulation is a pure supposition. Perhaps we should
rather say that vv. 7 f. are Paul's formulation, while v. 9, which says 'that we should
go to the Gentiles and they to the circumcised' is a citation of the agreement.

which James was not called, nor do we know whether John was called by the risen Lord to be an apostle.[1] But when an apostle speaks of the apostleship, he speaks of it as a whole, and in doing so he does not distinguish in the modern way between the Church authorities and the mission going out from them to the Jews, as if he wanted to put these two bodies on the same level. It is therefore natural to suppose that Paul saw in Peter a man with a call that, like his own, was unique of its kind, and who was therefore engaged in a service that was likewise of critical importance for the last days. But we cannot infer from the short text how near equality Paul supposed his position and Peter's to be.

From this we cannot make Paul a witness for Matt. 16.18.[2] There is a fundamental difference between the two apostles with regard to the tradition of their call. Within the tradition the call plays a great part in both cases, and special weight is laid on the unworthiness of the person called, in view of Peter's denial and Paul's persecution of Christ. But whereas in Paul's case the traditions about the call do not vary greatly and, apart from external circumstances, agree remarkably with each other (as we saw in ch. 1) and can therefore be traced back to Paul's own account as part of the preaching of the mission, there exist for Peter several traditions which vary on important points.

Apart from Matt. 16.18, we have the call to be a fisher of men in Matt. 4.18–20 and Mark 1.16–18, and in Luke 5.1–11 Peter's catch of fish. We have a parallel to this in John 21.1–19, where Jesus reveals himself to seven disciples by Lake Tiberias, asks Peter whether he loves him, and tells him to feed his lambs. Besides these there are short passages that are presumably connected with Peter's call; e.g. John 1.42, where Jesus gives the name Peter to Simon the son of John (cf. Mark 3.16), and the words to Peter at the Last Supper in Luke 22.31 f., whereby he receives a call with regard to his brethren 'when you have turned again', and also the brief remarks about the risen Lord who had appeared to Peter (Luke 24.34 and I Cor. 15.5), which may have been the outer framework containing the account of the call in Matt. 16.[3]

[1] John in Ephesus is long called μαθητὴς τοῦ Κυρίου, and only later apostle; but on this see 'Paul, the Apostles, and the Twelve', p. 103.

[2] Thus J. Chapman, 'St Paul and the Revelation to St Peter, Matt. 16.17', *Revue Bénédictine* 29, 1912, pp. 133–47, thinks that Paul knew Matt. 16.16 f. because of the close parallels with Gal. 1.12, 16. Chapman also thinks that Paul's use of 'Peter' in Gal. 2.7 f. is explained by his having in Q an account in Greek of Peter's confession and Jesus' answer.

[3] Cullmann on the other hand would put Jesus' words to Peter (Matt. 16.17 ff.) in the story of the Passion and originally in conjunction with the prophecy of Peter's denial (*Peter: Disciple, Apostle, Martyr*, ET 1953, pp. 178–84). While Cullmann is right in saying that Matt. 16.17 ff. is a tradition that did not originally belong to the narrative of Peter's confession at Caesarea Philippi, he has not succeeded in showing convincingly that the words were originally part of the story of the Passion.

Among these varying traditions about the call of Peter, Paul must have known one that told of his call as apostle to Israel. The comparison in Gal. 2.7 f. aims indeed at showing that Peter too is an apostle, but an apostle for Israel. It may refer to one of the accounts already mentioned of his call to be a fisher of men or to feed Jesus' lambs; but it may also be a tradition that we do not know of; or it may be Matt. 16.18 f., though in the latter case the present form of v. 19a cannot be the original one.

But the most important thing about Paul's words in Gal. 2.8 is that he neither shares Jerusalem's view of Peter as one of the pillars, second to James, nor contents himself with pointing to Peter's mission to the Jews and his own mission to the Gentiles (as 'those of repute' do in v. 7), but that he lays it down as his own opinion that Peter is an apostle just as he himself is, and that Peter in his call in relation to Israel can justifiably be compared with Paul in his quite unique mission to the Gentiles. In this recognition of Peter as an apostle of equal rank, far beyond his then more modest rank in Jerusalem among 'those of repute' and the 'pillars', we have a witness, not only for Paul's assessment of himself, but also for his free and independent judgment of another whom God had called through Christ to an outstanding work at the end of time.

VII

In later texts too we can find the apostle Paul described in terms of an outstanding figure in redemptive history. In Rev. 11.3–13 he and the apostle Peter are represented as the witnesses who are to precede Antichrist,[1] and in Acts 20.17–38 and I and II Timothy we get from the sub-apostolic age the picture of Paul as one who is taking leave of his friends and whose death will bring to the churches persecution and inward strife.[2] In all these texts we can confirm what I have tried to show in the above-mentioned treatises, that it is not a question of free inventions by a later generation, but that their ideas go back, with changes here and there, to the apostle himself. Nothing more and nothing greater has been said about Paul in these later texts than in Rom. 11 and 15, II Thess. 2, and Gal. 2. As we saw (in ch. 1) that the account of his call went back to the apostle himself, so we can now safely say here that he spoke of himself in the same way as the later time described him. We cannot speak of the increase of mythologizing; such an explanation would be most profitable to modern dogmatic

---

[1] See my *Petrus und Paulus in der Offenbarung Johannis*.
[2] See my article, 'Discours d'adieu dans le Nouveau Testament', in *Aux Sources de la Tradition Chrétienne: Mélanges Goguel*, 1950, pp. 159–63.

theories; but that kind of mythologizing would not be capable of explanation from the currents and inclinations of primitive Christianity.

Pauline research has been engaged for long periods in what might be called, in the language of modern theology, secularization and demythologization. Purely secular ideas have been used to describe the apostle and his call, and those secular ideas have been imposed on the apostle himself as if they were his own thoughts and motives. In the same way people have tried to transform his personal and concrete way of thinking into a modern, abstract line of thought and to stretch it on the Procrustes' bed of every fleeting philosophy that happens to be in fashion.

A few examples will show this, and what follows in this book will bring further examples here and there, arising unsought in the course of the historical work. We begin with a quite innocent example: we have inherited from the older generation a view of Paul as a great missionary strategist. He follows with his clear gaze the main lines of communication through the Roman world by sea and land, and founds in the large centres viable churches that may serve as missionary bases for the adjacent towns and provinces. We met this view above (see pp. 52 ff.) in dealing with Rom. 15.23. In that way his missionary outlook has been modernized and rationalized to make it agree with modern ideas, and he has been taken far away from the world of apocalyptic thought where his roots are. Only when we realize that the end of the world is at hand, that the salvation of the Gentiles and of the Jews are bound up together, that Paul is called to prepare the fullness of the Gentiles to usher in the coming of Antichrist and the coming of Christ in glory, that all this is true for the small Pauline churches of former pagans, that these churches arise where the apostle works among the nations so that the opportunity may be given them to define their attitude to the Gospel—only when we have realized all this is it possible to understand Paul's biblical conception of his mission.

We misunderstand Paul much more fatally if, as has been usual, we regard him as a theologian.[1] We theologians easily make this mistake, recreating everything according to our own picture; and in Paul's case it is generally the systematic theologians who possess themselves of his letters and stamp him as a systematizer, not always as a good

---

[1] This tendency, however, is decreasing; see Goguel, *Les Premiers Temps de l'Église*, p. 92: 'Paul was not a theologian in his study, reflecting at leisure on the problem of human destiny. He was a missionary whose thought was shaped and formulated in the course of an exceptionally active life.' Cf. p. 98: 'What the apostle wanted was not to solve a theological problem, but to bring as many souls as possible to enjoy the benefits of the redemptive work of Christ . . .' : and Dibelius and Kümmel, *Paul*, p. 40, 'His thinking is opportunist, not systematic.'

systematic theologian, though often as a considerably better one than an ordinary expositor would expect after studying the apostle's letters.

One of the reasons for the wrong conception of Paul that has been current since the time of the Tübingen School is just this one-sided view of him as a theologian. People make him a Christian thinker who goes out from his study into the rough-and-tumble of the day's controversy as the keen logical representative of his own particular ideas (Paulinism) and at the same time as the supple, clever church politician who is unfortunately not always morally unassailable. The liberal period, with its emphasis on the deep emotions of the apostle's religious life, reflected freely and unchanged in his letters, wanted to break with the idea of Paul as a theologian—Paul's place is not in theology but in religion, so Deissmann could say[1]—but in the place of Paul the thinker it merely succeeded in putting an apostle swayed by his feelings and always autobiographical. This misunderstanding of Paul's capacity for thinking must of course be rejected. He certainly can think, and he does. But on the other hand it must be stressed that he is not a theologian in the modern sense. Just as we cannot trace in his letters the course of his intimate feelings—what, if anything, we learn of his feelings is determined solely by the needs of the churches—so Paul has never in his letters presented Christian thought in a connected form; on the contrary, he has spoken his mind about current problems; and, if behind that there is a line of connected thought, we do not know what it is, but only how it works out in discussions of practical questions. This point of view also holds good for the letter to the Romans, which was certainly not written in relation to any direct controversy and was not provoked by conditions in the church at Rome, its object probably being to come to an understanding about the results of the struggles during the third journey, among other things the disputes with the Judaizers, when these were over (see pp. 197–200). As we shall see, such a discussion had its practical aim. Paul wrote the letter to give the Gentile churches and the Jerusalem church an account of what was achieved in the mission field and what problems now confronted them.

Instead of the thinker clinging at all costs to his own line of thought, or the excitable sentimentalist carrying the churches along with him and laying bare in his letters his most intimate feelings, it is the *apostle* Paul with whom research has to do. He is the man who has been called, who has a unique task to perform in the last great drama of salvation. It is the apostolic task, that of the emissary who is to go to the Gentiles to preach the Gospel, so that this hindrance to the coming of Christ and final salvation shall be cleared away. In this connexion Paul's

[1] *St Paul*, p. 6.

feelings play no part; we know very little about them, and he himself attaches no importance to them. On the other hand, his thoughts become clear in his letters, yet not as *his* thoughts, but as the language of the Scriptures, as the words of Christ or the tradition of the Church, or his own exposition, given him by divine grace, of what was not already established in God's revelation or in the usage of the churches. Throughout his letters the questions that he has treated are problems that have had to be discussed in consequence of his apostolic work as the man called by God to be the apostle to the Gentiles, and they are missionary problems that Paul met with in his work. For the churches' sake he discusses them and tries to find their practical solutions according to which the Christians can regulate their lives. That is what his theology, if we can call it that, consists of. He is no Albert Schweitzer, continuing his theological work during his missionary activity. No, all Paul's work as a thinker arises from his missionary activity, and its object is missionary work. We can say of Paul's theology, *mutatis mutandis*, what has been said of Goethe's religiosity, that it is primarily an accompaniment of his activity. His theology arises from his work as apostle and directly serves that work.

This is also the reason why this long book about Paul does not contain a single chapter about his theology. On the other hand it deals with the apostle's call and with his conception of that call, with his relation to Jesus' earliest disciples and to his own churches, with his conception of the missions to the Jews and the Gentiles, and finally with his journeys and their destinations, Jerusalem and Rome;[1] and all this is in the deepest sense Paul's theology. We propose to explain this in more detail by means of the last two examples, his journeys, which seem to be the least promising. They will bring before our eyes the thoughts that he had on those journeys; and so we shall concern ourselves with his theology, but only in the form in which he himself saw it, in relation to his work. Thus he has considered Jerusalem and Rome theologically, but at the same time they are the places where he was to develop his work by virtue of his call. Both Jerusalem and Rome are the subject of theological consideration: what do they signify within the framework of the plan of salvation, how can the Gospel be taken to them, and what work is Paul called to do in these very cities? Thus Jerusalem and Rome are, if we will, theological problems that have to be solved; but the solution is no coherent theory—rather it carries in itself the answer that the missionary needs. He discovers through it the work to which Christ has called him, in Jerusalem and Rome.

[1]Wrede, *Paul*, p. 30: 'An active character like Paul can only be clearly recognized in its activity.'

VIII

As already mentioned at the beginning of this chapter, we have not dealt with all the texts that describe Paul as the eschatological messenger who is to prepare the way for the coming of Christ for judgment and salvation. The following chapters will put before the reader other texts and various related passages in his letters, which will thus become more easily intelligible and will confirm our presentation. But we cannot escape the impression that Pauline research, speaking generally and in spite of individual contributions that point in the same direction as this book, has been orientated differently. In the last hundred years it has quietly and steadily contributed—to use a modern expression—to a demythologizing and secularizing of Paul and his letters. It will therefore be necessary to give a short account of this hundred-year-old tradition, and to show the weaknesses from which it suffers. The decisive texts on which the traditional view was founded are dealt with in the following pages to show that those texts cannot properly be used in that way. The controversial texts, in fact, agree with the uncontroversial ones that have already been discussed. In both cases we meet the apostle to the Gentiles who has had the eschatological call; and the numerous passages that have hitherto been explained in a different way within the tradition receive in the new interpretation a meaning that is more fruitful and historically more probable.

3

THE TÜBINGEN SCHOOL AND PAUL

AT the end of the previous chapter we mentioned the obstacles put in the way of regarding Paul as a figure in redemptive history, and of understanding his letters in their original sense. These obstacles come from the Tübingen School. For more than a hundred years Pauline research has taken its stamp from that source. Led by Ferdinand Christian Baur, the Tübingen School decisively changed the main points of view both in Pauline research and in the treatment of the earliest history of primitive Christianity.

We may hear many people speak of F. C. Baur and his school as if the latter were something entirely in the past. That is true if we are thinking of its literary standpoint. No one seriously supposes today that the New Testament Scriptures were written in the course of the first two centuries, and that they reflect a development of more than a hundred years from the sharp contrast between Paul's teaching and the primitive church in Jerusalem to a progressive weakening of these originally contrasting standpoints till they finally merged in the Catholic Church. By the time that Harnack wrote his well-known preface to the *Chronologie der altchristlichen Literatur* in 1896 the literary hypotheses of the Tübingen School had been rejected, and the standpoint had been reached that we now know from modern introductory books on the New Testament with the quite small deviations between them.

But though the literary hypotheses were dropped, the historical points of view of the Tübingen School were still regarded as valid. While the Scriptures were assigned to the first and early second centuries, the contrast between Paul and the primitive church, between Gentile and Jewish Christianity, remained. The contrast that was originally thought to have lasted through two centuries was transferred to approximately the three decades between Paul's conversion and his death; and the constant tensions in the sub-apostolic age between a Christianity more and a Christianity less under Jewish influence were inadequately treated.

With regard to Paul and Jerusalem, the view is still adhered to that there was opposition between Jewish and Gentile Christians, and that attempts to bridge the gap were bound to come to grief. The picture of

Paul therefore becomes the picture of a lonely apostle, giving all his strength in the unparalleled effort of calling into life church after church of newly converted Gentiles, but losing those churches at once to the Judaizing emissaries from Jerusalem who follow hard on his heels.

If we choose the contrast between Gentile and Jewish Christianity (if we can use the term Christianity, as Baur does, in the latter case) as the *leitmotiv* in the history of primitive Christianity, we are compelled to support this hypothesis with literary conjectures, as Baur quite rightly did. But without such supports it cannot be maintained; and when the literary conjectures then ceased to be taken into account, the historical conjectures ought to have been revised; it was not enough merely to transfer the problem from the two centuries to the three decades.

The immense simplification that Baur's theory brings with it by finding everywhere in all Pauline texts the same contrast between the apostle and Jewish Christianity (as a rule its chief leaders in person) has ever since lain like a load on the exposition of the Pauline letters. Instead of a richly faceted historical reality, there has been found a colourless homogeneity, caused by making inferences everywhere from a one-sided interpretation of early Christianity. The picture of Baur that at any rate the author of this book has received by reports and accounts that were sympathetic towards Baur was that of a systematic theologian, who by virtue of his philosophic efforts for co-ordination turned a living history into a rationalized and dead abstraction.

But the study of Baur's writings reveals a researcher who achieved his results only gradually, and who distinguished clearly between what was certain and what needed to be re-examined and verified. I do not think he would have been pleased if he had lived to see his opinions turned into an authoritative tradition, and I am sure that he would welcome a fresh discussion.

I

Baur's view of the development of early Christianity stresses the party contrast between the primitive Church and Paul.[1] He makes the apostles and the whole Church stand on Jewish ground throughout, apart from their belief in the crucified Jesus as the coming Messiah. Everything about Jesus that was the expression of a new religion was

---

[1]The following account is taken from the article by H. Schmidt and J. Haussleiter 'Ferdinand Christian Baur' (see p. 56 n. 1). Besides Baur's exegetical works, his presentation of his own contribution in his *Kirchengeschichte des neunzehnten Jahrhunderts*, 1862, pp. 395–9, and E. Zeller, 'Die Tübinger historische Schule' and 'Ferdinand Christian Baur' in *Vorträge und Abhandlungen geschichtlichen Inhalts* I, 1865, pp. 267–353 and 354–434, have been used.

either forgotten or completely disregarded in the apostles' memory. When Paul rediscovers the universalism and freedom that Jesus represented, it puts him out of line with the primitive Church, which refuses to approve his message. The older apostles, indeed, incomprehensibly do not oppose him, but consent to give their authority to the mission to the Gentiles and to give Paul an equal status with themselves; but he is opposed all the more violently by those of the Church who do not agree with the recognition given him by the apostles.

In our time the sharpest criticism of Baur's view comes from Sundkler,[1] who says rightly (p. 38): 'The opposition between particularism and universalism is the product of a modern cosmopolitan outlook, and has nothing to do with the biblical conception of the mission.' One may add, as I did in 'Israel and the Gentiles in the New Testament',[2] that the very opposite of Baur's view is right. The primitive Church and Paul were universalistic as Jesus was, because they knew that the Gospel was for Gentiles as well as Jews, whereas the later Catholic Church lost that universalism. It no longer divided the human race into Israel and the Gentiles, but turned with its message to the Gentiles.

Baur has been taxed with not giving a sufficiently clear picture of Jesus' attitude to the Gentiles;[3] but even after him it was generally assumed that Jesus was a universalist, though the assumption was variously expressed.[4] Sundkler was the first to describe clearly Jesus' attitude towards Israel and the Gentiles in its relation to the existing Jewish points of view, so that it is no longer an abstract theory, but can be considered in conjunction with Old Testament lines of thought.[5]

On the other hand the picture of the primitive Church and the apostles, who are supposed to be standing entirely on Jewish ground, has been subjected to only slight criticism. Yet it is quite incredible that Jesus' disciples, who were those nearest to him during the whole of his ministry, learnt and retained nothing of his life and teaching, but continued to have a Jewish point of view—apart, of course, from their belief that the crucified Jesus was identical with the coming Messiah; but that additional belief was strangely enough regarded as unessential. Again it is impossible for such an essential completion of their faith not to have changed the purely Jewish point of view that the earliest disciples are supposed to have represented. Only the peculiar way in which the earlier New Testament research put away the individual

---

[1]'Jesus et les païens', *AMNSU* 6, 1937, pp. 1–38, also printed in *RHPR* 16, 1936, pp. 462–99.
[2]*JTS*, n.s. 2, 1951, pp. 3–16.
[3]Thus Schmidt and Haussleiter, pp. 475.44–50; 477.41–47; 478.42 ff.
[4]Harnack's view in *Mission*, pp. 39–48 (ET, pp. 36–43) (ch. 4, 'Jesus Christ and the Universal Mission'), is of special interest.
[5]See later, pp. 258 f.

objects in different drawers, and was thus unable to see things in their obvious connexion, made it possible to label that addition as unimportant, although, taken as it stands with the main assertion, it comes to this, that they represented an entirely Jewish point of view, which could not be Jewish at all if they believed that the crucified Jesus was the same as the coming Messiah.

According to Baur, Paul is supposed to have rediscovered the universalism and freedom that Jesus represented, but to have thereby become in the eyes of the primitive Church a stranger whose message it had difficulty in acknowledging. In this sharp contrast between the Church and Paul the accusation made above is relevant: the individual objects were put away in different drawers, and so the numerous connexions that exist between Paul and the earliest disciples were not discovered. Paul is no more than they an unconditional representative of universalism and freedom in Baur's sense. Just as Jesus and the earlier disciples did, so Paul makes Israel the most prominent and central feature of God's plan of salvation. And his aloofness towards the primitive Church, perhaps the most confidently held dogma in New Testament research, is not attested by the Pauline letters, but has come to us from Baur's exposition of Acts and of some of the controversial texts from Paul's hand.[1] The more strongly one stresses the aloofness between the primitive Church and Paul, the more unlikely it becomes that, as Baur maintains, the older apostles consent with really incomprehensible submissiveness to recognize the validity of the mission to the Gentiles and to put Paul on an equality with themselves. This essential part of Baur's theory might have been accepted if, in the course of things that gradually brought the two great opposing parties in early Christianity closer together, it had been considerably postponed, so that the agreement of the Council at Jerusalem became a scene of later invention, reflecting the ending of the originally irreconcilable antagonism. The 'really incomprehensible submissiveness' is in fact less an explanation than a historical problem still waiting to be solved.

II

It is not our task here, where the history of research is of interest only as an aid to exegesis, to investigate the fortunes of the Tübingen School's

[1] If Paul's opponents are emissaries of the church in Jerusalem, with its leading men behind them, we are bound to regard Acts as evidence of a Christianity that deviated from Paul and had a Jewish complexion. But, as we shall see later, Acts does not testify that the very early church in Jerusalem held to a purely Jewish point of view and therefore had quite a different character from that of the Gentile Christian churches. See ch. 8 (pp. 210–46 below).

ideas in later times; but it is important to be clear how many of Baur's ideas still meet us in the most recent discussion of Paul and primitive Christianity. If one takes up a handful of the most recent books about Paul, all written by recognized masters whose words are rightly respected, we find that in spite of progress in details, many of the fundamental ideas in Baur's theory live on.

It will be realized that I am reluctant to discuss the works of writers towards whom I feel gratitude and in several cases the deepest respect, and in relation to whom it would otherwise be my task to emphasize their merits and to establish what we can learn from their researches. But here the discussion must serve to ascertain what we ought not to learn from them, where in fact they are tied to an attitude that in my opinion blocks the way to a real understanding of Paul.[1]

Students of primitive Christianity usually still cling to the view that, apart from only slight deviations, it was Jewish.[2] But they find in this Jewish Christianity different gradations. That might seem to be a step forward in relation to Baur; but in reality these nuances serve only to hide the weaknesses contained in his view of the matter.

Lietzmann speaks (e.g., pp. 151–3) of the great contrast between Jewish Christianity and the Antiochene Hellenists and Paul,[3] but Jewish Christianity melts away into different points of view. There are difficulties between Peter and John on the one hand and James, the Lord's brother, on the other (pp. 67 f.). Peter's compromise solution in Corinth can be called semi-Judaism (pp. 151 ff.),[4] while James can be described as a righteous Jew, in high esteem among the Jews, as Hegesippus said (pp. 66 f.).[5]

Goguel makes a difference between the views of the leaders and those of the church on the agreement at the Council at Jerusalem. The church did not come into line with its leaders, but was confirmed in its Judaistic attitude and its hostility to Paul.[6] The opposition

---

[1]W. L. Knox, *St Paul*, 1932; H. Lietzmann, *The Beginnings of the Christian Church*[3], 1953 (ET of *Geschichte der alten Kirche* I, 1937); A. D. Nock, *St Paul*, 1946; M. Goguel, *Les Premiers Temps de l'Église*, 1949; M. Dibelius and W. G. Kümmel, *Paul*, ET 1953.

[2]Lietzmann, pp. 62 f., 66, 68; Nock, pp. 52, 67; Goguel, p. 53; Dibelius and Kümmel, pp. 27, 91, 125.

[3]Goguel thinks (pp. 103 ff.) that although Baur exaggerated the importance of the conflict between Jewish and Gentile Christianity, it was nevertheless of great importance.

[4]Goguel thinks (p. 73) that Peter's attitude to the question of the obligation of the Gentiles to observe the Law was inspired by an opportunist point of view, not by reasons dictated by principles.

[5]Cf. Nock, pp. 63, 168 ff., and Goguel, p. 57 (also with reference to Hegesippus). On the other hand, Dibelius and Kümmel (p. 142) speak of a difference between James and the extreme Judaizers.

[6]Goguel, pp. 64 ff. Cf. Knox, p. 64.

sharpens, and this becomes clear in the changed attitude towards Paul between the Council in 44 and his last visit in 58 (pp. 66 ff.). Goguel also sees changes in the primitive church, underlining this Jewish standpoint. One such change already takes place after the death of Jesus (p. 49), and becomes more evident when Peter is replaced by James as the leader of the church (p. 57). The dynastic principle, by which Jesus' relatives become the leaders of Jewish Christianity, has led to closer ties with Judaism (p. 66). The later Ebionism shows us what the primitive church was (pp. 70 f.).

In the midst of all this Jewish idyll the Hellenistic Jews stand out as an extraneous element. Stephen and the Hellenists slighted the religion of the temple and rejected the Jewish ritual laws,[1] and so it is only the Hellenists who are persecuted.[2] Speaking generally, these Hellenists represent only a passing phase.[3]

The relation between the primitive church and Paul becomes clear at the Council at Jerusalem and the incident that followed in Antioch. Instead of the unanimity that Paul and Luke jointly describe as the keynote of the Council, opposing positions are supposed to be taken up which no bridge can join; and the result is that the agreement arrived at cannot be permanent; in fact it fell to pieces at the first opportunity, over the incident at Antioch (Gal. 2.11 ff.). It is assumed that there were not one but two meetings held in Jerusalem, the first between the leaders of the Jerusalem church and Paul and Barnabas, and later a second at which these two were not present and which ended with the issuing of the apostles' decree from Jerusalem.[4]

The encounter between Paul and Peter in Antioch is generally placed after the Council at Jerusalem.[5] The brethren coming from James presumably had the task of trying to establish the Jerusalem point of view in Antioch; but it is also possible that they arrived fortuitously.[6] With

---

[1]Lietzmann, p. 71.

[2]Baur takes this view (*Paul the Apostle of Jesus Christ*, ET 1873, I, p. 39). Nock maintains (pp. 61 ff.) that in contrast to Jesus the disciples must at first have appeared harmless, but that the new religion had possibilities of development that were soon to put a different face on things. Stephen returns to Jesus' freer critical attitude in relation to Judaism, and so the church in Jerusalem is persecuted; cf. pp. 168 ff. Goguel thinks (pp. 56 f.) that the church in Jerusalem was not persecuted—on Stephen's death it was only the Hellenists who were persecuted and had to leave the city—apart from the persecution by King Agrippa I, which was produced by the Jews' anger at the concessions that the leaders of the church in Jerusalem had made to Paul at the Council at Jerusalem.

[3]Goguel, p. 52.

[4]Knox thinks (pp. 62 ff. and 77 ff.) that Paul was present at the second meeting too. Goguel's opinion (p. 64) is that no synthesis of the two points of view was reached, but that on the other hand a breach was avoided, and that the Jerusalem leaders (but not the church) recognized Paul's gospel.

[5]Knox, p. 64; Lietzmann, pp. 107 f.; Dibelius and Kümmel, p. 131.

[6]Goguel, pp. 63 f. and 73 n. 2.

regard to this episode it is supposed that the dispute did not end in a victory for Paul's point of view, but that it meant the collapse of the agreement of the Council at Jerusalem, and that the breach had far-reaching consequences for Paul.[1]

So the encounter in Antioch is supposed to form the introduction to the hostile relations between the two opponents.[2] The apostles' decree (Acts 15.23–29) has been interpreted in various ways. It is supposed to have been brought into existence at a new meeting after the Council at Jerusalem, as we have already seen (p. 74 with n. 4), and caused to be circulated from Jerusalem behind Paul's back, and he is not informed of it till near the end of his career, when he arrives in Jerusalem (Acts 21.25).[3] It is regarded as a compromise that goes a long way towards meeting the Gentile Christians.[4] The apostles' decree, that Jerusalem compromise solution, is in remarkable contrast to the belligerent situation that has now overtaken all the Pauline churches. Everywhere the Jerusalem Judaizers are dogging Paul's steps.[5]

If the Jerusalem leaders are thus placed, with or without reservations, behind Paul's opponents, the apostle himself is drawn with the familiar features of the Tübingen School. Although Paul never sat at the Master's feet, yet he is the only one of the apostles who really understood him.[6] And about the agreement at Jerusalem we hear the familiar strains when Goguel writes (p. 100 n. 1) that the Jerusalem leaders made concessions, but Paul none, because with them the feeling of the unity of the faith was stronger than 'the logic of their principles'. By thus separating their principles from their feelings, Goguel avoids the natural

[1]Knox does not think (p. 65) that agreement was reached between Peter and Paul. Lietzmann (p. 108) and Nock (pp. 110 ff.) are of the opinion that the encounter led to a permanently irreparable breach between Paul on the one hand and Peter and Barnabas on the other. Goguel assumes (p. 104) that the Jewish Christians regarded the compromise as repealed by Paul's action in Antioch, while Dibelius and Kümmel think (p. 131) that what happened in Antioch shows how lightly the Jerusalem agreement was to be regarded. Whereas Paul had thus broken with the church in Antioch, it is extremely unlikely (p. 135) that Peter was completely at odds with him and had taken sides with the Jerusalem Judaizers and taken an active part in the counter-mission against him. He mentions Peter later in such a way that no opposition of a serious kind can be detected (I Cor. 3.22; 9.5).

[2]Knox thinks (pp. 65, 68 ff.) that Paul's first missionary journey was arranged as a counter-thrust against Peter's compromise in Antioch, and that the strict Jewish Christians in Jerusalem began their activity in Antioch and in the Galatian churches when that journey was announced.

[3]Thus Lietzmann, pp. 108 f.; Nock p. 116, and Goguel p. 68, who places it after the Antioch affair.

[4]Lietzmann, p. 151; Goguel, p. 68.

[5]Thus Lietzmann (pp. 109 f.), who assumes that the first apostles were always behind those Judaizers; but this is denied by Dibelius and Kümmel (p. 124). Nock (p. 111) is of the same opinion as Lietzmann. Goguel (p. 69) leaves the question open whether the leaders in Jerusalem shared the feelings that animated Paul's opponents in Corinth and the Galatian churches.

[6]Lietzmann, p. 112.

explanation that the Jerusalem church's principles may not have been so different from Paul's as is generally supposed. We hear that there was only one Church, the earthly Jerusalem, to which the newly formed churches, among them the Pauline Gentile churches, unquestionably belonged,[1] and that Jerusalem therefore had the right to claim support, and the right to supervise the other churches.[2] Paul does not deny this, because he could not do without the testimony of the men who had seen Jesus after the Resurrection.[3]

So we see in the four principal Pauline letters how the situation develops. In Galatians Paul shows by the irony with which he mentions the 'pillars' in Jerusalem that he makes the church leaders responsible for what is happening among the Galatians.[4] In Corinth he is supposed to have first preached a message that could give no offence, but later the whole Gospel, so that the breach with the Jews followed inevitably.[5] The church splits into parties, some following the Judaistic agitators from outside the church and forming the so-called Cephas party,[6] and others, presumably some personal disciples of Jesus, refusing Paul the right, as an apostle, to take precedence over them.[7]

So too Paul's letter to the church in Rome arose from the opposition to Jewish Christianity. This church had to be prevented from being led by the work that Peter accomplished there into opposition to Paul.[8]

III

As regards method, this modern Pauline research suffers from having broken with the Tübingen School's literary theory, but not with its

---

[1]Lietzmann, pp. 72 f.; Goguel, pp. 61 ff.

[2]Lietzmann, pp. 73 f.; Knox, pp. 111 ff.; cf. Goguel, p. 100.

[3]Knox, pp. 77, 112; Dibelius and Kümmel, pp. 125 ff., 156; Lietzmann (unconvincingly) gives point to this in his treatment of Paul's visit (p. 106).

[4]Goguel, p. 108; otherwise Dibelius and Kümmel, p. 132.

[5]Knox, pp. 85 f.; so too Baur, *Paul* I, pp. 334–6; but this does not fit in with I Cor. 2.1–5.

[6]Knox, p. 94. Lietzmann assumes that Peter brought the apostles' decree to Corinth in 52 (p. 151); Goguel (p. 106), that the Peter party originated from Palestinian preachers who played off Peter's authority against Paul's. Paul does not know whether they come from James or from Peter, and whether they have exceeded their instructions (p. 106). It is not, however, a matter of Judaistic preaching, as Paul's controversial writing in Galatians has a different sense (p. 107). Dibelius and Kümmel (pp. 132 f.) see behind these emissaries not the apostles but the extreme Judaizers in Jerusalem who had demanded at the Council at Jerusalem that the Gentile Christians should keep the Law of Moses. This is especially so in II Corinthians (pp. 137 f.). Cf. Nock, p. 200.

[7]Knox, p. 100; cf. Lietzmann, *An die Korinther I–II*, on I Cor. 1.12 and II Cor. 10.7.

[8]Lietzmann, *The Beginnings of the Christian Church*, p. 111. Knox (p. 120) makes the letter to the Romans take account of the contrasts between the Jewish and Gentile Christian circles in the church at Rome.

historical theory. Baur found the material for his interpretation in the first two centuries A.D. He was able to quote the pseudo-Clementines with a confidence that later students of Paul have not been able to summon up.

If the struggles that Baur thought were carried on throughout two centuries were to be squeezed into the three decades between Paul's conversion and his death, the value of references to movements and texts from the second century became very doubtful. And the learned and fruitful studies that put an end to the literary fantasies of the Tübingen School, as for example T. Zahn's and J. B. Lightfoot's researches about the Apostolic Fathers, also led to the useful realization that the historical changes in the period from 30 to 200 A.D. are so far-reaching and decisive that we cannot unhesitatingly use arguments from the second century to prove what happened in the first century.

It is remarkable that this realization has been accepted with regard to the points that were untouched by the Tübingen School's view on the development of primitive Christianity. If it is a question of the apostle John's stay in Ephesus, or of the tradition about the way in which the other apostles or disciples went to the Dispersion, it is clear that we cannot build on the late traditions of the second century; indeed, the traditions from the beginning of the second century are often treated very rigorously, and as a rule the sources about the death of Peter and Paul in Rome are treated with the same rigour. In research into Jewish Christianity, on the other hand, arguments are constantly used that presuppose the Tübingen School's literary theories. From the second-century sources conclusions are drawn about relations in the primitive Church, for example with regard to the tension between Jewish Christianity and Paul. It is believed that in the original sources of the pseudo-Clementine literature there are sources of information that are valuable for the earliest period. Indeed, Hegesippus' legendary account of the death of James, the Lord's brother, dating from the end of the second century, is regarded as a valuable source for James' life and death, in preference to Josephus' more sober account which is nearly a hundred years older.

In this range of studies people are still working from an obsolete method of criticizing the sources—one that does not feel obliged to give an account of the *Sitz im Leben* of the individual sources and of their different recensions. The first period of the Christian Church had indeed no antiquarian interest which would have led it, as nowadays, to preserve things both important and unimportant from the past and occupy itself with them; and so we cannot take it that documents from the second century can serve as direct sources for the first century. We

can only venture indirectly, taking full account of the later sources'
Sitz im Leben, to question them, hoping that they will lift the veil from
the first Christian period, which was nearly as far from them as it is
from us.

But this method of procedure also holds good for the first century.
Here too we have to classify our sources, and must not be content merely
to criticize them in rough outline. If, as is often the case, no distinction
is made here in practice between Acts and Paul's letters in respect of
their value as sources, the fundamental mistake is made of using a later
document like Acts as a source of the same value as the letters that Paul
wrote. But whereas those letters were written at the same time as the
events that they deal with, the presentation in Acts rests on a more or
less fortuitous assortment of sources that was collected and retold by a
Christian of a later time.

It is possible that there are included in Acts sources of the same value
as Paul's letters; but because they are later retold and fitted into the
framework of Acts they can no longer be regarded as primary sources.
We may here compare Acts with Eusebius' *Church History*, which
contains many invaluable quotations, otherwise lost, from early Christian writings. In the case of Eusebius we can distinguish clearly the
quotation and his application of it, so that the quotation has still kept
the value of a primary source, while his later use of it shows the period
to which he belongs, and also in certain cases the theological views that
he upholds.[1] In the case of Luke, on the other hand, it is impossible to
distinguish the primary sources that he may have collected and separate
them from the setting into which he has put them in his narrative;
and it cannot be ascertained with any certainty which are the primary
sources and where we have Luke's additions or adaptations.

John Knox has tried in a valuable book, *Chapters in a Life of Paul*
(1950), to clear up the relation between Acts and Paul's letters. He certainly makes the editor of the letters assemble the material, add to it
and omit from it, to make the apostle's purpose plain; and the editor,
by adding the letter to the Ephesians, even furnishes a piece of pseud-
epigraphical writing.[2] But the letters are of much greater value than Acts.
In fact, the author of Acts feels freer in that work than in Luke's Gospel;

---

[1] We may mention as an example Eusebius' treatment of Papias of Hierapolis
in *h.e.* III. 39.

[2] See Knox's investigation, *Philemon among the Letters of Paul*, 1935, in which
Goodspeed's hypothesis about the publication of the Pauline corpus (which I know
only through his later publications *New Chapters in New Testament Study*, 1937,
and *Christianity goes to Press*, 1940) is developed and confirmed by Knox's assumption that Philemon as Bishop in Ephesus (Knox demonstrates Ignatius' dependence
in his *Letter to the Ephesians* 1-6 on the letter to Philemon) was the editor of the
Pauline corpus.

can only venture indirectly, taking full account of the later sources' *Sitz im Leben*, to question them, hoping that they will lift the veil from the first Christian period, which was nearly as far from them as it is from us.

But this method of procedure also holds good for the first century. Here too we have to classify our sources, and must not be content merely to criticize them in rough outline. If, as is often the case, no distinction is made here in practice between Acts and Paul's letters in respect of their value as sources, the fundamental mistake is made of using a later document like Acts as a source of the same value as the letters that Paul wrote. But whereas those letters were written at the same time as the events that they deal with, the presentation in Acts rests on a more or less fortuitous assortment of sources that was collected and retold by a Christian of a later time.

It is possible that there are included in Acts sources of the same value as Paul's letters; but because they are later retold and fitted into the framework of Acts they can no longer be regarded as primary sources. We may here compare Acts with Eusebius' *Church History*, which contains many invaluable quotations, otherwise lost, from early Christian writings. In the case of Eusebius we can distinguish clearly the quotation and his application of it, so that the quotation has still kept the value of a primary source, while his later use of it shows the period to which he belongs, and also in certain cases the theological views that he upholds.[1] In the case of Luke, on the other hand, it is impossible to distinguish the primary sources that he may have collected and separate them from the setting into which he has put them in his narrative; and it cannot be ascertained with any certainty which are the primary sources and where we have Luke's additions or adaptations.

John Knox has tried in a valuable book, *Chapters in a Life of Paul* (1950), to clear up the relation between Acts and Paul's letters. He certainly makes the editor of the letters assemble the material, add to it and omit from it, to make the apostle's purpose plain; and the editor, by adding the letter to the Ephesians, even furnishes a piece of pseud-epigraphical writing.[2] But the letters are of much greater value than Acts. In fact, the author of Acts feels freer in that work than in Luke's Gospel;

[1]We may mention as an example Eusebius' treatment of Papias of Hierapolis in *h.e.* III. 39.

[2]See Knox's investigation, *Philemon among the Letters of Paul*, 1935, in which Goodspeed's hypothesis about the publication of the Pauline corpus (which I know only through his later publications *New Chapters in New Testament Study*, 1937, and *Christianity goes to Press*, 1940) is developed and confirmed by Knox's assumption that Philemon as Bishop in Ephesus (Knox demonstrates Ignatius' dependence in his *Letter to the Ephesians* 1–6 on the letter to Philemon) was the editor of the Pauline corpus.

regard to this episode it is supposed that the dispute did not end in a victory for Paul's point of view, but that it meant the collapse of the agreement of the Council at Jerusalem, and that the breach had far-reaching consequences for Paul.[1]

So the encounter in Antioch is supposed to form the introduction to the hostile relations between the two opponents.[2] The apostles' decree (Acts 15.23–29) has been interpreted in various ways. It is supposed to have been brought into existence at a new meeting after the Council at Jerusalem, as we have already seen (p. 74 with n. 4), and caused to be circulated from Jerusalem behind Paul's back, and he is not informed of it till near the end of his career, when he arrives in Jerusalem (Acts 21.25).[3] It is regarded as a compromise that goes a long way towards meeting the Gentile Christians.[4] The apostles' decree, that Jerusalem compromise solution, is in remarkable contrast to the belligerent situation that has now overtaken all the Pauline churches. Everywhere the Jerusalem Judaizers are dogging Paul's steps.[5]

If the Jerusalem leaders are thus placed, with or without reservations, behind Paul's opponents, the apostle himself is drawn with the familiar features of the Tübingen School. Although Paul never sat at the Master's feet, yet he is the only one of the apostles who really understood him.[6] And about the agreement at Jerusalem we hear the familiar strains when Goguel writes (p. 100 n. 1) that the Jerusalem leaders made concessions, but Paul none, because with them the feeling of the unity of the faith was stronger than 'the logic of their principles'. By thus separating their principles from their feelings, Goguel avoids the natural

[1]Knox does not think (p. 65) that agreement was reached between Peter and Paul. Lietzmann (p. 108) and Nock (pp. 110 ff.) are of the opinion that the encounter led to a permanently irreparable breach between Paul on the one hand and Peter and Barnabas on the other. Goguel assumes (p. 104) that the Jewish Christians regarded the compromise as repealed by Paul's action in Antioch, while Dibelius and Kümmel think (p. 131) that what happened in Antioch shows how lightly the Jerusalem agreement was to be regarded. Whereas Paul had thus broken with the church in Antioch, it is extremely unlikely (p. 135) that Peter was completely at odds with him and had taken sides with the Jerusalem Judaizers and taken an active part in the counter-mission against him. He mentions Peter later in such a way that no opposition of a serious kind can be detected (I Cor. 3.22; 9.5).

[2]Knox thinks (pp. 65, 68 ff.) that Paul's first missionary journey was arranged as a counter-thrust against Peter's compromise in Antioch, and that the strict Jewish Christians in Jerusalem began their activity in Antioch and in the Galatian churches when that journey was announced.

[3]Thus Lietzmann, pp. 108 f.; Nock p. 116, and Goguel p. 68, who places it after the Antioch affair.

[4]Lietzmann, p. 151; Goguel, p. 68.

[5]Thus Lietzmann (pp. 109 f.), who assumes that the first apostles were always behind those Judaizers; but this is denied by Dibelius and Kümmel (p. 124). Nock (p. 111) is of the same opinion as Lietzmann. Goguel (p. 69) leaves the question open whether the leaders in Jerusalem shared the feelings that animated Paul's opponents in Corinth and the Galatian churches.

[6]Lietzmann, p. 112.

explanation that the Jerusalem church's principles may not have been so different from Paul's as is generally supposed. We hear that there was only one Church, the earthly Jerusalem, to which the newly formed churches, among them the Pauline Gentile churches, unquestionably belonged,[1] and that Jerusalem therefore had the right to claim support, and the right to supervise the other churches.[2] Paul does not deny this, because he could not do without the testimony of the men who had seen Jesus after the Resurrection.[3]

So we see in the four principal Pauline letters how the situation develops. In Galatians Paul shows by the irony with which he mentions the 'pillars' in Jerusalem that he makes the church leaders responsible for what is happening among the Galatians.[4] In Corinth he is supposed to have first preached a message that could give no offence, but later the whole Gospel, so that the breach with the Jews followed inevitably.[5] The church splits into parties, some following the Judaistic agitators from outside the church and forming the so-called Cephas party,[6] and others, presumably some personal disciples of Jesus, refusing Paul the right, as an apostle, to take precedence over them.[7]

So too Paul's letter to the church in Rome arose from the opposition to Jewish Christianity. This church had to be prevented from being led by the work that Peter accomplished there into opposition to Paul.[8]

III

As regards method, this modern Pauline research suffers from having broken with the Tübingen School's literary theory, but not with its

[1]Lietzmann, pp. 72 f.; Goguel, pp. 61 ff.
[2]Lietzmann, pp. 73 f.; Knox, pp. 111 ff.; cf. Goguel, p. 100.
[3]Knox, pp. 77, 112; Dibelius and Kümmel, pp. 125 ff., 156; Lietzmann (unconvincingly) gives point to this in his treatment of Paul's visit (p. 106).
[4]Goguel, p. 108; otherwise Dibelius and Kümmel, p. 132.
[5]Knox, pp. 85 f.; so too Baur, *Paul* I, pp. 334–6; but this does not fit in with I Cor. 2.1–5.
[6]Knox, p. 94. Lietzmann assumes that Peter brought the apostles' decree to Corinth in 52 (p. 151); Goguel (p. 106), that the Peter party originated from Palestinian preachers who played off Peter's authority against Paul's. Paul does not know whether they come from James or from Peter, and whether they have exceeded their instructions (p. 106). It is not, however, a matter of Judaistic preaching, as Paul's controversial writing in Galatians has a different sense (p. 107). Dibelius and Kümmel (pp. 132 f.) see behind these emissaries not the apostles but the extreme Judaizers in Jerusalem who had demanded at the Council at Jerusalem that the Gentile Christians should keep the Law of Moses. This is especially so in II Corinthians (pp. 137 f.). Cf. Nock, p. 200.
[7]Knox, p. 100; cf. Lietzmann, *An die Korinther I–II*, on I Cor. 1.12 and II Cor. 10.7.
[8]Lietzmann, *The Beginnings of the Christian Church*, p. 111. Knox (p. 120) makes the letter to the Romans take account of the contrasts between the Jewish and Gentile Christian circles in the church at Rome.

historical theory. Baur found the material for his interpretatio first two centuries A.D. He was able to quote the pseudo-Clen with a confidence that later students of Paul have not been summon up.

If the struggles that Baur thought were carried on through centuries were to be squeezed into the three decades betweer conversion and his death, the value of references to moveme texts from the second century became very doubtful. And the and fruitful studies that put an end to the literary fantasies Tübingen School, as for example T. Zahn's and J. B. Ligl researches about the Apostolic Fathers, also led to the useful rea that the historical changes in the period from 30 to 200 A.D. are reaching and decisive that we cannot unhesitatingly use arg from the second century to prove what happened in the first cen

It is remarkable that this realization has been accepted with to the points that were untouched by the Tübingen School's view development of primitive Christianity. If it is a question of the John's stay in Ephesus, or of the tradition about the way in wh other apostles or disciples went to the Dispersion, it is clear t cannot build on the late traditions of the second century; inde traditions from the beginning of the second century are often very rigorously, and as a rule the sources about the death of Pe Paul in Rome are treated with the same rigour. In research into Christianity, on the other hand, arguments are constantly use presuppose the Tübingen School's literary theories. From the s century sources conclusions are drawn about relations in the pri Church, for example with regard to the tension between Jewish tianity and Paul. It is believed that in the original sources pseudo-Clementine literature there are sources of information th valuable for the earliest period. Indeed, Hegesippus' legendary a of the death of James, the Lord's brother, dating from the end second century, is regarded as a valuable source for James' li death, in preference to Josephus' more sober account which is a hundred years older.

In this range of studies people are still working from an ob method of criticizing the sources—one that does not feel oblig give an account of the *Sitz im Leben* of the individual sources a their different recensions. The first period of the Christian Churc indeed no antiquarian interest which would have led it, as nowa to preserve things both important and unimportant from the pas occupy itself with them; and so we cannot take it that documents the second century can serve as direct sources for the first centur he composes speeches that are supposed to be an expression of the apostle's teaching, and he narrates his material, including what he has to say about Paul, rather as an author than as a compiler.

Paul's letters are therefore more reliable sources than Acts. For the apostle's intimate history, i.e., for his thoughts, character, and religious experience, the letters provide the authoritative source. Even someone who would cite Paul's speech before King Agrippa as a source equal in value to a text from Romans, gets his picture of the apostle's personality and message from the letters. On the other hand the letters bring us no connected picture of Paul's outward history; and we are therefore inclined to interpret Acts from the point of view of the letters when Paul's intimate life is being considered, but conversely to look at his letters from the point of view of Acts when we want to know about the external data of his life.

If we had only Paul's letters, we should know considerably less, for most of the outlines in our picture of Paul's life are taken from Acts. In the letters, only Gal. 1–2 tells about the time from his conversion up to the second visit to Jerusalem. About his work among the Galatians, in Asia, Macedonia, and Achaia, especially about the work of collecting for the church in Jerusalem, we are told in I Cor. 16.1–4, II Cor. 8–9, and Rom. 15.25–32. From the first and last of these passages we hear about his last visit to Jerusalem. From these correct observations Knox then draws far-reaching conclusions; but it would take us too far to go into them in more detail here.

It is very important that an outstanding scholar like John Knox draws attention to the faulty method, hitherto adopted, that uses Acts as a source equal in value to Paul's letters. But while fully recognizing this service, I feel obliged to raise two critical objections to his exposition. The first is that his criticism of the indiscriminate use of Acts is too narrowly conceived. It is not only with regard to external data that people are inclined to interpret Paul's letters from the point of view of Acts. Our whole picture of Paul, not only the outward circumstances but also his inner life, is determined by the indiscriminate use of Acts as a primary source when the controversial passages in his letters and the contents of Acts are made the basis of the exposition of the letters as a whole, and thus of his life and work. The evidence that will be produced here and in the next four chapters will fully confirm this.

The second critical observation that I would make about Knox's book seems to point in exactly the opposite direction, and to cancel what I have just said regarding my agreement with his criticism of the use of Acts. Its point is that Acts as a secondary source contains a quantity of material that is valuable as a primary source, although this has been revised and cannot in its present form be used as a primary source. While therefore I agree with Knox that Acts can never be used as a source where it disagrees with the letters, I would take a more positive attitude towards Acts than he does in a number of cases in which the letters are silent. We agree that the individual passages of Acts must be examined as to their degree of probability, but in practice I would adopt a less sceptical attitude as to the value of those that have no counterpart in the letters.

I will illustrate this by one or two examples. When Acts 9.26–30 speaks of Paul's first visit to Jerusalem after the Damascus call, and describes how Barnabas brings him into touch with the apostles, that description contradicts Paul's own account in Gal. 1.18 f.[1] While according to Acts he gets into touch with the apostles, according to Paul's own account in Gal. 1.19 the only apostle whom he saw was Cephas, except for James, the Lord's brother. Therefore if we regard the account in Acts as historically reliable in its present form, it cannot be dealing with the same visit that is recounted here; and the account in Galatians excludes the possibility of his having undertaken more than the two visits mentioned in chs. 1–2. Knox is also right in pointing out that it is only in Acts that we are told that Paul was born in Tarsus, and in still holding the opinion that we can rely on that information (p. 34). On the other hand, I disagree with his criticism of some points of detail in Acts, which are not mentioned in Paul's letters and are therefore not regarded as correct. I would give as an example the statement that Paul had been a pupil of the Jewish scribe Gamaliel in Jerusalem. Knox may be right in several remarks that cast doubt on the credibility of the statement (p. 35); for example, he rightly points out that Luke stresses the part played by Jerusalem in the earliest period of the Church (pp. 25 ff.). But it is not right to emphasize Paul's complete silence as to his connexion with the well-known Jewish teacher, and to suggest that we might expect an allusion to this fact several times in the letters. In doing this, Knox points to the passages in which Paul boasts of the purity of his Judaism and of his zeal for the faith of his fathers; but he overlooks the fact that this was plainly comprehensible to the Gentile Christians, whereas the name Gamaliel told them nothing at all. Although he was known among his own people and in his own country, there would be no point in mentioning his name to Gentile

---

[1] Knox, *Chapters in a Life of Paul*, pp. 36 f. It is not certain whether the account in Acts contradicts the 'after three years' in Gal. 1.18, though it seems as if the events in 9.1–30 follow in quick succession (Knox, p. 36). If Luke knew nothing about the relation of the individual events in point of time, and therefore did not want to express himself clearly, he could do nothing else than choose, in 9.19, 23, the vague terms that remind one of the transitional formulae in the Synoptic Gospels.

Christians in Asia Minor and Greece, as they probably did not know
by name even Athenodorus in Tarsus or Seneca in Rome.

Thus, while exception may be taken in certain details to the rejection
of those statements made only in Acts, we can also, on comparing Paul
and Acts (while fully recognizing the secondary value of Acts as a
source in relation to Paul's letters) find a number of small and apparently accidental agreements between Paul and Acts, with the result that
we can attach greater value to the narratives of Acts than is usual from
the critical point of view. We have already seen in ch. 1 that Paul's
narrative of his call and the three accounts in Acts agreed on many
points, which became more numerous the nearer we got to the interpretation of the occurrence (see pp. 24–28). We shall also find several
times later in this book points of agreement between Paul and Acts—
often, indeed, where we should not expect to.[1]

The important thing in this connexion is that we agree with Knox
that Paul's letters are the primary source and that Acts represents only
a secondary source, written at a later time and testifying to views that
the Church then held. Although some genuine source-material has been
fitted into Acts, this has been so shaped by its insertion and adaptation
that it can no longer be regarded unconditionally as a primary source.
Some indeed may think that what Knox has so meritoriously clarified
is a matter of course and is generally recognized. To that, however, it
may be replied that one may approve of a thing in principle and at the
same time act quite differently in practice. Thus, many people have
rejected the account in Acts 9.26–30 of Paul's visit to Jerusalem, but have
based the explanation of his second visit on the Council at Jerusalem
(Acts 15), and interpreted his description of a meeting in Jerusalem
(Gal. 2.1–10) as if this were the Council at Jerusalem, or, in other words,
as if a very subjective description were given of a meeting of which we
already possessed Luke's excellent report. When Paul has to do with
opponents in his letters, it has always been asked whether the people
concerned were not Peter or James or some of the apostles from
Jerusalem who were his opponents or at any rate were standing behind
them. Here people have disregarded Paul's account of these men and
their view of the mission to the Gentiles, but have formed a one-sided
and certainly incorrect view of the account in Acts, and have assumed
the correctness of that interpretation in their reading of Paul's
letters.

But that brings us to the third problem in our approach to the reading of Paul's letters. Baur made controversy the criterion of the real

---

[1]See, e.g., pp. 112 f., 293–97, and 332 f.

Paul.[1] Here the bias of his critical theory becomes clear, and we realize that from such a point of departure we shall arrive at a picture of Paul that is fixed and dogmatically assumed in advance. The controversial passages become the more important texts, while the uncontroversial ones are pushed aside as being less important or even unauthentic.

If a modern ecclesiastical controversialist were treated in that way and all his positive utterances were disregarded, he would necessarily be misunderstood. Paul has been treated even worse.

An example of the method of treatment is as follows. The starting-point was the assumption that we have a clear picture of the earliest church at Jerusalem, with reference both to its external and to its internal relations. As we saw above, the source used was Acts. We can probably say without exaggeration that we have in Acts only inadequate and not always clear original material in the narratives of the earliest church in Jerusalem. But if the accounts given there do not agree with Paul's letters (e.g., Acts 15 with Gal. 2), the definite picture in the secondary source is used to subject our primary sources, the Pauline letters, to criticism and to interpret them.

Scholars also had a clear picture of Paul's opponents; but on dispassionate reflection we find that we are inadequately informed about them too. That is because our only sources are the controversial passages in Paul's letters. As primary sources the letters are excellent; but in controversy no objective picture of his opponents emerges, and the readers of the letters were so well informed that it did not seem to the writer necessary to give the exact particulars that we should have liked to find in them; and our information is therefore inadequate. Pauline research is inclined to identify the opponents mentioned in the different letters with each other; and it was thus possible to simplify matters, so that everywhere we meet either Judaizers or libertines or both.

As we shall see later (chs. 4–7), the letters show us different situations with different opponents, so that this interpretation gives a mistaken view of the matter. But the result for research of the supposedly clear picture of Paul's opponents has been that the picture that was thought to be clearly seen of the church in Jerusalem, and to which we have already referred in section 1, appeared more probable. If Paul's opponents were so often thought of as Judaizers and therefore

---

[1]"Thus the apostle Paul seems to be permanently armed for battle; and any of his writings in which he meets us in any other form must be suspect in advance.' In the sub-apostolic age, which emphasized the unity of the Church, it was a different matter. 'So that where an irenic tone can be noticed in a letter, where there is mention of the Church, its unity, its faith, it can be taken as a clear sign of sub-apostolic origin.' H. Schmidt and J. Haussleiter on F. C. Baur (*op. cit.*, p. 475.29–31, 34–37).

as being connected with the church in Jerusalem, it confirmed what people thought they read about that church in Acts.

The result was that primitive Christianity, apart from the libertines, who appeared only here and there, was dominated by the contrast between Paul and Jerusalem.

One therefore had a reliable picture of the Jerusalem church, based on the secondary source of Acts; and one had likewise, from the secondary source of Acts and with the help of an exposition of the controversial and therefore less clear passages in the letters, made out a reliable picture of Paul's opponents. But now came the difficulty that Paul, about whom we possessed primary sources in his letters, telling, among other things, about the Jerusalem church and his opponents, must be fitted into the picture that had already been made from the secondary sources. Instead of asking Paul himself about Jerusalem and his opponents, people took the opposite way. And when they reached the only place where they were on firm ground, namely Paul and his apostleship—Paul having himself described the apostleship and the events in which it was expressed or developed, the description being nearly simultaneous with the events—well, they already knew so much about him that they were in no position to understand or use his own words. They knew his background in advance, and now they were able to fit at the most a part of his own words into the detailed picture that they had already made with the help either of secondary sources or of Pauline texts that had been understood in relation to those secondary sources. And they were so sure of standing on firm ground with their picture of Jerusalem and Paul's opponents that his letters, apart from certain controversial passages that were wrongly interpreted, were of no use in deciding about the earliest history of primitive Christianity.

From the point of view of source and method, things are thus made to stand on their heads. The secondary sources are allowed to invalidate the primary ones. It is just topsy-turvy, as far as method goes, to shut one's eyes to Paul's assertion that his work is to prepare for the Lord's return and that he has been recognized by the leaders in Jerusalem as the apostle to the Gentiles, and to maintain instead that he was dependent on the apostles in Jerusalem, and to put him alongside his opponents as if he were of the same kind as they.

Thus the method of work that has been usual hitherto in Pauline research is of great and serious import for the picture of Paul. First, it is assumed that his opponents were always right. For instance, if it is held against him that he is dependent on Jerusalem, his defence of his independence is listened to coldly, and his dependence on Jerusalem is reaffirmed with the mere assertion that he will not admit his dependence on Jerusalem.[1] The authority of the picture that Paul draws for us of the Jerusalem leaders as the earliest disciples, well disposed towards him, is denied; and instead it is firmly asserted that the real state of affairs is exactly what his opponents believe, namely that Jerusalem did not recognize him.[2] Jerusalem is said to have demanded contributions from the Pauline churches, so the fact that Paul speaks of a voluntary gift from the churches (e.g., II Cor. 8–9) tells us nothing—the truth simply is that it is a question of a contribution or tax extorted from them.[3] When Paul wants to induce his churches to make the gift, and declares that it is voluntary, it is for him to make his own statements square with a quite different situation (which people have found in the primary sources when they started from the secondary ones).[4] Such interpretations of the apostle's words and deeds add up to make a picture of a Paul who is cunning, double-tongued, and, to put it bluntly, untruthful. The answer is, in the jargon of liberal theology: we see the apostle's faults, but we must not overlook the greatness of his personality.

This picture of the controversialist who is not too particular about the truth is not attractive. Everywhere Paul is on the watch, stopping in the middle of a sentence to shout 'No' at his opponents, being irritated and answering the attack. He is never at peace, nor can he wait patiently on events. He is concerned with himself, and again with himself, and then about the other people who treat him so badly and who are therefore to be blamed and punished and anathematized. We get an unpleasing picture of a not very agreeable man who is self-centred and suffers from a mild form of persecution mania. And so there are good reasons if, in spite of the greatness of his personality, some people have not been able to forget the apostle's faults.

All this is, in brief, the result of bad method in modern Pauline research. From force of habit people have continued to use second-century sources to understand first-century texts. Acts, with its many details, has determined the interpretation of Paul's letters. And here the controversial passages have played a larger part than the uncontroversial ones, as the former, whose meaning was taken from Acts and later sources, gave us a finished picture of Paul into which the uncontroversial passages could not be fitted.

The course that we have taken here, and that we shall follow out in

[1]Knox, *St Paul*, pp. 77, 112; Lietzmann, *The Beginnings of the Christian Church*, p. 104, cf. pp. 108 f.; Goguel, *Les Premiers Temps de l'Église*, pp. 61 ff.; Dibelius and Kümmel, *Paul*, pp. 125 ff.; cf. p. 156.
[2]Lietzmann, pp. 108 f.
[3]K. Holl, 'Der Kirchenbegriff des Paulus' etc., *Gesammelte Aufsätze zur Kirchengeschichte* II, 1928, pp. 55–62; Knox, pp. 111, 112–14; Goguel, pp. 100 f.
[4]See pp. 287–90.

the following chapters, marks a return to sound historical method. We start from Paul's letters, which originated in the events that they report. Here, if anywhere, it must be possible to get information about primitive Christianity. Paul's possible faults, on which traditional exegesis puts its finger in its efforts to make his letters agree with Acts, the pure truth of which is presupposed, are of minor importance compared with the fact that his letters are primary sources and that Acts is a secondary one. Admittedly Paul becomes vehement, is an interested party, expresses himself diplomatically, and so on, and so on; none of this can bridge the chasm between primary and secondary sources and so enable us to return to the traditional procedure of pruning the former in such a way as to make them agree with the latter.

The principles underlying the inquiries that are here presented are as follows: 1. Paul's letters are to be interpreted as such. Statements from other sources, especially Acts and the post-Pauline letters, may be used if they agree with or do not clearly contradict what we are told in the letters, but those statements must not determine the exposition of the letters. 2. Paul's individual letters, and the situation that forms the background of each individual letter, must be viewed on their own merits in each case, and the material in the letters and behind these supposed situations may be unified only if such a procedure does not violate the individual nature of the particular letter and of the situation that lies behind it. 3. A historical situation, in this case a situation that is the background of a particular Pauline letter, is not always the expression of a clearly systematized theological position, and it is therefore possible that we cannot subject such a situation to any exhaustive philosophic or systematic theological explanation; but this does not cast doubt on its historical character.

If we thus release Paul's letters from the traditional exposition that goes back to the Tübingen School, we shall not only get a more coherent picture of Paul, but we shall discover greater riches and variety in early Christianity than tradition made possible. Besides that, Acts will gain greatly by leaving its dominating position and no longer having its exposition so closely bound up with Paul's letters. It will then appear, not only that the Tübingen School's theories falsified our picture of Paul, but also that Acts, freed from the load of tradition, gives us a much clearer picture of primitive Christianity, and that its presentation of Jewish Christianity does not open between Paul and Jerusalem the deep chasms that the Tübingen School took for granted, but that, with all the difference between the earliest disciples and Paul, there does exist a connexion that brings them close to each other where tradition made it impossible.

But we have spoken long enough of method. It is now time to follow the correct principles whose superiority to the traditional bad usages we have made plain. Unfortunately custom breeds certainty, and an oft-repeated assertion gains, merely by repetition, a weight and plausibility that a fresh assertion cannot expect, even if its evidence is of the best. And in our case the traditional assertions are so venerable that from time out of mind no one has felt called on to bring forward any evidence on their behalf. The reader therefore needs an open mind and considerable tolerance if he is to follow the course that is taken in the following chapters.

Each of the next four chapters (4–7) deals with one of the four great Pauline letters, and ch. 8 examines Acts to clarify the picture of Jewish Christianity in that document. That paves the way for ch. 9, which tries to draw a new picture of the history of primitive Christianity corresponding to the exegetical arguments of the five preceding chapters. In this way we get here a first sketch of primitive Christianity in a presentation aimed at replacing the Tübingen School's theories, which have hitherto been those traditionally accepted.

4

THE JUDAIZING GENTILE CHRISTIANS
Studies in Galatians

ALBERT SCHWEITZER says of Baur, 'The great merit of the Tübingen critic was that he allowed the texts to speak for themselves, to mean what they said.'[1] Our task will be to show that the central Pauline texts, which for so long have been expounded on the traditional lines of the Tübingen School, do not support Baur's interpretation, but that they gain in meaning and depth when their exegesis is relieved of that hundred-year-old yoke.

The sequence of the four great letters that are to be dealt with will be Galatians, I Corinthians, II Corinthians, and Romans. It is a chronological order for the last three letters. As it is difficult to decide with any certainty the time of the writing of Galatians in relation to I Corinthians, and as Galatians is dealt with first in the natural course of things, that is done here without further discussion.

According to the usual view, the letter to the Galatians is supposed to be the main source for the opposition between Paul and Jerusalem, for the continual struggle that no dishonourable compromise could end. Both before and after the meeting in Jerusalem (Gal. 2.1–10) Paul contends with the emissaries from that city, who try to make his churches disloyal to him; and behind those emissaries there stand the great figures of the original church, James the brother of the Lord, Peter, and John. We shall try to show in this chapter that in the letter to the Galatians Paul tells quite a different story, that in spite of the clash at Antioch there was no permanent discord between him and the Jerusalem leaders, and that the conflict that the apostle wages in that letter concerns a problem in the Gentile mission field that does not touch Jewish Christianity in Jerusalem and the eastern world.

The Judaizing opponents in Galatians are Gentile Christians. That emerges from 6.13, which reads, 'For even those who receive circumcision do not themselves keep the law, but they desire to have you circumcised that they may glory in your flesh.' The present participle

---

[1] *Paul and his Interpreters*, p. 13.

with the article οἱ περιτεμνόμενοι is rightly applied by Lietzmann[1] to the Gentile Christians who become circumcised under the pressure of Judaistic demands; but, as v. 13b shows, these Gentile Christians are those who are agitating among the Galatians for Judaism. People have tried for a long time to get round this difficulty and maintain the traditional view that the agitators in the Galatian churches were Jewish Christians, by making the present participle with the article denote 'those belonging to the class of those . . . who are circumcised according to the established custom, the class of Jews who receive circumcision' (Sieffert). Sieffert refers to Winer, § 45.7,[2] on the present participle (with the article) in substantival use that excludes any fixing of time, and points to *Acta Petri et Pauli* (ed. Tischendorf) 63. It is to Hirsch's credit that in the above-mentioned article he maintains that with such an expressive writer as Paul the present form περιτεμνόμενοι is not to be regarded as a 'careless' mode of expression (Lietzmann's original point of view). Such a view would provide a way out only if other statements in the letter made it clear that the opponents with whom Paul is contending were Jews by birth; but there are no such statements.

O. Holtzmann[3] has defended the traditional view of the verse about circumcised Jews. He asserts here, 'But the present participle here says more than the substantive ἡ περιτομή used elsewhere by Paul. He is referring not merely to the actual experience of circumcision, but to an attitude towards circumcision that is based on principle, and continues in the present. "Those who receive circumcision" are those who as far as they are concerned adhere to circumcision as a duty, so that they never want to renounce it. They therefore demand circumcision for Gentile Christians too. The same participle is used in just the same way in 5.3.' This last remark cannot be sustained at all. But Althaus thinks that in 6.13 Paul may have used the present form loosely; and Schlier thinks that οἱ περιτεμνόμενοι means ' "those who are in the state of circumcision" or "those who practise circumcision", without reflecting that the Judaizers are themselves already circumcised.' He refers to Lietzmann (!) and other commentators, and brings in the same quotation as Sieffert. Anyone to whom Tischendorf's edition of the Apocryphal Acts is not available cannot necessarily know that his *Acta Petri et Pauli* 63,[4] is identical with *Martyrium Petri et Pauli* 42 in Lipsius and Bonnet:[5] Σίμων εἶπεν· Ἱερώτατε βασιλεῦ, μὴ πίστευε

---

[1] According to Hirsch, 'Zwei Fragen zu Galater 6', *ZNW* 29, 1930, pp. 192–7.
[2] G. B. Winer, *Grammatik des neutestamentlichen Sprachidioms*[7], revised by G. Lüdemann, 1867. Cf. Blass-Debrunner, § 413.
[3] 'Zu Emanuel Hirsch, Zwei Fragen zu Galater 6' *ZNW* 30, 1931, pp. 76–83.
[4] *Acta Apostolorum apocrypha etc.*, ed. C. Tischendorf, 1851, p. 28.5 f.
[5] *Acta Apostolorum apocrypha*, ed. R. A. Lipsius et M. Bonnet, I, 1891, p. 156.4.

αὐτοῖς, ὅτι οὗτοι οἱ περιτεμνόμενοι πανοῦργοί εἰσιν. This passage is certainly very inappropriate as an argument for interpreting οἱ περιτεμνόμενοι in Gal. 6.13 as a substantival present participle with no connotation of time, as this rejoinder of Simon Magus is not very intelligible. But the passage becomes clear in the context by producing Paul's answer which uses the verb περιτέμνω in a figurative sense.[1]

It is peculiar that we are invariably presented with exactly the same passage as an argument. Probably there are no others—it really seems so. The present participle of περιτέμνω does not occur in the LXX, and in the New Testament only in Gal. 5.3 and 6.13; it is not found in the Apostolic Fathers. It is however used in Justin's *Dialogue*, 27.5 and 123.1, twice in each place. Here there is no doubt that the meaning is 'receive circumcision'. Even if it is not out of the question, it seems difficult to take uncritically in the present participle with no temporal significance a verb that denotes an action that can take place only once; and it is quite obvious that Sieffert's and O. Holtzmann's all too detailed expositions do not rest on the grammatical construction, but proceed from the context as they understand it.

As the present participle in the middle voice of περιτέμνω never means 'those who belong to the circumcision',[2] but everywhere else 'those who receive circumcision', that must also be the case in Gal. 6.13. That is made specially clear by the connexion between the two sentences. The thought here is not of the Jews or Judaizers in general, but specifically of the Judaizers among the Galatians. Paul's opponents, who are agitating for Judaism among the Gentile Christian Galatians, are therefore themselves Gentile Christians. Their circumcision is still in the present, so that all this Judaizing movement is of recent date.

II

These Judaizing Gentile Christians have been canvassing among the Galatians for their own particular conception of Christianity (1.7; cf. 1.9; 3.1; 5.7, 10, 12; 6.12 f.), and they have succeeded partly in putting the churches into a state of uncertainty, and partly in winning them over to themselves. But on this point, as on others, we get no clear picture of the actual state of affairs.

These churches were founded by Paul,[3] and consist of Gentile

---

[1] Paul's answer reads, Πρὸ τοῦ ἐπιγνῶναι τὴν ἀλήθειαν, σαρκὸς ἔσχομεν περιτομήν· ὅτε δὲ ἐφάνη ἡ ἀλήθεια, ἐν τῇ τῆς καρδίας περιτομῇ καὶ περιτεμνόμεθα καὶ περιτέμνομεν (p. 156.5–7).

[2] It is rather the perfect participle in Justin, *Dial.* 19.3, and the aorist participle in *Dial.* 114.4, that can express this timeless meaning.

[3] 4.13; cf. v. 19. This verse is no adequate foundation; but we must take into consideration Paul's attitude to the churches, as it becomes clear in the whole letter.

Christians (4.8; 5.2 f.; 6.12). At first they led their Christian life in the Holy Spirit (3.1–5), but now, when the letter is written, some of them have come to the view that they must be circumcised (5.2 f., 11 f.; 6.13; cf. Paul's arguments in 2.3 f., 15–21; 5.1, 6, 14; 6.12, 15) and keep a part, if not the whole, of the Law (4.21; 5.3; cf. 3.10; 6.13).

They combine this new conception with a new outlook on Paul. He is an apostle through others (1.1, 11 f.; 1.13–2.21) and therefore not a missionary who was called and sent out by a revelation of the risen Lord, but an emissary of the churches—in fact, of the churches in Judaea and Jerusalem and of people who were apostles before him (1.16–19, 22–24; 2.1–10, 11–21).[1] Unfortunately Paul, in order to please men (1.10; 5.11; 6.12 f.), has abridged the message entrusted to him in Jerusalem (5.11),[2] so that it needs to be completed (2.6; cf. 3.12a); and that is what the Judaizing Gentile Christians are now striving for, by demanding from the Galatians circumcision and obedience to the Law.

This new picture of Paul and of the nature of Christianity also involves a new conception of Jerusalem, not corresponding to the one with which the Galatians were familiar from Paul's account. The Galatian churches now believe that Jerusalem and the earliest disciples there preach circumcision and observance of the Law—if not the whole Law, at least part of it. Paul therefore has to contend with three falsifications: the false picture of himself, of Jerusalem, and of the nature of Christianity.

It is remarkable how Pauline research for the last hundred years has relied more on the Judaizers than on Paul. It has taken the view that Paul was dependent on Jerusalem,[3] that the leaders of the church there preached circumcision and the observance of the Law,[4] and that, apart from Paul and his theology, the Church was then preaching precisely those two things, while preaching in addition that the crucified Jesus would reveal himself in glory as the promised Messiah.[5] It may well be time now to try to hear what Paul has to say, and to rely on his telling the truth, not only about his own attitude to the Law and to the Judaizers, but also about his apostleship and the leaders of the church in Jerusalem.

[1]Paul's opponents have spoken only of the churches of Judaea and of those who were apostles before him. But against those very clumsy ideas Paul gives precise explanations of quite a different kind, which reveal the Judaizers' ignorance about the relations in Jerusalem and about his supposed connexion with the church there.

[2]M.-J. Lagrange rightly remarks on 5.11, 'The best way for the Judaizers to confuse the Galatians was for them to plead the authority of Paul himself in favour of circumcision.'

[3]See p. 84 n. 1.

[4]See p. 73 n. 2.

[5]See pp. 72–75.

III

Paul refutes the Galatians' misapprehensions about his apostleship by referring to the history of his call, about which they know, at any rate partly (1.13). ἠκούσατε could of course mean either 'You have heard (from me)' or 'You have heard (from my opponents)'; but as only the first point, about Paul as a persecutor, can have been mentioned for the purpose of controversy, it seems likely that the interpretation suggested on p. 29 is correct, that Paul used the history of his call as a part of his missionary preaching.[1] In such a case only those points of view are considered which are necessarily involved. The first point is that Paul has persecuted God's Church. That can serve as evidence that his call was not of human origin, but must have been God's work (cf. pp. 13 f. and 15 f.). But another possible reason for mentioning the fact is that it was used by Paul's opponents to denigrate him in the eyes of the churches. The deliberate repetition in 1.23, μόνον δὲ ἀκούοντες ἦσαν ὅτι ὁ διώκων ἡμᾶς ποτε νῦν εὐαγγελίζεται τὴν πίστιν ἥν ποτε ἐπόρθει, καὶ ἐδόξαζον ἐν ἐμοὶ τὸν Θεόν, where both διώκειν and πορθεῖν are repeated from v. 13, suggests that Paul wanted to emphasize that the churches of Judaea, in contrast to those of Galatia, had formed a favourable impression of the former persecutor. It may also be that in 2.6 the thought is of the persecutor and the persecuted: ὁποῖοί ποτε ἦσαν οὐδέν μοι διαφέρει· πρόσωπον [ὁ] Θεὸς ἀνθρώπου οὐ λαμβάνει, but this text can be interpreted in different ways (see pp. 98 f.). It may be in this connexion that Paul mentions in 5.11 that he is being persecuted, and that his opponents' object in urging the Galatians to be circumcised is to avoid being persecuted as Christians (6.12). This might give the impression that Paul is here trying to counter the accusation that he has removed circumcision from the Christian Gospel to please the Gentiles who are flocking in (5.11). If τὰ στίγματα τοῦ Ἰησοῦ (6.17) is to be interpreted as marks of persecution, Paul is here referring to himself as to the one who is hard hit by persecution.[2]

The next point, Paul's Jewish past, where he stresses his zeal and progress in Judaism (1.14), can hardly have been related by his opponents with any controversial intent.[3] Paul's object in this reference is

---

[1] The most detailed inquiry that we have of Paul's missionary preaching is that of A. Oepke, *Die Missionspredigt des Apostels Paulus* (Missionswissenschaftliche Forschungen 2), 1920, which proceeds from the assumption that Paul's missionary preaching is nowhere directly transmitted to us. If we want to reach conclusions as to its form and scope, it is a purely subjective undertaking, even if we proceed very cautiously, as Oepke does.

[2] Persecution is also spoken of in 4.29.

[3] Paul's preaching of circumcision cannot relate to his Jewish past or prove that he was an apostle even as a Jew.

rather to emphasize the authority with which he expresses himself in
what follows about the Gentile Christian attitude to the Law. If, as
shown above (p. 90), the Gentile Christians thought that part of the
Law ought to be kept, but not the whole Law, that is probably an
expression of their wish to keep the Law to the best of their ability. To
a former rabbinic pupil that attempt was bound to seem pitifully
amateurish.

The decisive point of the argument is, of course, the third, the call at
Damascus itself. Here it is stressed (*a*) that the call is from God, and
(*b*) that it concerns the Gentiles (see also pp. 24–26). The former point
is to disprove that he is an apostle from men, while the latter anticipates
2.7–9, where Paul's apostleship to the Gentiles is the presupposition
for the separation in Jerusalem of the mission to the Jews and the
mission to the Gentiles.

But Paul brings in these allusions to his call only as introductory
evidence that in his work after his call he did not show himself dependent
on the churches of Judaea and their leaders. When God had called him,
he did not at once ask men for advice (σαρκὶ καὶ αἵματι, cf. Matt.
16.17), or to put it more accurately, the men on whom his opponents
asserted that he was dependent—τοὺς πρὸ ἐμοῦ ἀποστόλους,[1] but went
to Arabia, and was later in Damascus. It was three years after the call
that he made his first visit to Jerusalem as a Christian. The object of
the visit was to make Peter's acquaintance, and his stay there lasted
only a fortnight. Besides Peter he met only James, the Lord's brother[2]—
God can be his witness. The addition of the confirmation by oath shows
us that on this point it is necessary to refute his opponents' assertions.
They asserted that he went to Jerusalem immediately after the call,
and that he there made the acquaintance of the leading men and became
their disciple, just as he later went out on his missionary work to the

[1]The opponents have not spoken of Peter, James, and John, and they knew just
as little about the details of Paul's visits to Jerusalem. They only asserted that Paul
was dependent on the churches of Judaea and on the people who were 'apostles'
before him. It is Paul who sets out his journeys, their time, and their more detailed
circumstances. The details have therefore been produced by his own free choice,
and do not depend simply on his opponents' assertions and accusations.

[2]It is difficult to decide whether James is an apostle, because the text in 1.19,
with its ἕτερον δὲ τῶν ἀποστόλων οὐκ εἶδον, εἰ μὴ Ἰάκωβον τὸν ἀδελφὸν τοῦ
Κυρίου, is not clear. Some will think that this means, 'but I saw no other apostle
(than Peter) except James, the Lord's brother', while others will take it to mean,
'but I saw no other apostle (than Peter), but I saw of all the great names in Jerusalem
only James, the Lord's brother'. We do not know whether James, the Lord's brother,
was an apostle in the wider sense, 'a missionary sent by Christ', which might be
meant here. We cannot infer from I Cor. 9.5 that James may have been an apostle,
as the Lord's brothers as well as Cephas are not here included in the group of the
'other apostles', but are named separately. As there is nothing to indicate that James
was one of the missionaries sent out by Christ (as Cephas and Paul were), but he
is always shown as a leader in the Jerusalem church, it is natural to follow the
interpretation that does not include him among the apostles.

Gentiles as their messenger and the messenger of the Judaean churches. The last three verses in ch. 1 show that there was no personal connexion between Paul and the churches in Judaea, but simply that they had heard that the former persecutor was now preaching the Gospel, and that they rejoiced at it (cf. p. 91).

'Then after fourteen years' there followed the second visit, this time with Barnabas and Titus. It was God who by a revelation sent Paul on this journey (2.2). By that remark Paul wishes again to refute the idea that he had then gone to Jerusalem to learn or to be sent on a mission. The argument has hitherto been related to his independent position with regard to Jerusalem and had a negative character: he did not confer with flesh and blood, nor did he go up (at once) to those who were apostles before him (1.16 f.). In Jerusalem he saw none of the apostles but Peter, but he also saw James, the Lord's brother (1.19). He was personally unknown to the Christian churches in Judaea (1.22). Now there follows a piece of more positive evidence, which, however, has negative elements. Paul set out in consequence of a revelation, i.e., not on the orders of his superiors, to give an account of his work (2.2). Titus was not compelled to be circumcised (2.3). 'We' did not yield submission even for a moment to the false brethren who slipped in (2.4 f.). 'Those who were of repute' added nothing to Paul (2.6). The rest is positive, and shows that in spite of his special call and his special gospel Paul was fully acknowledged by the leaders in Jerusalem. The Galatians had not been informed about the Jerusalem meeting,[1] but only supposed, as in the case of his first visit, that on his visits to Jerusalem he was dependent on the leaders there, who had sent him and given him the gospel that he was to preach, and which contained more than the Galatians heard (2.6). When Paul is not content merely to correct their misunderstandings, and gives his account in more detail, the reason is that the leaders in Jerusalem are not at one with the Judaizers, but have recognized the mission to the Gentiles under his direction as an independent missionary work alongside their own work among the circumcised.[2] There was no suggestion that Paul's gospel needed supplementing, for instance by any of the things that the Judaizers are now demanding. So the Gentile Christians' Judaism hangs in mid-air, and their pleading an earlier and more comprehensive Pauline gospel with Jerusalem's authority is a pure invention.

[1]Another view is put forward in O. Linton's 'The Third Aspect. A neglected Point of View', *ST* 3, 1950, p. 92. Linton also holds the view that other missionaries —in the Galatians' opinion—had to follow agreements made in Jerusalem. But in any case it is not certain that the Galatians knew any other missionaries than Paul and his fellow-workers. See pp. 104 f.

[2]Just as the churches of Judaea joyfully recognized Paul's work as missionary to the Gentiles (1.24).

Paul's report of the meeting in Jerusalem has usually been interpreted differently. People have started from Acts 15, sketched the background of the meeting, and assumed that members of the church in Jerusalem have demanded the circumcision of the Gentile Christians in Antioch (Acts 15.1; cf. v. 5; this has then been read into Gal. 2.4 f.). Paul therefore has to go and see the leaders there and come to an agreement with them so that the whole Gentile mission shall not be ruined. But the agreement that the apostle reaches in Jerusalem is in the long run useless. Even when Peter visits Antioch soon afterwards, some emissaries of James succeed in making the Jewish Christians unfaithful to the agreement,[1] and in the following period Paul has to wage a continual conflict in his churches with the Judaizing emissaries from Jerusalem, so that he speaks here with great bitterness about the state of affairs.[2]

But that cannot be how matters really stood. If it is supposed that it was possible for Paul to use the story of the Jerusalem meeting in his argument with the Galatians, who have heard that he is dependent on Jerusalem and was therefore preaching circumcision and the observance of the Law, it is not enough to point to the meeting where he brought about an agreement and with it the recognition of his apostleship to the Gentiles. For in that case the understanding would have come to grief soon afterwards at the Antioch encounter and would have been invalid ever since, as is made clear by the numerous agitators from Jerusalem (as the scholars suppose) of whom the Galatians must know something, if this assumption were correct. The narratives of the meeting in Jerusalem and the subsequent episode in Antioch must be important elements in Paul's argument, and cannot be counter-evidence that he presents to his opponents. The narrative of the discussion in Jerusalem must therefore be evidence of his independence, and show that nothing was decided there apart from what the Pauline gospel contains. In other words, in fact, Paul and his preaching are recognized by the leaders in Jerusalem. And in the same way we must read between the lines the point of the story about the encounter in Antioch, as it is an absolutely necessary assumption for Paul's argument—namely, that Peter gave way and allowed that Paul was right.[3]

[1]According to the Jewish Christians' view, Paul was the one who broke his word and so caused the conflict and the breach in Antioch. Thus Goguel, *Les Premiers Temps de l'Église*, p. 104.
[2]So Knox, *St Paul*, pp. 64–70; Lietzmann, *The Beginnings of the Christian Church*, pp. 109 ff.; Nock, *St Paul*, pp. 110 f.
[3]We cannot be content merely to remark with Lietzmann, on Gal. 2.11–14, 'The result is of course tacitly assumed to be that Peter gives way and accepts Paul's rebuke, and thus the leader of the Twelve acknowledges Paul's authority. Whether the incident was regarded in the same way by the other side is a different matter.' This last sentence of Lietzmann weakens Paul's argument, which is transformed into an illusion out of touch with the actual state of affairs. But Paul's words, spoken

If we look away from Acts 15 and simply at Gal. 2.1–10, the essential points also become clear, and speak in Paul's favour. God sends him up to Jerusalem. The leaders there agree with Paul on a division of the work, and this assumes a full acknowledgement of his apostleship. It is more difficult to get a clear picture of the details in vv. 3–5, which are a break between v. 2, which speaks of 'those who were of repute', and v. 6, where they are again mentioned at the beginning of the verse.

Of course, we are dealing here, not with a historical report, but with a sustained argument against the Judaizers and their followers among the Galatians in these churches. We do not know what the Judaizers' accusations were, but from the alleged facts that are denied, and from the way in which it is done, we can infer some of these accusations, as we did on pp. 91 ff. But we must be clear that these inferences are hypothetical. As to the narrative of the meeting in Jerusalem (a more detailed narrative, as we mentioned above) we must adopt an even more cautious attitude than on ch. 1, and not suppose that there is historical information everywhere behind Paul's argument. When he denies something, it may be that a misconstruction of a historical fact is in question; but it may also be an assertion by the Judaizers that has nothing to do with the facts. Finally it may be Paul himself, throwing words in his opponents' faces: 'On that view you would believe that this or that must have happened; but that is not the case at all, and so your view of the Judaean churches and the earliest disciples is absolutely perverted.'

These possibilities must all be considered in connexion with the remark in v. 3 that Titus was not compelled to be circumcised. If one emphasizes that Titus was not *compelled*, it is a question of a historical fact, namely that at the time of the Jerusalem meeting Titus was circumcised, while Paul denies that any demand from the Jerusalem side lay behind that fact; the circumcision was performed because of a voluntary decision of Titus (and Paul). This interpretation is, of course, impossible, because it assumes that Paul consented to the circumcising of a baptized Gentile—a thing that is out of the question. If we therefore decide to take the verse to mean that Paul denies that Titus was circumcised at the time of the conference, it may be a question of an assertion by the Judaizers. 'The standpoint of Jerusalem can be seen in the fact that Titus received circumcision.' To that Paul answers quite simply, 'But it is not true that he was circumcised.' But what Paul denies may

publicly before the churches, are a more trustworthy historical reality than is the theory about the apostle's spiritual life—a theory that is built up on the testimony of the secondary sources, and therefore requires that the testimony of the primary sources be disregarded.

also be an inference at which he arrived through his opponents' attitude towards the first disciples in Jerusalem, namely, 'If you were right in your attitude, Titus would have had to be compelled to be circumcised at once, but nothing of the kind happened.'

The same possibilities must be considered in vv. 4 f. It may be a question of a historical fact which Paul claims to have interpreted differently from his Judaizing opponents. In such a case there were present at the meeting not only 'those who were of repute' and Paul with his companions, but also some of the apostle's opponents, who presented demands that would enslave the Christian freedom of the Pauline churches. If we combine the passage here with Acts 15.5 about the Pharisees who had become Christians, and at the meeting demanded from the Gentile Christians circumcision and observance of the Law, everything seems clear.

Lietzmann regards vv. 4 f. as a more detailed explanation of what is told of Titus in v. 3; but that view is by no means obvious. The verse about Titus is a link connecting vv. 2 and 6 ff., which in common with this last passage shows clearly the agreement between Paul and the Jerusalem leaders. Vv. 4 f., regarded as a more detailed explanation of v. 3, are an explanation that explains nothing, but the verses confront us with a number of problems. If we accepted Lietzmann's exposition, it would be natural at vv. 4 f. to think of the opponents at the Jerusalem conference;[1] but he is right in maintaining that the κατασκοπῆσαι must of course take place in the Pauline churches.[2] But if these false brethren are not present at the Jerusalem conference, who are οἷς in the sentence οἷς οὐδὲ πρὸς ὥραν εἴξαμεν τῇ ὑποταγῇ? Here there seem to be only two possibilities. The first is that these false brethren from the Pauline churches are present at the Jerusalem conference. But this was not said in Acts 15. Those who come down from Jerusalem and teach the brethren in Antioch that they can be saved only if they are circumcised according to the Law (v. 1) are not identified with the former Pharisees in the Jerusalem church. These Pharisees demanded that 'they'[3] should be circumcised and ordered to keep the Law (v. 5).[4] At any rate, 'those who had some standing' did not wish to make any demands or to add anything.

---

[1]So Lagrange.

[2]On the other hand it is erroneous to follow Lietzmann in thinking that these people are to be regarded as spies and trouble-makers in the Pauline churches, who compel Paul to fight for his rights in Jerusalem; nor should we interpret Gal. 2.12 as an example of such espionage in Antioch. That would mean interpreting the text of Galatians from Acts 15 and from an erroneous view of Gal. 2.11 ff.

[3]αὐτούς, see Lake and Cadbury *ad loc.*

[4]The identification is undertaken in the Western Text; see *Beginnings* 3, The Text, 1926, ed. J. H. Ropes, pp. 140 f., and Wendt *ad loc.*

The other possibility is that what Paul narrates in vv. 4 f. does not take place in Jerusalem at all. Because we all have in mind the Acts narrative of the Council at Jerusalem (ch. 15), I want to point out that we are in the course of explaining Gal. 2.1–10 without regard to that text. And because we are thinking historically, we allow ourselves to be led into regarding controversial texts like Gal. 2.1–10 as historical accounts. But in Gal. 2.1–10 the participation of only two groups is mentioned, namely the apostles to the Gentiles, who had come to Jerusalem, and 'those who were of repute', besides the churches in Judaea of which Paul has just been informed that they are praising God because the former persecutor is now preaching the faith. In vv. 4 f. he speaks of the false brethren who are depicted as are the Judaizers[1] among the Galatians; they have stolen in to act as spies in the Pauline churches in the Gentile mission field. If we therefore take the view that they did not appear at the discussion in Jerusalem—nothing in Galatians except this verse indicates that they did, any more than Acts 15.1, 5 insists that they are the same opponents in Antioch and Jerusalem—then in vv. 4 f. it is not a question of a historical fact, namely that Paul had a discussion with the Judaizing opponents in Jerusalem, which the Judaizers among the Galatians regarded as a piece of compliance on his part, while Paul himself claims that his attitude there was one of firmness with no yielding.

Here again there are two possibilities: either there is an accusation by the Galatian opponents which Paul rejects as groundless, or Paul himself constructs such an accusation and rejects it. In the first case the Judaizers have taxed him with having given way in Jerusalem. In accordance with their view of him as the pupil and emissary of Jerusalem who began to go his own way, they have maintained, 'When Paul is in Jerusalem, he has to comply obediently on the matter that we have now raised, that of circumcision.' The apostle rejects the imputation that he had been obedient. He has never made any concessions regarding circumcision in deference to the false brethren (this is a correction of the Judaizers' assumption that he was obedient in Jerusalem on account of 'those who were of repute') who had stolen into the mission

---

[1]The false brethren have tried to combat the freedom of Christianity and to make the Gentile Christians into slaves. We know these expressions from other passages in Galatians, so that we can be sure of their meaning here at once. The Galatians are called to freedom (5.1, 13); of special help in understanding 2.4 is 5.1 with its τῇ ἐλευθερίᾳ ἡμᾶς Χριστὸς ἠλευθέρωσεν· στήκετε οὖν καὶ μὴ πάλιν ζυγῷ δουλείας ἐνέχεσθε. We do not meet καταδουλόω again in Galatians, but we have δουλεία in 4.24 as well as in the passage already quoted, 5.1; δουλεύω in 4.8, 9, 25; δοῦλος in 4.1, 7; and δουλόω in 4.3; all the passages are directly or indirectly in relation to the Judaizing in the churches. That means that the opponents who are described in Gal. 2.4 f. are pictured as are the Judaizing Gentile Christians who have stolen in among the Galatians.

field—of course not into Jerusalem—to spy out Christian freedom so that they could enslave the Gentile Christians, his object being to preserve the Christian freedom of the latter.

It may, however, not be a matter of an accusation by the Galatian Judaizers, which Paul had taken up after the charge that at the meeting at Jerusalem Titus was compelled to be circumcised. It may be an accusation that Paul himself formulates so as to reject it at once. The words about Titus may be Paul's own remark, designed to show that the leaders in Jerusalem would have been bound to have Titus circumcised if the opponents had been in the right in their view about Jerusalem; but this did not happen. When he has made this point about the Jerusalem leaders, he adds that he would never have agreed to anything of the kind in deference to the Judaizing opponents in the Gentile Christian churches. He then, in effect, says this: 'If you were right in your view of Jerusalem, Titus, who went with me, would have been compelled to be circumcised. But that is not how things are in Jerusalem. And in this connexion there is something else that you forget. I have never, in deference to people like the Judaizers among you, whose only aim inside the church is to spy out our Christian freedom and to enslave us, given way on this question of circumcision. In fact, I have refrained from it so that the truth of the Gospel may remain with you, in contrast to the Judaizing propaganda that is now the rule among you.'

Paul has rejected three assertions about the meeting: (1) he went up to Jerusalem in consequence of a revelation from God (this is of itself a purely positive statement, from which, however, there is usually inferred the corresponding negative form '*not* on the orders of my superiors there'); (2) Titus was not circumcised during the meeting in that city; and (3) Paul never submitted to the demands of the Judaizing opponents, whenever and wherever he met them in the Gentile Christian churches. After he has made these negative points the positive one follows: 'those who were of repute', who are mentioned in v. 2, are those who are again referred to in v. 6 after the rejection of the wrong conceptions in v. 3 and vv. 4 f.

V. 6 (ἀπὸ δὲ τῶν δοκούντων εἶναί τι) and v. 4 (διὰ δὲ τοὺς παρεισάκτους ψευδαδέλφους . . .) both begin with a prepositional phrase which is extended by a qualifying sentence (οἵτινες κτλ. in v. 4, and the parenthetical sentence ὁποῖοι κτλ. in v. 6) and which thereby reaches such proportions that Paul begins a fresh construction with a main sentence in which the noun of the prepositional phrase is again taken up, in v. 5 in the dative and in v. 6 as the subject.

The parenthetical sentence ὁποῖοι κτλ. in v. 6 is generally interpreted as follows: however close 'those who were of repute' formerly were to

Jesus in his life on earth, that makes no difference; God attaches no importance to it. Thus the remark would be a controversial one directed against the exaggeration of the Judaizing opponents as to the value of 'those who were of repute'. In such a case we should have a remark by Paul with the object of having his apostleship recognized as being on the same plane as that of the earliest disciples. But here there is scarcely a thought of any contrast between 'those who were of repute' and others such as Paul, but rather of the contrast between what these people seem to be and now are, and what they were formerly, which was something less.[1] In that connexion Paul may have had in mind that they were unlearned, that they had left Jesus in the lurch, that James was unbelieving till he received a revelation from the risen Lord, and that Peter had denied Jesus. I am not suggesting that Paul wants to conduct a campaign against the earliest disciples in Jerusalem by means of any such comparison; he speaks in the text of their full recognition of and unity with him. But he may want to shake his opponents' position with regard to the 'pillars'. In his opponents' view there were in Paul's past life a number of things that one might talk about: was he still seeking to please men, was he still preaching circumcision, had he not been a persecutor of God's Church? Possibly this rejoinder may be in the nature of a sword-thrust that Paul makes purely as a remonstrance: the 'pillars' too have a past, but God does not raise it either with them or with me.[2]

Paul says that 'those who were of repute' added nothing (v. 6), and it has been thought that he was alluding to canonical decisions, like the one that follows in v. 10, which is supposed to mean that the Gentile Christian churches are to pay the church in Jerusalem a contribution, or like the so-called 'apostolic decree' that according to Acts 15 is supposed to have been decided on at a meeting in Jerusalem. Therefore, it is thought, the negotiations in Acts 15 cannot be identical with

[1] It is therefore superfluous to pose the following dilemma, as does Heussi in 'Galater 2 und der Lebensausgang der jerusalemischen Urapostel', *TLZ* 77, 1952, cols. 67–72 (col. 68): 'We must conclude either that the first apostles have meanwhile forfeited their "quality" and therefore their esteem as "pillars" (a thing that cannot be considered), or that, as Paul wrote, they no longer dwelt among the living.' See also Stauffer against Heussi in 'Zum Kalifat des Jakobus', *ZRGG* 4, 1952, p. 203 n. 11a.

[2] We must not forget that the dilemma 'from God or from men' is seen not by the Judaizers but by Paul (1.1, 11 f.). The opponents were not by any means pronouncing sentence on Paul when they regarded him as being dependent on the earliest disciples in Jerusalem. But it gave them a standard by which to judge him, for they thought they knew the disciples in Jerusalem and their attitude to Christianity (see later, pp. 130–34). Wherever Paul was different from the Judaizers' picture of the earliest disciples, his preaching must be supplemented, namely by the demand for circumcision and observance of the Law. So it may be useful for Paul to remind his readers that the men on whom he is supposed to depend have a very human past indeed, even though his main concern is to report their acknowledgement of his independence and of his preaching to the Gentiles.

the discussion described by Paul in Gal. 2. It is by no means certain that the two meetings are identical, but the supposition from which people start here is certainly wrong. The expression 'added nothing' has nothing to do with the remaining decisions reached in the negotiations— they could, if they had liked, have laid down a whole *corpus juris canonici*—but means that nothing was added of what, in the opponents' opinion, Jerusalem would have been bound to demand. We are dealing here with the picture of Paul as the Judaizers wrongly imagined him, as the one who, originally the emissary of Jerusalem, preached a message of which circumcision and observance of the Law were part (cf. 5.11), but who later, in order to please men, i.e., the Gentiles, dropped those demands, which were so burdensome to them, and confined himself to preaching what was easiest in the Jerusalem message. A meeting face to face between Paul and the leaders in Jerusalem must therefore lead, in the Judaizers' view, to some arrangement by which anything that Paul left out of his preaching was again 'added'. In that sense—but in our context in that sense only—nothing was added. It is therefore also unjustified to take the addition to the Jerusalem agreement (v. 10) to mean that Jerusalem here imposed on Paul and his churches a contribution to the mother church. But we shall deal with this question of the Pauline churches' liability for contributions to Jerusalem in another connexion (see pp. 287–91). We shall return shortly to the agreement reached at the conference.

IV

The encounter between Paul and Peter in Antioch, mentioned in the next verses, 11 ff., is generally regarded as an episode that took place after the Jerusalem meeting. The events are, in fact, narrated in that order, and it is therefore assumed that the agreement between Paul and the 'pillars' did not last, but broke down when Peter visited Antioch soon afterwards.[1] That agrees quite well with the traditionally supposed sharp opposition between the leaders of the Jerusalem church and the apostle to the Gentiles. But here it is overlooked that the text at least leaves open the question whether the clash in Antioch took place before or after the conference in Jerusalem. And what is still more important, people have shut their eyes to the fact that such an assumption, that the episode in Antioch invalidated the Jerusalem agreement, is not consistent with the text of Galatians. For the narrative of the encounter

[1] See pp. 74 f. Zahn assumes (pp. 110 ff.) that the Antioch episode took place before the Jerusalem meeting, and mentions in n. 39 what led to this interpretation.

is an argument that turns to the advantage of the Judaizing opponents, not to Paul, if the clash brought to light the deep cleavage between him and Jerusalem, a cleavage that was only superficially covered at the meeting there. We may be sure that Paul did not wish by adding this last episode to undermine his whole argument as to his independence of Jerusalem and the recognition that he did in fact receive there at his last visit.

If we look at the chronological arrangement, the first two chapters of Galatians are a refutation of the opponents' view of Paul's apostleship as a call that made him dependent on the leaders of the mission to the Jews. Paul is extremely anxious to prove his independence of Jerusalem by showing that he did not at once ask the older apostles there for advice (vv. 16b–17), and did not go to Jerusalem till three years later, and then for only fifteen days. At last, 'after fourteen years', there followed the momentous visit at which Paul was fully acknowledged by the 'pillars'. To emphasize the fact that in the time between his call at Damascus and the two visits he had no communication with Jerusalem, he expressly mentions that he stayed in Arabia (and Damascus) and then in the regions of Syria and Cilicia (vv. 17, 21).[1] Regarding the last interval he says plainly that the churches of Judaea had only heard of the Christian preaching of the former persecutor.

This account is built up as follows. It begins with ὅτε δὲ εὐδόκησεν in 1.15 ff., where the call is mentioned. The report of the first visit to Jerusalem is introduced with ἔπειτα μετὰ τρία ἔτη (v. 18), and the information about Paul's going to the regions of Syria and Cilicia with ἔπειτα ἦλθον (v. 21). The narrative of the second visit is again begun with ἔπειτα διὰ δεκατεσσάρων ἐτῶν (2.1). But after that the construction changes. We are not told where he stayed between this second visit and the clash in Antioch, and there is no introductory ἔπειτα. Instead he begins with a ὅτε δὲ ἦλθεν, which is an exact parallel to the ὅτε δὲ εὐδόκησεν of 1.15. So we have here a fresh beginning as in the presentation of the case in 1.15 ff., but going beyond the latter by containing even stronger proof of Paul's independence. The section 1.15 ff. is designed to refute the assertions that he is dependent on Jerusalem. This is done in a negative way, and leads on to his positive recognition by the 'pillars' on his second visit. Paul can now, in 2.11 ff., bring forward an even stronger argument for his independence as an apostle

---

[1] Linton rightly observes, p. 84, 'Arabia is here mentioned only with the purpose to prove an *alibi*. The meaning is, he was in *Arabia* and consequently *not in Jerusalem*.' As the names of these places are mentioned to show that he was not in Judaea, it is wrong to assume with John Knox, *Chapters in a Life of Paul*, pp. 78 ff., and Dibelius and Kümmel, *Paul*, p. 59, that in the intervals that he mentions Paul was in quite different places, such as among the Galatian churches, in Macedonia, Greece, and Asia.

than that recognition, namely that on one occasion of unspecified date he opposed Peter and gained his point.

Thus it is not for chronological reasons that 2.11 ff. has been brought in here; it is put last as the clearest proof of Paul's independence. Not only was he not dependent on the Jerusalem leaders, but he was recognized by them, and on a certain occasion he even opposed Peter and the latter had to concede him his point. The question of the time at which this incident happened is therefore open. If we start from the traditional opposition between the Jewish Christians in Jerusalem and Paul, it is possible, but by no means certain, that it happened later than the Jerusalem meeting. If we think, on the other hand, that the mutual relation of both sides was on the whole harmonious, as Paul describes it, although not without differences of opinion, it seems reasonable to place the incident before the conference in Jerusalem (2.1–10). It was a case where for the first time the people from Jerusalem, namely Peter and 'certain men from James', met a mixed church of Jewish and Gentile Christians, and were compelled to decide on their attitude to problems that they had not known at Jerusalem.

The explanation of Peter's changing points of view may well be that he is meeting the problems for the first time. The influence exercised by 'certain men from James' is generally explained by assuming that James' standpoint was outspokenly Jewish Christian, and that he interfered through emissaries in the affairs of the church in Antioch. This assumption, however, rests on the traditional view, not on the text. 'Certain men from James' may be simply some Jerusalem Jewish Christians.[1] They may have been on a journey unconnected with church affairs. In any case, when confronted by meals taken in common by Jewish and Gentile Christians, they are at a loss. But during his stay Peter had hitherto taken part in what was a custom in the Antioch church. Their attitude causes him to change his, and thereupon the other Jewish Christians, and even Barnabas, do the same, so that the Gentile Christians remain with Paul only. If it is Paul whom this narrative, with the account that follows of a clash between him and Peter, puts in a favourable light—we have here, indeed, not a historical report, but an attack on the Judaizing propaganda among the Galatians—it is bound to culminate in the recognition by Peter, Barnabas, and the other Jewish Christians in Antioch that Paul is in the right. That is not said, but it must be assumed. Whether that also holds good of the people who had come from James, we cannot know, but it is not out

[1] J. B. Lightfoot writes (p. 112), 'Of these nothing more can safely be inferred than that they belonged to the Church of Jerusalem.' But he also adds, 'It is not improbable however, that they came invested with some powers from James which they abused.'

of the question. If the Jerusalem Christians thought as James did, they must have adopted a friendly attitude towards Paul and the Gentile mission. We shall be able on another occasion (see pp. 111–19) to consider James' positive attitude.

V

For the present, however, we shall continue our discussion of the meeting in Jerusalem (Gal. 2.1–10). Presumably the above description of Paul's second visit to Jerusalem will be regarded with some uncertainty, as he went there in consequence of a revelation. In Acts 15 we read that the visit was preceded by a dispute in Antioch; so we are accustomed to assume that Paul had some reason that was more substantial (in the modern sense) than a revelation. Many people therefore, in order to harmonize Acts and Galatians, have combined the outward struggle and the decision that the apostles should go to Jerusalem (Acts 15.2) with Paul's revelation. That might be possible, but it is not a happy solution. If the revelation had coincided with external events, the latter would certainly be mentioned in Gal. 2.2.

But what we are anxious to do here is to find the correct interpretation of Gal. 2.1–10, and we do not want to misunderstand the text by trying to save Acts 15 from the charge of unreliability. The assumption that the meeting of which Paul speaks really came about as the result of a revelation is quite natural, and we therefore need not be surprised to find at the meeting, apart from the whole church, only Paul with his companions and 'those of repute'. No one had come from the areas where the Gentile mission operated to ask for the implementation of the Judaistic claims, nor do any former Pharisees appear with similar claims on behalf of the Jerusalem church. In any case we hear in Galatians none of what is in Acts 15, and we shall therefore find it best to refrain from reading what comes from Acts 15 into Galatians. The meeting ends with an agreement between Paul and Jerusalem, and here we must investigate the problem with which Paul had to contend till the revelation referred to caused him to go to Jerusalem to solve the problem there with the earliest disciples.

We can take it from v. 2 that the mission to the Gentiles had already begun at the time of the journey. Paul goes up and puts before 'them', i.e., the churches of Judaea, the gospel that he is preaching to the Gentiles ('but privately before those who were of repute'), lest somehow he 'should be running or had run in vain'. It is usually inferred from these words that the Judaizers were in the right—Paul was dependent on Jerusalem and had to go up there to obtain the recognition of his gospel. And when, under the pressure of Paul's words, people had to admit that they could not maintain that he was dependent on Jerusalem, they narrowed the meaning of the passage. It then signified a historical fact—Paul could not carry on a mission to the Gentiles and allow a Christianity without circumcision and observance of the Law if Jerusalem emissaries were continually coming along and inciting to apostasy. He therefore had to try to win over the leaders in Jerusalem for his work, so that they should not in the future take up a position behind the Jerusalem emissaries and trouble-makers.

Those Jerusalem emissaries who appeared again and again in the Pauline churches and tried to put them under the jurisdiction of Jerusalem are, however, the product of a groundless assumption. We certainly read in Acts that the apostles in Jerusalem send Peter and John to Samaria on hearing that Samaria has received God's word (8.14). In the same way the church in Jerusalem sends Barnabas to Antioch when it hears the news that the Gospel is being preached to the Gentiles in that city (11.22). But the members of the churches in Judaea who are mentioned in 15.1, who demand of the Gentile Christians in Antioch circumcision and observance of the Law, are not sent by the apostles and the elders in Jerusalem (15.24). On the contrary, the latter send Silas and Judas with the so-called 'apostolic decree' (15.27 ff.).[1] We hear nothing in Acts about emissaries from Jerusalem to the Pauline churches, and nothing about Jewish Christians from Palestine who visit those churches; and the official emissaries mentioned, Peter and John, Barnabas and Silas and Judas, are certainly first described as such by the writer of Acts, the idea coming from the sub-apostolic Church. According to Acts, the history of the Church is the history of the Christian centres of Jerusalem, Antioch, etc. Jerusalem has a care for the mission, including that in Antioch, and Antioch in its turn becomes the starting-point of a mission (13.1 ff.).[2] Even if the history of the Church has always been also the history of the Christian centres, it is reasonable to suppose that the people who carried on the first Christian mission and founded those centres were missionaries like Paul, sent out by the risen Christ, with fellow-workers whom they, like Paul, had won on the way. Emissaries of the Christian centres and their churches they certainly were not.[3]

[1]Apart from the people already mentioned we hear of some prophets who go from Jerusalem to Antioch and prophesy an imminent famine (11.27 f.), and of Agabus, the only one of them who is mentioned by name, who goes down from Judaea to Caesarea, where Paul is, and prophesies his arrest in Jerusalem (21.10 f.).
[2]See Dibelius and Kümmel, pp. 69 ff.
[3]According to Acts it is the fugitive members of the church in Jerusalem who begin preaching among the Gentiles in Antioch (11.19 f.), and it is Philip the Evangelist who, put by Luke among those fugitives, evangelizes in 'a city of Samaria'

The presuppositions for the continual visitation of the Pauline churches by emissaries from Jerusalem would of course have to be sought in a genuine interest of Jerusalem in the Gentile Christian churches. That, however, did not exist, as we shall see later (pp. 255–64). From the very beginning the Jewish Christian church saw its task as that of spreading the Gospel among the Jews, as Israel's conversion was for them of decisive importance for the salvation of the Gentiles. And when Paul goes up to Jerusalem (Gal. 2.1–10), the agreement is made that 'those of repute' shall go to the Jews, and Paul to the Gentiles. So we meet no Jewish Christian emissaries in the Pauline churches, either before or after the meeting in Jerusalem.

It is true that people have claimed to find such emissaries in Paul's letters, namely Peter and 'certain men from James' (Gal. 2.11 f.), the leaders of the 'Cephas party' and of the 'Christ party' in Corinth (I Cor. 1–4; cf. II Cor. 10.7), the opponents in II Corinthians (see particularly chs. 10–13), and the Judaizers who caused in the Roman church the antagonisms that Paul tried to overcome in the letter to the Romans. But we shall see in the coming chapters that there are no parties in the church at Corinth, and that there is therefore no Judaism either, so that before I Corinthians there is no trace of Jerusalem emissaries to be found in that church (see ch. 5). The opponents in II Corinthians are certainly Jews, but not Judaizers; and their importance in the struggle between Paul and the church has been greatly exaggerated (see ch. 6). The antagonisms in Romans are not an expression of difficulties in the church that Paul did not know, but throw light on the conditions in the east during the third journey. They show how the apostle has overcome those difficulties and now gives an account of the results of his struggle, which he carried on in the best interests of the Jews and Gentiles inside and outside the Church (see ch. 7).

While referring to the later chapters to show that the other three great letters are not about Judaistic emissaries from Jerusalem, we will meanwhile consider here Gal. 2.11 f. We have seen above (pp. 100–3) that the Antioch incident did not necessarily take place after the meeting in Jerusalem. We have expressed our view that the clash took place before that meeting, as Peter and 'certain men from James' were there for the first time confronted with a mixed church. Their reactions

---

(8.4 ff.; cf. what follows about Philip in ch. 8). In Acts, as in the Pauline letters, it is clear that Paul is not tied to a centre. Some connexion with Jerusalem is spoken of, but not in the sense of a Christian centre that has sent him out and is standing behind his activity (see later, pp. 231–38). Rom. 15.14–24 (cf. pp. 49–55) shows how an apostle can use for the benefit of his missionary work a Christian centre that already exists.

are therefore unpremeditated, and are subject to changes through outside influences.

We know that Peter was an apostle in the original Christian sense, a missionary called and sent out by the risen Lord.[1] His stay in Antioch may be explained in more than one way—it might be a stopping-place on his way after he had left Jerusalem (Acts 12.17)[2]—but we cannot infer, from his participation in the common meals of Jewish and Gentile Christians according to the church's custom,[3] that he had come for an inspection and with rigid directives from Jerusalem. The same applies to 'certain men from James', of whom we are only told that they came to Antioch while Peter was there and was taking part in the common meals. They may have been Christians from Jerusalem coming on their private affairs but possibly having no particular commission to discharge in Antioch.[4] But they stayed long enough to exercise some influence on the church. How those Christians from Jerusalem could produce such an effect as is related in vv. 12 f., namely that first Peter and then the other Jews, including even Barnabas, drew back through fear of the Jews, is not explained. The words φοβούμενος τοὺς ἐκ περιτομῆς, which are given as Peter's reason, may give us a hint of what in Paul's opinion led to that unhappy result. They are usually applied to Jewish Christians, either Jewish Christians generally, or the Jewish Christians from Jerusalem sent out by James.[5] It is by no means certain, however, that that is a correct interpretation. In v. 12 we have both τὰ ἔθνη and οἱ ἐκ περιτομῆς, and the same expressions have already occurred in v. 8. The last expression refers to Peter's missionary task, the first, to Paul's. Even if τὰ ἔθνη here in v. 12 can mean nothing else than the Gentile Christians, the words belong to a context in which the

[1]Gal. 1.19, 2.8. See 'Paul, the Apostles, and the Twelve', p. 107. I am no longer of the opinion that Peter's journeys in Acts can prove that he was an apostle in the original Christian sense, as those journeys were for visitation, not for missionary work.

[2]Thus Zahn *ad loc.*, pp. 111 f.

[3]It is not certain that the text speaks of a mixed church, as οἱ λοιποὶ 'Ιουδαῖοι may denote the other missionaries (cf. Col. 4.11: οἱ ὄντες ἐκ περιτομῆς . . . συνεργοὶ εἰς τὴν βασιλείαν τοῦ Θεοῦ), as indeed most of them were Jews. If we judge by Acts 11.20 f., it must be a mixed church.

[4]Goguel, *Les Premiers Temps de l'Église*, p. 73 n. 2: 'It is impossible to decide—and Paul certainly did not know—whether these followers of James had come to Antioch by chance, or whether they had been sent from Jerusalem to try to put pressure on the church . . .'

[5]The expression is applied to Jewish Christians generally by Sieffert, Lagrange, Lietzmann, Beyer and Althaus. G. S. Duncan makes the expression mean 'the circumcision party', namely those inside and outside the Church for whom the main distinction was between Jews and non-Jews. Zahn makes it refer to the circle round James, not to James himself (p. 115), while E. de Witt Burton, D. A. Frövig and Schlier think that the reference here is to the Jewish Christians from Jerusalem sent out by James. The same view is probably taken by Lightfoot, whose attitude to this question is not quite clear (see in particular the rendering of the contents of vv. 11–14).

expression is used of the Gentiles in contrast to the Jews. The question is now whether οἱ ἐκ περιτομῆς must necessarily mean the Jewish Christians[1] in a context where περιτομή in vv. 7 f. is used of Jews (cf. the contrasts between Jew and Gentile in v. 14). The decision must be made on general considerations. As we shall show later, the Jewish Christians do not regard circumcision and the observance of the Law as a *sine qua non* of salvation (see pp. 109 ff., 122 ff., 247 ff.). These things are not at the heart of their religion, but they are part of the national manners and customs among Christians of Jewish origin. If we consider the independent attitude of the Gentile Christians towards these things, the question repeatedly presents itself how the Jews will regard that independence. In James' speech at the Council at Jerusalem (Acts 15.21), this is made quite clear. He seems to assume that the mission to the Gentiles is to be carried on from the synagogues of the Diaspora (cf. pp. 112 ff. and 234 f.); and in his speech on Paul's last visit to Jerusalem the hearty welcome and the praise of God are carried over into the consideration of how the Jews will behave when Paul visits the Jewish Christians.[2] We have the same experience in the first part of Acts, where Luke emphasizes that the church enjoyed 'favour with all the people'. How important this regard to the Jewish people as a whole was, we can realize from the point of view of the Jewish Christians' missionary duty towards Israel. A public disregard of the Jewish laws about food might cause Peter, the apostle to the Jews, difficulties in carrying on his work.[3] As he sees the newcomers' horror at his participation in the common meals, which has hitherto seemed quite right and proper, it becomes clear to him that it may make his work among the Jews difficult. Paul's rather inappropriate version of this consideration is 'fearing the circumcised'.

We shall return later to what such behaviour caused Paul to say to Peter. But nothing in v. 12 makes it likely that 'certain men from James' were emissaries commissioned by James and Jerusalem to carry out any inspection in Antioch. And as in the other letters too we shall meet no emissaries from Jerusalem in the Pauline churches, the assertion

[1] οἱ ἐκ περιτομῆς means the Jews in Acts 10.45; Rom. 4.12; Col. 4.11 (cf. the use of περιτομή in Rom. 3.30; 4.9, 12; 15.8; Gal. 2.7–9; cf. Eph. 2.11; Phil. 3.3; and Col. 3.11), and the same is probably the case in Titus 1.10, where the commentators apply the expression to either Jews or Jewish Christians. Acts 11.2 uses the expression for circumcised Christians (D reads οἱ δὲ ἐκ περιτομῆς ἀδελφοί). For τὰ ἔθνη something similar holds good; it denotes as a rule the Gentiles in contrast to the Jews. If it is to mean the Gentile Christians, the expression is written more precisely, as in Acts 15.23 and 21.25. There is indeed nothing to prevent its being used of the Gentile Christians, but where it is so used the contrast between Gentiles and Jews is tacitly assumed, as in Rom. 11.13; 15.27; Gal. 2.14; cf. Eph. 3.1.

[2] See below, pp. 238–42.

[3] Cf. G. Kittel, 'Die Stellung des Jakobus zu Judentum und Heidenchristentum', *ZNW* 30, 1931, p. 153.

cannot be maintained that Paul was compelled to enter into negotiations with the leaders in Jerusalem because emissaries came from their church to his churches, interfering in his affairs, having a different gospel, and trying to detach the churches from him so as to put them under Jerusalem.

We therefore have to find another reason for the agreement that was made in Jerusalem, and to prepare which Paul put his gospel before the churches and particularly before 'those of repute'. If we look more closely at the expressions in vv. 1 f., we shall notice especially the last sentence in v. 2: μή πως εἰς κενὸν τρέχω ἢ ἔδραμον. The expression εἰς κενὸν τρέχω connects the image of the running[1] with κενός.[2] Apart from I Cor. 15.58, Col. 2.8, and Eph. 5.6, κενός is used of Paul's apostleship. In Phil. 2.16 we have κενός in an eschatological context.[3] In vv. 14–16 the church in Philippi is urged to make every effort to become blameless to the glory of Paul in the day of Christ, ὅτι οὐκ εἰς κενὸν ἔδραμον οὐδὲ εἰς κενὸν ἐκοπίασα.[4] This summons to do everything so that Paul may glory in the church on the day of judgment is followed by the remark that the apostle rejoices even if he himself is to be given up 'upon the sacrificial offering of your faith'. This has reference to the fullness of the Gentiles (cf. pp. 42–49), which Paul is preparing by his work. As Gal. 2.1 f. and Phil. 2.16 are closely related, it is a justifiable assumption that the first passage too refers to an eschatological day of reckoning, so that Paul's anxiety before the Jerusalem conversations has to do with the relation between the mission to the Jews and the mission to the Gentiles. Paul, who has already been to Jerusalem once, even though for quite a short time (Gal. 1.18), must have information as to the position of the Jerusalem church and its leaders with regard to the mission to the Gentiles. They regard it as secondary in comparison with the missionary work to Israel, in which they themselves are occupied. Jerusalem had no need to interfere with Paul's work in any way. But Paul, proceeding from his view of the central position of Israel in the plan of salvation, could not continue his work among the Gentiles without connecting it with the mission to Israel. He could not

---

[1]τρέχω: Rom. 9.16; I Cor. 9.24 (twice) and v. 26; Gal. 5.7; II Thess. 3.1; besides Gal. 2.2 and Phil. 2.16, where τρέχω is combined both times with εἰς κενόν.

[2]κενός: I Cor. 15.10, 14 (twice) and v. 58; II Cor. 6.1; (Eph. 5.6); Col. 2.8; I Thess. 2.1; 3.5, and also the text Gal. 2.2 here and Phil. 2.16 (twice).

[3]Also in I Cor. 15.58, but here it is a question of the Corinthians, not Paul.

[4]κοπιάω is used by Paul in Rom. 16.6, 12 (twice); I Cor. 4.12; 15.10; 16.16; Gal. 4.11; cf. Eph. 4.28; Phil. 2.16; Col. 1.29; I Thess. 5.12; cf. Acts 20.35. Cf. Paul's use of κόπος. Of these passages I Cor. 4.12; 15.10: περισσότερον αὐτῶν πάντων ἐκοπίασα, Gal. 4.11: μή πως εἰκῆ κεκοπίακα εἰς ὑμᾶς, and Phil. 2.16 relate to Paul. Of the κόπος passages we notice the above passage, I Cor. 15.58: εἰδότες ὅτι ὁ κόπος ὑμῶν οὐκ ἔστιν κενὸς ἐν Κυρίῳ, besides I Thess. 3.5: μή πως . . . εἰς κενὸν γένηται ὁ κόπος ἡμῶν.

leave Israel in the lurch and go to the Gentiles without assuring the leaders of the mission to the Jews that his work too had consciously, as its fixed object, the conversion of Israel and the glorification of Jerusalem. It is therefore not the mission to the Gentiles about which Paul fears that the work has been in vain, but his own call, concerning Israel as well as the Gentiles, that is at stake.

VI

We still have to look at the important agreement reached at the discussion in Jerusalem (Gal. 2.7-10). Before we deal with these verses, which report on the settlement between the Jerusalem 'pillars' and Paul, we must first examine what we happen to know about the 'pillars' and the churches of Judaea, and their position in relation to the mission to the Gentiles. The final discussion of this question must be deferred to ch. 9; but here we already have so much material at our disposal that we have a good foundation on which to form an opinion about the Jerusalem agreement and the subsequent rebuke of Peter in Antioch.

First as regards the churches in Judaea, Paul speaks kindly of them, not only here in Galatians, although in this connexion he mentions only their positive attitude to his work among the Gentiles. In I Thess. 2.14 he tells the Thessalonians that by their sufferings under persecution by their own countrymen they have imitated the example of God's churches that are in Jesus Christ in Judaea, as the latter have suffered the same things at the hands of the Jews.[1] And about the Jews Paul says in v. 16 that they 'hinder us from speaking to the Gentiles that they may be saved'. This remark would sound strange if the Christian churches of Judaea did their best to prevent him from saving the Gentiles. About the oldest churches, which have also been suffering, he speaks freely and frankly, and names them in the same breath with the

---

[1]Goguel has tried to weaken the force of this passage, proceeding from his view that apart from rare and easily explained exceptions, Jewry behaved extremely tolerantly towards the Jerusalem church, which, indeed, held firmly to all the Jewish traditions (*Les Premiers Temps de l'Église*, p. 56). He points out (pp. 57 ff.) that when Paul wrote I Thessalonians he had not been in Judaea for seven years, and that there is nothing to indicate that he was informed about what happened there. In Goguel's opinion therefore it is not only possible, but even probable, that Paul's remarks allude to the persecution of the Hellenists and the persecution ordered by King Agrippa. The expression 'churches of Judaea' is, however, not a suitable one in connexion with these two short persecutions in Jerusalem. Paul, indeed, is said to have extended the first of these persecutions to places outside (Acts 26.11), but it is difficult to imagine that he should speak here of a persecution in which he himself took part as a persecutor, and not of a persecution of later date, about which he was informed as a Christian. Finally, it is unlikely that he was cut off from news from Jerusalem and Palestine during his journeys. Especially for anyone who expects Jerusalem emissaries to be going in and out of the Pauline churches, it seems out of the question for any such important news as the persecution of the church in Jerusalem to have escaped Paul.

most recent converts who were being persecuted, so as to encourage the latter. It would be most remarkable if at that particular time Paul's experiences with the churches of Judaea had been anything but good.[1]

Later on, the collection for the poor among the saints of Jerusalem gives Paul the chance to mention these people repeatedly, and he does so, as we shall later have occasion to see in detail, so unconstrainedly and confidently that it is only by questioning the apostle's trustworthiness that we could read out of the texts the opposite of what they contain (see pp. 286–89).

The relation to Peter—the apostle John need not be considered here, as the evidence is inadequate—is subjected to a severe strain in the next section, 2.11–21. But only just before this, vv. 1–10 show the strong fellow-feeling that forms the background of the Jerusalem agreement; and we generally meet that sympathetic attitude when Peter is mentioned. There is no need to give any special weight to I Cor. 15.5, where Peter is mentioned as a witness of the Resurrection. But in I Cor. 1.12 and 3.22 he is mentioned as a leader whom some of the Corinthian church members invoke, but nothing bad is said about him. Paul condemns the setting up of different Christian leaders as teachers of wisdom, but he finds no word of censure for the leaders named. If anyone invokes Paul himself in that way, he criticizes this attitude. As Peter, according to our interpretation in ch. 5, is not to blame for the Corinthians' faults, the effect of these passages is of course not as convincing as when they are made to refer, as they traditionally are, to the Cephas party of which either the apostle himself or some of his disciples laid the foundations while they were in Corinth. The most apposite is the last passage that we have to mention, I Cor. 9.5, in which Paul, in referring to the right to ask for maintenance, speaks of the justified claim for the maintenance of an apostle and his wife, and in that connexion quotes 'the other apostles and the brothers of the Lord and Cephas'. In this and the next verse, where Barnabas is named, Paul speaks quite unconstrainedly about those leaders of the Jewish Christian church, and of his old travelling companion with whom, according to Acts 15.36–39, he is supposed to have fallen out. As I Cor. 9 is not, as is generally supposed, full of polemics against people who are attacking Paul's apostleship, the mention of those great names is an innocent remark. It shows that there was no reason to avoid naming Peter or the others.[2]

---

[1] Nock says on I Thess. 2.14 (*St Paul*, p. 151), '. . . Paul speaks in a very appreciative way of the churches in Judaea: presumably if the "Decrees" had been passed, there was as yet no active opposition of the type described in Galatians.'

[2] Dibelius and Kümmel, *Paul*, p. 135: 'Paul himself mentions Peter later on in such a way that no kind of serious disagreement can be detected (I Cor. 3.22; 9.5)'.

For the rest, research is in two minds about Peter. In the discussion by Hirsch and Lietzmann that is mentioned at the beginning of this chapter, the former has expressed himself against regarding him as a Judaizer. Peter does not want to break with James and Jerusalem, and therefore the compromise that is expressed in the apostles' decree is probably his distinctive contribution. This view of Peter as the representative of a policy of compromise has become the usual one.[1] If we take Cullmann's book about him,[2] we see a picture of Peter who, as the leader of the Jewish Christian mission, was dependent on the Jerusalem church, and in that position of dependence occupied an immeasurably more difficult position that did the independent Paul. Peter therefore, as the earlier and first head of the Church, is confronted with a particularly painful dilemma by the conflict in Antioch (Gal. 2.11 ff.), because in fact he was much closer to Paul than to James on questions of Gentile Christianity and observance of the Law (p. 51).

This mediating position with its compromises assumes that James' standpoint was rigid and uncompromising. He represented Jewish Christianity, which Baur defined so sharply (see pp. 70 f.) that it cannot properly be called Christianity. To be sure, James had had a few rough edges knocked off him since them. Some people have even tried, as we have just said, to make the church take up the uncompromising attitude, and to make James a new man of compromise, together with Peter. But in the main, scholars still regard him as Paul's opponent, as a righteous Jew who enjoyed great prestige among the Jews.[3]

The inquiry must therefore fasten on this point, if we want to form a picture of the resistance to the mission to the Gentiles and of the

---

[1] Thus Lietzmann, *The Beginnings of the Christian Church*, 1937, p. 151; Goguel, *Les Premiers Temps de l'Église*, p. 73; Dibelius and Kümmel, p. 135. Although unanimous that Peter is the man of compromise, the experts are of different opinions as to where that compromise is to be sought. Lietzmann speaks of Peter's semi-Judaism in Corinth. Goguel thinks that Peter's attitude to the validity of the Law for the Gentiles was influenced by opportunist points of view and did not arise from reasons of principle. Dibelius and Kümmel emphasize not only the explicit contrast between Peter and the Judaizers of Jerusalem, but also between James and the extreme Judaizers. The same is true of G. Kittel, 'Die Stellung des Jakobus zu Judentum und Heidenchristentum', *ZNW* 30, 1931, pp. 145–57; cf. 'Der geschichtliche Ort des Jakobusbriefes', *ZNW* 41, 1942, pp. 97–99. But here the question arises: Who were the Judaizers in Jerusalem, if they included neither Peter nor James? Goguel tried to answer the question by drawing a distinction between the attitude of the leaders and that of the church in Jerusalem (pp. 64 ff.).

[2] *Peter: Disciple, Apostle, Martyr*, ET 1953.

[3] Knox, *St Paul*, p. 17: 'A pattern of the Pharisaic type of righteousness'; Lietzmann, p. 66: 'Moreover James, the leader of the church, belonged at bottom to those who were strangers to Jesus, and strove for the ideal of a Jewish "righteousness".' Goguel, *Les Premiers Temps de l'Église*, p. 57: '. . . James, the brother of Jesus, who earned the epithet "the Just" by his devotion to Judaism and its Law, and by the zeal with which he made intercession in the temple on behalf of his people.' In Stauffer, 'Zum Kalifat des Jakobus', *ZRGG* 4, 1952, pp. 200 ff., we find a still stronger revival of the Tübingen School's outlook.

persistent clinging to the Jewish religion inside the Jerusalem church and the whole of Jewish Christianity. The others could vacillate, but James stood firm. It is therefore of the greatest importance for any real understanding of primitive Christianity to see clearly that modern research has made a quite unhistorical picture of James, and in doing so has worked with a late source of little or no historical value. The righteous Jew, with his hostile attitude to Paul and the Gentile mission, arises from this untrustworthy source, and has been read into our older and much more trustworthy sources.

Here too, as so often elsewhere in primitive Christianity, we must begin by recognizing that we are very imperfectly informed—in this case about James the brother of the Lord. In the New Testament we find his name when Jesus' brothers are mentioned (Matt. 13.55, Mark 6.3).[1] In Acts 12.17 he is mentioned by Peter in such a way that many people see in it an allusion to his leading position in the Jerusalem church. Paul says in I Cor. 15.7 that the risen Lord appeared to James,[2] and he also speaks of James in Galatians in connexion with his first and second visit to Jerusalem, and here in Gal. 2.12. We hear about him in more detail only in Acts 15.13–21 and 21.18–26. In the first text a speech is reproduced that James is said to have made at the so-called Council at Jerusalem. As at the meeting in Gal. 2.1 ff., he recognizes the *raison d'être* of the mission to the Gentiles, but he does not see it with the same eyes as Paul. As we shall see later, he takes the Jerusalem standpoint regarding the mission to the Gentiles.[3] He knows that God wants to win from out of the Gentiles a people for his name; that is already affirmed by the prophets. And he quotes Amos 9.11 f. according to the LXX: 'After this I will return, and I will rebuild the dwelling of David, which has fallen; I will rebuild its ruins, and I will set it up, that the rest of men may seek the Lord, and all the Gentiles who are called by my name.' Here the mission to the Gentiles is regarded as a consequence of the conversion of Israel. James adheres to the 'to the Jew first and also to the Greek' of Rom. 1.16. That is probably how the last part of the speech too (v. 21) should be understood; it is brought in as a reason for the proposed prohibitions (v. 20). He expects that in the synagogues, where the Law is read, the Gentiles will hear of Christ and be converted to him; and that conversion, he thinks, is the consequence of the conversion of Israel.[4]

---

[1]Cf. Mark 3.31–35; John 7.3 ff.; Acts 1.14.

[2]It is on this that Holl forms his views of James (*Gesammelte Aufsätze* II, pp. 47 ff.).

[3]See later, pp. 255–64.

[4]This passage is, so to speak, strongly illuminated by Paul's description of the complete fiasco of the mission to the Jews (Rom. 10.14–21).

The picture of James at the Council at Jerusalem in Acts in no way corresponds to the traditional picture of him in recent research. The case is no better in the narrative of Paul and James in Acts 21.18–26. When Paul comes to Jerusalem, the brethren receive him gladly (v. 17), and after he has given a full report of his missionary work among the Gentiles, James and all the elders praise God (vv. 18–20). The text that follows is obscure, the responsible leaders of the Jerusalem church not knowing what to do because their own church members misunderstand Paul's mission to the Gentiles. Instead of boldly taking their stand beside Paul, they propose to him that he should show by his acts that he observes the Jewish customs. The present form of this text cannot be the original one (for a fuller discussion, see pp. 238–42); but if we want to use it in this form, James' attitude to Paul and the Gentile mission is sufficiently clear—he fully acknowledges Paul. It is therefore not about his attitude to Paul that the text leaves us in doubt, but simply whether he was suitable to be the leader of others. It is true that he acknowledges Paul, but he faint-heartedly leaves him to settle the matter alone with James' own fellow church members, who have quite a wrong estimation of him. James has therefore effectively concealed his own different standpoint, and has never allowed it to be expressed in defence of the apostle to the Gentiles. In later church history there may well have been some fairly plain and not exactly eulogistic opinions expressed about this.[1]

In the New Testament we still have the letter of James, which some scholars regard as authentic, while most put it later. We shall therefore consider the letter to James here together with the other later evidence about him supplied by Josephus and Hegesippus.[2]

Josephus tells us about the death of James the Lord's brother in *Ant.* XX.9.1, §§ 199–203. This report has been regarded very critically, partly because Hegesippus' narrative was preferred,[3] and partly because Josephus assumes that the Sanhedrin could not carry out a death sentence without the procurator's confirmation, and this contradicts the view of a number of researchers.[4] But the narrative gives an impression

[1] See later, pp. 238–41.
[2] The appearance of the risen Lord to James, related by Jerome, *De Viris Illustribus* 2 (*PL* 23, 611C f.), if it represents old tradition at all, has no importance in this connexion.
[3] Thus Zahn, *Forschungen zur Geschichte des neutestamentlichen Kanons*, 6, 1900, pp. 301–5. J. Juster, *Les Juifs dans l'Empire Romain* II, 1914, pp. 140 f., regards the Josephus text as a Christian interpolation.
[4] A discussion about this was carried on in *ZNW* 30, 1931, and 31, 1932, viz., F. Büchsel, 'Die Blutgerichtsbarkeit des Synedrions', 1931, pp. 202–10; Lietzmann, 'Bemerkungen zum Prozess Jesu', 1932, pp. 78–84 (the article with the same title in 1931 is a reply to Dibelius' article of the same year); Goguel, 'A propos du procès de Jésus', 1932, pp. 289–301. See also Juster, *op. cit.*, pp. 133–44, and K. Bornhäuser, *Studien zur Apostelgeschichte*, 1934, pp. 71–88.

of much greater credibility than does Hegesippus' history, which is different from Josephus'. We hear how Agrippa II, in the interval between the procurators Festus and Albinus, installs as High Priest Ananus, a son of the High Priest Annas who is well known from the Gospels. The new High Priest was of a headstrong disposition; moreover he belonged to the party of the Sadducees, who were stricter in their judgments than any other Jews. As the vacant procuratorship gave him a favourable opportunity, he convened a court, condemned James and some others to be stoned to death, and had the sentence carried out. The Pharisees in Jerusalem were indignant at what had happened, and sent a secret message to Agrippa, asking him to require Ananus to refrain from such proceedings in future. Some even went to meet the new procurator and declare to him that Ananus was not authorized to hold a court without his sanction—a statement that is to be understood with certain qualifications.[1] Albinus thereupon wrote Ananus a threatening letter, and Agrippa deposed Ananus as High Priest.

It has been thought that this account cannot be historical, because an interregnum does not mean lawlessness, and because the Pharisees had no right to tell Albinus what his duties as procurator were. But these details that are given by Josephus and that are mentioned here are not unlikely. If the account as such is believed to be historical[2] and it is not interpreted through Hegesippus,[3] what it amounts to is this: The newly installed High Priest Ananus uses the interval after Festus' death to summon a court,[4] and this court condemns to death James the Lord's brother[5] together with some other Christians.[6] The indignation

---

[1]Schürer, II, p. 262 (ET, II. i, p. 189), says rightly: 'All that is meant by the statement is that the high priest had no right to hold a court of *supreme jurisdiction* in the absence and without the consent of the procurator.'

[2]Thus M. Dibelius, *Der Brief des Jakobus* (Meyer 15) [7], 1921, pp. 12 f.; E. Meyer, *Ursprung und Anfänge des Christentums* III, 1923, pp. 73 ff.; H. J. Schoeps, *Theologie und Geschichte des Judentums*, 1949, p. 415.

[3]Goguel does so (*The Birth of Christianity*, ET 1953, pp. 124 ff.) when he writes (p. 127): 'How too could James have been accused of violating the law, when a tradition which was so widely scattered that it cannot be dismissed as pure fiction held him to be a rigorous legalist?'

[4]Presumably with 23 judges (cf. Sanhedrin IV, 1) from the party of the Sadducees within the Sanhedrin.

[5]The wording of the Josephus passage, 'the brother of Jesus who is called Christ; his name was James' is presumably original; see A. Schlatter, *Der Chronograph aus dem zehnten Jahre Antonins* (TU 12.1), 1894, pp. 75–77; cf. also M. Dibelius, *Der Brief des Jakobus*, p. 13.

[6]It is therefore a question of a persecution of the Christians. It is true that the others are not stated to be Christians and might be other Jews whom the High Priest Ananus wanted to clear out of the way. But if only James is mentioned by name, we must presume τινὰς ἑτέρους to refer to some of his less well known fellow believers. Goguel assumes (p. 127) that if James' death took place as part of a persecution of the Christians, Jewish public opinion must still have been favourably inclined to-

and protest caused by Ananus' procedure are concerned here, not with substance, but with forms, probably not only with the expressly mentioned infringement of the procurator's rights, but rather with the highhanded actions of which Ananus was guilty in holding the court[1] and passing sentence.[2] The High Priest is himself guilty of παρανομῆσαι, the very offence with which he had charged James and the other accused persons. For our picture of James it is not unimportant that, like Paul, he is accused of a breach of the Law. It shows how careful we must be if we want to make James the brother of the Lord a Jew in every respect—though of course with the exception that for James the coming Messiah is identical with the crucified and risen Jesus.

We now come to the text that set scholars off on the wrong track. We refer to Hegesippus' account of James' death in Eusebius, *h.e.* II. 23.4–18. Hegesippus describes James as a Jew who lives an upright life according to the Law, but who believes Jesus to be the Messiah. We have here palpably before us the Tübingen School's view of James and the Jerusalem church, and here is perhaps also the reason why the credibility of Hegesippus' legendary narrative has been so unreservedly accepted. The same scholars who have rejected such a well-attested tradition as that of the apostle John's stay in Ephesus and a number of other second-century traditions about the apostles do not hesitate to approve an account of James the Lord's brother which comes from the end of the second century and is in itself unlikely.[3]

James is described here as an ascetic and a priest (Eusebius, *h.e.* II.

---

wards the Christians (thus too Nock, *St Paul*, p. 169). This, however, is a conclusion that does not necessarily follow from the text. The protest is directed, not against the persecution of the Christians, but against the infringement of the Law by the holding of the court. We may also suppose that this protest is an expression of the struggle for power in the inner circles of Judaism. According to Goguel, Ananus had James executed because of his popular influence. But it is only from Hegesippus that we hear of any such influence.

[1] There can hardly have been any Pharisees among the judges who were convened.

[2] Josephus alludes to this with his remark about the Sadducees' strictness in legal matters.

[3] Thus Lietzmann, *The Beginnings of the Christian Church*, p. 66; Goguel, *Les Premiers Temps de l'Église*, p. 57. J. Weiss's mention of James in *The History of Primitive Christianity* II, ET 1937, pp. 711 f., is very characteristic: 'The later account permits a conclusion *a posteriori* in regard to the character of James only in so far as the complete Judaization of his character in Hegesippus corresponds to the original James himself: he must have felt himself a Jew through and through, and must himself have observed the Law to the highest degree. When Hegesippus tells how he prayed so continuously in the temple for forgiveness for his people that his kneecap became calloused like that of a camel, even this would suit the actual attitude of a man who was chief leader in the endeavor to gain and convert Israel. But this statement cannot be given much credence as an historical account.'

23.5 f.).[1] He is called 'the Just',[2] and was holy from his mother's womb.[3] Besides 'the Just' James is called 'Oblias', which is said to mean in Greek 'the people's stronghold',[4] and righteousness', as the prophets say of him.[5] Here and in what follows the text seems to be confused. § 7 repeats what was said in § 4, and James is questioned in both §§ 8 and 10 about Jesus, in the latter case so that he 'may persuade the people not to fall into error about Jesus', although by his first answer he has already inspired many people's faith (§ 10; 'some' in § 9). The seven Jewish parties (mentioned in IV. 22.7) believe neither in Christ, nor in the resurrection, nor in judgment according to works (§ 9)! All believe in James, and want to follow his words;[6] so people[7] turn to him and ask him to help all those—both Jews and Gentiles [*sic!*]—who have come together for Easter Day,[8] to the right conviction, namely

[1]For the account of James as priest or High Priest in II. 23.6 (cf. Epiphanius, *haer.* 29.4; 78.14), we may use in comparison what is related about the apostle John in Polycrates' letter (Eusebius, *h.e.* III. 31.3): ὃς ἐγενήθη ἱερεὺς τὸ πέταλον πεφορεκὼς καὶ μάρτυς καὶ διδάσκαλος. Presumably B. P. Grenfell and A. S. Hunt in *A Fragment of an Uncanonical Gospel*, 1908 (= *Oxyrhynchus Papyri* V. No. 840), in lines 7 ff. of the fragment, show Jesus as a man with priestly privileges; but cf. J. Jeremias, *Unknown Sayings of Jesus*, ET 1957, pp. 40 ff. James'|prayer for the forgiveness of the people (ἄφεσις τῷ λαῷ) has no direct background in the LXX or in the New Testament, and is difficult to interpret. Has it to do with the sin of the people, expressed in the hardened attitude against Christ?

[2]James' title ὁ δίκαιος is used of Jesus (without any mention of his name) in Acts 3.14; 7.52; 22.14; see on this Lake and Cadbury's remark (p. 83). The only example known to me where δίκαιος is added to a personal name is the High Priest Simon the Just, the son of Onias I; see Josephus, *Ant.* XII. 2.5, § 43; cf. 4.1, § 157 and Pirqe Aboth I, 2; see Strack's remark in *Pirqe Aboth*,[4] 1915, p. 1 note k. Schürer, II, p. 420, makes Simon the Just the later High Priest of the same name. Dibelius, in *Der Brief des Jakobus*, p. 14, is hardly right in his assertion that this additional name in Hegesippus' legend has Old Testament roots. It is not impossible that it existed independently of Hegesippus' legend. If Peter can be called 'the rock', and Paul 'the messenger', James too could have been given a Messianic term as an additional name, and he might be called 'the Just'. Stauffer is not right in saying (Jüdisches Erbe im urchristlichen Kirchenrecht', *TLZ* 77, 1952, col. 203 n. 1) that the surname Justus is not rare, in which connexion he is thinking of the above-mentioned Simon and Jesus Justus in Col. 4.11. It is true that Justus means 'just' or 'righteous', but as a name it has little or nothing to do with the quality of righteousness. Billerbeck's examples of the name Justai (II, p. 595), to which Stauffer calls attention, show it in use as a personal name, not as a descriptive surname.

[3]Cf. the application of this expression to Paul in ch. 1, pp. 25 f.

[4]The name ὠβλίας has given rise to various interpretations, e.g. H. J. Schoeps, 'Jacobus ὁ δίκαιος καὶ ὠβλίας', in *Aus frühchristlicher Zeit*, 1950, pp. 120–25.

[5]The last remark has been referred to Isa. 3.10, which is quoted in § 15. We have found Isa. 49.6, applied to Paul, quoted in Acts 13.47 (p. 27 n. 4).

[6]23.7, 9–12, 14 f.; cf. § 17. It is said about Paul too, in *Epistula Apostolorum*, 31 (42), Schmidt, p. 98, 'He will acquire authority among the people, and will preach and teach.'

[7]The subject is presumably 'Jews and scribes and Pharisees', and is identical with the above-named seven Jewish parties.

[8]The expression εἰς τὴν ἡμέραν τοῦ πάσχα must cause surprise in the mouth of a Jew. We meet it neither in the LXX nor in the New Testament, Apostolic Fathers, and Apologists (apart from Justin, *Dial.* 111.3, ἐν ἡμέρᾳ τοῦ πάσχα), nor in Melito's *Homily on the Passion* (ed. Campbell Bonner, *Studies and Documents* XII, 1940), but in Eusebius, *h.e.* IV. 14.1, where Eusebius repeats the narrative of Irenaeus, and V. 24.2, 6 in Polycrates' letter. The last passage shows that Easter Day in the Hege-

not to believe in Jesus. This request is made in words that are addressed to Jesus in Luke 20.21.[1] James is therefore placed on the pinnacle of the temple, so that all can see and hear him; but when he confesses Jesus, he is hurled down from the pinnacle of the temple and stoned, his head being finally crushed by a fuller.[2] He was buried near the temple,[3] and soon after his death Vespasian besieged Jerusalem.[4]

It is difficult to understand why a number of scholars have attached any historical value at all to this text with its numerous contradictions.[5] It has even been preferred to Josephus' account of James' death, or, like J. Weiss, people have admitted that we have here a legend, and have then used it as the authentic picture of James the brother of the Lord. We maintain, on the contrary, that this narrative, and the possibly separate accounts of which it was originally made up,[6] are not to be regarded as sources of historical value. The picture of James here is too ambiguous and contradictory. Both the historical framework and the Jewish touches are wrong, so that we cannot help doubting whether Hegesippus is a source of any value at all.[7]

In going on from this point, it is important to note that it is through Hegesippus, and only through Hegesippus, that we know James as a

---

sippus text must be the 14th Nisan, but it is Christian and not Jewish to term this day 'Easter Day'. Billerbeck in his index, Vol. IV, pp. 1252 f., uses the word 'Passahtag' of the 14th Nisan; but the texts quoted by him give no kind of authority for this. For the rest, the Old Testament texts Ex. 12.14, Lev. 23.5, 7 might have given rise to such an expression.

[1] James is compared to Jesus, because Jesus' words in Matt. 26.64 and Luke 23.34 are put into his mouth (II. 23.13, 16) and because, like Jesus, he dies at the festival of Easter. Cf. also p. 116 n. 2, and E. Schwartz, 'Zu Eusebius Kirchengeschichte', *ZNW* 4, 1903, p. 52, 'The brother of Jesus, who, being himself holy and acknowledged to be righteous, prays to God for the sinful people, is the exact counterpart of Jesus himself.'

[2] This gives rise to great difficulties. If we regard this narrative as historically probable, it is certainly right to suppose with Schlatter (*Der Chronograph* etc., pp. 75-77) that James was thrown down from the outer wall of the temple into the Kidron valley, and it was perhaps there that a fuller was able to carry on his trade.

[3] This statement, and the assertion that his grave is still there, have rightly been doubted.

[4] In the connecting of James' death with the destruction of Jerusalem we have the usual *motif*—misfortune follows closely on the death of the righteous; cf. the doubtful quotation from Josephus in Eusebius, *h.e.* II. 23.20, ταῦτα δὲ συμβέβηκεν Ἰουδαίοις κατ' ἐκδίκησιν Ἰακώβου τοῦ δικαίου, ὃς ἦν ἀδελφὸς Ἰησοῦ τοῦ λεγομένου Χριστοῦ, ἐπειδήπερ δικαιότατον αὐτὸν ὄντα οἱ Ἰουδαῖοι ἀπέκτειναν. Cf. E. Schwartz in *ZNW* 4, 1903, p. 59; Lietzmann in *ZNW* 31, 1932, p. 79 n. 1; and Goguel, *The Birth of Christianity*, p. 125 n. 5. Cf. also my remarks on Acts 20.29-30 in 'Discours d'adieu', p. 160 with n. 3.

[5] Attention is drawn to these, e.g., by Goguel, *op. cit.*, pp. 127-32.

[6] See, e.g., Schlatter, *op. cit.*, pp. 75-82.

[7] The assumption of Zahn (*Forschungen* etc. 6, p. 251), and today for instance of Altaner (*Patrologie*[2], 1951, p. 110), that Hegesippus was a Semite domiciled in Palestine, does not seem compatible with Eusebius, *h.e.* II. 23.17, εἰς τῶν ἱερέων τῶν υἱῶν Ῥηχὰβ υἱοῦ Ῥαχαβείμ, as the last word is presumably an incorrect reproduction of a Hebraic plural.

pious Jew who is a Christian only in his inmost soul. As we have said, we find James described here in Hegesippus as the Tübingen School imagined the earliest church in Jerusalem, the original church representing a wholly Jewish standpoint, apart from believing in the crucified Jesus as the coming Messiah.

All the other sources draw quite a different picture. According to them James is the Christian leader of the church in Jerusalem, who himself feels the duty to evangelize among the Jews, but who acknowledges Paul as an apostle called by Christ, and his work among the Gentiles.

There is one more witness who ought to be heard. We refer to James' letter, which is said to have been written by James the brother of the Lord. If this letter is genuine, it must tell us something about James' attitude to Judaism. But if the letter, as is most probable, is of later origin, it testifies to the tradition about James within the Gentile Christian church. The letter speaks of the perfect law, that of liberty (1.25), the law of liberty (2.12),[1] and of the royal law of the love of one's neighbour (2.8), and also of the genuine worship of God that expresses itself in ethical conduct. These expressions do not picture to us a legalistic Jew for whom the ceremonial law is binding. Of course, this cannot be used as an objection to the assumption that James is the author of the letter,[2] as indeed James' piety is primarily Christian, and only then Jewish. The traditional picture of James goes back to Hegesippus, and not to reliable texts.[3] If we assume that the letter of James was written by James the brother of the Lord, we can without difficulty assimilate it to the rest of the New Testament evidence about him. If, however, as I suppose, the letter is not authentic and is of later date, then tradition, apart from Hegesippus, knows only a Christian James in Jerusalem, not a pious Jew who was secretly a Christian.

[1]Stauffer claims, in *ZRGG* 4, 1952, p. 205 n. 12a, a relation between the rule of the Order of Jericho, DSM (which I should like to call the Discipline Roll of Qumran, DSD, now called 1 QS), and the letter of James, so that the date and origin of the latter must be investigated afresh; and he mentions 1 QS 10.6, 8; cf. James 1.25; 2.8, 12. But it is uncertain whether 'cheruth' should be translated by 'liberty'; presumably it means 'engraved' in 10.6, 8, 11; cf. Bo Reicke, *Handskrifterne från Qumran* (Symbolae Biblicae Upsalienses 14), 1952, p. 90 n. 40.

[2]As to this, see the discussion in Michaelis, *Einleitung in das Neue Testament*, 1946, p. 285, where consideration is given to K. Aland, 'Der Herrenbruder Jakobus und der Jakobusbrief', *TLZ* 69, 1944, cols. 97–104.

[3]G. Kittel has worked this out clearly in his two valuable articles, 'Die Stellung des Jakobus zu Judentum und Heidenchristentum', *ZNW* 30, 1931, pp. 145–57, and 'Der geschichtliche Ort des Jakobusbriefes', *ZNW* 41, 1942, pp. 71–105 (esp. pp. 97–99). As the picture that is to be drawn here and in what follows of James and Jewish Christianity differs on certain vital points from Kittel's presentation, I will not enter into a detailed criticism here. But I will add that it is out of the question that at some earlier time, as Kittel thinks, James addressed himself in Greek to the Greek-speaking Diaspora, as the church in Jerusalem did not carry out, either earlier or later, any missionary work among the Jews of the Greek Diaspora.

Indeed, we shall not come to know a legalistic Jewish Christian fighting for the strict observance of the Law, whether the letter be thought to be authentic or to have been written later.

VII

According to our trustworthy sources, none of the people with whom Paul dealt in Jerusalem was disposed to be hostile to the mission to the Gentiles. We shall not be able to produce further support for this view till later, but we already have enough material to enable us to see that in all probability it is correct. Therefore the problem at the meeting in Jerusalem is not that stated by Luke in Acts 15, namely the demand for circumcision and the observance of the Law, raised by Jerusalem Christians and put before the Gentile Christians. As we said before, we have to look for the subject of the negotiations in the agreement that was made between the earliest disciples in Jerusalem on the one hand and Paul and Barnabas on the other.

Galatians 2.9 reads, 'And when they perceived the grace that was given to me, James and Cephas and John, who were reputed to be pillars, gave to me and Barnabas the right hand of fellowship, that we should go to the Gentiles and they to the circumcised.' The two groups, in fact, receive their mission field, and the division is based at the same time on religious and geographical considerations. It is religious by dividing the world according to the basic division of the Jewish-Christian plan of salvation, into Israel and the Gentiles, and by laying down that Peter is to go to the Jews, and Paul to the Gentiles.[1] But the division is at the same time geographical, as we must assume that according to it Peter received Palestine, Syria, and presumably also the eastern districts inside and outside the Roman empire, where for a very long time there had been large Jewish colonies. Paul was allotted the whole of the Greek Diaspora stretching westwards from Syria as far as the Roman domination extended.[2]

It is probably true that in Peter's sphere of work this geographical division was also a religious one. He represented, in fact, the Jerusalem point of view that when Israel was won, the salvation of the Gentiles too would be thereby guaranteed. Any possible conversion and baptism of Gentiles would therefore presumably be an exception for Peter, like the Cornelius incident. With Paul it was different. He certainly

---

[1]The verb is missing in both the sentences, which read simply ἵνα ἡμεῖς εἰς τὰ ἔθνη, αὐτοὶ δὲ εἰς τὴν περιτομήν, but it must be taken from the expression εἰς ἀποστολὴν τῆς περιτομῆς in v. 8.

[2]Unfortunately we know nothing about the large oriental Greek-speaking Jewish population in Egypt and its missionary history.

knew (Rom. 11) that the salvation of the Gentiles would not be brought about by the conversion of the Jews, but that on the contrary the fullness of the Gentiles would lead to the saving of all Israel. But, as we know from Acts, Paul did not cease to preach in the Jews' synagogues, to go on from there to begin the mission in the towns, and to persevere till the obdurate and unbelieving Jews drove him away. The accounts in Acts are indirectly confirmed by his letters.[1] We hear, for instance, in II Cor. 11.24, 'Five times I have received at the hands of the Jews the forty lashes less one', which presupposes that he was condemned in the synagogue and that he submitted in spite of the freedom of a Roman citizen from the Jewish administration of justice. We could, however, put these incidents back in such places of his activity as Damascus, Antioch, and similar places of his earliest missionary work, where there were great numbers of Jews; but in I Thess. 2.16 Paul says of the Jews, 'by hindering us from speaking to the Gentiles that they may be saved'; and it is more natural to relate this remark to his recent experiences in Thessalonica, Beroea, and Corinth (Acts 17.5 f., 13 f.; 18.5 f.). And in I Cor. 9.20 he says, 'To the Jews I became a Jew, in order to win Jews; to those under the law I became as one under the law—though not being myself under the law—that I might win those under the law.' This rule, which together with others is meant to show that he has 'become all things to all men, that I might by all means save some', confirms, in conjunction with the two other passages quoted, that there are good grounds for regarding as reliable the description in Acts of Paul's missionary activity; in each city he begins in the synagogue, but is soon compelled to leave it, and generally takes with him at most a few of the proselytes and God-fearing Gentiles to the new church which the Christian preaching has won from among the former pagans.[2]

We can now try to carry further our earlier remarks (see pp. 108 f.) about Paul's problem, which a revelation from God caused him to take to Jerusalem to be decided. It might be essentially a question of the mission to the Gentiles, as has hitherto been thought; and in that case Paul seeks to have the work recognized. He cannot carry the mission further unless the leaders in Jerusalem are behind him. Jerusalem itself feels the call only for a mission to the Jews, but for Paul it is important to obtain recognition of his work among the Gentiles as well as the present mission to the Jews. He succeeds in doing so. The Church, hitherto Jewish-Christian, recognizes that it has alongside it another

[1] Cf. Vielhauer, 'Zum "Paulinismus" der Apostelgeschichte', *EvTh* 10, 1950–1, p. 6.

[2] See Acts 13.43–50; 14.2, 4 f., 19; cf. v. 27; 17.4 ff., 13; 18.6, 12 f., 28; 19.9; 20.3. Otherwise 14.1; 17.11 f.; 18.2, 8, 24 f.

section in the churches gained by Paul, that that section constitutes a part of the same Church, but that for geographical as well as religious reasons it will be right to build it up as something new beside Jewish Christianity. Peter is not 'sent' on this occasion, but he is confirmed in his mission to the Jews as Paul is confirmed in his mission to the Gentiles. So in this agreement the division of the Church becomes more important than its unity. It is emphasized that the two sections are to be separate from each other, and Paul's introductory words about the race that he is running, which is not to be in vain (Gal. 2.2), are spoken, as we know from Rom. 11, with his thoughts on the connexion between the saving of the Gentiles and the salvation of the Jews. For Paul, however, the emphasis in such a case is on the certainty that his work will have a positive influence on the mission to the Jews because the two missionaries have been 'sent' by Jerusalem. The fullness of the Gentiles does not then become a purely Gentile Christian concern; its importance to Israel is guaranteed by the connexion with the church in Jerusalem. In this way unity too plays a part, although it is rather in Paul's interest and is more his work than a common concern of both sections of the Church.

There is also, however, the possibility that the agreement concerned not only the mission to the Gentiles, but the mission to the Jews too. Paul cannot lightly leave the regions in Syria and Cilicia with their numerous Jewish colonies, and go on to the Gentile regions where the Jews are a small minority, without being sure that the Jewish Christian missionaries are caring for the Jews in the provinces that he is leaving. What he gets, then, is a division by which Peter takes over Antioch and Syria etc. and at the same time the duty of evangelizing among the Jews outside Jerusalem. Thus the discussion in Jerusalem may signify the turning-point at which the Christian leaders in that city give up the policy hitherto followed of confining themselves to Jerusalem, and agree to send Peter to the Jews.[1] Only on the assurance that the Gospel is being preached to the Jews outside Jerusalem and Palestine can Paul leave those parts and hasten along the way where Christ called him at Damascus. James, Peter, and John must in the future visit the regions where Barnabas (Acts 11.22 ff.) and other Jerusalem preachers (11.19–21) and Paul himself have hitherto worked. Barnabas and Paul are also sent out at the same time by the 'pillars', who thus consent to their

[1]As we shall see later (pp. 210–13), the earliest disciples were to stay in Jerusalem till Israel had been converted; after that they were to go to the Gentiles. Such a change in the missionary practice of the earliest disciples must be due to discussions on points of view as to man's salvation, and we may guess from the later arguments in Rom. 9–11 what Paul may have said just then about Israel's salvation and the saving of the Gentiles. But unfortunately nothing more than a guess is possible.

going out on the Gentile mission outside the thickly populated Jewish regions in the east.

This interpretation is more probable than the first-mentioned. If the discussion in Jerusalem in Gal. 2 is thus moved to a point before Paul's first missionary journey, it is reasonable to put the request to Paul for support for the poor in Jerusalem shortly after Agrippa's persecution. At the same time, the request must have been of a hypothetical and anticipatory nature, as Paul can hardly have been asked to organize a collection for Jerusalem at once when the churches which it is hoped will make it do not yet exist. On the basis of this second and more probable interpretation of the Jerusalem meeting the unity of the Church occupies a more important place in the negotiations than does its division.

VIII

Just as it is not a question of circumcision and observance of the Law at Jerusalem, these things play no part at Antioch either. Here, as everywhere else, when there are difficulties between Jewish and Gentile Christians, the questions at issue are not the demands of the Judaizers. Those demands are made only by the Gentile Christian Judaizers and, according to Luke, by some Jerusalem Christians (Acts 15.1, 5). But when Jewish and Gentile Christians meet, the problems arise over their common meals.

By the time that Peter returned to Jerusalem after the Cornelius incident in Caesarea, the problem formulated by Luke was not, as we should expect, 'Did you demand circumcision and observance of the Law from those Gentiles that you have had baptized?' but surprisingly —perhaps Luke chose his words in view of the meeting in ch. 15— the accusation against Peter reads (11.3), 'Why did you go to uncircumcised men and eat with them?' At the ensuing discussion in Jerusalem the demand is made that the Gentiles are to be circumcised and conform to the Law (15.5);[1] but the upshot of the discussion is the apostles' decree (15.23–29), which is partly concerned with laying down rules as to food.[2] In the Cornelius story Peter receives through a vision

---

[1] Cf. 15.1, 24, where Luke puts the Gentile Christian Judaizers in the mother church and makes them Jewish Christians.

[2] On the text see Ropes' edition in *Beginnings* 3, pp. 265–9, especially p. 269. Harnack, as his first evidence against the interpretation of the three (or two) regulations as prohibitions concerning food, makes the following assertion (*The Acts of the Apostles*, ET 1909, p. 255): 'In the whole of St Luke's book, where it deals with the Gentile Christian controversy, there is no other reference to the question of prohibited meats, but only to questions of capital importance—namely, to *Circumcision and the Mosaic Law as a whole*. It is most strange that in a single passage so important, St Luke should suddenly introduce rules concerning meats without making any further remark, or giving any reason for their appearance.' This argument is

the command to go to Gentiles, and that vision in its figurative language alludes directly to the Jewish food laws and God's annulment of them (10.15): 'What God has cleansed, you must not call common.'

This focusing on common meals with the Lord's Supper leads one to suppose that Jewish Christianity did not take the view that the Gentile Christians should be incorporated into the Jewish community. If we recognize 15.5 as a historical account, it can have been at most only a minority that temporarily demanded anything of the kind. But the general view was that the Gentiles were to be received into the Church not as Jews but as Gentiles. Then difficulties arose when Jewish and Gentile Christians met each other in the same church. That very rarely happened. Jewish Christianity evangelized only within Israel, and Paul, although he preached to Jews and Gentiles, generally won only Gentiles.[1] In the very early Church, therefore, mixed communities were rare. We do not venture to contest that the church in Antioch was a mixed church, as we are given to understand in Acts 11.19–21; but we pointed out above (p. 106 n. 3) that the Jewish Christians who were present according to Gal. 2.13 as elsewhere in the Pauline churches, may be Christian fellow-workers, while the church itself consists only of Gentiles.

After Peter has been taking part in the common meals of the church for some time, 'certain men from James', that means some Jerusalem church members, come and cause Peter to withdraw from the meals. The result is that the remaining Jews, and even Barnabas, also withdraw. Because of that disunion Paul reproaches Peter publicly.

In dealing with Gal. 2.11 ff., as with Gal. 2.1–10, it is necessary to point out that the passage is both a reference to historical facts and a polemic against the Judaizers. But while it has been usual to judge the narrative of the meeting in Jerusalem as a historical report (on occasion as a bad historical report), and in doing so to forget that it is being used in a controversy against Judaizers, the opposite is done with the textual passage of the clash between Paul and Peter in Antioch. Here, as a rule, it is Paul who does the arguing and presents his own view of justification by faith and not by works; but the historical suggestions in the text are allowed almost or completely to disappear, as Paul has quickly turned to current controversy.[2]

---

quite wrong. Controversies arise at common meals, but do not revolve round the questions of circumcision and the observance of the Law (see pp. 242–45; cf. pp. 233 ff.). On the other hand, that is the problem with the Judaizing Gentile Christians among the Galatians.

[1] See above, p. 120 n. 2, and later pp. 200–9.
[2] See Sieffert on 2.15, and Lietzmann, Zahn, and Schlier on 2.15–21.

It is very difficult in 2.11 ff., as in the preceding passage, to distinguish between controversy and historical recollection—where is Paul
speaking to Peter, and where is he arguing against the Judaizers? Or
is he speaking mainly to the former or mainly against the latter in the
separate verses? It is true that Paul is finally speaking, no longer to
Peter but to the readers, but where is the transition? As is so often the
case with Paul, it is not possible here to find an answer satisfactory to
everyone. But there are in the text details which have so far remained
disregarded, but which may contribute to a better understanding of
the text and of the conflict that it relates.

We may expect to meet controversy with both Peter and the Judaizers, and it is therefore right, before we come to the text, to be
clear in what respect his point of view differs from theirs. Peter is a
Jewish Christian, but as such he does not assert the claim that Gentiles
are to be circumcised and conform to the Law. On the contrary, while
he is visiting Antioch he takes part in the common meals with the
Gentile Christians—who are in the Jewish sense Gentiles—and does so
without reservation and without protecting himself from impurity (as
provided, for instance, by the regulations of the apostles' decree). The
Judaizers are Gentile Christians, and they demand from their erroneous
point of view that all the Gentiles who are received into the Church
shall be circumcised and conform to the Law. If these Judaizing Gentile
Christians come to Gentile Christian churches—as, for instance, the
Galatian churches—they are not content, as Peter is, to take part
peacefully in the life of the church. No, they raise a storm by refusing
to accept the authority of the apostle to the Gentiles, putting the distant
leaders of the Jerusalem church in his place, and wanting to have those
leaders' Jewish practices accepted in all the Pauline churches, so that
the Gentile Christians may thereby become true Christians.

The essential difference between Peter and the Judaizers is therefore
that Peter makes no demands—the constraint that he exercises is only
indirect (2.14)—but participates as fully as possible in the church life
of the Gentile Christians, whereas the Judaizers cannot recognize the
Gentile church as Christian, and therefore demand that circumcision
and observance of the Law, as well as other practices, be 'added' to the
Pauline gospel. In our exegesis we can use this difference as a guide to
help us to distinguish correctly between what is said to Peter and what
is really meant for the Judaizers.

The question of common meals is not a trifling one for Paul, even
if it seems to be of small importance when compared with the demands
of the Judaizers. The apostle can see here no difference of principle.
It is possible, however, that he draws his conclusions indirectly *a minore*

ad maius—'In Antioch there was no disunity because of the food regulations, and I succeeded in clearing the matter up with Peter; therefore
there is no reason to demand circumcision and compliance with the
Law'—as though the sum of those things constituted the religious
practice of Jerusalem and its claims on the Gentile church. But the two
questions are of equal importance from the point of view of principle,
because there is in Peter's attitude an indirect demand on the Gentile
Christians to take over Jewish customs as necessary for their Christian
life. Anyone who feels free with regard to these customs can, like Paul,
observe them with a good conscience, but the Gentile Christian must
not accept them as conditions of salvation. Therefore the dispute about
meals during his stay in Antioch, a dispute that threatened the common
celebration of the Lord's Supper, is important in the struggle against the
Judaizers; for they deny something on which Jewish and Gentile
Christians have hitherto agreed, that 'a man is not justified by works
of the law but through faith in Jesus Christ'.

When Paul sees that Peter and the other Jewish Christians are not
walking according to the truth of the Gospel, he says to Peter, in the
presence of them all, 'If you, though a Jew, live like a Gentile and not
like a Jew, how can you compel the Gentiles to live like Jews?' (2.14).
We might imagine that these words were addressed by Paul the rabbi
to the unlearned Peter: 'If you, as an *am haaretz*, observe the Law so
badly that you can be regarded rather as a Gentile than as a Jew, how
can you get the idea of wanting to compel the Gentiles to behave like
Jews?' We have seen above that in some passages in the letter Paul
takes a pride in his Jewish learning, and also points to the amateurish
attempts of the Judaizing Gentile Christians to keep the Law (pp. 91 f.);
but it is better to regard v. 14 as an allusion to Peter's behaviour in
Antioch, which has just been described.

In vv. 15 f. we hear further remarks from Paul directed to Peter:
'We ourselves, who are Jews by birth and not Gentile sinners, yet who
know that a man is not justified by works of the law but through faith
in Jesus Christ, even we have believed in Christ Jesus, in order to be
justified by faith in Christ, and not by works of the law, because by
works of the law shall no one be justified.' Attention has rightly been
called to the repetitions in v. 16, especially to the twice repeated 'not
by works of the law', and of course, this has its importance in Paul's
controversy with the Judaizers in Galatians. But what is more important
is that Peter and Paul meet at this point. Attempts have, of course, been
made to regard the words as an expression of Paul's own point of view,
and to doubt whether Peter could share it; but here a difficulty has been
overlooked. When v. 16 reads, 'yet who know that a man is not justified

by works of the law but through faith in Jesus Christ, even we have believed in Christ Jesus, in order to be justified by faith in Christ, and not by works of the law', this is in fact not Paul's own experience, as he did not, as Luther did, first despair under the Law and only then believe in Christ (cf. p. 11 n. 2). As is shown by Phil. 3.7, it was only by meeting Christ outside Damascus that Paul learnt to break with the Law and to count as loss whatever apparent gain he had from his Jewish past. Paul's rejoinder must therefore be directed at the experiences that Peter, and presumably the other Jewish Christians, have had.

We now have to inquire whether this interpretation can be correct. Did Peter believe in Christ in the conviction that there was no justification by works of the Law? We know very little about Peter's theology, as the two letters that are attributed to him were composed after his death, and in contrast to the post-Pauline letters, show no trace of any connexion with the circles that had the apostle's authentic tradition. Peter, the apostle of Israel, did not leave behind him either letters or tradition, as Paul did. Or, to put it more accurately, if he left anything of the kind, those traditions (apart from those preserved in the Gospels and Acts) perished with the Jewish people during the rebellion of 66–70. We therefore have to inquire whether there are in Acts any traditions confirming Paul's view in Gal. 2.14 ff. that Peter saw the Jews' acceptance of Christianity from that angle.[1]

In Acts 15 we have a speech by Peter, pointing the moral of the Cornelius story, that God makes no distinction between Jews and Gentiles; and he goes on with these words: 'Now therefore why do you make a trial of God by putting a yoke upon the neck of the disciples which neither our fathers nor we have been able to bear? But we believe that we shall be saved through the grace of the Lord Jesus, just as they will.' We are confronted here with the realization that the Law cannot be fulfilled, and that salvation is bestowed on all by grace. This tradition from Acts therefore can only strengthen our belief that in Gal. 2.14 ff. Paul is really quoting Peter.

The formula that Paul uses to introduce the view of Peter and the other Jewish Christians, εἰδότες (or οἴδαμεν), occurs frequently in his letters, usually introducing a dogmatic proposition as something commonly known.[2] As the formula introduces a commonly accepted

---

[1] In the Gospels we find no such material. Here Peter appears in general rather as a mouthpiece for the circle of the twelve than as the representative of a special Petrine standpoint.

[2] Thus Rom. 2.2, οἴδαμεν δὲ ὅτι τὸ κρίμα τοῦ Θεοῦ ἐστιν κατὰ ἀλήθειαν ἐπὶ τοὺς τὰ τοιαῦτα πράσσοντας, and Rom. 3.19; 5.3; 6.9; 7.14; 8.22, 28; cf. I Cor. 6.2, 3, 9; 8.4; II Cor. 1.7; 4.14; 5.1, 6; Col. 3.24; 4.1; I Thess. 3.3; 5.2; II Thess. 3.7; cf. Eph. 5.5; 6.8, 9; I Tim. 1.8, 9; Titus 3.11; James 3.1; I Peter 1.18; I John 3.2, 5, 14, 15;

proposition that is not identical with his own experience, and which in this context can only be a Jewish Christian experience, the obvious interpretation is that we have here in vv. 15 f. Paul's words to Peter at Antioch. The emphasis expressed by the repetition may very well come from their later appearance in Galatians, where the controversy with the opposing Judaizers may have made the emphasis necessary.

In vv. 17–20 Paul asks the question, 'But if, in our endeavour to be justified in Christ, we ourselves were found to be sinners, is Christ then an agent of sin?' and he answers at once, 'Certainly not!' This question usually calls to people's minds what had happened a little while before in Antioch: 'But if we Jewish Christians, in our endeavour to be justified in Christ, are ourselves found to be sinners—as you were when you were in Antioch, because you had sat at table with the Gentile Christians, and then when the Jerusalem brethren came, felt in your conscience that you had acted wrongly—is Christ then an agent of sin?' The difficulty about this interpretation is that we can hardly suppose Peter to have thought on such lines if he seriously maintained what v. 16 says. We should rather be compelled to suppose that Paul is thinking here of the Judaizers. But the Judaizers cannot follow Paul and Peter in what these two formulate as the acknowledged Jewish Christian theology (v. 16); and the dispute over the common meals can therefore have no controversial interest for them. Thus it may be supposed that v. 17 expresses something that is generally valid for the Jewish Christian who is seeking justification in Christ—he is himself found to be a sinner. In v. 15 indeed Paul had drawn a distinction between 'we' who are Jews by birth and those who are Gentiles by birth and therefore sinners. From this the question in v. 17 is clear: If the Jewish Christians, who seek their justification only in Christ, are found to be unrighteous or sinners like the Gentiles, is not Christ then an agent of sin? If we understand v. 17 in this way, then from that verse (inclusive) onwards the thought is no longer of Peter. Paul is no longer thinking of the incident in Antioch, but it is possible that he is thinking of the Judaizers. It was difficult for those Gentile Christians within the Church of Jews and Gentiles not to belong to Israel, but to be ἐξ ἐθνῶν ἁμαρτωλοί. In their opinion indeed the Law justified (5.4; cf. 3.2, 5, 11, 21), and the point was that they should have both Christ and the

---

5.15, 18, 19, 20. Many of these passages have the effect of crystallized traditional material; but they have escaped A. Seeberg in his works, as for instance *Der Katechismus der Urchristenheit*, 1903. Bultmann, in 'Analyse des ersten Johannesbriefes', in *Festgabe für Adolf Jülicher* etc., 1927, pp. 146 f., has noted these passages, but has not evaluated them. This also applies to Bultmann's new contribution on I John, 'Die kirchliche Redaktion des ersten Johannesbriefes', *In memoriam Ernst Lohmeyer*, ed. W. Schmauch, 1951, pp. 189–201.

Law (5.2–4; cf. 3.12). But all the Jewish Christians, with Peter at their head, are agreed that 'a man is not justified by works of the law but through faith in Jesus Christ', and therefore when they are justified by faith, they are justified as sinners. They have rejected the righteousness of which the Jews and the Gentile Christian Judaizers speak, as being insufficient before God in Christ. And here it might seem as if the Jewish Christians had renounced the righteousness that they possessed as Jews, and were therefore now standing as sinners with the unrighteous Gentiles. Is there not a misunderstanding here of Christ and his work, of him who is righteousness and who justifies us? Has not Christ then become to the Jewish Christians an agent of sin? This question is of importance not only for the Jewish Christian, but also for the Judaizing Gentile Christian, who wants to be just as good as the Jewish Christian, whom he imagines in his ignorance to be at once Jew and Christian, not as v. 16 describes him. If it can be proved that the Jewish Christian has made Christ an agent of sin, the Judaizing Gentile Christian is justified in expanding the conception that both Jewish Christianity and Paul have of Christianity, by adding to the Pauline gospel that was first preached to the Gentile church, namely by circumcision and the observance of the Law.

Paul reveals in this passage that the Judaizing Gentile Christians are not only, as they thought, at variance with him, but because of that disunity they are at the same time at variance with Jewish Christianity, and therefore with the earliest disciples and Jerusalem. Paul has already shown that there was no opposition between Jewish Christianity and himself or his message. He therefore shows here that the salvation of the Jewish Christian through faith without works of the Law does not make Christ an agent of sin, for through the Law the Christian has died to the Law, that he may live to God (v. 19); this invariably applies to the Jewish Christians, and is not true for Paul's own experience; on the contrary, it was through Christ that he died to the Law.

After the emphatic 'Certainly not!' v. 18 reads, as a continuation of the question of v. 17, 'But if I build up again those things which I tore down, then I prove myself a transgressor.' This sentence has been applied to Peter's breach of the Jewish food laws and to his renewed observance of those laws on the arrival of the Jerusalem brethren (v. 12). But if Paul had Peter in mind, why does it read 'I' and not 'you'? And, as we saw above, this 'I' certainly cannot refer to Paul, who neither came to Christ through the realization that there is no justification through the Law, nor built up again what he had torn down. This 'I' in vv. 18 f. is neither Peter nor Paul, but is in the first person to denote any person at all.[1] And there can be no doubt from the context that v. 18 is meant for the Judaizing Gentile Christians, though indeed we cannot say of them that they built up again what they had torn down. But the Gospel that they received meant a tearing down of Jewish practices: circumcision and the observance of the Law (it was possible to be received as a Gentile into God's Israel)—practices which they now want to build up again. And for the Gentile Christians who had been connected with the synagogue before they were baptized it is still truer that they want to build up again through their Judaism what they tore down at the time that they were received into the Christian Church. It may sound strange that Gentiles who once found it difficult as God-fearing Gentiles to accept circumcision and the observance of the whole Law should now feel strongly urged, through the acceptance of the Gospel, to be received into Israel through circumcision and the observance of the Law, yet not for the sake of anything that the salvation of the Jews could give, but as a true Israelite to be made one with Christ.

But circumcision and the Law, says Paul, do not exist for one who has been crucified and has died with Christ, and who is indwelt by Christ, not himself.

IX

Thus Paul and Jerusalem agree that the Judaizers are in the wrong. This would be true even if, as traditional Pauline studies hold, there were a Judaizing movement in Jerusalem behind the Judaizers in Asia Minor. If, as we have done here, we proceed from the assumption that greater weight should be given to Paul's words than to Acts, which was not written till after the events that the writer of Galatians had just experienced, such a movement can represent at the most an unimportant group, of whose existence we know nothing except from Acts 15. And the unity between Paul and Jerusalem does not become less probable if, as was shown here, there is no such movement behind the Judaizers, but if the Judaizing attitude was built up among the Gentile Christians. The Gentile Christians' ideas about Jerusalem were wrong, as they were bound to be if one painted a picture of a far-off ideal Christianity and thought it was already a reality in Jerusalem.

The fact that this puts everything in a new light cannot surprise us; it is inevitable if we keep to what Paul wrote, remembering that he represents the primary source, and not giving him an interpretation that is based on the secondary sources and does not agree with the Pauline texts. Jewish Christianity and Paul are of the same opinion,

---

[1] Blass-Debrunner, § 281.

that both Jew and Gentile are justified by faith in Jesus Christ and not by works of the Law, and therefore Jewish Christianity acknowledges Paul and the mission to the Gentiles, while evangelizing for its part only among the Jews. Many will certainly find it difficult to see things that are 'standing on their heads', even if the witness of the texts is clear and on some points irrefutable. It was once no simple matter to get used to the idea that the earth goes round the sun, and not *vice versa*. And difficulties will arise which are involved in the new conception, and which were unknown to the old, well-worn, traditional outlook.

It will, for example, be asked—and rightly—where Judaizing comes from, if not from Jewish Christianity. The answer is to be seen in the fact that it has its antecedents in Paul and the Old Testament, while its error arises from a Jewish interpretation of the Old Testament, with the result that both the Old Testament and Paul were misrepresented. We must, in fact, insist that Judaizing cannot have proceeded from Jewish Christianity. Jewish Christianity carried on its mission only within Israel, holding that Israel's conversion would result in the saving of the Gentiles. It is therefore difficult for Jewish Christianity to realize and acknowledge a missionary problem relating to the Gentiles, because the fate of the Gentiles depended on whether Israel accepted or rejected the Gospel. Jewish Christianity therefore has among its traditions only a few narratives, as exceptions, of any concern shown by Jesus, and afterward by Peter, for an individual Gentile. On the contrary, Jewish Christianity neither thought about nor laid down regulations for the admission of Gentiles into the Church; it merely defined its attitude on the question of common meals for Jewish and Gentile Christians.

It is clear that the Judaizing movement presupposes Paul's idea of his mission. As long as the mission is only to Israel, the conditions for the admission of Gentiles into the Church present no problem; it is not till Christianity goes to the Gentiles and asks for faith in the Gospel that the question arises whether that is the right message. And that is exactly what the texts show us: after the Gentile Christians have received Paul's gospel, they begin to doubt its truth and validity. They therefore reject Paul as an independent 'apostle', and want to live in the same way as the Jewish Christians in Jerusalem. They cling at the same time to the gospel that Paul has preached to them, and to circumcision and the observance of the Law, the things that they know as the Jewish conditions of admission to membership of Israel.

But the Judaizing movement has its roots not only in Paul's idea of his mission. The apostle's view of Jewish Christianity and Israel may, in a distorted form, have helped to give the Judaizing Gentile Christians a wrong conception of Jewish Christianity and the nature of Christianity. What the Gentile Christian churches know of Jewish Christianity they know only through Paul. As we said above, there was no stream of Jerusalem Christians and messengers on the way to the Pauline churches; it was the apostle himself who gave them their information about Jerusalem, the earliest disciples, and the Judaean churches; and from it the Judaizers drew a distorted picture of Jewish Christianity. We have also seen (pp. 110 f.) how Paul spoke of Peter and the Lord's brothers and the missionaries sent out by Christ, the people whom Paul calls 'the apostles'. His words about Jerusalem and the Judaean churches were full of sympathy and understanding (pp. 109 f.). Thus the Gentile Christian churches had a sympathetic picture of the whole Jewish Christian world. They learnt that the Church was divided into Jewish and Gentile Christian churches, and the members of the former lived among Jews, were circumcised, and made a practice of observing as many of the ordinances as was necessary in a Jewish *milieu*. That is the picture that Paul showed them without giving them the impression that what was strange to them was of inferior quality.

On the contrary, Jerusalem is not only James, Peter, and John, but God's chosen city, and the mission to the Jews is concerned with God's chosen people. Paul is a Jew, and in fact it is as a Christian that he feels himself to be a true Israelite who, in spite of all the unbelief of his own people, is in the true Israelite tradition, which is now the Church's possession. In Jerusalem the great saving acts in the Old Covenant took place. It was there that Christ died on the cross and was raised from the dead. There too the last things will take place before the end of the world comes. Antichrist will appear in Jerusalem and take his seat in the temple of God, proclaiming himself to be God (II Thess. 2.3 f.). But here Christ too will manifest himself and slay Antichrist with the breath of his mouth (II Thess. 2.8). The liberator will come from Zion, as we read in Rom. 11.26 in a quotation from Isa. 59.20. Even if Paul can describe the Jews as the enemies of the Gospel, as in I Thess. 2.14–16, we see in Rom. 9–11 and II Cor. 3.9–18 the apostle's expectation that Israel will be saved before Christ's return, and his confidence that his own work among the Gentiles is the necessary preliminary to this culminating point in man's salvation.

These two lines along which Paul taught his Gentile Christian churches—to think lovingly of the Jewish Christians and the earliest disciples, and lovingly of God's chosen people, which is to be saved in spite of its present obduracy and persecution of the Gospel—are an important presupposition for the Judaizing movement. 'Presupposition' is applied here, as earlier in connexion with Paul's idea of his mission, to positive features which in the Judaizing movement are used negatively by being turned controversially against his own views.

The other important presupposition lay, as we saw above, in the Jewish interpretation of the Old Testament. The Pauline churches used as their Bible the LXX translation of the Old Testament, and here there are many utterances that make it appear as if God cared only for the physical Israel, and left other nations to their own devices. Only when Israel needed correction he made a Gentile nation rise and march against Jerusalem, but when the punishment was completed and the Gentile king boasted of his power, God hurled the arrogant monarch from his throne. At the last the Gentiles were to be subjected to Israel, and Jerusalem was to be exalted to share in God's glory. Then the Gentiles would go up to Zion as subject peoples, and would have to pay taxes and bring their gifts to the chosen people.

In the short time that Paul spent with the church before he felt justified in leaving it and going on to the other Gentile nations, all these Old Testament texts were clear and intelligible. Everything spoke clearly about God's salvation of the Gentiles. But when Paul had gone, they remained alone with the Old Testament. Some of the church members had taken part as Gentiles in the services at the synagogue, and had learnt there to read the Old Testament as a Jewish book, so that when the Bible was used in these newly converted Gentile communities there was a great risk of misunderstandings; they could very easily drop into habitual Jewish ways of thought.

That might happen in two ways. These Gentile Christians, who had learnt from Paul that they were to inherit all God's promises to Israel, could discover on reading the Old Testament that only Israel, and not the Gentiles, had the title to God's salvation. Or it could happen that, while not doubting that they would inherit everything that was promised to Israel, they supposed from their reading of the Old Testament that God required of his people that they should be circumcised and observe everything that he had commanded in his Law. This latter possibility, through which Pauline Gentile Christians might become Judaizers, is the more likely, as we see here in Galatians that they did not reject what they had learnt from Paul; they wanted to add to it something that they later considered to be necessary.

What influence had Paul's preaching and exegesis from the time when he was with them, in comparison with the constantly repeated witness of all those texts that the Gentile Christians looked at through the Jewish spectacles to which they had become accustomed through their former attendance at the synagogue? And wherever salvation by faith without the works of the Law is preached, we find people who cannot satisfy their longing for holiness—it was then called righteousness; they want to be doing something, they want to build up a world of holiness, or at any rate their own life of holiness; they do not want to be content with the grace that they feel is debased and sullied by every-day human life, but to prepare a human vessel that is worthy to receive God's heavenly grace.

Nor we must forget that the Church was in fact divided. Not all Christians lived 'without the Law'. In Jerusalem they were circumcised and observed the Law, so the Gentile Christians thought. This division of the Church made it still more difficult for the Pauline Gentile Christians who felt attracted by the Judaizers' point of view. If Israel had received the promises, then Israel and Jewish Christianity would without any question be able to attain salvation; but what could the Gentile Christians expect? In this connexion we must not forget that Paul believed, as did Jewish Christianity, that Israel *and* the Gentiles were to be saved. But he did not believe, as did the later Gentile church, that Israel had said a decisive No to the Gospel and was therefore finally rejected, and that therefore God sent his Gospel only to the Gentiles. That later arrogance was far from the minds of the first Gentile Christians, who were thankful to be allowed to share in Israel's promises. Yet those promises were a theological problem, as we may gather for example from Rom. 9.6, 'But it is not as though the word of God had failed.' It is quite understandable that the Gentile Christians could have doubts about the promises which Israel had received but which had not been fulfilled for Israel; how then could the promises be fulfilled for the Gentile Christians? The latter, therefore, seeing in despair how Israel rejected the Gospel that meant the fulfilment of God's promises for the chosen people—in concrete terms, saw how the synagogue as a whole rejected Paul, while only a part of the God-fearing Gentiles accepted baptism—longed for Jerusalem, of which Paul spoke so warmly, where the Christians lived as Jews, formed a part of the chosen people, and at the same time believed in Christ. Was it not better and safer for a Gentile to become not merely a Christian but also a Jewish Christian?

If we regard the Judaizing movement as one that arose and spread among the Gentile Christians, we must not disregard the fact that the Old Testament, not only in its Christian-Jewish but also in its purely Jewish features, has repeatedly influenced Gentile Christians during the history of the Church up to our own time. The tension between what is Jewish and what is Christian belongs to the structure of Christianity; Jesus' and Paul's critical exposition of the Old Testament is a permanent and present concern. In the history of the Church the Old Testament, viewed in a way not derived from Christ, has played a part reminiscent of the Judaizing movement. Certainly the Judaizers' demands of circumcision and observance of the Law are not put forward after the time of the apostles; but Jewish piety repeatedly finds expression within the Church, playing a large part even in sub-apostolic times.

The presuppositions mentioned here help to send the Gentile Christians off on the wrong track, so that the Judaizing movement arises, wanting to unite the Pauline missionary conception and the Pauline gospel with Judaism. When this movement criticizes Paul, it does so because he is supposed to have brought them only a fragment of true Christianity. If the Judaizing movement makes Jerusalem the norm of true Christianity, the cause is to be found in what Paul has reported about the original church and Jerusalem's importance in the past, present and future, and also in the idealization of the Jerusalem of that time on the basis of the Old Testament presentation of Jerusalem and Palestine.

To sum up, we may say that the Judaizing movement does not, as the Tübingen School thought, represent the original Christian conception of the Church in the period from Jesus to Paul, but that it is a Gentile Christian heresy that was possible only in the Pauline churches.

5

THE CHURCH WITHOUT FACTIONS
Studies in I Corinthians 1–4

THE foundation of Ferdinand Christian Baur's work on the history of primitive Christianity was laid in an article that he wrote on the factions in the church at Corinth.[1] In it we already meet the characteristic features that we mentioned above as the *historical* side of the Tübingen School theory. The four factions in Corinth mentioned in I Cor. 1.12 ff. are narrowed down, on the basis of our common knowledge of Paul and Peter in their mutual relations,[2] to two—a Petrine, in the form of the Cephas and the Christ faction, and a Pauline, composed of the Paul faction and the Apollos faction. In other words, Baur again finds here the two main factions that he constructed within the whole Church (not only in Corinth), that is the Jewish Christian and the Gentile Christian, with their own particular views about the two apostles.

Instead of that view of conditions in Corinth and of a contrast between Petrine and Pauline Christianity—a contrast hiding behind those conditions and of decisive importance for the whole of primitive Christianity—we shall offer another and, we hope, a convincing exegesis of the texts that have hitherto been used as evidence for Baur's views, and shall try in doing so to refute the assumptions and conjectures of Baur and later scholars. For this purpose we wish not only to show that that conception rests on an exaggeration of certain much less serious party contrasts in the Gentile Christian church in Corinth—the commentators are gradually coming to recognize this—but to make it clear in the course of our argument that the first letter to the church in Corinth does not speak of factions among the Christians there, but that

[1] 'Die Christuspartei in der korinthischen Gemeinde, der Gegensatz des petrinischen und paulinischen Christenthums in der ältesten Kirche', *Tübinger Zeitschrift*, 1831, No. 4, pp. 61–206. Of this, pp. 61–107 are by and large reproduced in Baur's book, *Paulus, der Apostel Jesu Christi*, 1845, on pp. 260–97 (ET of 2nd ed., I, 1873, pp. 269–92); also pp. 3–32 of an article in the same periodical for 1836, No. 4, 'Einige weitere Bemerkungen über die Christuspartei in Corinth', are reproduced on pp. 298–326 of the book (ET, more briefly, I, pp. 298–308).
[2] Baur, 'Die Christuspartei' etc., pp. 76 ff. (ET, I, pp. 273 ff.).

the texts that have hitherto been used as evidence for that assumption mention only disunity and bickerings.

I

First it must be shown that it can be clearly seen, from the terms that Paul uses about the situation in Corinth, that it is not a question of factions. The Greek word for faction, αἵρεσις, is used in I Cor. 11.19: 'For factions among you must come in order that those who are genuine among you may be recognized.' There is a saying of Jesus of later tradition[1] which reads, for example in Justin, *Dialogue* 35.3, ἔσονται σχίσματα καὶ αἱρέσεις.[2] This saying of Jesus may be older than Paul and have been used by the latter in I Cor. 11.19; or it may have its origin in this remark of Paul's; in any case Paul intends the verse to be taken eschatologically. In the last days, which are not far off, many in the Church will fall away, and thereby endanger the Church's continued existence (Matt. 24.10 f.; cf. Acts 20.30).[3] αἵρεσις is also thought of eschatologically in the other two cases where the word is used in letters (in Acts it refers to the Jewish sects—Sadducees, Pharisees, and Christians), namely in enumerating the works of the flesh in Gal. 5.19–21, where we find one after the other διχοστασίαι, αἱρέσεις, φθόνοι,[4] and in II Peter 2.1 αἱρέσεις ἀπωλείας.[5] The divine purpose (ἵνα after δεῖ in I Cor. 11.19) behind these heavy afflictions that will come on the Church consists in the recognition of those who are genuine. The many, as is shown in Matt. 24.10 f. par., will fall away and be seduced, their love growing cold; and it is of the few that we read further on, 'But he who endures to the end will be saved.' So the disputes over the

---

[1]Resch, *Agrapha* (TU 30.3, 4)[2], 1906.

[2]See also J. Jeremias, *Unknown Sayings of Jesus*, pp. 59–61.

[3]Cf. my article 'Les discours d'adieu' etc., pp. 159 ff., and Schlier in *TWNT* I, p. 182.

[4]In enumerating the works of the flesh, the text says that those who do such things shall not inherit the kingdom of God. With reference to the supposed factions in Corinth, it is interesting to see that the catalogue of vices in II Cor. 12.20 f., which resembles Gal. 5.19–21 so strikingly (ἔρις, ζῆλος, θυμοί, ἐριθεῖαι from Gal. 5.20 form the introduction to the list in II Cor. 12.20, while the first three items of the catalogue in Gal. 5.19 f. close the list in II Cor. 12.20 f., only in a different order [πορνεία, ἀκαθαρσία, ἀσέλγεια in Galatians, but ἀκ., π., ἀσ. in II Corinthians]) does not mention διχοστασίαι and αἱρέσεις at all. The comparison between Gal. 5.19–21 and II Cor. 12.20 f. might perhaps also help to show that the commentators' difficulties over the mentioning of the sins of unchastity in II Cor. 12.21 are probably due to the fact that the catalogue of vices in vv. 20 f. represents something already referred to in an earlier context (cf. Gal. 5.19–21), and that Paul in his agitated style of writing in II Corinthians separates some of the items from the rest and gives them a different construction in v. 21, but without exactly giving the sins of unchastity special emphasis. (Also ἔπραξαν in II Cor. 12.21, corresponds to πράσσοντες in Gal. 5.21.)

[5]This refers to the false teachers of the last days; cf. 'Discours d'adieu', pp. 161 f. ἀπώλεια is a favourite word in II Peter (Oepke in *TWNT* I, p. 396.7–9).

Lord's Supper open out to the apostle a sinister prospect, for he recognizes here the first signs of coming tribulations, which, however, remain hidden from the unconcerned Corinthians. The explanation of this verse must therefore start from the recognition that the apostle looks on suffering as the Christian's natural lot—a view that is expressed not only in I Corinthians, but even more strongly in II Corinthians.[1]

The last clause in v. 19, 'in order that those who are genuine among you may be recognized' (ἵνα [καὶ] οἱ δόκιμοι φανεροὶ γένωνται ἐν ὑμῖν), is probably also in itself an eschatological statement.[2] We not only find it said in the New Testament that Christians are destined to afflictions (I Thess. 3.3), and that 'we' must through many tribulations enter the kingdom of God (Acts 14.22), but we read in James 1.12, 'Blessed is the man who endures trial, for when he has stood the test (δόκιμος γενόμενος) he will receive the crown of life. . . .' Resch quotes as Agraphon 90 a saying of Jesus,[3] which reads in the Old Latin fragment of the *Didascalia* edited by Hauler, 'vir, qui non est temptatus, non est probatus a D(e)o'[4] (cf. the Greek form in Nilus, ἀνὴρ ἀπείραστος ἀδόκιμος παρὰ [τῷ] Θεῷ).[5] This saying, which is also discussed by Jeremias (pp. 56–59), has in its form no resemblance to the last clause in I Cor. 11.19. But if we are right in taking the first clause of the verse to mean that factions and divisions must of divine necessity visit the Church in the last days, the verse's second clause has as its content the same line of thought as the saying of Jesus just quoted. Affliction is necessary. He who has experienced nothing of the kind has not proved himself genuine. Therefore we see that the divine aim of affliction is that those who prove themselves genuine will emerge from it victorious. But the rest succumb to temptation and fall away.

So it is not as yet a matter of factions; they are part of the future misfortunes, of the Messianic sufferings, which the apostle to the Gentiles has already encountered, but which the Corinthians have so far been spared.[6] On the other hand, we are told of divisions, σχίσματα, in the church. In John's Gospel we read in three places that a σχίσμα arose, among the people (7.43), the Pharisees (9.16), and the Jews

---

[1] I Cor. 4.8 ff.; 7.28; II Cor. 4.7 ff.; 6.3 ff.; 11.23 ff.

[2] See *Epistula Apostolorum* 36 (47) (TU 43, p. 111): 'Thereby shall the elect be known, that they, being plagued with such afflictions, come forth.'

[3] Resch, *op. cit.*, pp. 130–2. With this we should also compare Agraphon 68 (pp. 89 f.).

[4] E. Hauler, *Didascaliae Apostolorum Fragmenta Veronensia Latina* I, 1900, p. 17, lines 19 f.

[5] *PG* 79, 896D. Resch quotes the passage as Nilus, *Peristeriae* 4.6, but it is in 10.6. In Migne there is no article before Θεῷ and no οὐκ in the introductory formula, which is not quoted here.

[6] Whereas the Corinthians, according to I Corinthians, have not yet suffered, II Cor. 1.6 f. is evidence that they now 'endure the same sufferings'.

(πάλιν, 10.19). In these passages the word does not imply a lasting separation, but means that some people want or think something in which others cannot concur. We find it in I Cor. 1.10; 11.18; 12.25. σχίσματα (or σχίσμα in 12.25, though some important manuscripts have the plural) may signify here a division that is not of such short duration; and this is confirmed by the fact that the apostle wishes to define his attitude to it from a distance. In the text that we investigated earlier, 11.18 ff., it is a question of happenings at the common meal, where the church members fall apart into cliques for eating and drinking. The commentators usually relate the separation ὃς μὲν πεινᾷ ὃς δὲ μεθύει to the poor and the rich.[1] No one thinks that this might refer to the factions that are supposed to be in the church, and that these factions take the Lord's Supper separately and so cause the grievous division.

The same holds good for 12.25. It is true that here Paul is not speaking directly of the relations in the church at Corinth. He tells a parable of the human body and the relation of its members to each other, applying it to the Corinthian church (which is the body of Christ), and the church members' mutual service with the gifts of the Holy Spirit, where among other things the thought is of Christians endowed with charismatic gifts, who are to have at heart the welfare of those who have received no such spiritual gift of grace. We therefore cannot be certain that each separate feature of the parable refers to the conditions at Corinth. But if we do so, and relate vv. 24 f. directly to the unhappy conditions there, then we have to think of the church members who did not share in the gifts of the Holy Spirit. God has given greater honour to these people than to those endowed with charismatic gifts, so that there may be no cleavage(s) in the body, and the different parts may care for each other in the same way. If (as must not be too readily assumed) this is the correct interpretation, then the real state of affairs is that there is no split in the church, whereas we can see by the detailed statements in ch. 14 what might indicate such a split. But it is all so uncertain that we must regard σχίσμα as a temporary division among the church members.

The third passage in which Paul speaks of σχίσματα is in 1.10. After the greeting and thanksgiving (1.1–9) he exhorts the church to be united and to avoid dissensions among themselves. It is justifiable to give σχίσματα the same meaning here as in 11.18 and 12.25, where the thought was of cliques at the Lord's Supper and cliques based on the apparently unequally distributed gifts of the Spirit. It is therefore a question, not of factions, but simply of divisions among church members for non-

[1] It would be more prudent to speak of the more prosperous.

theological reasons. We must agree with Lietzmann in his interpretation of τὸ αὐτὸ λέγειν as *consentire*, and on the other hand reject the view of Heinrici and Schmiedel, who think that the passage is concerned with 'credal declarations' because of λέγει in v. 12.[1]

In v. 11 Paul describes the prevailing condition as ἔριδες. On this Bachmann remarks pertinently (p. 56), 'Not only the plural (which is apparently less usual with Paul; cf. e.g. Titus 3.9) but also the explanation that follows in v. 13 show that ἔριδες is meant to include antagonisms working themselves out in words, that is, bickerings; thus the idea is much more restricted than that of σχίσματα, and this is confirmed at the same time by the precision with which in this case (though not in v. 10) the ἔριδες are described as actually present. Paul therefore takes care not to describe the σχίσματα as already present. But he indicates clearly enough by the context that at least they will come if the ἔριδες do not go.'[2]

Paul therefore describes the conditions that he is combating not as factions but as bickerings, arising because the individual church members profess as their teacher Paul, Apollos, Cephas, or Christ, and exclude the others.[3]

II

If the first four chapters of I Corinthians really dealt with four different factions, to which the greater number of the church members attached themselves, we should necessarily expect to hear of those factions elsewhere in the letter. But the letter's commentators do not think that any references to factions are to be found outside chs. 1–4. It is true that in the following chapters a number of problems are mentioned on which we suppose the most diverse views to have been held by the Corinthians, for instance by the strong and weak on the question of meat offered to idols, by those ascetically or otherwise minded on questions of sex, and so on. But very few have expressed the opinion that these differences expressed the points of view of the four factions that were thought to be found in chs. 1–4.[4] It is, in fact, not

[1] Lietzmann and G. Heinrici *ad loc.*; P. W. Schmiedel, 'Die Briefe an die Thessalonicher und an die Korinther', *Hand-Kommentar zum NT*[2] II, 1893, on I Cor. 1.10–13.

[2] Nothing in *TWNT* s.v.; J. Weiss writes on p. 15, 'The expression implies, not that world-shaking false doctrines or grave moral errors or far-reaching constitutional struggles are in question, but dissensions of a more personal kind. . . . There may have been a good many petty squabbles of that kind in a church so full of vigour and of such motley composition.'

[3] See 4.6, ἵνα μὴ εἷς ὑπὲρ τοῦ ἑνὸς φυσιοῦσθε κατὰ τοῦ ἑτέρου.

[4] Thus W. Lütgert, *Freiheitspredigt und Schwarmgeister in Korinth. Ein Beitrag zur Charakteristik der Christuspartei* (BFCT 12.3), 1908, pp. 119 ff. Hirsch, 'Petrus und Paulus', *ZNW* 29, 1930, concedes (p. 72) that it is not easy to connect the weak and the strong in I Cor. 8–10 with factions, but it seems clear to him (proceeding from 9.1–5) that the 'weak' are the followers of Peter.

possible to allot those points of view to the factions mentioned. Only in a few places have people thought they found allusions to antagonisms like those that are described in the first four chapters, viz., in 9.1 ff. and 15.1–11. Here people claimed to see attacks on Paul which corresponded to the accusations made against him in chs. 1–4. On this, however, we must observe at once that these later passages become worthless as evidence if it is not a question of factions in the first four chapters.[1]

If it is factions that are referred to in chs. 1–4, they appear there only to disappear completely later. That is strange if we reflect that these factions are supposed to have had such importance that they embodied the decisive forces in the history of early Christianity. It has, however, been supposed that there is a reference to factions in II Corinthians. What is in mind here is the Christ faction, which is supposed to be mentioned in 10.7, and from that it is inferred that the polemic in II Cor. 10–13 is concerned with that faction. What ground there is for that assumption will be considered later. For the present we may confine ourselves to the remark—given the assumption just mentioned—that in his second letter to the church which cannot have been written much later than the first, Paul defines his attitude to the Christ faction, but not to the three others. It is difficult to understand how these three factions could vanish so completely in the course of six to eighteen months, or that they should have played no part at all while so much was happening in Corinth.

III

We now turn to the first four chapters of I Corinthians, to see what enlightenment we can get there about the four factions. We have already seen that the factions play no part in the rest of the letter, or, if we disregard the Christ faction, in II Corinthians. From that we may go on to infer that on practical questions there are no differences between the factions. They did not differ in their point of view as to sexual problems, the spiritual gifts of grace, and so on. If it was a matter of something different from and more important than bickerings, it meant that dissensions were traceable to differences of doctrine; and so our problem now is to produce what material we have as to the various doctrinal standpoints.

It is usual to assume with regard to the first faction, the Paul faction, that it is composed of those Corinthians who are Paul's adherents.[2]

---

[1]See now my article, 'Paulus tamquam abortivus (I Cor. 15.8)', in *New Testament Essays*, ed. A. J. B. Higgins, pp. 180–93. The mention of Peter and James etc. in 9.5 was described on p. 110 as uncontroversial.

[2]Lietzmann: 'Those who "belong to Paul" take the same view as their master' (excursus on 1.12; see the article cited on p. 141 n. 2).

But Paul reproves them in the verses that follow. It therefore cannot be correct to say that those who exclaim 'I belong to Paul' are the same as those who follow the apostle. It is quite possible that Paul had adherents at Corinth, whom his rebuke in the first chapter did not concern.[1] There is, in fact, nothing wrong in learning from Paul; his criticism is that by taking him as their authority and professing him as their teacher of wisdom they put themselves into a wrong relation to the Founder of the Church, and change Christianity into a form of pagan wisdom.

The same may be said of the Cephas faction. The teacher of wisdom on whom some Corinthians rely is Peter, who works far away in Palestine and among the eastern Diaspora as the apostle to the Jews, but whom the Gentile Christian Corinthians regard in a specially favourable light because of what Paul has told them about him.[2] Paul says nothing about this 'faction' and its particular doctrine; and there is therefore no reason to agree with the usual assumption that the 'Cephas faction' attached itself to the original apostles and refused to recognize Paul as an apostle.[3]

The only passage that might possibly convey to us something about the Cephas faction and its doctrine is 3.10–17. It is J. Weiss's opinion that in these verses the tone has been so changed that Apollos can no longer be the person referred to. Formerly, because v. 4 mentions Paul and Apollos, whereas Paul, Apollos, and Cephas appear in v. 22, he concluded that vv. 10–17 are meant for the leader or leaders of the Cephas faction; but in his commentary (1910) he is content to remark that it is difficult to say whom Paul had in mind. In my opinion, only one single (and uncertain) circumstance can be adduced as evidence that the Cephas faction is mentioned in 3.10–17, namely Paul's emphatic assertion that no one can lay any other foundation than that which is

---

[1]Presumably Crispus and Gaius (1.14) and Stephanas' household (1.16) do not belong to the 'Paul faction'; other people than these could have asserted that they were baptized 'in Paul's name'.

[2]Things were not the same here as in the Galatian churches, where Peter is first mentioned by Paul, while the churches have spoken only of the apostles and the Judaean churches; see p. 90 n. 1. Peter has not been in Corinth, as Lietzmann maintains in the excursus on 1.12 in 'Zwei Notizen zu Paulus', *Sitzungsberichte der Berliner Akademie, Philos.-hist. Klasse*, 1930, pp. 151–6 (see 2, 'Die Reisen des Petrus', pp. 153–6), and in *The Beginnings of the Christian Church*, pp. 110 f. Knox, *St Paul*, p. 94, and Goguel, *Les Premiers Temps de l'Église*, p. 106, think it is a question of Jewish Christian newcomers, who play off Peter's authority against Paul's. But his work as apostle to the Jews is in Palestine and among the eastern Diaspora (Gal. 2.7 f.), whence he is later taken to Rome as a prisoner and dies (see my *Petrus und Paulus in der Offenbarung Johannis*, pp. 69 f.). Even at the time when Peter, like the rest of the twelve apostles, is regarded as an apostle to the Gentiles (see 'Paul, the Apostles, and the Twelve', *ST* 3, pp. 109 f.), his original mission field, Babylon, is remembered (I Peter 5.13).

[3]Thus Lietzmann on 1.12.

laid, which is Jesus Christ.[1] This might be a Pauline criticism of a wrong use of Jesus' words to Peter, 'On this rock I will build my church' (Matt. 16.18). It is then stressed that Christ, not Peter, is the foundation, as was pointed out in 1.13, that Paul was not crucified for the Corinthians, and that they had not been baptized in his name. But the presupposition of this view is that those who acknowledge Peter as their teacher have known and misrepresented the passage about Peter as a rock. That, of course, is uncertain. It is uncertain not only whether, as some assume, the saying about Peter is older than I Corinthians, but also whether a Cephas party existed which misrepresented the saying. It can hardly be imagined that Paul would have merely touched the surface of this matter if a false doctrine of that kind had existed. It is therefore probable that the criticism in 3.10–17 is directed, as is the whole context, at the church and its bickerings.

We therefore know nothing at all from I Corinthians about these two 'factions', the Paul faction and the Cephas faction; and we can draw a picture of them only on the basis of highly uncertain inferences from other New Testament writings. The case is the same with regard to the 'Christ faction'. Here too we have only the words 'I belong to Christ' to help us to understand this party which is supposed to have existed.[2] People have tried in two ways to draw a picture of the 'Christ faction', partly by stamping its members as extreme Judaizers, and partly by regarding them as Christians who professed direct revelations by Christ and put them above Paul and his apostolic authority. In both cases we learn more about them in II Cor. 10 (v. 7 and vv. 10 ff.).

The new interpretations of II Corinthians view with great reserve the possibility that 10.7 mentions the Christ faction. Lietzmann explains the interpretation that is based on Paul's use elsewhere of Χριστοῦ εἶναι: 'I am just as good a Christian as other people', but he abandons this interpretation, thinking that those adherents of Christ would not conform to Paul's directions, but that they wished to follow the commands of Christ as their only master, whether those commands

---

[1]Fridrichsen, in *TZ* 2, 1946, pp. 316 f., is of a different opinion. He regards ὁ κείμενος (θεμέλιος) as an 'architectural formulation'.

[2]This sentence has led to many speculations. 1. People have tried to regard ἐγὼ δὲ Χριστοῦ as something that the three previous sentences gave as their special password (Räbiger, quoted by R. Perdelwitz, 'Die sogenannte Christuspartei in Korinth', *TSK* 84, 1911, pp. 180–204; see pp. 182 ff. and Reitzenstei, *Hellenistische Mysterienreligionen*[3], 1927, p. 334); but this is not possible. 2. The sentence has been regarded as a personal observation of Paul's in contrast to the party passwords (Harless, quoted by Perdelwitz, p. 184), but it would have to read ἀλλ' ἐγὼ Χριστοῦ . . . 3. Χριστοῦ is changed to Κρίσπου, namely the Crispus mentioned in v. 14 (also κόσμος to Κρίσπος in 3.22 (Perdelwitz's suggestion on pp. 193 ff.), but there is hardly any convincing reason for this change. We should rather concede that there were in Corinth Christians who let it be known that they followed Christ as their teacher of wisdom.

might come from words of his that had been handed down or from revelations in visions. In this way we can draw a line from Paul's reference to his visions and revelations in ch. 12 to the opponents' revelations of Christ. But most commentators think that Paul uses Χριστοῦ εἶναι in the usual sense of 'to be a Christian' (Koch) or 'to be an apostle' (Windisch, Strachan, Bachmann, and Plummer). In that case, however, any allusion to the Christ faction is untenable. Windisch suggests that the Christians mentioned in II Cor. 10.7 have only the expression Χριστοῦ εἶναι in common with those in I Cor. 1.12, but that they either had not been in evidence so early or were to be found in the Cephas faction.

We are, of course, more likely to find in the Gentile Christian church in Corinth people who profess direct visions of Christ and detach themselves from obedience to an apostle, than to meet Judaizers there who make a point of their Palestinian tradition of Jesus Christ and cannot recognize Paul's free preaching of the Gospel to the Gentiles. However, the following treatment of the 'Apollos faction' will take us still further into Jewish circles and connexions.

IV

Finally we still have to consider the Apollos faction, which scholars have treated differently from the other three factions. Here the opinion is that in 1.18 ff. Paul is waging a controversy directly with those adherents of Apollos who despised Paul's simple preaching and were striving after wisdom. Apollos was, in fact, an Alexandrian Jew, and as such he was brought up in the Hellenistic Jewish philosophy and allegorical interpretation of the Scriptures.

It is not from Paul that we know Apollos to have been an Alexandrian Jew, but from Acts 18.24,[1] where he is described as Ἰουδαῖος . . . Ἀλεξανδρεὺς τῷ γένει,[2] ἀνὴρ λόγιος . . . δυνατὸς ὢν ἐν ταῖς γραφαῖς. And from that Alexandrian origin people draw conclusions about his philosophy and allegorizing; but they have firmly shut their eyes to the uncertainty involved in that method of drawing conclusions. One can quite well be a Jew and come from Alexandria without being influenced by the allegorical interpretation of Scripture and the Hellenistic Jewish philosophy that flourished in that city.[3] Paul, for instance, comes from

[1] Wendt follows Blass-Debrunner, § 29.4, in saying that Acts originally contained not only the variant form, but the other name Ἀπελλῆς, which was later changed to that of I Corinthians.

[2] We are told about Barnabas of Jerusalem that he was Κύπριος τῷ γένει (Acts 4.36), and about Aquila of Rome, that he was Ποντικὸς τῷ γένει (Acts 18.2).

[3] Likewise Schlatter, *Paulus der Bote Jesu*, 1934, p. 20, and he adds, in a reference to Apollos' earlier preaching of John's baptism, 'Presumably he was a man who had

Tarsus without its being possible to show any connexion with the Stoic philosophy of his native city.[1] As a rule it is rash to try to infer too much from the fact of a person's coming from a certain town.[2] The word λόγιος can mean both 'learned' and 'eloquent', and it is not certain which of those meanings should be chosen here.[3] Finally, if we consider Apollos' familiarity with the Old Testament, it may be a matter, as with Paul, of the biblical knowledge of a Jew of the Dispersion, which, however, need not be an allegorical scriptural interpretation of the Alexandrian type that looks behind the written word for a deeper philosophical meaning.[4]

Nothing therefore can be quoted about Apollos to make it likely that he was striving for wisdom in the way that—as Paul thought—the Greeks strove for worldly wisdom. No, Paul always speaks about Apollos in the same loyal and appreciative way that he is accustomed to do about his other colleagues. It seems out of the question that 1.17 ff. can be a polemic against Apollos and his adherents who laid stress on what was peculiar to his preaching.[5] Only by entirely separating those who are attacked in 1.17 ff. from Apollos and his preaching shall we understand the meaning of Paul's polemic.

Attempts have recently been made in various ways to give Paul's words here a Jewish basis, without taking account of Apollos and his possible dependence on the Alexandrian Jewish philosophy and exegesis. We have in mind here an article by Cerfaux written in 1931, and also some observations by Thackeray in 1920 which were taken up and carried further by Erik Peterson in 1951. Cerfaux has tried to show

---

been caught up by the baptismal movement, far away from any theology tinged with Greek thought; and the instruction that he received from Aquila could give him nothing but what Aquila had received from Paul, and that was quite different from mysticism based on Platonism.'

[1] See the attempt in Böhlig, *Die Geisteskultur von Tarsos* etc., pp. 117–27.

[2] In introductory studies of the New Testament it is quite the usual thing to attach an exaggerated importance to the character of the cities of antiquity and to their general reputation, as if we had here a reliable key to the nature of the churches in those cities. Thus people explain to themselves that in the case of Corinth, the port with decidedly low moral standards, Paul was bound to take account of sexual offences. However important it may be to get all available information about the places where Paul worked and his churches were, conclusions based on it and applied to conditions in the churches are as a rule quite arbitrary.

[3] Thus Wendt and Lake. See also Emil Orth, *Logios*, 1926, which was not available to me.

[4] In any case we read in Acts 18.28 about the use of the Scriptures by Apollos, ἐπιδεικνὺς διὰ τῶν γραφῶν εἶναι τὸν Χριστὸν Ἰησοῦν, as in Acts 17.3 about Paul, διανοίγων καὶ παρατιθέμενος ὅτι τὸν Χριστὸν ἔδει παθεῖν καὶ ἀναστῆναι ἐκ νεκρῶν, καὶ ὅτι οὗτός ἐστιν ὁ Χριστός, ὁ Ἰησοῦς, κτλ.

[5] Lietzmann thinks (on 1.12) that this faction arose without Apollos' co-operation, the latter working with Paul, as appears from 3.4 ff. and 16.12. The same view is expressed by Héring, p. 18.

that in the passage quoted Paul follows a *florilegium* of Scripture passages.[1] Cerfaux emphasizes that the quotations of this part of the letter show a text which departs from the LXX, and which is attested by later writers. It is therefore a very probable assumption that Paul uses here a *florilegium*. If we compare in their complete form the Scripture passages quoted (Cerfaux, p. 523), they fit in together so exactly that it is unlikely that Paul can have quoted parts of them simply by keeping them accurately and unabridged in his memory. One would rather suppose that he found in a *florilegium* those passages that he often quotes in an abridged form, and that it contained them all in their complete form and was to be used to refute human wisdom. Paul did not himself collect the passages, but took over the collection during his rabbinic studies in Jerusalem, where he was warned by his teachers against Greek wisdom.

The passages which, in Cerfaux's view, Paul took from a Jewish *florilegium* of Old Testament quotations that warned against Greek wisdom are as follows (my critical remarks are on the right):

Isa.	29.14	I Cor. 1.19 quotation.
	19.11 f.	1.20 allusion.
	33.18	1.20 allusion.
	40.13	2.16 quotation.
	44.25	1.20 allusion.
Job	5.12 f.	3.19 quotation.
Ps.	33.10	1.19 only one word, should be deleted.
	94.11	3.20 quotation.
Jer.	9.23 f.	1.31 a clearer allusion.

If we exclude the weaker allusions (Isa. 19.11 f.; 33.18; 44.25) and delete the entirely superfluous passage, Ps. 33.10, there remain four quotations and a clearer allusion, namely Isa. 29.14; 40.13; Job 5.12 f.; Ps. 94.11; and Jer. 9.23 f. Except for Job 5.12 f., Paul also quotes these verses elsewhere, namely Isa. 40.13 from I Cor. 2.16 in Rom. 11.34,[2] and Jer. 9.23 f. from I Cor. 1.31 in II Cor. 10.17 (agreeing word for word, and in a form which departs from the LXX, and which seems to be Pauline), or he quotes or alludes to the corresponding chapter or Psalm in other passages. For instance, he alludes in Rom. 9.20 to Isa. 29.16, while he quotes v. 14 in I Cor. 1.19. He quotes Ps. 94.11 in I Cor.

[1]"Vestiges d'un florilège dans I Cor. 1.18–3.24?', *Revue d'Histoire Ecclésiastique* 27, 1931, pp. 521–34. See also J. Moffatt, pp. 17 f.

[2]There is, however, the difference that in Rom. 11.34 the first of the last two sentences of Isa. 40.13 is quoted, ἢ τίς σύμβουλος αὐτοῦ ἐγένετο, on which Cerfaux lays special stress (see p. 523), whereas I Cor. 2.16 quotes the second sentence, ὃς συμβιβάσει αὐτόν.

3.20, and at the same time he alludes to v. 14 of that Psalm in Rom. 11.1 f. The allusion to v. 2, which Nestle[1] thinks he finds in I Thess. 4.6, is less probable. Only in the case of Job 5.12 f. can we assume that in I Cor. 3.19 alone Paul reveals a knowledge of those verses and their context.[2] These observations help to show that Cerfaux's hypothesis cannot be regarded as proved or even probable, unless we maintain that Paul remembered the individual verses and used them without regard to their original context in the Old Testament. In that case Isa. 29.14, Job 5.12 f., and Ps. 94.11 might have belonged to a *florilegium* of that kind. In the case of the two other Scripture passages that Paul quoted in another place, and of the quotation from an unknown source in 2.9 (which is not discussed at all), there is still the possibility that they do not come from the *florilegium*, and that therefore its use in the other cases is open to doubt.

Moreover, the fact that Paul's quotations do not agree with the LXX is not conclusive evidence that they were taken from a *florilegium*. It is more likely to indicate that he quotes from memory, because it is in that way that one is easily led to combine several scriptural passages and to condense or change individual passages.[3]

In *The Septuagint and Jewish Worship*[4] Thackeray has assumed that Baruch 3.9–4.4 is a sermon on wisdom, intended for the 9th of Ab. The text is taken from Jeremiah,[5] and the sermon is closely associated with the final verse of the Jeremiah text, 'Let not the wise man glory in his wisdom, let not the mighty man glory in his might, let not the rich man glory in his riches; but let him who glories glory in this, that he understands and knows me, that I am the Lord', etc. This sermon, Thackeray thinks, should be compared with Paul's argument about false and true wisdom in I Cor. 1.18–2.16, where we can see an obvious agreement indicating a dependence on sermons to which Paul, as a Pharisee, had often listened on the 9th of Ab. In a note, Thackeray points out the agreement between Baruch 3.16 and I Cor. 2.6 ff. *(οἱ ἄρχοντες),* and

[1]*Novum Testamentum Graece*, ed. Nestle, 20th ed., 1950, Index locorum etc. pp. 658 ff.

[2]About Paul's relation to the Book of Job, see R. P. C. Hanson. 'St Paul's Quotations of the Book of Job', *Theology* 53, 1950, pp. 250–3. Hanson thinks (p. 251) that Paul was thinking of Job 12.17–22 while he was writing I Cor. 1.25–29.

[3]The agreement between I Cor. 1.26–31 and Jer. 9.23 f. is not as complete as Cerfaux assumes, as Jeremiah speaks of σοφός, ἰσχυρός, and πλούσιος, so that the similarity with Paul consists more in the triad than in the three links. Only the first link is the same, the second is in I Corinthians sometimes δυνατός (cf. I Kingdoms 2.10), sometimes ἰσχυρός (in the neuter), while the third is εὐγενής.

[4]The Schweich Lectures for 1920, 2nd ed., 1923, pp. 95 ff.

[5]Thackeray gives the text as Jer. 8.13–9.24 (23), and in doing so builds on a remark by Abaye in T.b. Meg. 31a (*Der babylonische Talmud*, ed. L. Goldschmidt, Vol. 3, 1933, p. 667; the text lines 17 ff. and the translation lines 13 ff. from bottom; but here only the beginning of the text is given, Jer. 8.13).

between *(οἱ) ἐπὶ (τῆς) γῆς* in Baruch 3.16, 20, 23 and the repeated ὁ αἰὼν οὗτος and ὁ κόσμος in I Cor. 1.20 f. and v. 27, and 2.6. The preacher's text is quoted in I Cor. 1.31*(ὁ καυχώμενος ἐν Κυρίῳ καυχάσθω)*.

Proceeding from these observations and from Thackeray's hypothesis, Peterson has discussed[1] Paul's conflict with false wisdom. To Thackeray's observations Peterson adds, among other things, the three questions that are introduced with *ποῦ* in I Cor. 1.20 and Baruch 3.16. *συζητητὴς τοῦ αἰῶνος τούτου* in I Cor. 1.20 corresponds to *ἐκζητηταὶ τῆς συνέσεως* and *οἱ ἐκζητοῦντες τὴν σύνεσιν ἐπὶ τῆς γῆς* in Baruch 3.23. Baruch's remark in 3.27 about the giants, *οὐ τούτους ἐξελέξατο,* corresponds to Paul's in 1.27 about God's choice of the weak *(ἐξελέξατο)*. They perished *(ἀπώλοντο)* in Baruch 3.28, just as in I Cor. 1.18 'the word of the cross is folly to those who are perishing' *(ἀπολλυμένοις)*.

From these observations Peterson concludes that in I Cor. 1.18 ff. Paul, like the preacher in the Book of Baruch, is expounding the Jeremiah text of the Day of Atonement. We may therefore—here he agrees with Thackeray—not explain as literary associations the connexions that have been shown between Baruch and Paul. Those contacts must be understood as coming from the same homiletic liturgical situation.

Thackeray has shown that the giants are also mentioned in a Jewish morning prayer that shows obvious points of contact with the Baruch text and with I Cor. 1.[2] In 'Henoch im jüdischen Gebet und in jüdischer Kunst'[3] Peterson finds a parallel to that prayer in one taken from the Jewish collection of prayers in the *Apostolic Constitutions* VII. 33.3. This maintains that *πίστις* is above *γνῶσις,* thus differing from the Jewish mystics, who found in Enoch's ascent to heaven a proof that mystic *gnosis* has precedence. Paul too argues in I Cor. 2.6 ff. against a mystical doctrine of *sophia,* with which he contrasts God's wisdom (2.7). Such argument against a mystical doctrine of *sophia* was connected with the theme of the Day of Atonement, and Paul took this into account in I Cor. 2.6 ff. It is not, as Reitzenstein thinks, against Hellenistic mysticism that the apostle is arguing, but, as is made clear by a comparison with the prayer from the *Apostolic Constitutions,* either against Jewish mystics or at any rate against representatives of the Jewish apocalyptic doctrine.

Unfortunately, Peterson concludes, it is impossible to fix precisely that Day of Atonement on which Paul delivered the homily contained

---

[1]In 'I Korinther 1.18 f. und die Thematik des jüdischen Busstages', *Biblica* 32, 1951, pp. 97–103.

[2]Thackeray, p. 98 n. 2.

[3]*Miscellanea Liturgica in honorem L. Cuniberti Mohlberg,* Vol. I (Bibliotheca 'Ephemerides Liturgicae' 22), Rome 1948, pp. 413–17.

in I Cor. 1.18 ff. Very likely it was the 9th of Ab. And it would be tempting to be able to regard the text as a sermon that Paul preached in the synagogue.

But it is difficult to imagine how Paul's words against false wisdom can be a sermon that he preached in a Jewish synagogue where, as we must suppose, he wanted to preach the Gospel. Nor is there any good reason to think that this passage is older than the letter and was fitted into it in the same way as has been supposed, for example, about ch. 13. One cannot see why the argument in chs. 1–2 is to be separated from the following chapters (3–4), as it stands in such close and necessary relation to them.

Of course, there is no reason why Jewish reflections on wisdom should not lie behind Paul's words, and indeed the Old Testament quotations at any rate were originally used in that sense. But it is not necessary to infer from that that the concrete situation from which he speaks in the Gentile Christian church at Corinth has a Jewish background.

V

So far our inquiries have given us only negative results. The expressions that Paul uses in I Cor. 1–4 about the unhappy conditions in the church show that he is not writing about factions: and in fact outside these chapters we hear nothing about the supposed factions. But not even here are we enlightened about the points of view of the four 'factions'; we learn nothing even about the 'Apollos faction' from Paul's argument. But what does I Cor. 1–4 tell us about? We now have to estimate what Paul's argument in these first chapters tells us about the situation.

1. It is not a question of Jewish wisdom. In the passage 1.18 ff. people have claimed to see, in the fact that Paul is not speaking here only of the Greek striving after wisdom, but also has the Jews in mind in vv. 22–24, evidence that the argument is directed against the Alexandrian Jew Apollos. It is therefore not a purely Greek phenomenon with which Paul is concerned here, but something that is of importance for the Jews too.[1]

It may be observed here, however, that it is in vv. 22–24, where it is supposed to be proved that the argument against false wisdom is of importance for the Jews too, that the Jews are characterized as people who do not strive for wisdom; for v. 22 reads, 'For Jews demand signs

[1] J. Weiss on 1.18, and H. Mosbech on 1.18 ff., still maintain that the passage refers to Apollos. This is denied by Moffatt on 1.17 (pp. 11 ff.) and by Robertson and Plummer on 1.17; they assert, as does H.-D. Wendland, that these words are directed at all factions, or at the whole church.

and Greeks seek wisdom' (ἐπειδὴ καὶ 'Ιουδαῖοι σημεῖα αἰτοῦσιν καὶ "Ελληνες σοφίαν ζητοῦσιν). This passage, therefore, cannot contain any argument against Jewish wisdom.[1]

In vv. 19 f. Paul lays it down that what passes for wisdom in this world, and all sorts of wise men, are already destroyed. By his work of salvation (σταυρός) and the preaching of the Cross (λόγος) God has characterized the world's wisdom as foolishness. For as in its worldly wisdom the world did not recognize God in the works of creation (1.21) which testified to his wisdom, God determined to save, by the foolishness of preaching, those who believe. As in Rom. 1.20 f. and 10.3 ff., we see the disobedience of the Gentiles to the Creator, and the disobedience of the Jews who strive to plead their own righteousness. Christ is the turning-point in history, in whom God shows mankind a new way, because the one hitherto taken has been shown to be impassable. This new way is a way of salvation, just as the Gentiles thought that their wisdom and philosophy were. Salvation now comes by faith.[2] And yet Jews and Greeks go on behaving just as before, the Jews for their part demanding signs (1.22). 'We wish to see a sign from you', the Jews said to Jesus (Matt. 12.38; 16.4). If Jesus had revealed himself in glory, the Jews might have believed that he was the Messiah. But the Messiah on the cross was foolishness to all except those on the way of salvation. The Greeks for their part sought salvation, as always, through philosophy; they sought wisdom, and the Gentiles who have just been converted in Corinth go on doing the same thing. But we Christians—and no doubt you Corinthians too, Paul continues in v. 23—preach Christ crucified. This preaching must seem blasphemy to the Jews. Here the force of the miraculous and the sublimity are lacking; the Messiah dies on the cross like any criminal, abandoned by God and man. And the preaching must sound like foolishness to the Gentiles, because salvation is to be found only in worldly wisdom. But to us, Jews and Greeks, who have heard God's call, the Crucified One is the power of God, though the Jews rejected him because of his weakness; and he is the wisdom of God, though the Greeks saw in his person and in his work only foolishness (1.24).

[1]A. Schlatter has tried in *Die korinthische Theologie* (BFCT 18.2), 1914, to give the Corinthian problems an entirely Jewish basis. Thus on pp. 68 ff. he tries to show that in chs. 1–4 there is a Jewish background of wisdom in spite of the plain statements in 1.22. Schlatter writes, 'The argumentative force of the sentence that it is the Greek who seeks wisdom remains fully unimpaired even if the Corinthians borrowed nothing from the Greeks, but only from the tradition of the synagogue. For the worldly nature of wisdom is seen in the very fact that the Greek demands it and snatches at it.'

[2]It should be noted that Paul can apply the same line of thought in different ways. Here it is not, as in Romans, the Jews who are disobedient, and the Gentiles who flock to the Church.

If, in a context concerned with converted Greeks, Paul brings the Jews too into his treatment of the Christ-event by which the world's wisdom became foolishness, he does so because he is speaking of man's salvation and its effect on the two species of which the human race consists, Jews and Greeks.[1] By v. 26 the Jews have already disappeared from the train of thought.

2. Paul's argument is directed, not against the persons whose names are invoked, nor against the factions that have gathered round them, but against the church as such.

It is usual to suppose that the attacks in individual texts refer to the factions—the above-mentioned 1.18 ff., for instance, to the Apollos faction, or 3.10–17 (as used to be the case) to the Cephas party. In neither case is it likely that any such controversy was behind it. In connection with Paul's treatment of the supposed factions it is a matter of marked indifference to him what the different faction leaders represented, or what was preached by the leaders who were invoked. It is not those leaders, but only the Corinthians' attitude towards them, that Paul is attacking. At bottom it is only the word 'I', in the sentences 'I belong to Paul' etc., against which he argues.

It is the church itself that loves those wrangles in which the church members exalt themselves by supposing that their wisdom has been taken over from one of the great Christian sophists, one of those close and well known to them, Paul and Apollos, or one of those known by what Paul has told them, Peter, the apostle to the Jews, or by the Lord and Master himself, Christ.

Besides 1.18 ff., 3.10–17 in particular has been regarded as a polemic against other teachers. From 3.5 onwards Paul has been speaking about the Christian leaders and the way they should be regarded. As God is everything, we must make no distinction between those people; but at the judgment each of them will receive his reward according to his efforts.

This last idea, which is in contrast to the Corinthians' hasty judgment on the Christian teachers, leads Paul to mention the judgment on the Corinthians themselves. Thanks to his apostolic gift of grace,[2] Paul, as a wise architect, has laid the foundation in Corinth, but others are continuing to build on it. But each of them must take care how he continues to build (3.10). Paul therefore does not contrast himself with

[1] One could draw a comparison with his reference to the Jews and the Greeks in 12.13, where these and the following sentences—so J. Weiss and Lietzmann think—have the effect of breaking into the context.

[2] The thought here is of Paul's special apostolic call; see ch. 2 (pp. 36–68), perhaps especially of his call to preach the Gospel where Christ had not already been named (Rom. 15.20).

the other Christian leaders who have performed a task in Corinth after him.[1] That would indeed be in complete contradiction to all the earlier argument of the chapter, which is concerned to show that there was no distinction in relation to the Christian teachers, and that none ought to be made. On the other hand, the Corinthians and the apostle are contrasted with each other. The apostle has laid the proper foundation, for which no other can be substituted; but it is of decisive importance how the Corinthians continue to build on it. It will be seen on the day of judgment what they are building, whether the material is precious or worthless (3.10–12).[2] Paul reminds them that a day will come when everything will be revealed and a righteous judgment can be pronounced. What is the use of the Corinthians' hasty and foolish judgments on their leaders? Christ's incorruptible judgment will soon bring the real conditions to light (3.13). Three different things may happen to the Corinthians: (1) The good architect, whose work stands the test, will reap the reward of his labour. That reward is not salvation, but is added to salvation. Just as salvation comes from grace, so the reward will be given from grace, but the reward is in proportion to the good, well-tried work.[3] (2) If, on the other hand, the work of the individual architect does not stand the test, he goes without his reward; but he is

[1]This view is represented by J. Weiss on 3.10–15 (leaders not mentioned, perhaps the leaders of the Apollos faction); also by Heinrici on 3.10 ('not only Apollos, but all the later teachers of the Corinthians'), and also Lietzmann on 3.10–15. Moffatt finds in 3.10 a possible allusion to the Peter clique's criticism of Paul's apostolic authority; but an allusion to Apollos is not possible in view of the previous remarks about him. Bachmann thinks that in 3.10 Paul is speaking in quite an abstract way about the relation between the one who begins and the one who continues.

[2]As elsewhere in Paul's writings, his picture is not 'seen', and therefore not at once obvious; but it is constructed from the traditional images taken from the Old Testament. The temple—and vv. 16 f. are speaking of God's temple—is made of gold and silver and precious stones (and of wood), I Chron. 22.14–16; 29.2; II Chron. 3.4–9; 4.20–22; cf. Ex. 27.10; 38.10; Isa. 54.11 f. (cf. Rev. 21.19); Esth. 1.6; II Chron. 1.15. Gold and silver are refined by fire (Ps. 12.6). This is often applied figuratively to people: Mal. 3.3; Dan. 12.10; Ps. 66.10; Prov. 17.3; Zech. 13.9; Wisd. 3.6 (see the whole context, vv. 5–9); Ecclus. 2.5. It is an exception when it is said in Lam. 4.1 that gold became dim, etc.; cf. Isa. 1.22. Of the combustible materials, wood was already mentioned in connexion with the building of the temple (see above). χόρτος is described in Isa. 10.17 as very inflammable. Something that is consumed by fire in a moment is, in the LXX, only καλάμη in Ex. 15.7; Joel 2.5; Isa. 5.24 (33.11 f.; 47.14); Nahum 1.10. ξύλον and καλάμη are both named in Zech. 12.6. Mal. 4.1 is important not only for καλάμη, but as a parallel to the whole picture given by Paul. See also W. Straub, *Die Bildersprache des Apostels Paulus*, 1937, pp. 85–88.

[3]Even for Paul himself, the question of reward or praise exists in relation to his churches. Each of the Christian leaders will receive his reward according to his work (I Cor. 3.8). According to Phil. 2.16 the church in Philippi will be to Paul's credit on the day of Christ. In I Thess. 2.19 he describes the church in Thessalonica as his hope or joy or crown of boasting; cf. II Cor. 1.14; I Cor. 15.31. His economic independence, the apostle thinks, redounds to his glory, which is not to be denied to him in the regions of Achaia (I Cor. 9.15–18; II Cor. 11.10).

to be saved 'as through fire'.[1] (3) But because the church in Corinth is God's temple in which God's Spirit lives, God will destroy those who seek to destroy his temple (3.14–17).

4.15 too, which speaks of countless guides, is meant for the Corinthians themselves, who have tried to continue Paul's work in their own way.

3. Paul is not arguing in chs. 1–4 against false doctrine. As we shall see later, the Corinthians' wrong conception of the Gospel as wisdom is connected with their misunderstanding of other points; but there is no dogmatic controversy in the first four chapters. We saw in the above treatment of the 'factions' that it was impossible to get a clear picture of their points of view. That is connected with the fact that Paul is not arguing against the individual factions and their false teachers, since there are no factions and since the Corinthians' shortcomings in respect of their bickerings are regarded in this section as primarily ethical failures. The usual attempts to find a Judaizing movement behind the factions, and Peterson's efforts to see a Jewish contrast between true and false wisdom, must therefore be rejected.

4. The Corinthians regarded the Christian message as wisdom like that of the Greeks, the Christian leaders as teachers of wisdom, themselves as wise, and all this as something to boast about. Paul asserts, on the contrary, that the Gospel is foolishness, that the Christian leaders are God's servants whom God will judge, that the Corinthians are of the flesh and therefore without wisdom, and that none of this redounds to the glory of any human being, but that he who boasts is to boast of the Lord.

I Cor. 1–4 shows us something taken from a Hellenistic *milieu* which has received the Gospel, but which introduces into the Gospel certain elements of that *milieu* which falsify the Gospel. In others of Paul's letters too we find such misunderstandings and falsifications in people's outlook on the Gospel and its preachers. Dibelius has rightly pointed out, with reference to I Thess. 2, that the Christian preachers, like the better of the itinerant philosophic preachers of the time, were early compelled to draw a sharp dividing line between themselves and the many itinerant teachers who tried by all means to satisfy their craving for applause, riches, and fame.[2]

In Colossians we meet a church that received the Gospel much as the Corinthians did, adding to it and falsifying it by their existing pagan ideas. They venerate the cosmic powers and teach asceticism, and

[1] One cannot help thinking of Ps. 65 (EVV 66), 10–12: ὅτι ἐδοκίμασας ἡμᾶς, ὁ Θεός,/ἐπύρωσας ἡμᾶς, ὡς πυροῦται τὸ ἀργύριον·/εἰσήγαγες ἡμᾶς εἰς τὴν παγίδα,/ἔθου θλίψεις ἐπὶ τὸν νῶτον ἡμῶν./ἐπεβίβασας ἀνθρώπους ἐπὶ τὰς κεφαλὰς ἡμῶν,/διήλθομεν διὰ πυρὸς καὶ ὕδατος,/καὶ ἐξήγαγες ἡμᾶς εἰς ἀναψυχήν. Cf. Zech. 13.9.

[2] M. Dibelius on 2.5 and the excursus after 2.12. The same view in Nock, *St Paul*, p. 149.

describe these additions to the Gospel as 'philosophy'. 'Philosophy' is used, as so often, to describe a religious doctrine or cult. It is not only in the simple circles where Christianity gains entrance at that time, that religion appears as philosophy. It is, indeed, a sign of the time that philosophy turns with its preaching to the public at large. If we look at all the representatives of various philosophic trends, we find, beside the philosophers of the schools proper, numerous writers and preachers who are only loosely connected with their philosophic school, but who take part in speech and writing in the religious debate of their time.[1]

The *milieu* to which we are introduced in I Cor. 1–4 reflects processes that we know from literature and the upper classes. It is a question here, not simply of philosophy, but of a mixture of philosophy and sophistry, typical of that age. When Christianity becomes combined later in Alexandria with the highest civilization of the time, it first meets sophism in its more philosophic form in the person of Clement, before it finds in Origen a representative who matches the learned philosophers of the schools. In the simpler circles in Corinth we meet a more popular brand of mixture of philosophy, religion, and rhetoric.

It is a question of something that is philosophy or wisdom by name, but Christian life by content, as the Corinthians experience it in the firm consciousness of being rich, free, and equal to anything. To describe that experience they use the most imposing expressions that they know from their Greek *milieu*. That new, overflowing life is wisdom, and they have received it from a teacher of wisdom; and in their childish vainglory each boasts of having had the best and most eminent teacher of wisdom. And because they know only the popular philosophy and the professional orator or sophist, who understood how to captivate a Greek audience by his learning and eloquence, the outward form is conclusive for them. The apostle, who has not forgotten the apprehension with which he began to preach about Christ in Corinth, suddenly sees himself compared with a professional sophist who, with painted face and theatrical gestures, invites an audience of a thousand people to suggest to him a theme on which to improvise.

It is clear from the conjunction of 'word' and 'wisdom' that we have here Hellenistic features of Greek complexion. Wisdom appears in the guise of rhetoric (1.17, 20; 2.1, 4, 13). In Jewish wisdom literature such a high valuation of form is unknown.[2] The same may be said of Philo

---

[1] We are thinking here of men like Apuleius and Maximus of Tyre, Plutarch and Dio of Prusa (Dio Chrysostom).

[2] We cannot say that λόγοι and σοφία have nothing to do with each other, but it is the word of the Lord that gives wisdom (e.g. Prov. 4.10 f.), and, as regards men who hand wisdom on, the words are mentioned indeed, e.g. in Elihu's first speech, Job 32–33 (cf. 34.3), but in quite a different way from that used by the Corinthians (I Cor. 1.18 ff.).

of Alexandria, who, as we saw above, is even supposed to be the source of the Hellenistic Jewish philosophy and allegorical interpretation of Scripture of Apollos and his faction. If we examine what Philo says about word and wisdom, we find that, as with Clement of Alexandria later, his attitude to rhetoric is twofold: on the one hand he thinks that the art of rhetoric is necessary like all the other branches of higher instruction, and on the other hand he sharply condemns empty sophistical talk.[1]

This seems to suggest that we must not look for the origin of the Corinthians' striving after wisdom in connexion with Jewish philosophy and scriptural interpretation from Alexandria.

We should rather suppose, on the contrary, that the acceptance of the Gospel led the Corinthians to feel rich and wise in the possession of new life and spiritual gifts. That feeling was expressed in their calling Christianity a kind of wisdom, its leaders teachers of wisdom, and themselves—this was the most important thing for them—wise men who had drawn on that wisdom through the Christian leaders. The poor, insignificant Corinthians, with neither distinguished ancestry nor pagan wisdom to support them, had become so rich through the new proclamation that they seized on the Greek terminology that was there for them, and used it to express their new glory. They did not realize that by the very use of that wisdom terminology they were betraying the message that was their wealth, and that the feeling of being up on the pinnacle and pitying the others was a betrayal of Christ and his apostles.

VI

In Paul's view there are three things that the Corinthians have misunderstood: (a) the Gospel, (b) the Christian leaders, and (c) their own position.

(a) First of all, as regards the Gospel, it is not wisdom, but in the world's eyes foolishness, but it is by means of this foolishness that God

---

[1]Philo condemns the sophists: *Quod Deterius*, §§ 72–74 (Cohn and Wendland, Vol. I, pp. 274 f.); *De Post. Caini* 86–88 (II, 18 f.); cf. *De Leg. Alleg.* I, 74 (I, 80 f.); *ibid.* III, 232 (I, 164 f.); *Quod Deterius* 38 (I, 266 f.); *De Post. Caini* 101 (II, 22); *De Sobrietate* 9 (II, 217); *De Migr. Abrahami* 172 (II, 302); *De Somniis* II, 281 (III, 303); *De Vita Mosis* II, 212 (IV, 249); *Quod Omnis Probus* 4 (VI, 2). But at the same time he thinks that the art of rhetoric is necessary: *Quod Deterius* 39, 41–44 (I, 267 f.); *De Ebrietate* 48 f. (II, 179); *De Somniis* I, 103–6 (III, 226 f.); cf. *De Josepho* 269 (IV, 118); *De Vita Contempl.* 31 (VI, 54). Philo's ideas of the relation of the word to knowledge and action are to be found in *Quod Deterius* 125–37 (I, 286–9). Like Philo, Clement of Alexandria rejects the art of sophistry; see *Strom.* I, 3 and 8; but rhetoric, like other philosophy, is useful for the fear of God and wisdom; *Strom.* I, 5–7.

at the crucifixion of Jesus determined to save those who believe. True, there is a wisdom that the Christian leaders proclaim to mature Christians, but of that wisdom the Corinthians have not heard and cannot hear, because, as their bickerings clearly show, they are still of the flesh.

A more detailed consideration of this Christian wisdom will help to make clear the difference between the Gospel and the Greek wisdom. The Christian preachers have a wisdom to take to the mature Christians (2.6 ff.), but there is a great difference between this wisdom and the wisdom that belongs to this world. And this latter is characteristic of the leaders of this world, who come to grief. This wisdom of God is expressed in a mystery; it is God's wisdom which was hidden, which God decreed before the ages for our glorification. Proceeding from the expression εἰς δόξαν ἡμῶν in v. 7 and the quotation in v. 9, which was taken as a description of heavenly glories, people have assumed that that wisdom dealt with the heavenly world and its blessings. Bousset has even suggested that it is a knowledge of paradise, what it looks like, what happens there, how many heavens there are, how the angelic hosts are ranged before the throne, and so on.[1] Here he cites Ignatius, *Trallians* 5, where he speaks of his insight into 'the heavenly things, the gradations of the angels, the coming together of the ruling powers, visible and invisible things'. The New Testament as a whole is very reticent on these questions, with which parts of Jewish apocalyptic literature were occupied, and so this explanation has no great probability. If, for instance, the revelation mentioned in II Cor. 12.1 ff. brought Paul any knowledge of those things, it did not give him at the same time the possibility of communicating it. It may be added that Ignatius too, who is quoted as an authority, communicates nothing to the churches about his special knowledge of heavenly things. Immediately before what has just been quoted he says (5.1), 'Could I not indeed write of heavenly things? Rather I am anxious not to harm you who are not fully mature. And you must forgive my reticence; as you are not able to receive it, it would choke you.'

But there are other passages in which Paul speaks of a hidden mystery, e.g. Col. 1.26; cf. Eph. 3.9; in both those passages there is an allusion to the salvation of the Gentiles. This allusion also occurs in Rom. 16.25 f.; in I Cor. 15.51 and Rom. 11.25 μυστήριον is used in explanation of the coming of salvation, but not about paradise or anything of that kind. This wisdom in 2.6 ff. must therefore refer to God's

---

[1]Commentary on I Corinthians in *Schriften des Neuen Testaments, neu übersetzt und für die Gegenwart erklärt*,[3] 1917, Vol. II, p. 85.

plan of salvation, and especially, it may be supposed, to the salvation of the Gentiles, which is the presupposition of Paul's work in Corinth and the creation of the church there.

In such a case there is meaning, too, in speaking of the rulers of this age. The Cross of Jesus means, indeed, that Jesus dies as the Jews' Messiah, but also that by his death he prepares the way for the salvation of the Gentiles.[1] If the Jewish rulers and Pilate had known of that wisdom, which was still hidden, they would not have crucified him who was the Lord of glory,[2] and who by his death on the cross completed the work that was to bring us glory (2.8).

Paul here quotes a passage unknown to us, probably from a Jewish apocryphal writing intended to express that what God has prepared for those who love him (a non-Pauline expression) has never yet been seen or heard, and, indeed, is something that no one can imagine (2.9). If that wisdom is so incomprehensible, it is because it is not of men, but a revelation from God through the Holy Spirit. That it is the Holy Spirit who mediates the revelation is because the Spirit penetrates into everything, even into the depths of God (2.10 f.). We Christians have not received the spirit of the world, the Greek *sophia* which is mentioned in ch. 1 and which is only of this world and can therefore get to know nothing beyond this world, but we have received the Spirit that goes out from God, so that we may realize what God gives us. This last expression means that it is a question, not of future glories in paradise, but of the present salvation of the Gentiles (2.12).

The next verse has been interpreted differently according to whether λόγοις has been deleted or not, and whether the first, middle, and last clauses have been made to refer to persons or words. The word συγκρίνοντες too can be interpreted either as 'comparing' or as 'interpreting'. The fact that v. 14 deals with persons is no adequate reason for making v. 13 refer to persons too. After Paul has spoken in v. 12 of the content of wisdom, σοφία in its real sense, he can very well speak here in v. 13 of the form of wisdom, i.e., of the λόγοι, and then resume,

---

[1] Cf. the use of Ps. 22.27–29 in II Tim. 4.16–18; see pp. 332 f.

[2] Cf. John 7.25 f.: οὐχ οὗτός ἐστιν ὃν ζητοῦσιν ἀποκτεῖναι; καὶ ἴδε παρρησίᾳ λαλεῖ, καὶ οὐδὲν αὐτῷ λέγουσιν. μήποτε ἀληθῶς ἔγνωσαν οἱ ἄρχοντες ὅτι οὗτός ἐστιν ὁ Χριστός; cf. the interpretation of Ps. 2.1 f. in Acts 4.27 f.: 'For truly in this city there were gathered together against thy holy servant Jesus, whom thou didst anoint, both Herod and Pontius Pilate, with the Gentiles and the peoples of Israel, to do whatever thy hand and thy plan had predestined to take place.' Without going into the gradually accumulating literature that interprets ἐξουσίαι in Rom. 13 and other texts, including I Cor. 2.8, as spiritual forces (see K. L. Schmidt, 'Die Natur- und Geistkräfte im Paulinischen Erkennen und Glauben', *Eranos-Jahrbuch*, 1946, p. 120 n. 1), I will confine myself to drawing attention to Campenhausen's excellent refutation of that interpretation in 'Zur Auslegung von Röm. 13: Die dämonistische Deutung des 'ΕΞΟΥΣΙΑ -Begriffs', *Festschrift für A. Bertholet*, 1950, pp. 97–113; cf. A. Oepke in *TLZ* 77, 1952, cols. 452 f.

from v. 14 onwards, the idea already expressed in v. 6, that that wisdom can be expressed in speech only among mature Christians.

An unspiritual man cannot receive the wisdom that God's Spirit gives, for it is foolishness to him, as is the preaching of the Cross to him who perishes, to the Greek who has not received the Gospel. He cannot in the least understand that he—or it—is judged spiritually (2.14). The 'spiritually endowed' man, who receives wisdom from God's Spirit, can judge everything, but he cannot himself be judged by one of those who have no access to the Spirit and his wisdom (2.15). The passage quoted gives as proof of this that no one has known the mind of Christ and no one can instruct him. But we, who are more mature Christians, have the mind of Christ, and it therefore holds good for us too that no one without God's Spirit can judge us (2.16).

There is therefore no distinction between the wisdom of the Gospel and the Gospel, and one who has already received the Gospel has the possibility of making the wisdom of the mature Christian his own. But the Christian life is the necessary condition for acquiring Christian knowledge; we cannot reach it by the roundabout route of worldly wisdom.

VII

(*b*) The Corinthians have chosen to regard the Christian teachers as teachers of wisdom. Their valuation of them is at once too high and too low. Too high, because they have given them the stamp of authority without regard to their position as servants of God and Christ, and at the same time too low because they have subjected them to their own (the Corinthians') judgment. If the Christian leaders are freed from Christ's service and God's judgment, they become dependent on human judgment, and here we get to what is really the heart of the matter for the Corinthians, as their view of the Christian leaders as teachers of wisdom really ministers to their own exaltation. It is true that they boast about these great names, but only to boast about themselves. A number of texts will make this clear.

In 1.26–31 Paul has spoken of the Corinthians' state before their encounter with the Gospel, and in 2.1–5 he continues, referring to his visit to Corinth. When he preached the Gospel, he did not take them words or wisdom (2.1). Behind all that he did was the determination to preach in Corinth nothing but Jesus Christ and him crucified. As he also preaches Christ crucified elsewhere, that determination is in no way contrary to his usual practice; in preparing for his visit to Corinth he decided to preach as he was accustomed to. But the result of the Corinthians' later behaviour, when they put the stress on speech and wisdom, is to make Paul emphasize this particularly; for his determination meant in those circumstances that the beginning of their Christian life knew nothing of that kind of worldly wisdom (2.2).[1]

Paul does not control the word. He knows that he is only a steward, from whom faithfulness is required (cf. I Cor. 4.1 f.). In Corinth he has planted, but it is no use unless God gives the growth (cf. 3.6 f.). So an apostle can feel his weakness and tremble at the task entrusted to him, that of preaching the word, where a rhetorician or a philosopher would be full of confidence.[2] The trembling apostle cannot be regarded

[1] Cf. the parallel remark to the Galatians (3.1–5): 'Did you receive the Spirit by works of the law, or by hearing with faith?' Paul's decision before he went to Corinth has been explained through a conjectural fiasco that he is supposed to have experienced in Athens on his attempting a philosophical sermon to a philosophical audience (Acts 17); thus H. J. Holtzmann on 17.33 f.; Bousset (*Die Schriften des Neuen Testaments,*[3] II, 1917), *ad loc.*; O. Holtzmann, *Das Neue Testament* I, 1926, on Acts 17.34, with reference to I Cor. 2.1 f.; F. J. Foakes Jackson on 17.33 f.; H. Mosbech on 17.33 ff.; H. W. Beyer on 17.34; Lake and Cadbury *ad loc.* justifiably reject the idea of only slight success. It is not true that Luke describes Paul's work in Athens as a fiasco—τινὲς δὲ ἄνδρες in v. 34 denotes an indefinite number, not a small number; cf. above, pp. 45 f.—and, as Wendland rightly emphasizes on p. 17, it is impossible that Paul has tried to deliver a philosophical sermon and then afterwards says here that there is unquestionably a difference between the Gospel and worldly wisdom.

[2] It was θάρσος that was demanded of a sophist. The following are praised for this: Pollux of Naucratis (Philostratus, *Vitae Sophistarum* [quoted here from W. C. Wright's edition of Philostratus and Eunapius, Loeb Classical Library, 1922], 592, p. 238, 1.7), Hermocrates of Phocis, of whom it was specially remarked that his bearing roused the admiration of the audience, ἣν ἐκπλήττονται ἄνθρωποι τοὺς τὰ μεγάλα μὴ ξὺν ἀγωνίᾳ πράττοντας (612, p. 276.24–27), and Polemo (537, p. 120.12). The speaker's confident bearing is of special importance when it is a matter of impromptu speeches, which are supposed to have been introduced by Gorgias (482, p. 8.9–14, here also θαρρέω). Thus Aeschines, the opponent of Demosthenes, is praised for his inspired way of speaking impromptu (ἀποσχεδιάζοντες, ὥσπερ οἱ τοὺς χρησμοὺς ἀναπνέοντες, 509, p. 60.11–16). The same thing is shown by the refutation of the charge against Scopelian (διθυραμβώδη καλοῦντες καὶ ἀκόλαστον καὶ πεπαχυσμένον, 514–15, pp. 70.22–72.19). It is told of Herodes Atticus that in his youth he liked only impromptu speeches, but that he lacked the necessary θάρσος, because he had not yet learnt from Scopelian, and had not realized what passion they needed (521, p. 86.17–21. σχεδιάζω is used in 528, p. 102.26). The opposite of θάρσος is δειλία, of which the sophist Antiochus is accused, because he did not come forward in public or take part in political life (568, p. 186.1–3). Nicetes of Smyrna was also twitted with being timid (511, p. 64.13–17). The sophist must not show fear; but the fact that very different feelings may be hiding behind his assurance is shown by a story about Polemo, who is said to have declared, on seeing a gladiator who was bathed in sweat through horror of the fight to the death, οὕτως ἀγωνιᾷς, ὡς μελετᾶν μέλλων. It may also happen that a sophist breaks down during a speech (ἐκπίπτω), as for instance Herodes Atticus in his early years (565, p. 180.9–13) and Heraclides of Lycia (614, pp. 280.25–282.9). In both cases excuses were made for the sophist concerned with conspicuous readiness, from which it is clear that it was regarded as an unpardonable offence. With regard to Herodes, it is pointed out that the same thing happened to Demosthenes when he was speaking before Philip. In the case of Heraclides, who, like Herodes, broke down completely in the presence of the emperor, excuses are made ungrudgingly—it occurred in the presence of the court and the bodyguard; it would have been unpardonable in an orator who was used to speaking in the forum, but a sophist who teaches boys every day can easily be disconcerted, etc., etc. It is scarcely necessary to prove that σοφία can denote the sophistical art, and that the sophist can be regarded as σοφός. λόγος can mean 'eloquence', e.g. Diogenes Laertius, II. 115. I Cor. 2.4 should presumably read

as a teacher of wisdom of whom one could be proud. What is effective is not the convincing force of words of wisdom that the apostle has at his command, but the demonstration of the spirit and power that goes out from God. In this way the faith of the Corinthian church rests on God's power, and not on the uncertain basis of human wisdom (2.4 f.).

After Paul has spoken of the Christian wisdom of the more mature Christians, he again turns in ch. 3 to the Christian leaders and their relation to the Corinthians, speaking not only of the time when the church was founded and of himself, but also of Apollos and his work: 'We preachers have the mind of Christ (2.16), but you Corinthians were and are of the flesh, and are babes in Christ. So you have had milk, not the solid food that was spoken of in 2.6–16 and is only for adults *(οἱ τέλειοι)*. And you are not yet adult so as to be able to change from milk to solid food, for your bickerings show that you are of the flesh and are walking as men without Christ.' The Corinthians' deification of men, and their boasting about certain teachers, are conclusive proof that they are still like people without baptism and faith, to say nothing of growth through the Holy Spirit (3.1–4). Paul now wants to show how it is fitting to regard the Christian leaders, and gives himself and Apollos as examples. The Christian leaders serve the Corinthians' faith just as the Lord has bestowed it on them. In this, therefore, it is already implied

---

ἐν πειθοῖ σοφίας . . . This word πειθώ is, of course, a mark of the great sophist. Philostratus therefore applies it to Dio of Prusa (488, p. 20.20), to Isocrates (503, p. 50.17), and to Scopelian (521, p. 88.12). Heinrici and J. Weiss have seen that ἀπόδειξις is a *terminus technicus* of rhetoric. It may seem surprising that in I Cor. 1.12–15, in view of the fact that individual Corinthians are pleading the various Christian leaders, as their teachers, Paul reproaches them with putting men into Christ's place. We have no valuable comparative material for this use of εἰμί with the genitive (v. 12), but the next verses show that the person who speaks like that esteems his human teacher so highly that he has to be asked whether it was Paul himself who was crucified for him or in whose name he was baptized. In 3.21–23 Paul reverses the genitive construction, so that everything, including Paul, Apollos, and Cephas, belongs to the Corinthians, while they themselves belong to Christ. These passages are evidence that in their relations with the Christian leaders the Corinthians are guilty of deifying men, as in fact we know happened among the sophists. The religious mystery language came in here early, and marks the sophistical literature with its varied subjects, often only loosely connected with any mystery theme, as it is found, for instance, in §§ 19–21 of the introduction to Aulus Gellius' *Noctes Atticae*. The professional orator's style too can be described as Bacchic (Philostratus 511, p. 64.7–12, on Nicetes of Smyrna; 588, p. 230.8 on Adrian of Tyre). Mysteries and different grades inside the mysteries are mentioned in the sophists' writings (e.g., Clement of Alexandria, *Strom.* I, 15.3, ἀγὼν γὰρ καὶ ὁ προαγὼν καὶ μυστήρια τὰ πρὸ μυστηρίων, ed. Stählin, *GCS* II, 1906, p. 11.21), and also by the professional orators. Philostratus tells of Adrian that he took part in the common meals of the chosen pupils of Herodes Atticus ὡς κοινωνὸς μεγάλου ἀπορρήτου (586, p. 224.3 f.). And it is told further of the same Adrian that the Athenians ἐθεράπευον αὐτόν, ὥσπερ τὰ γένη τῆς Ἐλευσῖνος ἱεροφάντην λαμπρῶς ἱερουργοῦντα. In that religious enthusiasm for a human being, a Christian apostle of Jewish origin was bound to see a danger to faith in Christ.

that God is everything, as he is working through the Christian leaders, and that accordingly God's judgment is the decisive one. The differences between the teachers are subject to God's judgment now and on the last day, but the Corinthians have not the right to sit in judgment on them (3.5). As what God does is decisive, he who plants and he who waters play no part, but God alone gives the growth. Yet at the last every one of them will receive his wages according to his labour (3.6–9).

The next section speaks of the Corinthians' judgment (cf. pp. 150–52), and in what follows they are exhorted to become fools, so as to be able to become really wise. In ch. 4 Paul again takes up the question of the Christian leaders and their position. In the first verse of the chapter he again uses the word mystery, μυστήριον, but in a different sense from 2.6 ff., for what is mentioned here is the concern which Paul and the other Christian leaders have for all the churches, including the Corinthians, who in fact are not yet able to receive God's wisdom. The emphasis is on God and Christ. As in 3.5–7, the decisive fact about the leaders is that they are serving God, who works through them. What they are in themselves, gifted people or teachers of wisdom, anything of which the churches can boast, recedes right into the background before the fact that they are called by God to serve.[1] Therefore nothing more is required from them, as men who are called, than faithfulness to the call that has come to them (4.1 f.). Paul rejects the judgment that the Corinthians with all their bickerings have pronounced on him and the other Christian leaders; indeed, every human tribunal—and Paul has often been accused—is a matter of indifference to him.[2] Nor does his own divergent view play any part for him. The only important thing is the Lord's judgment, and that is to be expected soon. So in the short time that is still left to them the Corinthians are not to judge, the more so because everything that is now hidden will then be revealed and so provide quite different possibilities of a sound judgment (4.3–5).

The object of everything that Paul has said above about himself and Apollos in 3.4 ff. is to teach the Corinthians not to go beyond what is written.[3] And indeed that is exactly what they are doing, as their self-

---

[1] Cf. S. Kierkegaard, 'On the Difference between a Genius and an Apostle', *The Present Age*, ET 1940, pp. 137–63.

[2] The remark anticipates 6.1 ff. with the complaints made there that the Corinthians are submitting their disputes to pagan judges. There is no reason to suppose that here in 4.3 Paul is alluding to any Corinthian court of examination relating to himself or any other leaders.

[3] On 4.6 see particularly O. Linton, ' "Nicht über das hinaus, was geschrieben steht" (I Cor. 4.6)', *TSK* 102, 1930, pp. 425–37. A recent suggestion by P. Wallis ('Ein neuer Auslegungsversuch der Stelle I Kor. 4.6', *TLZ* 75, 1950, cols. 506–8) that (τὸ) μὴ ὑπέρ is a catch-phrase, and that ἃ γέγραπται refers back to ταῦτα at the beginning of the verse, will hardly meet with assent. Dibelius remarks pertinently that if Peter

important behaviour at other people's expense makes clear. They are pluming themselves on a Christian teacher as if he were a teacher of wisdom, against another Christian who either swears by another teacher or does not boast of anything at all. As the apostles are only the recipients who can neither boast of anything themselves nor become the objects of other people's boasting, so it is with the Corinthians— no one sees anything different in them. Everything that they have, they have received from God; therefore they must not boast of it as if it were not a gift (4.6 f.).

The next section, 4.8–13, contains the concluding words in Paul's condemnation of the Corinthians' wrong outlook on the Christian teachers: they are not teachers of wisdom, but despised and suffering people. This will become clear as we proceed to discuss the passage.

VIII

(c) The Corinthians have been regarding themselves as wise. They have been boasting of the wisdom that they possessed as Christians, and they have also been boasting of the teachers from whom they received that wisdom; but above all they are boasting of themselves. Against this, Paul maintains that the assumptions on which they might appropriate that wisdom and so become wise are entirely lacking. Instead of judging the Christian leaders, they ought rather to think of the judgment that confronts themselves, and become fools in this world so as to become really wise. Their duty is not to judge, but to learn to emulate Paul, who is a suffering apostle.

In 1.26–31 Paul denies that before he came to them the Corinthians possessed wisdom or other privileges usually associated with worldly wisdom. In 1.25 he asserts that the foolishness of God and the weakness of the Cross of Christ, and Christ's Church which is founded on those things, are wiser and stronger than men. In v. 26 he gives that basic thought concrete form by asking the Corinthians to look round among their own numbers. God did not ask for wisdom or other human merit when he chose for himself a people in Corinth.[1]

---

had worked in Corinth, he would have been mentioned in I Cor. 4.6 ('Rom. und die Christen im I. Jahrhundert', *Sitzungsberichte der Heidelberger Akademie*, Philos.- hist. Klasse, 1941-2, 2, p. 28 n. 6).

[1] In I Thess. 1.4 Paul reminds the Thessalonians that they have been chosen, and in the text here he reminds the Corinthians that they have been called; in spite of a certain similarity in the two texts, the intention is different. In I Thessalonians Paul wishes to remind the Thessalonians of the abundant beginning of their Christian life, while in the other case he begins his argument from worldly weakness, wishing to prove that God attaches little value to worldly wisdom and other merit. Von Dobschütz, in 'Religionsgeschichtliche Parallelen zum Neuen Testament', *ZNW* 21,

Why does Paul say here, 'Not many of you were wise according to worldly standards, not many were powerful, not many were of noble birth'? Of course he wants to show that the Corinthians possess nothing of which they could be proud; but in that case the first part, 'not many of you were wise according to worldly standards', might be enough. Similarly it may surprise us to hear in 2.6 of the rulers of this age. Behind that there lies the idea of the contrast between this world, which is passing away, and the coming world, in which the Corinthians—but not yet, be it noted—are to be kings. But the triad 'wise, powerful, noble'[1] sounds strange, because the apostle seems to be unnecessarily hard in the way he impresses on them their undistinguished origin and their modest place in the universe. It is a relief to realize that these three terms point to quite normal assumptions and conditions of life among students (and teachers) of wisdom.[2]

1922, pp. 69–72 has claimed to see a parallel to I Cor. 1.26–29 in Baruch's Apocalypse (Syriac), ch. 70.3–5, whereas Paul, in contrast to Baruch, sees in the elevation of foolish and despised people the beginning of the time of redemption, not the collapse of the world into chaos. While I do not agree with Dobschütz in his view of this passage from Baruch as a parallel to Paul, I think, as he does, that Jewish parallels to Paul's writings are no sign of dependence or lack of originality on the part of the latter, but that they witness to the superiority of the new outlook, and show that quite new ideas are making headway.

[1]On the connexion with Jer. 9.23 f. see p. 146 n. 3.

[2]σοφοί, δυνατοί, and εὐγενεῖς may be used of those who are instructed in the sophist's art. If we compare Philostratus' *Vitae Sophistarum* and Eunapius' *Vitae Philosophorum et Sophistarum* with Diogenes Laertius, we realize that the first two attach special importance to the fact that those whom they portray are of good family, with respected relatives, and often that their family is well-to-do, while as a rule Diogenes Laertius does not speak about his philosophers' origin. While we can take it, without further evidence, that the sophists are σοφοί, there are various examples of their having parents or ancestors who are δυνατοί and εὐγενεῖς. Philostratus, for instance, says that Varus' father is ἐν τοῖς δυνατωτάτοις τῶν Περγαίων (576, ed. Wright, p. 202, l. 27), and other expressions, especially the superlatives of ἐλλόγιμος and ἐπιφανής are used about certain sophists to say that they are of good family, in fact that their ancestors had the rank of consul, had belonged to the city senate, or had been ἀρχιερεύς of the province: Critias (501, p. 46.20 f.), Marcus of Byzantium (528, pp. 100.24–102.1); Scopelian was ἀρχιερεύς in Asia, as were his ancestors before him, each inheriting the office from his father (515, p. 72.20–22); Polemo (530, p. 106.15 f.); Herodes Atticus (545, p. 138.2 f.); Antiochus (568, p. 184.27 f.); Athenodorus (594, p. 242.10–12); Euodianus (596, p. 246.15–18); Rufus (597, p. 248.8 f.); Damianus (605, p. 264.8–12); Antipater (606, p. 268.15 f.); Hermocrates (609, p. 272.11–14); and Heraclides of Lycia (612 f., p. 278.12–14). These sophists themselves also attained high office: Favorinus (490, p. 24.3); Antiphon (498, p. 38.25 f.); Theodotus (566, p. 182.6); and Rufus (597, p. 248.9 f.). Eunapius (cited from the same volume), who deals with philosophers, sophists, and doctors, specially mentions the aristocratic origin of Porphyrius (455, p. 352.23 f.) and Iamblichus (ἐπιφανής; 457, p. 362.6 f.); with reference to Aedesius (461, p. 376.17), Maximus (473, p. 426.18) and Libanius (495, p. 518.8 f.) it is emphasized that their ancestors belonged to τῶν εὖ γεγονότων; to this class there also belong Prohaeresius (487, p. 484.16); Oribasius (498, p. 532.13 f.); Ionicus (ἐπιφανῶς; 499, p. 536.16 f.); and Chrysanthius (500, p. 540.3–5). In Diogenes Laertius, I. 22, εὐγενής is used of Thales (in the superlative) and of Menedemus (II. 125); εὐγένεια of Anaxagoras (II. 6). It is emphasized that the following came from good or aristocratic families: Phaedo (II. 105); Plato (III. 1); Polemo (IV. 17); and Aristotle (V. 1). In Diogenes we do

To σοφοί there is added a κατὰ σάρκα, this term also being mentioned
positively in the previous verses: there is a wisdom of God, of which
we shall hear more later in 2.6 ff. This addition is therefore made so
as to avoid any misunderstanding—here in v. 26 it is a question of
people who are wise in the worldly sense.

In three parallel constructions Paul sets out in more detail the three
negative terms in v. 26: σοφοί, δυνατοί, and εὐγενεῖς, changing between
masculine and neuter without any difference in meaning. God has
chosen his Church in such a way as to shame the wise and the strong
(1.27). We see in the Gospels that Jesus gathers round him the tax
collectors and sinners, while the righteous think they have no need of
him; in Matt. 11.25 he says, 'I thank thee, Father, Lord of heaven and
earth, that thou has hidden these things from the wise and understanding *(ἀπὸ σοφῶν καὶ συνετῶν)* and revealed them to babes.' Some commentators are of the opinion that in Paul's writings no allusion to this
saying of Jesus is possible, as he does not quote any of Jesus' sayings
elsewhere, and does not seem to know any. But it seems to have been
overlooked that that takes us into one of those circular arguments
that are so dangerous. For if we assert, at every single place where Paul
may be alluding to one of Jesus' sayings, that he does this nowhere
else, then we shall gradually succeed in reaching the conviction that he
never does it at all—because he never does it.

In v. 28 Paul introduces the last of the parallel constructions about
God's choice of what is insignificant; in this case he has widened the
terms, first by adding the stronger τὰ ἐξουθενημένα, and after that by
the much stronger τὰ μὴ ὄντα, which may well be regarded as a summary
description of what is mentioned in all three constructions. The contrast
in the latter is carried to the clear-cut formula τὰ μὴ ὄντα in contrast to
τὰ ὄντα, and to that is added a statement of God's intention in making
that choice: 'so that no human being might boast in the presence of
God' (v. 29). Just as in v. 21 we found a connexion with Rom. 1–2 and
10,[1] here too we can draw a connecting line to the ideas about salvation

---

not find the same interest in the philosophers' social background as it had for the
two other biographers in relation to the people whom they described. And yet some
philosophers seem to be of undistinguished origin, whereas it is rarely the case
with sophists. If only a few of the sophists reached a postion by virtue of their innate
gifts, one of the reasons is the fact that high fees were demanded from the pupils:
see Philostratus 591, p. 234.26–29 and p. 236.12–14; cf. 600, p. 254.2 f.; 604, pp.
260.26–262.1; 605, p. 266.3–7; 606, p. 266.21–25; and 615, p. 284.14–16. Finally,
it may make it easier to understand the text of I Corinthians if we quote from
Philostratus (618, p. 292.1 f.) on Hippodromus: ἀγροικότερός τε ὢν τὸ εἶδος ὅμως
ἀμήχανον εὐγένειαν . . . ,and from Diogenes Laertius IV. 51 on Bion: τὴν δυσγένειαν
πονηρὸν ἔλεγον εἶναι σύνοικον τῇ παρρησίᾳ·
        δουλοῖ γὰρ ἄνδρα, κἂν θρασύσπλαγχός τις ᾖ.

[1]See p. 149.

in Romans. In Rom. 3.27 we have, 'Then what becomes of our boasting? It is excluded. On what principle? On the principle of works? No, but on the principle of faith.' And in Rom. 4.17 we read of Abraham, κατέναντι οὗ ἐπίστευσεν Θεοῦ τοῦ ζωοποιοῦντος τοὺς νεκροὺς καὶ καλοῦντος τὰ μὴ ὄντα ὡς ὄντα. Here we have the same basic themes—God makes all boasting impossible by creating something out of what is nothing. It is clear from Paul's presentation that the Corinthians are striving to be something and to be able to boast of their wisdom and their teachers. By that striving they belong to earthly wisdom, which God has brought to nothing (1.28 f.). It is from God that the Corinthians have their life in Christ, from him who has become for us not only the above-mentioned wisdom from God (in contrast to worldly wisdom), but also righteousness, holiness, and redemption; all our gifts come from him, and we can therefore boast only in the Lord (1.30 f.).

In 2.6–3.4 Paul tells the Corinthians that, though there certainly is a Christian wisdom, its place is not in the first missionary period, and that as they are still of the flesh, they have not been able to hear it (see pp. 154–60). In 3.10–17 he urges them to stop judging the Christian leaders, and to reflect instead that they themselves are to be subjected to judgment on the coming day of judgment (see pp. 150–52). In 3.18–23 he continues his exhortation of the Corinthians. The interpretation that we gave above of 3.10–17 is confirmed by the fact that it facilitates the transition to 3.18 ff.[1] Let no one deceive himself, or, with the day of judgment before his eyes, strive for worldly wisdom, but let everyone become a fool before the world but wise before God. What plays a part in the world's wisdom does not count here—boasting and giving oneself airs about an individual human teacher, and rejecting the other teachers of wisdom whom other people quote. No, they will be given everything—God's wisdom and all who work with God; but they themselves will belong to Christ, and therefore to God (3.18–23).

Paul wanted to show by his exposition, as we see in 4.6 f. (see pp. 160 f.), that the Corinthians, like the apostles, have only received, and have cause neither to be puffed up nor to be boasted of by anyone; no one sees anything different in them (4.7). Everything that they possess they have from God, and they must therefore not boast of it as if they had not received it. The following section, 4.8–13, shows that there is a close connexion between the Corinthians' bickerings founded on

---

[1] If the preceding verses were directed against the other Christian teachers and their work in Corinth, it is difficult to understand why Paul suddenly, without any preparation, admonishes the church as a whole in 3.18 ff. But all difficulty disappears if we accept the interpretation suggested, that the preceding section, 3.10–17, is addressed to the whole church.

men's self-glorification and the arrogant consciousness of possessing an abundance of spiritual gifts (8.1 f. and chs. 12–14), and the conception of the resurrection of the dead (ch. 15). The wisdom that the Corinthians thought they found in the Gospel consists in divine instruction about the deep mysteries of God, the world, and man. Thanks to the gifts of the Spirit, the newly won Corinthians believed that they were already on the same plane as the Christian leaders and were therefore in a position to criticize them. It was not necessary, they thought, to hold to the written word, nor to the unanimous witness of the Church, for the Spirit (as was held later among the enthusiasts) could give instruction about everything and make one independent of Bible and Church.

The next section, 4.8 ff., shows, as does ch. 15 later, that in the Corinthians' reckoning 'the resurrection is past already' (II Tim. 2.18), as the existence begun with baptism and the gifts of grace already represented the millennium or the final salvation. The kingdom of God is for them a reality already experienced, as we can infer from the expressions that Paul uses about it—'Already you are filled!' (cf. Matt. 5.6; Luke 6.21); 'Already you have become rich! Without us you have become kings!' (cf. Matt. 5.3; Luke 6.20; II Cor. 8.9). In the next sentence, 'And would that you did reign, so that we might share the rule with you!' Paul reveals the Corinthians' error. When the kingdom of God comes, it is for all Christians, not the Corinthians alone. And with this sentence the apostle begins to explain in what way there is a difference between the Corinthians and the apostles. The former think they are rulers, filled and rich, wise in Christ, strong and held in honour (4.8, 10). The apostles, on the other hand, are suffering and in disrepute among men, but in the midst of their sufferings they bless those who revile them (4.9–13). The Corinthians have been mistaken, and think they already have eternal life, but the truth is that the Church is still in the midst of this world, that the apostles are already suffering, and that the deluded Corinthians will soon themselves experience the Messianic distress (7.26–31). In the enumeration of the apostles' sufferings, and especially at the end (4.12 f.), we feel the same interest as in II Corinthians (chs. 4–6 and 10–12) in making it clear to the Corinthians how the true apostle contrasts with the falsified picture that they have made for themselves of a Christian leader of whom one may boast. Here the suffering apostle, whose lot is a proof that the kingdom of God is still in the future, is contrasted with the teacher of wisdom who turns the Gospel into worldly wisdom and so gives an occasion for boasting.

The last section of ch. 4 (vv. 14–21) points out to the Corinthians that though they have countless guides in Christ, they have only one father, namely Paul. Therefore they must imitate him in the apostolic sufferings of which he has just told them, and in his preaching of the Gospel. He has sent Timothy to them to remind them of his own teaching and practice in all the Gentile churches. Those who have been puffing themselves up because they did not expect to see Paul again will see him again and discover that what matters is not their words but their strength.[1] They imagine themselves to be in God's kingdom, but it is all words; they do not know the strength that God's kingdom will possess when it comes. He therefore has to ask whether he is to come to chastise them or to forgive them (4.21). The last question anticipates the coming events involving a collision between the apostle and the church in Corinth; it points to the Corinthians' disobedience, the severe letter, and the detailed teaching about the true apostle, as we find it in II Corinthians.

IX

On the basis of the interpretation submitted here, according to which the matter dealt with is one of bickerings between the Corinthians, but not of factions or of clear points of view as to doctrine and practice, Paul's line of thought is as follows (1.12–4.13):

After mentioning the present bickerings, Paul at once argues against putting the teachers who are invoked—he names himself as an example —in Christ's place. Paul is called to preach the Gospel, but not in lofty words of wisdom. In 1.18–25 he shows that God has made the wisdom of this world foolishness and will save, by the foolishness of preaching, those who believe. After this basic discussion, which draws a distinction between worldly wisdom and the Gospel, he shows in 1.26–31 that the Christian Corinthians were without wisdom when the Gospel reached them. Paul, the bearer of it, had decided to know nothing among them except Christ crucified, so that their Christianity might rest on the power of God and not on human wisdom (2.1–5). The Corinthians are therefore in error if they think that they possess wisdom. There certainly is a Christian wisdom, which is different from worldly wisdom, and is a gift of the Holy Spirit, which cannot be received by 'unspiritual' people (2.6–16). Paul could not give them this wisdom at the beginning of their Christian life, and even now it is impossible, because they are of the flesh, as their bickerings prove (3.1–4). And they have no right to alter the Gospel and regard the Christian leaders as teachers of wisdom,

---

[1]The conclusion of II Cor. 12.14–13.13 reminds us of what is said here. Paul speaks there about the relation between parents and children (12.14 f.), about Titus (12.18) as he does here about Timothy, and about weakness and power (13.2–6) corresponding to word and power in 4.20; and several passages at the end of II Cor. remind us of the last verse, v. 21.

as those leaders are dependent on God and are placed under his judgment (3.5–9). This is also true for the Corinthians, who will soon have to answer before God's tribunal (3.10–17), and therefore, instead of imagining that they are wise, they are to appear as fools before the world, so that they can become wise before God (3.18–23). Of the Christian leaders it is expected that they remain faithful to their call; but human judgment is a matter of indifference—the only important thing is God's judgment, which is at hand (4.1–4). The Corinthians are to stop pronouncing judgment on the Christian leaders and praising themselves; all that they have, they have received from God, and therefore they are not to boast of anything as if they had not received it (4.5–7). But they are sitting like kings in glory, while the apostles suffer and are in disrepute before men (4.8–13).

Thus Paul shows that the Corinthians were without wisdom when they became Christians, and that as such they have received no wisdom, at first because they were newly baptized, and then because they actually proved by their bickerings that they were not able to receive the Christian wisdom. The Christian leaders, whom they erroneously regarded as teachers of wisdom, are in everything dependent on God, whose decision it was to turn this world's wisdom into foolishness, and to save, by the foolishness of preaching, those who believe. In everything they are dependent on him, and he will judge them. The Corinthians will themselves stand before the judgment, and the safe position from which they judge others will be taken from them, for God's kingdom has not come, and the Messianic tribulations are at hand. In other words, everything that the Corinthians call wisdom is a misunderstanding of what they received as Christians.

X

If the interpretation submitted here is correct, then not only were there no factions, but there was also no Judaizing in the church at Corinth at the time when Paul wrote his first letter to the Corinthians.

6

THE TRUE AND THE FALSE APOSTLE
Studies in II Corinthians

IN the previous chapter on I Corinthians we saw that there are no factions in Corinth, but that Paul is addressing the church there as a whole, and that there is no trace of a Judaizing movement among the Corinthians. This finding is confirmed by the second letter to the church. Here too what is said is not of factions; it is the church which has rebelled against the apostle, but which then submitted and is now admonished as to how it is to behave till the apostle comes to it. Nor is the letter about Judaizing, for although 'apostles' of Jewish origin had arrived, they did not try to Judaize. In spite of the extremely sharp words that Paul uses about them, it is clear that those opponents played a subordinate part in an already existing state of opposition between the apostle and his church. Not till we come to the final phase of that struggle, after the 'severe letter' and the submission of the church, are these visiting brethren met with who have brought to a climax a situation that admitted of no further complication. Hence the severe words written with deep emotion in a letter which otherwise breathes so much joy, trust, and comfort.

I

It is generally held that of all Paul's letters II Corinthians is probably the most difficult to understand in detail. He alludes again and again to events of which we otherwise know nothing, but which were so familiar to the writer and the recipients of the letter that the least suggestion was quite enough to recall the whole situation to the readers' recollection. It is therefore extremely difficult for us to be clear about the circumstances that have to be assumed in order to understand the letter. The expositor has to construct here the letter's missing details that are necessary for the context, and also the events that gave rise to the apostle's words. It can be realized, therefore, that it has been very difficult to find a consensus of opinion among scholars.

This is seen, for example, in the discussion about the unity of the letter. An attempt has been made to deal adequately with this problem

168

by assuming that what we have here is not one single letter, but that it consists of three fragments from three different letters. In this way 6.14–7.1 has been separated in the opinion that we have here a fragment of another of Paul's letters to the church at Corinth. The general belief is that we are dealing here with the oldest of the letters known to us, the one mentioned in I Cor. 5.9 where Paul says that he has written in an earlier letter, 'You are not to associate with immoral men.' Although 'immoral men' are not mentioned in II Cor. 6.14–7.1, the whole of this section argues that one must 'not be mismated with unbelievers', and this agrees with what is said in the earlier letter referred to in I Cor. 5.9.

Another and more important view is that II Corinthians should be divided into two letters or fragments of letters, viz., chs. 1–9 and chs. 10–13.[1] This assumes that II Cor. 10–13 is an independent letter, or at any rate a fragment of such a letter, written before II Cor. 1–9—in other words, that we have recovered in the last four chapters of our II Corinthians at least parts of the severe intermediate letter which otherwise was thought to be lost. But others have supposed that the two letters or parts of them were composed in the order in which we have them, so that II Cor. 1–9 was written later than the lost (severe) letter, while chs. 10–13 is a still later letter, written shortly before the apostle arrived in Corinth, and showing a new situation with new complications in the church. Finally, it is still possible for us to hold to our present II Corinthians in the belief that it was written as one letter (with the possible exception of 6.14–7.1), in spite of the changed tone that has caused the above-mentioned constructions to be suggested. As this discussion about the unity of the letter is important for its interpretation, it is necessary to go into these questions more closely.

Synopsis of Paul's Correspondence with Corinth

	0	1	2	3
1. The lost first letter	lost, or II Cor. 6.14–7.1?			
2. Our I Cor.				
3. The severe letter		II Cor. 10–13	lost	lost
4. The next letter		II Cor. 1–9	II Cor. 1–9	II Cor. 1–13
5. One more letter, the last before the arrival (Acts 20.2 f.)			II Cor. 10–13	

According to the first of the views mentioned, II Cor. 10–13 is identical with the letter, or with a fragment of the letter, that Paul wrote between I Cor. and II Cor. 1–9, the last-named letter (or fragment of a letter), which consists of the first nine chapters of II Corinthians, thus

[1] Alternatively, the division may be such as to put 13.11–14 with chs. 1–9, as, e.g., in Strachan's commentary, pp. 145 ff.

being written in Macedonia not long before his visit at the end of the third journey (see Acts 20.2 f.). In fact, a letter from Paul to the church is spoken of in odd passages here. The apostle has been very anxious about the effect of a severe letter that he had sent to Corinth, and it is not till he meets Titus, who had been sent there in advance, that he feels freed from anxious suspense about the impression that the letter would make (2.3 f., 9, 12 f.; 7.5–12). He cannot have had I Corinthians in mind here; it must be a question of a later letter, in which he spoke severely and threateningly to the recalcitrant church. That letter, which caused pain to the Corinthians, but which also resulted in the change that Paul had demanded in their attitude towards him, should then be identical with chs. 10–13, or else these chapters should represent a fragment of the severe letter.

It seems as if much might be said for this view. It would explain the severer tone of the last four chapters. The reason for Paul's different tone is then that the two parts of the letter are parts of two quite different letters. And in that case the severe letter, which is referred to here in chs. 1–9, is not lost, but is contained in chs. 10–13. That is why the later letter, II Cor. 1–9, looking back on the dispute that ended with Titus' return (7.6 ff.), is so completely filled with relief at the ending of the strain caused by the severe letter, and so buoyed up by confidence and joy. Moreover, it may be pointed out that two or three times in chs. 1–9 Paul discusses the reproach, to which he has been subjected, of commending himself (3.1; 4.5; 5.12); and this could be related to what he says about boasting in 10.13–16 and 11.16–12.10.

And yet this assumption will not hold water. The only thing that we know for certain about the severe letter is that Paul demanded the punishment of one of the church members (2.5–11; 7.11 f.), and in chs. 10–13 there is not a single word about this. To deal with this objection the point has, of course, been made that the last four chapters are only a fragment of the severe letter, and that the missing demand may be contained in the part that was lost. But it is more than remarkable if in a search for identification the one thing that was certain to be found in the letter is not contained in what is believed to be a fragment of it. This is particularly striking when we read as part of the supposed severe letter the demands that Paul makes (12.14–13.10) before his visit to the church. There is nothing mentioned here about the punishment of a church member which has 'caused pain'.

At the same time it has rightly been pointed out that in chs. 1–9 too Paul controverts accusations made against him (1.12, 13, 17, 18; 2.5–9, 17; 3.1, 5; 4.2, 5; 5.12, 13, 16; 6.8; 7.2); so that the difference between the two parts of II Corinthians is not as great as is sometimes claimed.

It is important to keep in mind that the opponents in chs. 10–13, if this should be the severe intermediate letter, would be mentioned as a matter of course in Paul's retrospective view of the dispute (chs. 1–9); but in that section of the letter there are no certain allusions to such opponents as those mentioned in chs. 10–13. On the contrary, the past dispute seems to have been simply between Paul and the church, so that it is no accident that an important point in the severe letter was that the church ought to punish a single member who had offended.

It is therefore the more probable assumption that chs. 10–13 were written later than chs. 1–9, either as part of the same letter or as a later letter or a fragment of one. The advantage of dividing our II Corinthians into parts of two letters, written in the order in which we now have them, is not only that it explains the different tone of the two parts, but also that Paul may meanwhile have received fresh information from Corinth, drawing his attention to a new situation different from the one that we have to assume for chs. 1–9. But to judge by the numerous points of agreement, there may have been only a short interval between the two letters. And one wonders whether the intervening period is not getting so short that after all the two parts are only one letter.

Between the two last-mentioned possibilities there is the important point of agreement that the opponents in chs. 10–13 did not cause the dispute in Corinth. It had been raging before they arrived, as we can see from Paul's retrospective treatment of the dispute (chs. 1–9). They do not come on the scene till later. To recognize this therefore does not make it necessary to divide II Corinthians into two letters. The two parts may quite well belong to the same letter, of which chs. 1–7 look back, while chs. 8–9 are already looking at the present and future as they deal with the Corinthians' participation in the collection for the poor of Jerusalem. Chs. 10–13 then start from that forward-looking section about the forthcoming collection and the probability of Paul's early arrival in the church (his last before his final departure for the west, according to Rom. 15.23 f.), and go into the question of what the church still has to put right, especially in connexion with the Jewish 'apostles' who have lately arrived. The latter, by their different apostolic outlook and practice, are endangering the Corinthians' submission to Paul, and—what has so far not been noticed—they are draining the Corinthians by their claim to maintenance—just before the Pauline messengers are due to collect a generous gift for Jerusalem.

II

The background of II Corinthians has usually been described in such a way as to show us a Pauline church, which Judaizing emissaries from

Jerusalem sought to alienate from the apostle to the Gentiles, and to put under the authority of the original church. But voices have been raised to claim that the opponents were spiritual men boasting of visions and revelations.

If there are Judaizers behind the agitations,[1] then the situation is that in our letter most of the questions that provided the main interest in I Corinthians have receded into the background or disappeared completely. We hear nothing more either of the four factions or of the many practical questions of I Corinthians. That might be due to the effect of that letter, but we hear on occasion that their moral state still leaves much to be desired (12.20 ff.);[2] and so the reason is more likely to be that all the earlier problems are now overshadowed by a great new one.

In II Corinthians the whole interest is in fact concentrated on the teachers from outside who have appeared in the church.[3] They must have come with letters of introduction from Christians of other parts (3.1), but attempts to find out who gave them the letters have reached no certain conclusions.[4] In 3.6 ff. Paul describes himself—obviously in contrast to those teachers—as a minister 'of a new covenant, not in a written code but in the Spirit'. Moses and the Old Testament had only a glory that fades away, and hardness of heart and blindness are to blame if the Jews cannot see it. There can therefore—so it is argued—be no doubt that the opponents are Judaizers, and this is confirmed by Paul's direct attack on them in 11.22 ff., where we see that they called themselves 'servants of Christ' and at the same time insisted on their position of honour as 'Hebrews, Israelites, descendants of Abraham'.

The methods of the opponents in Corinth were marked by great cunning. While Paul is writing, they have not yet made their demand that the Gentile Christians should be circumcised and observe the Law. Paul would certainly have opposed that demand in the way that we know from Galatians; but of course the Judaizing party was afraid of any such retort, and its members therefore contented themselves for the time being with praising Moses and all his works, with surrounding themselves with an appearance of greater sanctity, and with giving the church to understand that real, genuine Christianity would be able to enter Corinth only through their work (10.16).[5] It may be that their carefully thought out tactics were connected with the expected arrival in Corinth of a specially eminent member of the party, and that they wanted to postpone the decisive struggle till he had arrived (11.4).

[1] The following presentation leans on Koch, pp. 20–27.
[2] But see p. 136 n. 4.
[3] Koch, p. 21.
[4] Koch, pp. 168 f.; see pp. 177 f. below.
[5] Koch, p. 22.

For the present they concentrated on a personal attack on Paul, using the smouldering criticism and annoyance inside the church, and calculating that, when they had once undermined the church's personal respect for him, it would not be difficult to win the Corinthians round to their view of the Law. When they twit him with being 'unskilled in speaking' (11.6), it is not a Jewish accusation, but an objection that the followers of Apollos had once raised from their Greek line of thought.

That personal attack on Paul had succeeded only too well. It is clear from II Corinthians that the church allowed itself to be greatly influenced by the teachers from outside. That can be seen from the apostle's repeated references to the mistrust and ill-will that had been shown him in the church.

No doubt one of the main points in the accusations that the opponents had spread among the Corinthians was that Paul called himself an apostle, though he had no right to (12.12; 3.2 ff.; cf. 11.5; 12.11).[1] In person he made a remarkably uncertain impression. His letters were very forceful, but his bodily presence was weak (10.1, 9 f.). In eloquence and other qualities necessary for a missionary he left a great deal to be desired (11.5 f.; 12.11). He was a schemer, and his conduct aroused suspicion (1.12 ff.; 3.12 f.; 4.1 ff.; 5.11). That he was incessantly commending himself was a sign of his uneasy efforts to keep the church's favour (3.1; 5.12; 12.19). By refusing to accept support from the Corinthians though other churches had supported him, he betrayed a lack of love for the church in Corinth (11.7–12; 12.13). He changed his plans capriciously, without thinking of his promises to the church (1.15 ff.); in fact, people went so far as to charge him with dishonesty. The collection for Jerusalem, which he carried out so zealously, brought in a great deal of money, but did not that find its way into his own pocket to remunerate him for his work without 'burdening the churches' (7.2; 8.20; 12.16 ff.)?[2]

We might get the impression that it was only a matter of time before there was no longer a Pauline church in the capital of Achaia. And indeed the letter is intended not only for Corinth, but for all the churches in Achaia (1.1; cf. 9.2; 11.10). In other words, what was involved was a whole mission field, in which the achievements were apparently to be obliterated.[3]

If the situation in Corinth is thus to be regarded as one of unrest stirred up by Judaizers coming from outside, it is, of course, the other letters, especially Galatians, that lead some scholars to such analogous

[1]Koch, p. 23.
[2]Koch, p. 24.
[3]Koch, p. 25.

conclusions. The fact that the visiting Jewish apostles did not preach a Judaizing message might be a decisive obstacle to such a view. But it is asserted that the opponents confined themselves—and this is stressed as being particularly cunning—to undermining Paul's authority in the church before they went on to preach their Judaizing message. But this assertion only says in other words that it cannot be proved that the opponents were Judaizers if they did not preach Judaism. And it can hardly be true that Paul's opponents were always Judaizers.

The two texts that were quoted above to support the view that the opponents were Judaizers (p. 172) do not prove the point. In 3.6 ff. Paul compares himself and his service with Moses and his service; but in this case the comparison is between Christianity and Judaism, not between Paulinism and the views of the Judaizers (see pp. 58–61). And if 11.22 ff. shows that the opponents called themselves 'servants of Christ' and at the same time stood on their dignity as 'Hebrews, Israelites, descendants of Abraham', that proves that they are Jewish Christians, but not that they are Judaizers.

And finally we must not ignore the fact that such cunning behaviour by the Judaizing opponents could not have been concealed from Paul. It is really remarkable that he does not see through this tactical manoeuvre by his opponents and attack their Judaizing efforts.[1]

Windisch's account of Paul's opponents (pp. 23–26) makes the state of affairs quite different from the one described above, according to which the opponents are supposed to be Judaizers. Of the factions, only the Christ faction is mentioned in II Corinthians, and it now seems to dominate the church. Relying particularly on Lütgert's attempt to regard this Christ faction as a gnostic-libertine movement which carries Paul's ideas to excess,[2] and on Schlatter's efforts to trace such spiritual-libertine gnosticism back to Jewish and Palestinian sources,[3] Windisch claims to be justified in regarding Paul's opponents in II Corinthians as gnostic spiritual men, the more so as a spiritual-gnostic current clearly appears in I Corinthians. It is possible that that movement, which we know from the first letter, developed into the opposing faction that we find in II Corinthians. To this there come itinerant Jewish preachers, who may have been active in Corinth even before I Corinthians, but who had no considerable following till after that letter.

Such an amalgamation of Judaizing views and spiritual *gnosis* among Paul's opponents is improbable. We have already criticized the assumption that those opponents were on a Judaizing errand, and in ch. 5

---

[1]See E. Käsemann, 'Die Legitimität des Apostels', *ZNW* 41, 1942, p. 39.
[2]W. Lütgert, *Freiheitspredigt und Schwarmgeister in Korinth*, (BFCT 12.3), 1908.
[3]A. Schlatter, *Die korinthische Theologie* (BFCT 18.2), 1914.

we saw that there was no Judaizing in Corinth before I Corinthians. Now spiritual and 'gnostic'[1] currents are from the outset more likely to be met with than Judaizing ones in the Greek and Gentile church at Corinth. But these vague statements must give way to more concrete definitions. We have already ascertained in ch. 5 that Paul is not combating a 'gnostic' *sophia* doctrine in I Cor. 1–4. Nor is it possible to find in II Corinthians that Paul's opponents have a definite doctrine. We know so little of the facts about them that it is only by an investigation of his polemics and of the situation in the church that we can arrive at a picture of them and their place in the struggle between the apostle and the Corinthian church.

III

Lietzmann writes on ch. 10 (p. 139), 'In II Cor. 1–9 Paul has spoken only to the church; now he is dealing with his opponents against whom his anger is flaring up, and with that all kinds of things about the church that he had kept back in chs. 1–9 are coming out again.' In that short statement it is true that in the first nine chapters the apostle spoke only to and about the church, but it is an exaggeration to claim that chs. 10–13 deal with his opponents, even with the reservation that Lietzmann makes. This section of the letter too deals with the church.

So ch. 10, which is generally thought to be meant for Paul's opponents, is really directed against the church. That is quite clear from vv. 1–11, which refer to his visit and letters before his opponents' arrival at Corinth (v. 1; cf. v. 7; vv. 9–10). The warning words to the church are repeated in 12.20–13.10, which are also directed at the church. In 10.2 we read of 'some who suspect us of acting in worldly fashion', and on this Paul argues in vv. 3 and 4, 'For though we live in the world we are not carrying on a worldly war, for the weapons of our warfare are not worldly. . . .' What he has in mind here is not his opponents, but the Corinthians themselves; they have, in fact, been reproaching him with being worldly, so that in 1.12 he has to deny that he behaved with 'earthly wisdom', and in 1.17 that his changed plans for travelling arose from worldly motives: 'Do I make my plans like a worldly man. . . ?' And in 5.16 he writes, 'From now on, therefore, we regard no one from a human point of view; even though we once regarded Christ from a human point of view, we regard him thus no longer.'[2]

[1] As no one yet knows what gnosticism is, I venture to put the cognate adjective in inverted commas.
[2] With Koch (pp. 266 ff.) I regard κατὰ σάρκα in the two passages where it occurs in v. 16 as the subjective norm of knowledge.

This reproach of being worldly is based on the Corinthians' conviction that they themselves are spiritual, as we know from I Corinthians. They have looked down on other people, because they thought that other people had not the Spirit. And when the apostle wants to intervene and correct them, they are convinced that he cannot possess the Spirit and must be worldly, because he cannot share their point of view.

In 10.12–18 Paul goes on to say that he does not venture to compare himself with some of those who commend themselves, but that he will boast only of the sphere of work that God has allotted as his task, namely to reach even the Corinthians. In this section it is usual to suppose that three parties are concerned: Paul, his opponents, and the Corinthians; but there is no conclusive reason to suppose that Paul is thinking here of his opponents; and his ironical remarks become even sharper if what is said here is only between the apostle and his church in Corinth. The most natural conclusion is, therefore, that it is the Corinthians who are commending themselves, while the apostle can boast only of what God has apportioned to him, namely to reach the Corinthians with the Gospel—a thing that in the Corinthians' view is probably not particularly glorious. But when their faith increases and they realize that God's sending his apostle to Corinth is a great thing, then the time has come when the apostle can press on further.[1]

The next passage that has been made to refer to Paul's opponents is 11.4: 'For if some one comes and preaches another Jesus than the one we preached, or if you receive a different spirit from the one you received, or if you accept a different gospel from the one you accepted, you submit to it readily enough.' It is usual to see in this an allusion to the false gospel of the Judaizing opponents who have already been preaching in Corinth; but this cannot be right. Even if, as we saw, the opponents could not be Judaizers, we cannot on that account at once regard them as spiritual men. We cannot approve the traditional point of departure of Pauline research where the opponents, if they are not Judaizers, automatically become spiritual men with no third possibility. There can be no question in the letter here of another gospel. If the opponents had had a false doctrine or been boasting of spiritual gifts that did not involve the confession of Jesus as Lord, Paul would have attacked them on that account, however hidden such deviations might be.

The interpretation of 11.4 is generally supported by connecting it with v. 5, but in that case the much more important connexion with v. 3 is overlooked. Here Paul expresses the fear that Satan will lead their thoughts astray and that they may thus lose their sincere and pure

[1] Rom. 15.23 f. shows how important this is for the apostle just at that time.

devotion to Christ. The ground for that anxiety is given in v. 4 (above-mentioned), and therefore that verse cannot be evidence of a state of affairs already existing in Corinth. In such a case Paul would express the fear that the Corinthians might fall away from Christ, and his ground for this would be that they had already done so. V. 4 must therefore express a possibility that makes it clear that the apostle is rightly distressed about the Corinthians. If anyone came preaching another gospel, they would submit to it readily enough.[1] 11.4 therefore speaks of the Corinthians and not of the opponents, and says, in effect, that the church is so weak that any new and strange doctrine would lead them to fall away.

The reason given in 11.5, 'I think that I am not in the least inferior to these superlative apostles,' refers back, not to v. 4, but to v. 1, which dominates the context. Paul's wish that the Corinthians would bear with him in a little foolishness is taken up again in v. 16, and it is therefore probable that he is thinking of it in this verse too. Thus v. 5 becomes a basis of v. 1, parallel with v. 2—the Corinthians must bear with his own self-praise, for indeed he is not inferior to the men of whom they think so highly.[2]

The term 'superlative apostles' has been supposed to refer to the apostles in Jerusalem.[3] Recent commentaries have not taken this view, but it is still generally held that they come from Jerusalem and are emissaries of the twelve, or at any rate of the Judaistic circles in the church there.[4] As regards the letters of introduction which, according to the generally accepted interpretation of 3.1, they are said to have brought with them to Corinth, these are still believed to come from Jerusalem.[5] These three opinions, however, must all be rejected. The expression 'these superlative apostles' occurs in 12.11 as well as in 11.5, and in both cases it must mean the Jewish apostles who are staying in Corinth. If we make 11.4 describe what is already happening there, the 'superlative apostles' in v. 5 must be the same persons. And if the interpretation that we prefer is approved, that v. 5 is a basis of v. 1,

[1]Koch, pp. 388 ff.
[2]Koch, pp. 391 f.
[3]This view is now supported by Käsemann, *op. cit.*, pp. 45–48.
[4]Thus Knox, *St Paul*, p. 102; Lietzmann, pp. 108 f.; Nock, *St Paul*, p. 200; Dibelius and Kümmel, p. 137.
[5]Thus Windisch and Bachmann. Strachan, who quite realizes that the opponents are Jews of the Diaspora, nevertheless makes them get their letters of introduction from Jerusalem. Regarding the letters' place of origin, Lietzmann writes, 'Jerusalem?', and Plummer says, 'perhaps leading persons in Palestine'. Heinrici denies that the letters of introduction come from Jerusalem, as does Koch. The latter, who regards the opponents as Judaizers, supports his denial with the obvious reason that if the Judaizers could later accept an introduction from a Gentile Christian church like that of Corinth (3.1), they could have brought with them just as good letters from other churches than that in Jerusalem.

while v. 4 presents a hypothetical possibility, then v. 5 too refers to opponents who have come to Corinth. The whole of the following passage, 11.6–12.10, refers to these opponents. Therefore the next verse, 12.11, where the 'superlative apostles' are again mentioned, must have in mind those opponents who are at work in the church. It is only by taking 11.5 and 12.11 out of their context that we can manage to find the twelve earliest disciples mentioned there.[1]

But it will not do to assert that the opponents come from Jerusalem as emissaries either of the twelve or of Judaizing circles there. We know from 11.22 that they are Jews, and as such they may come from almost any city in the eastern part of the Roman empire. If we now assume that they are emissaries from Jerusalem, we are faced with serious difficulties, if we want to regard II Corinthians as one letter. In chs. 8–9 Paul exhorts the Corinthians to contribute voluntarily a generous gift for the poor of the Jerusalem church. It is hardly conceivable that in the same letter Paul opposes emissaries from Jerusalem as Satan's servants, and, untroubled by that fact, tries to raise a generous contribution for the same church. Although modern research may have overlooked this, the Corinthians cannot have done so, and Paul would have been bound to refer to such an apparent or real contradiction. It is only by doubting the apostle's personal trustworthiness that we can manage to circumvent this difficulty (as to this, see pp. 287–89). In that case the arguments in chs. 8–9 do not express his real views, for he knows quite well that he has promised Jerusalem contributions from the Gentile Christian churches, while at the same time he makes the Corinthians imagine that it is a question of a free-will offering.

There is no reason to regard 'some' who need letters of introduction to or from the Corinthians (3.1) as the opponents who are mentioned in chs. 11–12. If the latter really arrived with letters from Jerusalem, we are confronted by the same problem as in the preceding section.

The next verse, 11.6, has caused surprise that Paul should be ἰδιώτης τῷ λόγῳ. If that should be meant to indicate a contrast with the Jewish apostles who have come, it means that the latter were conversant with Greek rhetoric, of which Paul has made no use (cf. I Cor. 1–4). It is therefore natural to suppose that the remark about his weaknesses as a speaker was a criticism of him by the church, such as we know from I Corinthians.[2] Nothing is said here about his opponents' being specially good orators. This gives us another indication that Paul's struggle was with the church, while his opponents, in spite of the uncommonly

---

[1] We also wish to point out that Paul mentions these earliest disciples as 'the twelve', but never as 'the apostles'. See 'Paul, the Apostles and the Twelve', *ST* 3, p. 101 and pp. 103 ff., and the remark on p. 213 of the present book.

[2] That is Koch's opinion, pp. 22 f.

severe attacks in what follows, are only shadows into whom life and substance were infused by the Corinthians' idea of them and enthusiasm for them.

In vv. 7–11 Paul goes into his refusal to accept support from the church in Corinth. Earlier, in I Corinthians, he found himself obliged to go into this question. The Corinthians have taken notice of the fact that he would not allow them to support him (I Cor. 9.3); and in dealing with the right attitude towards the claims of freedom and love (which he discusses in connexion with the question of eating meat sacrificed to idols), he shows them that, although he is an apostle and as such has a claim to support, he has renounced his right in view of the special nature of his apostleship and in order to win as many as possible. If that text is obscure, the text here too, in II Corinthians, is not entirely clear. Here in II Corinthians Paul does not bring forward the real reason for his attitude. He has indeed been able to violate his principle (I Cor. 9.15 f.) elsewhere, but not in Corinth and Achaia. Considerations regarding his opponents may be of decisive importance for the future, but not for the past, as he became needy at Corinth before his opponents had arrived there. He has not allowed himself to be supported by the Corinthians, but in that difficult situation he allowed others to pay for his support in Corinth. That seems to have annoyed the Corinthians. As we may infer from I Thess. 2.7–9, I Cor. 9.15–18, and Phil. 4.15 f., it was Paul's regular practice to be economically independent, the only exception to that rule being the church at Philippi, which had been allowed to support him from the beginning. II Cor. 11.10 f. gives us to understand that the Corinthians were dissatisfied with this, and the outward cause of the reopening of the question is the arrival of the Jewish apostles, who asked for and received support from the church. Now it is regarded as a sign of a lack of love on Paul's part that he accepted support from the Macedonians, but not from the church in Corinth.[1]

In vv. 7–11, together with the following passage in vv. 12–15, this question is broached from a much more serious standpoint. First Paul describes his attitude in the matter, emphasizing clearly that 'other churches' (v. 8)—probably the Macedonians, as in v. 9—have supported him while he was at Corinth. In future this boast of his shall not be silenced in the regions of Achaia (v. 10). This is said without explanation,

[1]One cannot help thinking that Paul was wise enough to know when he could accept support from a church, and when not. And if he had no other reasons to guide him, it would have been wise to refuse the Corinthians' support from the first, as in fact he did. The subsequent story, with the persistent controversies and the church's insubordination, showed that the Corinthians were not people from whom one could accept money or board without being misunderstood. So it was better to say No, and remain independent when the inevitable misunderstandings arose.

so we may think both of the explanation that was given in I Corinthians and of the remark that follows in vv. 12 ff. His opponents are people who boast of being apostles, and as such of accepting support from the churches. The sharp words that now come, about his opponents, might be taken to mean that this right, which Paul has renounced, has gained so much in importance in his opponents' view, that they can on that account be described as false apostles. They have really become itinerant preachers who strive with all their means to satisfy their craving for applause, riches, and fame.[1] But behind Paul's unusually sharp words there lie not only this less serious affair, but the whole great argument between these Jewish apostles and their admirers in Corinth on the one side and Paul on the other side, the former regarding and carrying out their apostleship in such a way that it is becoming clear that Satan, and not Christ, is lord.

This question of the church's money plays no unimportant part in chs. 11–12. In ch. 12.13–18 Paul comes back to it: 'For in what were you less favoured than the rest of the churches, except that I myself did not burden you? Forgive me this wrong!' he says with bitter irony. For the third time he is ready to come to Corinth, and this time too he will not be a burden to them, for (he goes on without any irony), 'I seek not what is yours but you; for children ought not to lay up for their parents, but parents for their children. I will most gladly spend and be spent for your souls. If I love you the more, am I to be loved the less? But granting that I myself did not burden you, I was crafty, you say, and got the better of you by guile. Did I take advantage of you through any of those whom I sent to you? I urged Titus to go, and sent the brother with him. Did Titus take advantage of you? Did we not act in the same spirit? Did we not take the same steps?'

Even before the opponents arrived, the Corinthians had accused Paul of untruthfulness and dishonesty, as we can see in chs. 1–9; and when the quarrel reached its climax it led to these accusations (which are never far away, though they do not appear in the first letter) of mendacity and deception. The same is true of the reproach of his having been guilty of acting irresponsibly because he did not carry out his original plan to visit Corinth twice (1.17 f.).

As early as 1.13 we read, 'For we write you nothing but what you can read and understand. . . .' In 3.13 Paul declines to act deceitfully, as Moses acted who put a veil over his face, so that the Israelites might not see that the splendour was fading from his face. In 4.2 the apostle says, much more clearly, 'We have renounced disgraceful, under-handed ways; we refuse to practise cunning or to tamper with God's

[1]See p. 152 with n. 2 with reference to Dibelius.

word, but by the open statement of the truth we would commend ourselves to every man's conscience in the sight of God.' Again, in 7.2 we
read, 'We have wronged no one, we have corrupted no one, we have
taken advantage of no one.' We may also quote 2.17, 'For we are not,
like so many, peddlers of God's word; but as men of sincerity, as
commissioned by God, in the sight of God we speak in Christ.' We see,
therefore, that the question of Paul's economic independence is an old
problem for the Corinthians, and that their reproach of untruthfulness
and unworthy motives had become vocal during the conflict between
the apostle and the church before the arrival of the Jewish apostles.
One last passage that might be quoted, viz. 11.31 with its solemn
declaration that he is not lying, is meant for the Corinthians, and was
not necessarily written on account of his opponents. But we do not need
to quote this passage as proof that Paul was accused of lying, as we
meet similar strong attestations, not only in Gal. 1.20, but also in
Rom. 9.1.

11.7–12 and 12.13–18 show us that the Corinthians knew nothing
about providing for the maintenance of apostles or their companions
before the visiting Judaizing apostles came. Nor had money been
collected for churches abroad, except for the collection set on foot by
Paul in I Cor. 16.1 ff. for the poor in Jerusalem. But we must assume
that this collection for church purposes outside Corinth was soon
stopped during the general insubordination towards Paul and during
the revolt. In that case the remarks about the collection in II Cor. 8–9
are the first attempt to reanimate what had lain dormant for so long;
and it was a race against time, because Paul would soon be coming to
them on his way to Jerusalem, to take their share of the gift for the poor
Jewish Christians.

Now that the church has submitted, Paul can send his collectors to it
with every hope of collecting a generous gift for the poor in Jerusalem.
From an economic point of view, neither itinerant preachers nor collections had impoverished the church, so that the apostle could count
on great eagerness for the cause and on generosity. But just at that
moment the Jewish apostles come to Corinth with their claim to be
supported. In 11.20 Paul puts it like this, 'For you bear it if a man
makes slaves of you, or preys upon you, or takes advantage of you, or
puts on airs, or strikes you in the face.' It seems as if the visitors exploited their claim to maintenance in a most barefaced way, but that is
not certain; a comparison with the modest behaviour of Paul and his
companions, who did not demand financial support, may be a reason
for drawing an exaggerated picture of the opponents' behaviour. The
great collection among the Gentile Christians for Jerusalem—a matter

to which, as we shall see in ch. 10, Paul gives an important place in the plan of salvation—is in danger of being wrecked in Corinth by those Jewish apostles who in no respect deserve the name of Christ's apostles. The church's economic resources are being drained, and in their enthusiasm for those wonderful apostles the Corinthians are forgetting the poverty-stricken Jewish Christians far away in Jerusalem. It is obvious, even in I Corinthians, that the Corinthians were not able to move beyond their own local Christianity. The apostle's allusions to the universal Church in the whole world point reproachfully to that provincial self-sufficiency (I Cor. 1.2; 4.17; 7.17; 11.16; 14.33).

However, the denunciation of the visiting Jewish apostles in 11.13–15 is not caused by their exercising in a different way the apostle's right to be supported by the church. It may be that they exploited their claim excessively, as is indicated in 11.20; it expresses an unchristian nature, but the matter does not of itself involve disunity. Paul has, in fact, shown clearly in I Cor. 9 that one who preaches the Gospel is to live by it. No, the question is whether they are real apostles, and it is on this point that he attacks them in vv. 13–15. The visiting apostles are false apostles, deceitful workmen. They have only disguised themselves as apostles of Christ, just as Satan has disguised himself as an angel of light. Such servants of Satan imitate their lord and disguise themselves as servants of righteousness, but their end will correspond to their deeds.

The reasons for Paul's condemnation of the apostles who have come from outside are to be sought in the passages that follow. We shall soon see how hard it is to form a picture of them. According to 11.16, 18 they are boasting: 'I repeat, let no one think me foolish; but even if you do, accept me as a fool, so that I too may boast a little;' and 'Since many boast of worldly things, I too will boast'. 10.12–18, which speaks of some who commend themselves, we relate to the Corinthians, but in 11.16, 18 the context shows that the opponents are referred to; Paul has been speaking of them just before. V. 12 deals with their boasting about being apostles (cf. v. 23) and of having the right to be supported by the church, and it is therefore likely that 'too' in v. 16 refers to the opponents' boasting. And this boasting of theirs, whether of their right to support in v. 12, or of their advantages as Jews in v. 22, is a boasting of worldly things.

Unfortunately this talk about commending oneself or boasting does not take us very far. The Corinthians have accused Paul of that very thing: 'Are we beginning to commend ourselves again? Or do we need, as some do, letters of recommendation to you, or from you?' (3.1). In 4.2 Paul uses the expression positively; 'But by the open statement of the truth we would commend ourselves to every man's conscience in

the sight of God'; cf. 6.4, 'But as servants of God we commend ourselves in every way' etc., and in 4.5 f. he goes on, 'For what we preach
is not ourselves, but Jesus Christ as Lord, with ourselves as your servants
for Jesus' sake. For it is the God who said, "Let light shine out of
darkness," who has shone in our hearts to give the light of the knowledge
of the glory of God in the face of Christ.' Finally we read in 5.12 (cf.
v. 11), 'We are not commending ourselves to you again but giving you
cause to be proud of us, so that you may be able to answer those who
pride themselves on a man's position and not on his heart.' The latter
might be the opponents, who are thus alluded to for the first time;
but in this generally expressed form the sentence may be meant for
anyone, and so it may refer to people in the Corinthian church.

This accusation by the Corinthians refers to something that Paul
has done earlier and is still doing in II Corinthians. He is describing the
true apostle, using himself as an example. It is according to his own
portrait that he describes the true apostle to the Corinthians, who up
to the arrival of the Jewish apostles knew none but Paul. He is convinced
that he has acted rightly towards them and has really shown them what
the true apostle looks like. For him such observations are of a purely
objective nature, and are not to be regarded as self-commendation.

As the Corinthians have reproached Paul with commending himself,
and as he accuses both them and his opponents of this, we have in these
accusations the language that one uses to opponents. When the expression 'boast of worldly things' is deliberately used in 11.18, the same thing
is true here, for the Corinthians have reproached the apostle with being
worldly and behaving in a worldly way (see pp. 175 f.).

We must therefore find out what the opponents are boasting of. We
know from 11.12 that they are boasting of the apostolic right to support
from the churches; and we now learn in 11.22 f. what else they are
boasting of: 'Are they Hebrews? So am I. Are they Israelites? So am I.
Are they descendants of Abraham? So am I. Are they servants of
Christ? I am a better one—I am talking like a madman.' The last question shows that they are boasting of being servants of Christ, and this
accords with their boasting in 11.12. We see from the other questions
that the opponents are Jews. As we do not know (see later, pp. 218 f.)
who 'the Hebrews' are, we learn nothing more about the opponents
from this description. As Paul is himself a Hebrew (here and Phil. 3.5),
this description cannot mean exclusively Palestinian Jews; and so we
are given no information as to where these Jews live or where they come
from (cf. pp. 177 f.).

It is therefore very little indeed that we learn about the opponents.
As we saw above (pp. 171–73), it has been thought that they tried to

undermine Paul's authority in the church so as to establish themselves
and their own preaching. But we can say nothing certain about their
attacks on Paul. The passages that have been thus interpreted really
contain accusations that the church has made in the past and is still
making against him—that is, both during the culmination of the struggle
at the time of the intermediate visit and at the time of the submission.

But the passage 11.22–12.10 brings us the key to the question of the
contrast between Paul and the Jewish apostles. He says that they are
servants of Christ far less than he himself, because they have had far
fewer 'weaknesses' (11.23 ff.). The true apostle does not boast of the
flesh, as the opponents are reproached with doing. We see in chs. 11–12
what a great effort Paul has to make when he tries to boast, and how,
when he has got so far as to boast, he boasts of something that contrasts strongly with any object of ordinary worldly praise. The true
apostle always carries in his body the death of Jesus (4.10); and the
suffering apostle is therefore the true apostle, while the false apostle
seeks his own honour in what seems to the worldly and fleshly man to
be valuable.

Here, then, is the explanation of Paul's strong words. As we have
seen, the opponents are not Judaizers, and we know nothing at all of
their doctrine; but if they preached anything, it cannot be false doctrine,
as Paul refrains from any attack on them on that point. On the other
hand, we know as regards their ethical code that they boast of worldly
things (11.16, 18), of their advantages as Jews (11.22), and of their
position as apostles (11.12) and as 'servants of Christ' (11.23). We learn
in another passage (Phil. 3.3 ff.) how Paul as a Christian regarded his
advantages as a Jew, and here in this letter he has tried hard to explain
to the Corinthians how the true apostle appears, and that, far from
being able to boast of honour and power, he is, like Jesus, a suffering
and dying figure, whose work and power and victory arise from his
weakness and infirmity and defeat.

This question is the vital thing in Paul's conflict with the Corinthians.
Although they have been taught by him and must have known what the
qualities of the true apostle were, they made themselves a picture of the
Christian leader, even before I Corinthians, as a man who had honour
and power in this world (I Cor. 1–4); and II Corinthians shows that
the continuing conflict with the church, reaching its climax during the
intermediate visit, was over this very question. It is not merely a
question of apostleship, for the apostle and his gospel are identical.[1]

---

[1]See A. Fridrichsen, *The Apostle and his Message*, 1947 (Inbjudning till Teologie
Doktorspromotionen vid Uppsala Universitet den 31.5. 1947), pp. 8 f. See also
Fridrichsen in *Norsk Teol. Tidsskrift* 13, 1912, p. 250.

In the true apostle there is also seen true Christianity, while the Christian leaders as imagined by the Corinthians are the embodiment of this world and its ruler.

When the Corinthians have submitted to Paul after receiving his severe letter, they choose to follow the true apostle and to lead the life that his gospel preaches—'(God's) power is made perfect in weakness' (12.9); but his exhortations in II Corinthians show how much they still had to learn. His instruction is concerned with the contrast between the false apostle for whom they have longed and whom they have wanted to imitate, and the true apostle who has belonged to them all the time in Paul's person, but whom they had not been able to appreciate properly, and whom they have not wished to follow along the way of suffering.[1]

Just at the moment when the dispute has culminated and the church has submitted, so that Paul can instruct them in what they are lacking, something unexpected happens. A few Jewish Christians, who are apostles—either emissaries of other churches or missionaries sent by Christ—come to Corinth. We do not know whether they preached in the church, and in any case they did not preach false doctrine, let alone a Judaizing one. In the matter of claiming support from the church they seem to have followed the usual manners and customs—possibly with certain divergencies. We know very little about them—to their disadvantage or otherwise. It is certain that such travelling brethren often went through other Pauline churches, had meals there, and took part in the services, without giving occasion for special comment.

It seems that what settled Paul's attitude towards them was the fact that they came when they did. They could have chosen no worse moment. The quarrel turned upon the true and the false apostle, and after a long struggle the Corinthians had given way and were willing to receive instruction about the true apostle and his true gospel. But at that point there came to Corinth some Jewish apostles, who were different from Paul and his picture of the true apostle, as the church was not slow to realize. Here were people who liked to sing their own praises, and who could boast about their advantages as Jews as well as about their authority as Christians. For them the mystery of the apostle and the Gospel was not in suffering.

The Corinthians received them kindly, and gave them what they asked. There was also a certain enthusiasm for these Christian apostles from outside. It is possible that Paul overestimated the impression that they made on the Corinthians. For him the vital factor was the present danger that the easily influenced Corinthians, who were at last set on the right road, might now through these false apostles again fall a prey

[1] 2.14–7.4, especially 4.7–18 and 6.1–10.

to their former errors, and that he might again have the experience of seeing the church—a difficult church, but one that was dear to him—heading for perdition.

In this way the Jewish apostles are not really Paul's opponents. As to their attempt to undermine his authority inside the church we know nothing; and we must reject the charge that they preached a different gospel from his. But their demeanour showed that they were serving Satan by their apostleship, and that their gospel was therefore a false message. The real opponents, here as elsewhere in the letter, are the Corinthians themselves, their false picture of the apostle, which now finds support in the behaviour of the apostles from outside, and their continued difficulty in humbling themselves under the suffering Christ and his suffering apostle and the message of the suffering for the Church in the world. So, in spite of the changing tone, the letter is a whole, and all of it is meant for the Corinthians. The visiting apostles are only a subordinate theme, which has become important because the Corinthians saw something great in them and their demeanour, and because Paul thought he saw in them a temptation to apostasy.

We still have to add a few remarks about 12.1–10. This text has been taken to mean that Paul's opponents are spiritual men, and that the apostle therefore feels obliged here to write about his visions and revelations, so as to show that he is himself a spiritual man, and a better one than the visiting apostles. This interpretation would presuppose that Paul began this section intending to boast of his visions, but that by degrees his intention changed, so that he became quite restrained in his boasting, and added that a thorn in the flesh was given him to keep him from being too elated. Such an interpretation, which assumes that he did not reflect before he began to write, is quite improbable. The section should be regarded as a unity, as Paul is thinking from the beginning about the contrast between the glorious revelations and the thorn in the flesh. His enumeration of his sufferings (11.23 ff.) is therefore concluded by this piece about the infinite gifts which Christ bestows on his apostle and which are a complement of the sufferings. In this way the section ends, like the earlier descriptions of the true apostle, with a contrast between inward glory and outward failure.[1]

Here again we have a description of the true apostle, loaded with gifts from his Lord and with suffering in the world. Outwardly the high honour that his service brings with it is unnoticed. His own existence is

---

[1]Cf. II Cor. 1.5 f., 9; 2.14–16; 4.7–18, especially v. 16; 6.3–10. As stated later (p. 325 n. 2), I agree with Koch (pp. 433–48) in taking the 'thorn in the flesh' to refer to the apostle's sufferings caused by incessant persecutions.

characterized by death; out of it there grows life, and only in that life can his service for Christ be recognized; and that is what makes it so easy for worldly Christians to despise the apostle, to think themselves his equal, and to defy him and his authority. The emissaries, skilled speakers who can boast of their advantages that make a noise in the world, arouse quite a different kind of pleasure, and may achieve high honours even inside the Church. But the Christlike apostle knows no better conditions than his Master. His honour may be violated, his life is in constant danger, and his death is not far off. But where honour and respect are bestowed on the false apostle, who is praised by the churches and the world without distinction, the true apostle reveals his outward weakness, and yet he is the emissary of Jesus Christ, whose message he carries and whose power he possesses. But if he carries out his task thus, his 'earthen vessel' has to bear the burden of that service by which life is given to others, while his portion is death.

IV

In what has been written above we have regarded the settling of the questions that stood between Paul and his opponents in II Corinthians as part of what he had to do to reach an understanding with the church.

That church had caused him difficulties from the first. Even before our I Corinthians Paul wrote a letter to the Corinthians, telling them 'not to associate with immoral men' (I Cor. 5.9). The Corinthians misunderstood that letter, and that is not the only misunderstanding between the apostle and that church.

We see in fact in I Corinthians that the Corinthians regard Christianity from the point of view of their Greek background—it is a form of wisdom (chs. 1–4) bestowed on them here and now as a gift of the kingdom of God (4.8 ff.). There is therefore no future resurrection or day of judgment to be expected (ch. 15), and the Corinthians are so perfect that they can regard everything as permissible from the ethical point of view (chs. 5–7), and yet at the same time demand that all Christians take the most advanced standpoint (chs. 8–10, 11–14). Behind that façade of spiritual wealth and intellectual progress there is always lurking an inward instability and a lack of love. There is a great deal to argue out with the Corinthians, and the apostle does not spare them; but he does not forget to comment encouragingly on the good points, when he can do so with a good conscience.

The letter hardly had a friendly reception in Corinth, for in spite of his urbane manner, the apostle had criticized them unsparingly. He had gone right to the heart of things that were dearest to them—their boastfulness about Christianity, their own fictitious gospel, and their fanatical appeal to the Holy Spirit when they were following their own desires. We can see in II Corinthians that all this, which the apostle censured in I Corinthians, has been living on in the church and is again dealt with by him.

Even if there were other reasons too, we must suppose that this disastrous development in the church during the period after I Corinthians was Paul's main reason for wanting to interfere by another visit. But that visit was a complete fiasco; the church rose in open rebellion, and one church member behaved particularly defiantly (II Cor. 2.5–11; cf. 7.11–12). The demand later made by Paul for the punishment of the church member showed that the latter's conduct was not condemned by the church, which must have been jointly responsible for it.[1]

The expressions used about this unhappy visit are so vague that we cannot say much about it; but it is clear that the Corinthians denied Paul's right to give them instructions, and rebelled against his apostolic authority. So he found himself compelled to say to them, 'If I come again I will not spare (you)' (13.2).

When Paul returned from that ill-fated visit, he wrote a letter confronting the church with an ultimatum—it is to submit to the apostle and show its obedience in various ways, in the first place by punishing the church member concerned (2.3–9; 7.8–12). He wrote that letter out of much affliction and anguish of heart and with many tears (2.4), for the purpose of testing them and knowing whether they were obedient in everything (2.9). Now he rejoices that the letter has caused godly grief, which produces a repentance that leads to salvation and brings no regret. Worldly grief, on the other hand, produces death (7.9 f.). And the apostle describes to the Corinthians the fruits of that godly grief: 'For see what earnestness this godly grief has produced in you, what eagerness to clear yourselves, what indignation, what alarm, what longing, what zeal, what punishment!' The Corinthians have shown that at every point they have proved themselves guiltless in the matter (7.11). Now, after the event, the Corinthians have dissociated their case from the one who did wrong, although earlier they had allowed him to rise against Paul and had not disavowed his action; indeed, they may have regarded his behaviour as expressing a view that was backed by the whole church. Paul will let that pass, but he will not allow the church now to push off all the guilt on to the individual. He is satisfied with the punishment that was inflicted on him by the majority (2.6); and in ch. 7 too he concludes his remarks about the letter by saying that his earlier

---

[1]The postponement of this episode to Paul's second visit to Corinth goes back to Weizsäcker (cf. *The Apostolic Age* I, ET 1894, pp. 341–46).

demand for the punishment of that one person had been intended to test the church (7.12).

If we consider how Paul succeeded in bringing this church, which was always being difficult, round to his own point of view, even when, as now, it was in open revolt, it is natural to point to his own personal gifts as a man and a speaker. If his letters still have such a powerful effect on us, how much more must their first readers have felt their force, even when the sting was directed against themselves. But that is not an adequate explanation. Although Paul had written I Corinthians and was later with the Corinthians in person, he had not succeeded in getting the better of their pride, wilfulness, and self-satisfaction, and their boasting of their home-made Christianity, all expressed in their rejection of the apostle and his gospel. This called for quite different methods.

An ultimatum presupposes two possibilities. They may submit in obedience to the apostle, as in fact they did. That leads to the situation in II Corinthians, where he acknowledges their obedience and at the same time tries to repair all the damage that their disobedience had involved, and to remedy all the things in which it had its roots. But what was the other possibility, which fortunately did not become a reality?

In spite of all the mildness in II Corinthians, there are threats contained here too, and we hear in ch. 13 that when Paul returns he will not spare the Corinthians. They demand proof that Christ is speaking in Paul, and they will get it if he punishes in a way that they do not expect and that he himself is anxious to avoid (13.2 ff., cf. 10.2–6). As a rule the commentators express themselves very vaguely about these severe words of Paul's. But Koch is surely right in saying that what is in mind here is not severe church discipline with exclusion from the church. That would assume the church's co-operation and therefore fresh negotiations. No, the apostle feels that he is acting single-handed; he has come to see clearly how he will interfere, and his programme obviously contains no point on which he needs other people's approval. They must comply or take the consequences.[1]

The way in which Paul speaks in 10.2 and especially in 13.7 about what he may have to do shows that he is thinking of something much worse than excommunication in the modern sense. In the latter passage we read, 'But we pray God that you may not do wrong—not that we may appear to have met the test, but that you may do what is right, though we may seem to have failed.' The clearest passage is 13.3 f.,

---

[1]Koch, p. 366 (on 10.11). So too P. W. Schmiedel, 'Die Briefe an die Thessalonicher und an die Korinther', *Hand-Commentar zum NT* II, p. 302 (on 13.2).

where the apostle says that he will bring them proof that it is Christ who is speaking in him, and that God's power will be effective in dealing with them. Koch thinks that Paul intends to inflict some miraculous punishment similar to that mentioned in I Cor. 5.4 f.: σὺν τῇ δυνάμει τοῦ Κυρίου ἡμῶν Ἰησοῦ παραδοῦναι τὸν τοιοῦτον τῷ σατανᾷ εἰς ὄλεθρον τῆς σαρκός. He alludes to this with τὸ ἔργον in 10.11: οἷοί ἐσμεν τῷ λόγῳ δι' ἐπιστολῶν ἀπόντες, τοιοῦτοι καὶ παρόντες τῷ ἔργῳ. Thus the apostle feels himself master of the situation; cf. Acts 5.1 ff., 13.9 ff.

This interpretation helps us to understand the second possibility in Paul's ultimatum to the Corinthian church in the severe letter—that is, the possibility that was to be tried if the church did not submit. If in that letter church discipline was demanded in respect of the church member whose conduct had caused grief, and if here in the last letter before Paul's arrival in Corinth the fear is expressed that the apostle may have to inflict a miraculous punishment if the Corinthians' obedience is not complete, it shows that a still more terrible possibility had been mentioned in the severe letter. If the church would not give way and comply with the demands that the apostle put forward to test its obedience, he intended to deliver the church over to Satan, and in that way to separate it from Christ and expose it to the sufferings which Satan controls.[1]

So we can understand the apostle's great distress, the fear in his heart, and his many tears. It was now a matter of bending or breaking. The apostle saw the abyss opening in front of him, and his friends and children in Christ vanishing in a satanic darkness even thicker than that from which his preaching had once delivered them. He would have the task of pronouncing the crushing sentence on a once flourishing Christian community, on the results of his own work, and on his incessant labours over a long period.

We know from the Gospels Jesus' lamentations over the Galilean towns in which he had worked (Matt. 11.20–24 and par.), and we know that the missionaries whom he sent out were to shake off the dust from their feet against a town that would not receive them (Matt. 10.14 f. and par.). And we hear in the passages quoted by Koch (Acts 5.1–11 and I Cor. 5.1 ff.) about the church discipline by which individual members of a church were handed over to Satan. But the only parallels to what is mentioned here by Paul are in Rev. 2.5 (cf. 2.16—not the whole church in this case; 3.3; 3.16). As Paul's view, like that of the apocalyptic writer, is determined by the eschatological hope, there is no difference between Christ's threatening summons to the churches in Asia Minor to repent in the last days and the apostle's threatening

[1] So too Knox, *St Paul*, pp. 101 ff.

letter during his apocalyptic missionary journey through the Gentile world.[1]

Although the severe letter achieves its object, and the apostle can speak comparatively lightly about it afterwards when the alternative terrifying possibility has been avoided, it is noticeable throughout the letter how very seriously he is considering the possibility of perdition. With all his joy over the Corinthians' obedience and his anxiety about all that they still have to achieve, his thoughts keep on returning to the terrible possibility that has been hanging over them, but has now, thank God, not materialized. The apostle cannot forget what runs like an undertone through all his joy. The letter is like the sea after a storm, when the wind has died down and the heaving waters still testify to the mighty forces that have been unleashed.

Again and again the thought is expressed that although the Corinthians are in the way of salvation, the way of perdition lies close by it. Paul hopes that the Corinthians will 'understand fully' (1.13), 'as you have understood in part, that you can be proud of us as we can be of you, on the day of the Lord Jesus' (1.14). His remark, 'But it is God who establishes us with you in Christ, and has commissioned us' (1.21), is also important. Paul's conduct towards the Corinthian church has been determined by his consideration for them, 'to keep Satan from gaining the advantage over us, for we are not ignorant of his designs' (2.11). The rebellion in the church was caused by Satan, who is trying to ruin the Christian churches, and is fighting particularly against the apostle himself (cf. 11.3).[2] When Paul describes his apostolic labours, then 'we are the aroma of Christ to God among those who are being saved and among those who are perishing, to one a fragrance from death to death, to the other a fragrance from life to life' (2.15 f.). The dispensation of condemnation in the figure of Moses is contrasted with the dispensation of righteousness in Christ (3.9). As in 2.15 f., there is in 4.3 f. a duality in the preaching of the Gospel—the Gospel is 'veiled only to those who are perishing. In their case the god of this world has blinded the minds of the unbelievers, to keep them from seeing the light of the gospel', etc. In 6.1 ff. Paul says with great earnestness, 'Working together with him, then, we entreat you not to accept the grace of God in vain' (6.1). In 6.14–7.1, a passage that is most frequently regarded separately as a fragment of a Pauline letter, there is a call to conversion, as for instance, 'What accord has Christ with Belial? Or what has a believer in common with an unbeliever?' (6.15). And

---

[1] The effect of the letter can be seen not only in 2.1 ff. and 7.8 ff. which refer to the pain that it caused, but even more in 7.11, which was quoted above (p. 188), and in 7.15, 'the fear and trembling with which you received him' (Titus).

[2] Cf. B. Noack, *Satanas und Soteria*, 1948, pp. 92 ff.

in 7.9 f. it is said clearly that the severe letter led the Corinthians into being grieved into repenting, 'for you felt a godly grief. . . . For godly grief produces a repentance that leads to salvation and brings no regret, but worldly grief produces death'. In the chapters that follow we find only scanty material; but it is there that we meet the weighty passage that was referred to above (11.3), 'But I am afraid that as the serpent deceived Eve by his cunning, your thoughts will be led astray from a sincere and pure devotion to Christ.' The Corinthians may perish quickly through the careless acceptance of a different gospel (11.4), but Satan's servants who bring that false gospel will meet with an end that accords with their deeds (11.15). Again in 13.5 Paul says to the Corinthians, 'Examine yourselves, to see whether you are holding to your faith. Test yourselves. Do you not realize that Jesus Christ is in you?—unless indeed you fail to meet the test!' In connexion with the threat, in the preceding verses, of a miraculous punishment, there can be no doubt that the Corinthians themselves are to test whether they are Christians before the apostle's sentence of punishment falls on them. If we compare these texts from II Corinthians with I Corinthians, we shall discover that the admonitions in the latter are to a much greater degree spoken to people who are regarded as belonging to the Church. The more serious tone and the references to the two possibilities, salvation and perdition, are characteristic of II Corinthians.

Once the severe letter had been sent off to Corinth, uncertainty and suspense gave the apostle no rest; he was still a constant prey to the distress and tears that had been with him while he was writing the letter. For example, when he came to Troas to preach the Gospel of Christ, 'a door was opened for me in the Lord; but my mind could not rest because I did not find my brother Titus there. So I took leave of them and went on to Macedonia' (2.12 f.). Either Titus had been sent with the severe letter, or he had set off shortly after its dispatch to report on its effect. In either case it was probably his task, if the effect had been favourable, to help the repentant church to a new beginning in its relation to the apostle. But till Titus has returned Paul has no rest. What he tells is not the expression of excited nerves or unstable *psyche*, but denotes an exceptional state. He has been so tortured by uncertainty that he, a man who could not help going on with his apostolic work, wherever he was, had to let his work go for once, so much had he the Corinthian church at heart.

Our II Corinthians was written on Titus' return or soon afterwards. The turning-point has been passed, and the church has submitted; but much remains to be settled before Paul can come to them in full happiness (2.1, 3) and exhort them once more before leaving the east for the last time to go on to his missionary work in the west.[1]

In the first seven chapters Paul reveals what he has experienced in relation to the Corinthian church since the severe letter, and in doing so he makes long digressions to prevent misunderstandings, and gives instructions in the right understanding of his conduct and apostolic work. He describes the state of mind in which he wrote the severe letter (2.1–11; cf. 7.8–12), and the restlessness that tormented him in the uncertainty about the Corinthians' reception of the letter (2.12 f.). He broke off a very promising piece of missionary work and went on through Macedonia so as to meet Titus as quickly as possible. Then he expresses his overflowing joy that the Corinthians have given the answer that he hoped for (7.5–16). That description of the apostle's personal state (1.8–11) and his relation to the church (1.12 ff.), with the many interruptions to justify himself or instruct the church, reminds us of I Thess. 1–3. In this letter we hear of his visit to Thessalonica, of how he had to leave the church, of his fruitless attempts to return, and of his sending Timothy, who brings him gratifying and reassuring news. And here too the account is interrupted for Paul to defend himself against accusations (I Thess. 2.3–12). This Pauline style of letter-writing breathes love and trust in spite of all the interwoven remarks and rebuttals of accusations.

When this first part of the letter is finished, the account that Paul is writing about himself has reached the point of time at which he is writing it. In the next main division of the letter (chs. 8–9) he gives advice on the collection that is about to be made for the poor in Jerusalem. We can infer from 8.16 ff. (cf. 7.13–16) that the bearer of II Corinthians is Titus, who is here the subject of the kindly praise that Paul so likes to give his fellow-workers when they are setting off on a journey and are to have an introduction to the churches. If we want to suggest the separation of any part of II Corinthians (cf. pp. 168–71), it is easiest to take out chs. 8–9. While there is controversy in chs. 1–7 and in chs. 10–13, nothing comparable is found in these two chapters that deal with the collection. For example, the other two parts of the letter contain Paul's answer to the church that accuses him of untruthfulness and dishonesty, but in 8.20 he writes without any reference to those accusations, 'We intend that no one should blame us about this liberal gift which we are administering.' That gives the impression that Paul may here be using almost formal expressions about the collection, without reflecting that the Corinthians might profitably receive a little correction on that point.

[1] This is not stated in II Corinthians, but we know about it from Rom. 15.23 f.

In chs. 10–13 the tone is sharper than before. From the very beginning Paul is uttering threats of miraculous punishments (10.2 ff.; cf. 13.2 ff.). The church's obedience is at stake because of some visiting Jewish apostles, whose behaviour and boasting of their Jewish and Christian advantages are endangering the continued submission and improvement of the Corinthians. Although we have no writings by Paul that fit in with this section, the ideas that it contains are familiar as a whole to us from chs. 1–7, some of them indeed from I Corinthians.

V

Paul's struggle with the Corinthians is vitally concerned with the apostleship.[1] Even in I Corinthians he had to define his position with regard to their fundamental misunderstanding in regarding the Christian teachers as teachers of wisdom. As the church did not receive that letter in the right spirit, but again manifested its obstinate attitude, Paul had to assert his authority as apostle. The severe letter gave them to understand beyond the shadow of a doubt that he was Christ's emissary to the Corinthians, with authority to command and to require submission. Now after the event, when they have submitted, he gives full expression to his love for them. He writes like a father who was compelled to punish his children, and who, when his children submit to the punishment and show penitence, ceases to punish, wants to explain his actions, and tries to renew the loving relation that indeed underlay all the chastisement.

We have already pointed out that it was not a Judaizing movement which caused the Corinthians to take up the struggle against Paul's apostleship; and we showed in ch. 5 that they thought they found the Greek rhetorician, with his eloquent religious and philosophical sermons, in the Christian teachers, whom they regarded as teachers of wisdom. During the further struggle it is the charges that we know from I Thess. 2.3 ff., against itinerant preachers and teachers of all categories, that we meet in the church's accusations against the apostle.

Paul's picture of the true apostle in II Corinthians is no improvisation; we already have it in I Cor. 4.8–13. If the paradoxical relation between suffering and glory, so characteristic of II Corinthians, is absent here, that is to be attributed to the ironical nature of the text, with only shame and suffering as the subject. But the irony of this passage assumes that only half the truth is told, and the enumeration of sufferings in II Corinthians shows what is left out.

Paul not only told of the true apostle's life; he lived it too. But he

[1]Cf. Käsemann, *ZNW* 41, pp. 48 ff.

found it difficult to carry out what was demanded of him as an apostle. He would have liked to stand there as the powerless man and look on the Corinthians as strong men; but instead of that he had to be strong and forceful, rebuking them, threatening them, and being ready to hand them over to Satan. The sincerity of his loving words to the church is shown by the fact that he does not abandon it, even though his doing so would enable him to proceed unhindered with his great plans, first for the collection for Jerusalem, and then for the mission in the west. On the contrary, he gives himself time, he visits the Corinthians and writes to them; and his patience bears fruit. He succeeds in keeping the church with Christ.

7

THE MANIFESTO OF FAITH
Comments on Romans

THE letter to the Romans, like Paul's other great letters, has been regarded as evidence of the contrast between Jewish and Gentile Christianity. Although it is clear that this letter is directed to Gentile Christians, it has been thought that it was written to a mainly Jewish Christian church;[1] or people have found in the discussion about the weak and the strong in Rom. 14–15.6 a contrast between Jewish and Gentile Christians, whereby it has been supposed that the church was predominantly Gentile Christian but with a large minority of Jewish Christians.

In part the arguments for these views have been sought in the subjects with which Paul deals in the letter—and which, it was supposed, presuppose Jewish Christian readers—and partly in people's belief that they were bound to find Jewish and Gentile Christians in the Roman church; and so they searched through the letter for traces of those contrasts.

The form of the letter to the Romans is rather different from that of Paul's other letters, and some scholars are of the opinion that it was intended to present Christian doctrine and to convince people of its truth.[2] This line of thought has been given greater emphasis by the numerous systematic theologians who have concerned themselves with the letter, which has thus very largely been regarded as a timeless presentation of Christian theology, and less interest has been shown in the circumstances connected with it, whether they were to be sought in Rome or with the writer. Another reason for this unfortunate development was that people took over from traditional Pauline research the view that Paul's theology, 'Paulinism', had originated independently of the rest of the Christian world, its problems, and its theological work. Modern commentators are therefore as a rule disinclined to relate the letter's contents to the rest of the New Testament writings.

[1]Thus Baur, *Paul* I, pp. 321 ff.
[2]Baur protests against any such assumption, p. 325.

196

I

However, there is no need to stop at these two possibilities, and to assume either that Paul is addressing himself to a church in which Jewish and Gentile Christians live side by side in a state of tension, or that the letter was written with no regard to his position and no consideration of the people who were to read the letter.

Thanks to an article by T. W. Manson, 'St Paul's Letter to the Romans—and Others',[1] it is possible to get beyond these traditional ways of putting the problem. For Manson the problem takes this form: Was Romans in its present form originally composed in one piece and destined for the church in Rome, and sent to it in the same form as we now possess? Manson arrives at this question by means of two preparatory investigations which concern the beginning and the last two chapters of the letter. First he investigates the evidence of the manuscripts in which the word 'Rome' does not appear in 1.7 and 1.15, the letter not appearing in these as addressed to the Romans. As with Ephesians, the manuscripts do not agree on the address.

Manson then inquires where Romans ends. The closing doxology, 16.25–27, appears in three different places in the traditional text of Romans—at the end of ch. 14, ch. 15, and ch. 16. A letter to the Romans that ends with ch. 14 goes back to Marcion, but it is a question how much he had to cut away to obtain that result. In the oldest Greek MS. of Paul that we possess, P[46], a third-century codex containing the Pauline letters,[2] the doxology is at the end of ch. 15, i.e., between the personal remarks to the church in Rome and ch. 16 with the many greetings to people specially named. We may infer from this that a text of Romans without ch. 16 existed before P[46] was written. A hundred years ago David Schulz put forward the hypothesis that Rom. 16 is a letter to Ephesus. This suggestion is now supported by P[46]. Rom. 1–15 thus seems to be the letter that Paul sent to Rome; and so Marcion, who published his Pauline text in the west, removed only ch. 15 from his original in Rome, as ch. 16 was already missing from the Roman text.

Rom. 1–15 in P[46] therefore shows us the form in which the letter was received in Rome, but the original pre-Marcion text has been altered by the insertion of the doxology and the addition of ch. 16. This chapter was probably added in Egypt. But how are we to explain

---

[1] *BJRL* 31, 1948, pp. 224–40. The next 4 pages summarize this article.
[2] The leaves of this codex, which were acquired partly through the University of Michigan and partly by Chester Beatty, have been published together by F. G. Kenyon as *The Chester Beatty Biblical Papyri*, Fasc. 3, supplement, Pauline Epistles, Text, 1936. Romans is on pp. 1–21.

that, apart from Marcion's curtailed edition which ends with ch. 14, Romans exists in two forms, one comprising the 15 and the other the 16 chapters of the letter?

The hypothesis that Rom. 16 is a letter to Ephesus has a strong argument in the many greetings to friends and acquaintances whom one would hardly expect in a church that Paul has never visited; and moreover, the friends whom we already know have connexions with Asia and Ephesus. At the same time the exhortation in 16.17–20 is natural if addressed to a church that Paul himself founded and where he worked for several years, but not if addressed to a church that he did not know. Lietzmann criticizes this hypothesis sharply by saying, 'A letter consisting of practically nothing but greetings, as ch. 16.1–23 would if it were a separate letter, is an absurdity' (p. 129).

But since then P[46] has been published and throws fresh light on the question. We may now take it that Paul wrote and sent to Rome a letter that consisted of Rom. 1–15. At the same time a copy of the letter was made, to be sent to Ephesus. That copy also contained the personal remarks in 15.14–33, which were originally intended for the church in Rome, but which contained explanations about Paul's plans that were of interest in Ephesus too. What follows then in ch. 16 is an introduction for Phoebe (who may have been the bearer of the letter) to which Paul added his greetings to his friends in Asia, and the exhortation in vv. 17–20. These additions to the letter form a unity with the first fifteen chapters which were sent to Rome, so that the letter that was sent to Ephesus forms a whole. This document then, as a copy, found its way to Egypt at an early period.

The Roman text, which forms the basis of Marcion's text of Romans, and the Ephesian text were worked in together during the text's later history, as we see in P[46], ch. 16 of the Ephesian text, which was the usual one in Egypt, having been added to the Roman text, which ended with ch. 15.

If the letter was written to Ephesus as well as to Rome, we have to consider Paul's motives for writing. As long as the letter was regarded simply as being addressed to Rome, the purpose of such a comprehensive presentation of the faith was supposed to be to obtain for the apostle a friendly reception in the church at Rome and support for the Spanish missionary enterprise. But if it was written in Corinth and sent to both Rome and Ephesus, we must reconsider the matter.

The letter was written in Corinth at the end of a bitter and violent struggle that involved the church in Corinth and the Galatian churches, and if the letter to the Philippians originates from the third journey, the Macedonian churches were also involved. The dispute was about the relation between Judaism and Christianity, the Law and the Gospel. Those questions were discussed passionately in Galatians and in Phil. 3, and more calmly in II Cor. 3–6; and finally they are discussed thoroughly and comprehensively in the first eleven chapters of Romans, where we find Paul's well-considered views on them. If we study the presentation of the argument in detail, we can hardly escape the conclusion that we have here the report of an actual discussion. Again and again Paul meets objections and encounters criticism of his own point of view. Are they only imaginary objections and hypothetical criticisms, or have they to do with discussions that really took place? Manson thinks it is a report of an actual discussion that was recorded by Paul and his colleagues. The arrangement and presentation presumably come from Paul himself, but the material is for the most part taken from the debate.

This impression is confirmed when we turn to the sections of the letter that deal with the Christian life, 12.1–15.13. Ch. 12 speaks of the Church's unity and organic cohesion, a question that was very important in relation to the church in Corinth, where factions had formed. 13.1–10 treats of the Church's relation to the authorities, a question that had presented itself in another connexion in I Cor. 6. Then 13.11–14 touches questions into which I Cor. 15 had entered in greater detail. Finally 14.1–15.13 deals with the problems that had been taken up earlier in I Cor. 8–10.

These observations seem to show that Romans is essentially a summing-up of the point of view that Paul had reached during the long struggle that begins in I Corinthians and Phil. 3. When he had worked out his statement of the case satisfactorily, he decided to send a copy of it to his friends in Ephesus, whom he did not intend to visit on his journey to Jerusalem (Acts 20.3, 16). That copy was to be used to enlighten the churches in Asia. At the same time he had the idea of sending a copy to Rome with a statement of his future plans. Possibly a copy remained behind in Corinth, but that need not be so, as the contents of the letter had presumably been discussed in detail with the members of the church there.

The situation therefore is that the Corinthian church has had the apostle's complete statement of the case by word of mouth. The church in Syria and Palestine can expect to hear about it in the same way in the near future. The church in Asia and the Roman church will be informed in writing. If we consider Romans in this way, it ceases to be merely a letter in which Paul introduces himself to the church in Rome; it becomes a manifesto presenting his deepest convictions on vital points and claiming the widest publicity, to secure which the apostle strives with all his might.

This valuable investigation by T. W. Manson is of great importance for any future treatment of Romans. It enables us to get a new understanding of the letter, by having regard to Paul's situation at the time when at the end of the third missionary journey he was getting ready to go to Jerusalem and afterwards to Spain. On one or two details I do not entirely agree with Manson; I think, for instance, that the background of the letter in the east is not only the struggle over the Law, but also the other struggles that we have been able to describe in chs. 5 and 6.

If we adopt Manson's view, scholars need no longer look in the church at Rome for the background of the letter to the Romans. We know nothing certain about that church, except what the letter tells us directly or indirectly; and if we follow Manson, our views on Rome are clarified merely by what the letter tells us directly, while indirect inferences from it can no longer be used to draw a picture of the Roman church.

At the same time, the fact that Manson has placed the letter in a particular situation in Paul's life has invalidated another widespread assumption, namely that it is a theological presentation unaffected by time and history. Paul certainly sets out his thoughts in the letter, but that is done in conjunction with a quite definite situation in his work as a missionary among the Gentiles. Thus it becomes possible for us to read Romans as a missionary's contribution to a discussion, and not as a theological work.

From Manson's view, with which we agree, it follows that Romans tells us nothing about Judaizing movements in the church at Rome; and so we have no reason to concern ourselves any further with this question. We are glad to stop at this point, referring the reader to a work dealing with Rom. 9–11, with some reflections on the letter's *Sitz im Leben*.[1]

II

We propose instead to examine a problem that has claimed a good deal of time and thought, and to try to substitute a clearer conception for the not very clear solutions at which people have generally stopped short. We refer to the composition of the Pauline churches. Were they essentially Jewish Christian or essentially Gentile Christian, or did they consist of a Gentile Christian majority with a large Jewish Christian minority? We shall try to show here that the Pauline churches were purely Gentile Christian. Even if a few Jewish Christians were to be found in them here and there, they were so few that it was of no

[1]*Christus und Israel, eine Auslegung von Röm. 9–11*, 1956.

importance, so that even those churches can rightly be regarded as purely Gentile Christian.

If we look at each of Paul's letters separately, there is no doubt in the case of several of them; it is said plainly that the readers are Gentile Christians. That is so, for instance, with the church in Thessalonica; in I Thess. 1.9 Paul says of the conversion of the Thessalonians to Christianity, '. . . how you turned to God from idols'. We can also refer to 2.14, which reads, 'For you, brethren, became imitators of the churches of God in Christ Jesus which are in Judaea; for you suffered the same things from your own countrymen as they did from the Jews.' This must mean that the Thessalonians suffered the same things from their Gentile fellow-countrymen as the churches of Judaea from the Palestinian Jews.

The modern 'introductions' to the study of the New Testament have raised no doubts about the Gentile Christian character of the church at Corinth. In the letters we have only one direct statement (I Cor. 12.2), 'You know that when you were heathen, you were led astray to dumb idols, however you may have been moved.' On the other hand, it is said clearly of the Galatian churches that they are Gentile Christian; Paul says in Gal. 4.8 f., 'Formerly, when you did not know God, you were in bondage to beings that by nature are no gods; but now that you have come to know God. . . .' We can infer from 5.2 f. and 6.12 f. that the readers are not circumcised, and are therefore neither Jews nor proselytes.

As to the church in Rome there can be no doubt. In his greeting at the very beginning Paul says that he has received grace and apostleship to bring about obedience to the faith among all the Gentiles, including the readers of the letter (1.5 f.). He goes on to declare in v. 13 that he has often intended to come to Rome, in order that he may reap some harvest among them as well as among the rest of the Gentiles; and after some further explanation in v. 14, he assures them in v. 15 that he is eager to preach the Gospel to the readers, who are in Rome. Again, he remarks in 11.13, 'Now I am speaking to you Gentiles. Inasmuch then as I am an apostle to the Gentiles. . . .' And in ch. 15, in which Paul again speaks, as in ch. 1, about his letter, he says in vv. 15 f., 'But on some points I have written to you very boldly by way of reminder, because of the grace given me by God to be a minister of Christ Jesus to the Gentiles in the priestly service of the gospel of God, so that the offering of the Gentiles may be acceptable, sanctified by the Holy Spirit.'

As regards the church at Philippi, we may infer from 3.3 ff. that it was composed of Gentile Christians; we read here, 'For *we* are the true circumcision, who worship God in spirit, and glory in Christ Jesus, and put no confidence in the flesh'. If the interpretation given of Phil. 2.17 above (see p. 50 n. 3) is correct, and that passage alludes to the same thing as Rom. 11.25 and 15.16, that verse too is evidence of the church's Gentile Christian character. Finally, it is also clear that the church at Colossae was Gentile Christian. 1.21 says of the Christian Colossians, 'And you, who once were estranged and hostile in mind, doing evil deeds. . . .'; and in 1.24 f. Paul speaks about his apostolic work among the Gentiles, among whom he counts the Colossians (v. 27). 2.13 is still more definite: 'And you, who were dead in trespasses and the uncircumcision of your flesh, God made alive together with him, having forgiven us all our trespasses.'

These statements are so clear that there ought to be no doubt that these churches consist of Gentile Christians. Paul is in fact the apostle to the Gentiles, as we see from the passages quoted above and from Rom. 11.13 and Gal. 1.16; 2.2, 8 f. The letters never remark that they are written to Jewish Christians, and they describe the Jews as unbelieving; e.g., Rom. 9–11; 15.31, and I Cor. 1.22 f.[1] The passage just mentioned, Rom. 15.31, also describes them as persecutors of those who preach the Gospel—Paul prays to be delivered from the unbelievers in Judaea. In II Cor. 11.24 the apostle mentions that he has five times received at the hands of the Jews the forty lashes less one; and in I Thess. 2.15 f. we get a detailed picture of the Jews as persecutors: '. . . who killed both the Lord Jesus and the prophets, and drove us out, and displease God and oppose all men by hindering us from speaking to the Gentiles that they may be saved.'[2]

If in spite of all this, it has hitherto been supposed that the Pauline churches consisted mainly of Gentile Christians but included a number of Jewish Christians, that is partly because people have added to the evidence of the letters—according to which the churches consisted of Gentile Christians—the pictures that Acts gives of the missions to the Jews and Gentiles, and the information that that document contains about the first members of the various churches. It must, however, be emphasized that the fact that the Jews were preached to does not mean that they believed or that they joined the Christian church.

We have maintained above that the evidence of Acts may serve as a historical source where it does not contradict Paul's letters (pp. 78–81). Now the statements in Acts on this question do not differ greatly from

[1] Cf. Rom. 2.17, 28 f.; 3.1.
[2] Paul's letters mention the missionary work among the Jews (Rom. 1.16; 2.9 f.; I Cor. 9.20; 10.32). The Jews are also mentioned together with the Greeks in the set phrases in which the pattern of salvation is expressed, 'Jews and Greeks': Rom. 3.9; 10.12; I Cor. 1.24; 12.13; Gal. 3.28; Col. 3.11.

the evidence in the letters, although if we think they are reliable, they may modify Paul's statements on certain points here and there.

In Acts too the Pauline mission is described as a mission to the Gentiles. Thus Barnabas and Paul declared at the end of the first missionary journey (14.27) 'how (God) had opened a door of faith to the Gentiles'. At the Council at Jerusalem (15.12) Paul and Barnabas related what signs and wonders God had done through them among the Gentiles. In the same way Paul related, on his last visit to Jerusalem (21.19; cf. v. 21), what God had done among the Gentiles through his ministry.

If all the weight is laid on the apostle's work among the Gentiles, although it is described as concerning the Jews too, the explanation is that the Jews' attitude towards the preaching of the Gospel was unbelieving (e.g. 13.44 f.). Although the apostle's first sermon in the synagogue at Pisidian Antioch made a great impression on the Jews, they rise against him when the Gentiles gather to hear him too; cf. 14.2; 17.5; 18.6; 28.24–28.

This unbelief readily changes to active resistance and persecution of the apostle—as early as in Damascus (9.23–25)[1] and in Jerusalem (9.29 f.). In Pisidian Antioch the Jews stir up persecution against him (13.50), and the same thing happens in Iconium (14.2), and again in Lystra (14.19). We see the same thing on the second missionary journey in Thessalonica (17.5 f.), and in Beroea (17.13) and Corinth (18.12–17). At the beginning of the last journey to Jerusalem a plot is laid against him on his leaving Corinth (20.3), for which reason he decides to travel *via* Macedonia; and in the speech that follows in Miletus to the elders from Ephesus Paul alludes to the Jews' persecutions in Asia (20.19), which had not been referred to previously. In Jerusalem it is Jews from Asia who stir up a tumult against him in the temple (21.27); and the further accusation against him is made by the Jewish authorities in Palestine.[2]

So, while the picture that Acts draws of Paul's missionary work and the Jews' attitude to it agrees in its broad lines with the picture that Paul gives of them, certain details given in Acts as to the origin of the individual churches may either modify or contradict the evidence of the letters. If we agree with the South Galatian theory and include the churches of the first missionary journey in those of Galatia, we shall see that Acts does not suggest that Jews joined the church in Pisidian

---

[1]Paul's own narrative in II Cor. 11.32 f., according to which the governor under King Aretas tried to seize him, must of course be preferred to Luke's account. It does not seem possible to harmonize the two accounts satisfactorily, as presumably Luke attributes any persecution to the Jews unless other people are mentioned as the originators.

[2]On the persecution of Paul by the Jews, see further pp. 309 f. and pp. 313–22.

Antioch. On the other hand, we are told of the work in Iconium that '. . . a great company believed, both of Jews and of Greeks. But the unbelieving Jews stirred up the Gentiles and poisoned their minds against the brethren' (14.1 f.). The expression 'a great company, both of Jews and of Greeks' seems to mean that a great number of Jews were already involved. In Lystra and Derbe Acts relates nothing about Jews in the infant church.

As regards Philippi, we are told of only one of the women at the place of prayer that she became a Christian (16.13–15). The narrative of the Thessalonica mission is not clear. First it is said of the Jews that 'some of them were persuaded' (17.4), but v. 5 goes on, 'But the Jews were jealous, and . . . set the city in an uproar.' In Beroea, according to 17.12, many of the Jews believed. In Athens, where Paul spoke in the synagogue (17.17), we hear nothing about Jews joining the church; and in Corinth Paul has to leave the synagogue (18.6). We are told that Crispus, the ruler of the synagogue, believed with all his household (18.8), but we do not hear whether Aquila and Priscilla were already Christians, or whether it was Paul who persuaded them to believe (18.2 f.). During the apostle's later work in Ephesus it is not clear from 19.8–10 whether it is many or few Jews who have joined the church.

As we see, the statements in Acts do not contradict the information in Paul's letters. If we agree with the South Galatian theory, we should expect that, according to Acts 14.1 f., there were more Jews in the Galatian churches than the letter to the Galatians assumes. Similarly Acts 17.4 f. can be so interpreted that there are a certain, though indefinite, number of Jews in the church at Thessalonica—a conclusion that does not agree very well with I Thessalonians. But in both cases the differences are due to an interpretation that is not to be regarded as the only possible solution, and the corresponding passages of Acts can therefore not be regarded as safe sources, nor on the other hand can they be used to dispute the value of Acts as a source. The usual result of the Jews' unbelief is that the church becomes a Gentile Christian one, the only clear exception being Beroea; and as we know nothing else about that church, it is possible that here the account in Acts is correct, but then we can say unreservedly that that church forms an exception.

The second reason for supposing that, in spite of the evidence of the letters, there were a number of Jews in the Pauline churches, is the nature of the subjects with which Paul deals. When he deals with Old Testament or 'Jewish' questions, the explanation—so it is supposed— must be sought in the circle of his readers. That, in fact, is proceeding from the assumption that such subjects could have no great interest for the apostle, who was regarded as the representative of Paulinism and the opponent of Jewish elements in the Christian religion. Nor could those subjects arouse any interest among the Gentile Christians, whom he had won for Paulinism. Therefore the sections in which he discussed those Old Testament or Jewish matters must have been due to the presence of Jewish Christians in the churches concerned.

It is not difficult to find examples of this line of argument. Baur himself took this view in his chapter on Romans;[1] and more recently Mangold,[2] and then Sanday and Headlam (p. xxxii), have expounded the argument as follows: the letter to the Romans is evidence that part of the readers are Jewish Christians. The questions with which the letter deals are, in fact, of a Jewish kind. They are the questions of the validity of the Law, the nature of salvation, the possibility of man's justification before God, and the election of Israel. At the same time the arguments in Paul's treatment of these questions are such as would make the best impression on Jews. The apostle links his own point of view directly to Old Testament doctrine, and he seeks evidence for it in the Old Testament itself. We are therefore justified in asking what effect such arguments could have on Gentile readers.

It is surprising that such an argument as that of Sanday and Headlam should have carried any weight; Galatians deals with the same subjects, and it does so with arguments that testify to Paul's rabbinical training. The validity of the Law and the nature of salvation (Gal. 3–4.11), the possibility of man's justification before God (3–5.6), the election of Israel (3–4.11; 4.21–31)—all these are discussed in the letter; and in its form Galatians is influenced more strongly than Romans by Paul's rabbinical schooling (3.16, 19; 4.21–31). We can say of the most important parts of the argument in Galatians exactly what Sanday and Headlam maintained, viz., that there is a direct connexion between the apostle's standpoints and Old Testament doctrine, and that he seeks support for them in the Old Testament (3.6–20; 4.21–31). As Galatians is addressed to Gentile Christians among whom there is no considerable minority of Jewish Christians, the same thing can apply to Romans. It is true that here, as is made plain by the tone of the letter, there is no immediate conflict with opponents in the church; but the arguments of the letter, as well as the form in which they are presented, are calculated to appeal to the Gentile Christian readers in the Pauline churches, and they do not in any way reveal Jewish Christian groups in the church at Rome.

---

[1] *Paul* I, pp. 321 ff.
[2] W. Mangold, *Der Römerbrief und seine geschichtlichen Voraussetzungen*, 1884. I have not had access to this work.

All the questions described above as Jewish questions are discussed in Galatians directly with Gentile Christian readers. They are dealt with here because of the penetration of a Judaizing movement into the Galatian churches; but even apart from those special circumstances, they are live problems within the Christian Church. Through its very existence the Church confronts Christians with the problem: Where is God's chosen people? Is it Israel after the flesh, or God's new Israel? For the Christian, who must needs reply that the Church is God's chosen people, the next question will be: Then what is God's revealed will for this his people? This necessarily involves dealing with the validity of the Law, the nature of salvation, and the possibility of man's justification before God. Those are exactly the problems with which the Church's Bible, the LXX, confronts its Christian readers; and the one-time Jews and the Gentiles who formerly attended the synagogue are faced with those problems, as are the Gentiles who come from outside, because they use the same Bible as the synagogue, though with a different interpretation of its contents.

In the external struggle of the Church against Judaism, people were more apt to remember and record the persecution of the Christians by the Jews than their mutual discussions and conversations about religion. At the same time we may take it that the Jewish colonies found themselves largely compelled, as minorities among Gentiles, to carry on this less bloody kind of struggle with their former adherents and attenders and with the increasing stream of Gentiles turning to the new Israel. It may have been dangerous for the Jewish minority to begin a persecution of the Christian minority, as the latter was much more representative of the native population than was the synagogue, and was not so easily exposed as the Jews to the xenophobia of anti-Semitism. It was therefore not only inwardly, but also outwardly, that the new Gentile Christian churches were compelled to apply themselves to so-called Old Testament and Jewish subjects.

In shaping the new Christian life the Gentile Christian was faced with the problem: What is God's will for the Gentile's life in Christ? He must, of course, change his manner of life and follow the commands and exhortations of the apostle. What validity then had the ethic of the Christian Church?[1] Was the Jewish Law which was in the Bible still

---

[1]How difficult it was for the former pagans to reach a right conception of the new Gospel that Paul brought them we can see from the ethical argument in I Thess. 4.1–8, where it is stressed persistently and in the most diverse ways that the new ethic is God's will and Christ's commandment: 'Finally, brethren, we beseech and exhort you in the Lord Jesus, that as you learned from us how you ought to live and to please God, . . . you do so more and more. For you know what instructions we gave you through the Lord Jesus. For this is the will of God, your sanctification; . . . not in the passion of lust like heathen who do not know God; . . . because

valid, or had it been essentially changed and modified by Christ? And in churches where the Holy Spirit with its rich gifts made its impress on life, the right of the man who was filled with the Spirit to judge everything—even the letter of the biblical ethic—was bound to become a burning problem.

The starting-point of Pauline ideas in the Old Testament, and the arguments resting on passages of Scripture and biblical material, are also characteristic of Christian thought in the early Church. The Church had begun as a movement inside Judaism, and Christianity was taken to the Gentiles by Jewish Christian missionaries; the oldest theology is therefore Jewish and biblical. It would not have been possible at that time to discuss and solve questions of Christian doctrine in Gentile (e.g., Greek philosophical) terms. It was not till about a hundred years later that Christian teachers began to clothe the Christian doctrine in philosophic terms. The fact that the oldest Christian theology is Jewish and biblical does not mean that it cannot be clearly separated from Jewish theology; its peculiarity is that it is more biblical than Jewish.

The third and most important reason for regarding the Pauline churches as Gentile Christian churches with a not very small minority of Jewish Christians is to be found in the picture that has been drawn of the development of early Christianity. That picture, which is determined by the general tradition within Pauline research, is on this point older than Baur and the Tübingen School. Jewish Christianity in Jerusalem is imagined as having a permanent mission to the Gentiles and close connexions with the whole Roman world. Paul is only one of the leaders of the mission, and his churches, even where they have been strongly Gentile Christian from the beginning, have gradually become intermixed with immigrating Jewish Christians, and have been taught by emissaries from Jerusalem.

But the picture is not accurate. Jewish Christianity did carry on a mission among Jews in Palestine and in the eastern Diaspora; but even before the agreement with Paul in Jerusalem (Gal. 2.1–10) it had no sort of mission among the Gentiles. Even at the time of the letter to the Romans the picture that Paul gives of the mission to the Jews shows that those who were called as apostles to the Jews have continued to preach the Gospel and have now finished, but that the Jews have not

---

the Lord is an avenger in all these things, . . . For God has not called us for uncleanness, but for sanctification. Therefore whoever disregards this, disregards not man but God, who gives his Holy Spirit to you.' This demonstration that the apostolic ethic is God's will in Christ goes quite parallel with Paul's struggle for right views about the apostleship.

been willing to accept salvation (10.12–21). While Paul has been the
apostle to the Gentiles, Peter and the other Jewish apostles have gone
on to preach to the Jews in the east. There is therefore no Jewish Christian mission in the Pauline mission fields.

But, as we have shown above (pp. 104 f.), no emissaries go from
Jerusalem to the Pauline churches to change their faith and their works,
to separate them from the apostle, and to bind them closely to the
twelve earliest disciples and the church in Jerusalem. It is only in II
Corinthians that we meet Jewish apostles in a Pauline church, and there
it is a question of people from outside about whose preaching and other
activity we learn nothing. Like 'certain men from James' in Gal. 2.11 ff.,
those Jewish Christians may have gone to the Gentile Christian church
from motives unconnected with the church.

We really must not imagine that the earliest Christian mission was
as systematically planned as the writer of Acts would have it. Jerusalem
is not the mother church of all the new churches, nor is Paul the only
missionary to the Gentiles. In the same way as he received his call,
without any connexion with the existing disciples and churches, by
meeting Christ on the road to Damascus, so other apostles—in the
early Christian meaning of the word—met Christ and were sent by
him.

Although Jewish Christianity, taken as a whole, continued to preach
the Gospel only to Israel in the period that followed, there are individual
apostles of Jewish origin who worked among the Gentiles, e.g., Andronicus and Junias whom Paul greets in Rom. 16.7 among his other
friends and acquaintances in Ephesus. They are his fellow-countrymen
and fellow-prisoners, men of note among the apostles, and were Christians before Paul. We may suppose that they worked with him, as they
were prisoners with him. Those Jewish apostles in Ephesus might have
enlightened us about the Jewish apostles in Corinth who are referred to
in II Corinthians. If we had known a little more about these latter, we
might have found that they were among the Jewish apostles of the same
kind as Andronicus and Junias, with whom Paul was glad to work;
but unfortunately those apostles in Corinth had gone astray and become professional apostles, and so servants of Satan instead of apostles
of Christ.

Besides such pre-Pauline apostles there are the innumerable types of
missionaries who were won by the work of the former and of Paul.
Acts shows us how Apollos became a fellow-worker within the Pauline
mission, and we hear in Colossians about Epaphras and the Colossian
church which seems to be a result of his work. So we see how the
Pauline movement is constantly setting new forces in motion.

Moreover, we do not get matters right if we always claim to see Jerusalem or Paul as the effective forces. We must assume that at that time Christianity was not spread only by people with a definite call or a clearly defined authority with missionary activity in view. Every Christian could be active in his immediate circle, or in the locality where he lived. If we think of Aquila and Priscilla, for instance, we can hardly say for certain that they were called or authorized to do missionary work; and yet the tent-maker and his wife seem to have taken part in the mission untiringly.

There are certainly many intermediate stages between the missionary who could devote the greater part of his time to spreading the Gospel, and the church member who could not stop telling about it and testifying to what he had received. The distinction that modern missionary history draws between traders or others from Christian countries and missionaries did not exist in primitive Christianity. The Christian merchant (e.g., Lydia of Thyatira) was presumably just as zealous an advocate of the Gospel as the Christian who by virtue of his calling or service was able to give up his whole time to missionary work.

III

We can choose from these various possibilities when we want to explain the origin of the church in Rome. It is wrong to trace it back to Jerusalem because it was not founded by Paul. It is a fallacy widespread in the world of learning to think that a phenomenon must be either A or B, and to think it must be B because it can be proved not to be A. In the rich and varied world in which we live, the phenomena can often be A, B, C, D, E, and so on; and only the limitations of our knowledge or field of vision are responsible for our choosing between A and B, instead of rediscovering the hitherto neglected C, or boldly seeking out the quite unknown D.

In the foregoing chapters we have often had occasion to remark how often in New Testament research people have tied themselves down to two possibilities—there are strained relations between Paulinism and Jewish Christianity; Paul's opponents are either Judaizers or spiritual men; if Paul did not found the church in Rome, we must go back to Jerusalem for its origin.

In the earlier chapter (ch. 4) we have given an account of Paul's view of Jewish Christianity; and in ch. 8, which now follows, we intend to draw the picture that Acts gives of Jewish Christianity. In that way we are seeking to gain a new understanding of the earliest Christianity, and one that will help us to a better insight into the letter to the Romans.

8

JEWISH CHRISTIANITY ACCORDING
TO THE ACTS OF THE APOSTLES

WE have to study Paul's letters if we want to learn anything about him, his background, and his surroundings; and in the four preceding chapters we have tried to do this in relation to the four great letters. But of course, we must not on that account cease to consult Acts too. If the interpretation of Paul's letters has been impeded and misdirected by the influence of the Tübingen School, the same is true of the interpretation of Acts. Indeed it is not always Acts that has been played off against Paul; the case is rather that a precise, one-sided interpretation of Acts has dominated first that document itself and then Paul's letters.

Let us test this in respect of one particular question. It has been thought that the very early Church took its stand entirely on Jewish ideas, except for the belief that the crucified Jesus was identical with the coming Messiah. We are not asking here whether that is correct according to our primary sources, Paul's letters; we are simply asking, Is it correct that we can find that picture of the very early Church in our secondary source, Acts, or does the assertion rest on an insufficiently careful exposition of the text of Acts, which cannot be so explained without further examination?

The answer to this question must be found through a number of individual inquiries, which will lead to some concluding reflections. The texts that are examined are taken from Acts 1–12, with the exception of 15.1–29 and 21.17–26.

I

The apostles are to stay in Jerusalem. According to Acts, the Christian message is at first tied, not only to Israel, but also to Jerusalem. In Acts 1.4 Jesus tells the apostles that they are to wait for the promise of the Father 'which you heard from me'. There seems here to be an allusion to the words of the risen Lord who said (Luke 24.49), 'And behold, I send the promise of my Father upon you; but stay in the city, until you are clothed with power from on high.' This is confirmed by Acts 2.33, where we read, 'Being therefore exalted at the right hand of

210

God, and having received from the Father the promise of the Holy
Spirit, he has poured out this which you see and hear.' The narration of
the earliest church history in Acts shows, however, that the outpouring
of the Holy Spirit at Pentecost did not have as a consequence that the
earliest disciples left Jerusalem to begin their activity in other places.

It is therefore doubtful whether Luke is right in interpreting the
promise—a usual expression in Acts[1]—as the outpouring of the Holy
Spirit. The expression rather means the salvation of Israel. When the
promise of Israel's salvation has been fulfilled, the twelve disciples
will leave Jerusalem and go to the Gentiles. It is nowhere related that
these disciples leave Jerusalem; on the contrary, it is expressly stated in
8.1 that in the persecution after the killing of Stephen all the Christians
were scattered except the apostles, who stayed in the city. Apart from
Peter's departure in 12.17, we hear only of journeys in Palestine by
Peter and by Peter and John, to exercise oversight in churches that had
already been established. It is not in itself certain that Peter's departure
from Jerusalem in 12.17 was regarded by Luke as a very far-reaching
event, so that James, the Lord's brother, takes over the leadership of
the church in Jerusalem from then. Peter's conduct at the Council at
Jerusalem (ch. 15) shows nothing about where he was living at that time.
We might well assume that he had gone back to Jerusalem and was still
living there, but nothing is said about it. But from ch. 16 onwards we
have no more information about the apostles. In ch. 21, which tells of
Paul's visit—the first, after the Council at Jerusalem, to be mentioned
in more detail (in contrast to the supposed visit in 18.22)—nothing is
said about the apostles, but it is James and the elders who receive Paul.

We can therefore say confidently that the apostles reside in Jerusalem,
and that it is only at odd times that some of them leave the city on a
journey of no great length, before they all, without any further explanation, disappear entirely from the narrative of Acts. Acts 15.2 is very
characteristic of the attitude of Acts towards the apostles; we read here,
'And when Paul and Barnabas had no small dissension and debate
with them [viz., with some from Judaea, who were teaching the brethren
in Antioch that they could not be saved unless they were circumcised],
Paul and Barnabas and some of the others were appointed to go up to
Jerusalem to the apostles and the elders about this question.' In Acts,
then, the contending Christians in Antioch proceed from the assumption
that they can go up to Jerusalem and thus be sure of finding the apostles
and elders at home there and ready to smooth out the dispute.

---

[1]In 2.33 (cf. Luke 24.49) ἡ ἐπαγγελία (τοῦ πατρός) is applied to the outpouring
of the Holy Spirit. Whether the same is true of Acts 1.4 is uncertain. In 2.39; 13.23,
32; 26.6 it is used in a wider sense of the coming of salvation to Israel.

We must, of course, consider whether this view of the apostles in Acts arose only in the later Church, or whether it has any value as a source for the history of the very early Church. When we reflect that the later Gentile Church regards the apostles as travelling missionaries to the Gentiles, it is natural to regard as historically valuable the view that we get in Acts—a view that is so different from, and in fact opposed to, that of later times. There is also in Paul's writings a passage that confirms the view that at quite an early period the 'apostles' were normally to be found in Jerusalem. It is Gal. 1.17, where Paul says that he did not confer with flesh and blood immediately after his call at Damascus, 'nor did I go up to Jerusalem to those who were apostles before me.'

In my article, 'Paul, the Apostles, and the Twelve',[1] I have taken the view that before Paul the word ἀπόστολος is used within the Church in only two senses—with the primary meaning of 'messenger', and of the missionaries who were sent out by Christ. To these Paul adds a new meaning by trying to signify by the word 'apostle' that he is the chosen messenger who has been sent to preach the Gospel to the Gentiles. This application by Paul of the word 'apostle' to a person elected and called by God in a special sense gives rise to the development of an apostolic idea which is partly Pauline, but which expresses a different view of the Church's origin.

After Paul the word 'apostle' is persistently used in its primary meaning, and is applied to the missionaries whom Christ sent out, but it is used preferably—and later exclusively—in a narrower sense of the twelve disciples whom Jesus had chosen. In the texts that we have from the post-Pauline period there are two ways of regarding those twelve who are now called 'apostles'. One, and presumably the older, which we have in Acts, regards them as a council residing in Jerusalem, and the other and later view has it that the twelve apostles are like Paul, continually travelling all over the world. If this is correct, it will be realized that the first view (a council of twelve apostles in Jerusalem) was already partly due to the influence of Paul's apostolic ideas. If this council, which does not consist of travelling missionaries, is given a name that denotes those very missionaries, it must be because the word 'apostle' has received a new meaning, viz., a person specially called by Christ; and that is just what we see in Paul's letters. But it is only in the other view (that the twelve apostles are travelling missionaries to the Gentiles) that the Pauline apostolic idea comes into its own. To be sure, it meant that he himself was overshadowed when his apostolic idea was merged into the figure twelve of the first disciples, to whom he

[1] *ST* 3, 1950, pp. 96–110.

did not belong. But his apostolic idea won the victory, because those twelve all became like Paul. For what happened was nothing other than that the Church of the Gentiles took over the twelve disciples who had been sent out by Jesus to Israel, and made them, like Paul, apostles to the Gentiles.

In that article I went into Gal. 1.17, and felt tempted to apply the word 'apostles' in the text—a word that Paul never uses elsewhere of the twelve earliest disciples whom Jesus chose to be with him and to be sent to preach and heal—to those twelve, so that we should have here the first passage where the post-Pauline meaning of the word 'apostle' occurred. But in view of the remaining Pauline material I kept to the meaning 'missionary sent out by Christ', and I still think that that meaning is justified. But it is possible to unite the two points of view, that the most obvious meaning of 'apostles' in Gal. 1.17 is the twelve, and that Paul never applies the word 'apostles' to those twelve. The sentence of disavowal, 'Nor did I go up to Jerusalem to those who were apostles before me,' may, like other such sentences in Gal. 1–2, be pole-mical and directed against the opponents' assertions, so that we have in this isolated use of the word 'apostles' by Paul a free quotation from the Judaizers' usage. The latter have therefore already transferred to the twelve disciples Paul's view of his apostolic calling.

In this way the letter to the Galatians confirms—or rather the Judaizing opponents in the Galatian churches confirm—Acts' view of the apostles as a council resident in Jerusalem, that view not only being preserved in Acts as a conception going back to the earliest period, but also being found in Galatians and written down as soon as it had been stated. Its existence can be proved in relation to the Galatian churches, but not for Jerusalem itself. As those Judaizers have no connexion with Jerusalem, but have only Paul as a source of information as to the circumstances there, the idea of that council of the twelve residing permanently in Jerusalem must go back to Paul; but the mentioning of the twelve as 'apostles' must, as we have already said, be because Paul's opponents have transferred his view of his apostleship to the distant earliest disciples of Jesus.

II

The importance of Pentecost. Both the miracle of Pentecost, and Peter's speech which is to explain more fully what has happened, show that the outpouring of the Holy Spirit is a sign for Israel.[1] In any case,

[1]Acts 2.5: 'Now there were dwelling in Jerusalem Jews, devout men from every nation under heaven.' Wendt is right in saying (on 2.5), 'The numerous people of

some of those who experience the miracle and hear Peter's speech are Jews of the Babylonian and Greek Diaspora who are living in Jerusalem; but that fact does not influence Peter's speech, except, perhaps, in v. 39, 'all that are far off, every one whom the Lord our God calls to him' (see p. 213 n. 1). Within the context of Acts the Church remains a Jerusalem enterprise, even if we assume that it evangelized from the beginning among the Jews living there, those who spoke Aramaic as well as those who spoke Greek, and among the many pilgrims in the temple.

If we want to reconcile the great events in Jerusalem with the localization of the apostles in the city, we may take it that Jerusalem with the temple as Israel's centre, to which the Jews of all countries flocked for the great festivals, offered the possibility of preaching the Gospel to all Israel both in Palestine and in the Diaspora; thus local limitations do not exclude a universal outlook.

III

The life of the Christian church in Jerusalem is distinct from Judaism. As we have seen above, it has been usual to assume that the first disciples in Jerusalem did not differ from the other Jews, except by their belief that the coming Messiah was identical with the crucified Jesus. It does not seem to have been clearly realized that that difference was great enough to make the Jerusalem Christians differ from their fellow-countrymen on all other points too. We can point to various circumstances that show clearly the difference between Jewish Christians and the Jews in Jerusalem.

Like John the Baptist, the Church required that the Jews who joined the new movement should be baptized. Like the Baptist and Jesus, therefore, the early Church could not recognize the election of Israel in the way that the Jews did. It was not enough to belong to Israel; salvation was to be reached only through baptism in the name of Jesus. Therefore the fact that only Israel was chosen is of no avail;[1]

---

other languages are at once described, in accordance with their religion and nationality, as Jews, so as to exclude the obvious supposition that they were Gentiles.' Peter's speech too shows that the sign is meant for the Jews: 'Let all the house of Israel therefore know assuredly' etc. (v. 36), and 'For the promise is to you and to your children and to all that are far off, every one whom the Lord our God calls to him' (v. 39). The last might refer to the Gentiles, but it may also mean the Jews of the Diaspora. It is an allusion to Isa. 57.19, a passage that is applied in Eph. 2.13, 17 to Jews and Gentiles (cf. Acts 22.21), but there is no need to interpret it so here; it may be said of Jews in Palestine and in the Diaspora. A different view is expressed by Preisker in *TWNT* IV, p. 376.36–43.

[1]So with Paul, Rom. 9.6 f.: 'For not all who are descended from Israel belong to Israel, and not all are children of Abraham because they are his descendants', etc.

the decisive turning-point comes only with baptism in the name of Jesus.

A number of texts in Acts show us how unbaptized Jews were regarded. We read in Peter's speech, 'Save yourselves from this crooked generation!' (2.40). In ch. 3 the speech is not in such sharp terms; here he says that his audience delivered Jesus up and denied him in the presence of Pilate (3.13 f.); but that it is an extenuating circumstance that they, like their rulers, acted in ignorance (3.17). Peter further urges them to repent, so that their sins may be blotted out, and that times of refreshing may come from the presence of the Lord (3.19 f.). In 3.23 the passage is quoted 'And it shall be that every soul that does not listen to that prophet shall be destroyed from the people.' Here, as in the other speeches, Israel's sinning against the Messiah does not necessarily mean the beginning of its ruin; God always has before his eyes the salvation of his people. Thus (3.26), 'God, having raised up his servant, sent him to you first, to bless you in the turning of every one of you from your wickedness.' Taken singly, the expressions in the speech seem to assume that the Messiah brings final salvation, if the individual Jews repent. In ch. 5, too, Peter points out that his audience was responsible for Jesus' death, and that God had nevertheless ordained him for the salvation of Israel (5.30 f.); 'The God of our fathers raised Jesus whom you killed by hanging him on a tree. God exalted him at his right hand as Leader and Saviour, to give repentance to Israel and forgiveness of sins.' And in his speech in Cornelius' house Peter speaks of the word that God sent to the sons of Israel by the preaching of peace by Jesus Christ (10.36). Although the people killed him, God commanded 'us' after the Resurrection to preach to the people and to testify that he is the one ordained by God to be judge of the living and the dead (10.39–42). Here it is emphasized in 10.41 that God made Christ manifest, not to all the people, but to those who were chosen by God as witnesses, 'us' (cf. 13.31). Again in Paul's speech in the synagogue in Pisidian Antioch it is told that the Jews— the Palestinian Jews—killed the Messiah; but now 'we' bring 'you' the good news that what God promised to the fathers he has fulfilled to 'us their children' by raising Jesus (13.32). Through him the forgiveness of sins is proclaimed to 'you' (the Jews), and Paul warns them lest there come upon them what is said in the prophets (Hab. 1.5; Acts 13.38, 40 f.).[1] While on the one hand it is constantly said that the Gospel is sent to Israel alone (even in Peter's speech in Cornelius' house, 10.36, 42), it is on the other hand clear that the Jews remain outside.

[1] Paul too, who distinguishes in Rom. 9–10 between the Jews' failure to believe in Christ (9.30 ff.) and to believe the apostles (10.4 ff.), has it that the apostles preach to the Jews the message of justification by faith after the Jews have rejected Christ as their Messiah.

The celebration of the Lord's Supper too shows us that those Jewish Christians in Jerusalem did not merely look back to the crucified Jesus or forward to him as the Lord coming back from heaven in Messianic glory. At that meal they became united with him in his heavenly life and work. In that living together with Christ something came to the Jewish Christian that was bound to separate him from his non-believing fellow-countrymen.

Of course, it is possible to suppose that Luke's account has been influenced on these points by the conditions of a later time, in such a way, for instance, that in the very early Church we meet baptism and the Lord's Supper only in a primitive form; but even in that case their mere existence testifies to the gap that existed between Israel and the Church.

IV

The persecution of the Church shows that it is different from Judaism.
We can produce conclusive proof that the Jewish Christians were different from their Jewish fellow-countrymen. If things had really been as Baur and his school imagined, the Jews would have had no occasion to persecute the Christians; but we see from the very beginning that the history of the Christian Church is a history of martyrs. Scholars have certainly tried to make light of the persecution, as if it were only the specially radical Christians like Stephen and Paul against whom the Jews turned; but that is not the case.

In Acts 1–12, where the life of the earliest Christians is described, persecution is reported in chs. 4–5, 6–7, 8, 9, and 12. In chs. 4 and 5 first Peter and John are thrown into prison after the healing of the lame man at the temple gate called Beautiful (4.1–22), and afterwards all the apostles are arrested and brought before the council (5.17–42). In chs. 6–7 we are told how Stephen is accused before the council and makes a speech in his own defence, but is afterwards lynched illegally and unjustly. In 8.1–3 we are told of a great persecution of the church in Jerusalem and of Paul's active participation in it. In 9.1–19 the narrative of the apostle's call involves a mention of his participation in the persecution of the Church (vv. 1 f.; cf. Ananias' remark in vv. 13 f.); and when Paul has become a Christian, the former persecutor is pursued by his one-time co-religionists, first in Damascus (9.23–25), and then in Jerusalem (9.29 f.). Finally, we hear in ch. 12 of Herod Agrippa I's persecution of the church in Jerusalem, beginning with the execution of James the son of Zebedee and continuing with the arrest of Peter; and we are then told of Peter's happy deliverance and finally of the just punishment of the persecutor (12.1 f., 3–19, 20–23). According to this,

Herod went on with the persecution when he saw that it pleased the Jews (12.3), as Peter says (12.11) that God has rescued him from the hand of Herod and from all that the Jewish people were expecting.[1]

It is remarkable that the constant persecution of the very early Church is disregarded, but scholars can excuse themselves by claiming that the writer of Acts was the first to take that view. We can observe in that work a peculiar incongruity between the narratives that he found and used, and the framework into which he put them. The passage about the church's 'having favour with all the people' (2.47)—cf. 4.33,[2] 'and great grace was upon them all'—are in the writer's summary of the life of the church. The people are said to have been an obstacle to the high priests in the persecution of the apostles; thus 4.21, 'And when they had further threatened them, they let them go, finding no way to punish them, because of the people; for all men praised God for what had happened'; and 5.26, 'Then the captain with the officers went and brought them, but without violence, for they were afraid of being stoned by the people.' These two statements show what the church's opponents were thinking, so they cannot be regarded as particularly valuable, even if they could be traced back to Luke's sources.[3] In 9.31 we meet the joyous proclamation, 'So the church throughout all Judea and Galilee and Samaria had peace,' etc., in a transitional formula of Luke's composition. It is only in 5.13 that we hear indirectly of persecution, in a summary by Luke, which because of its addition seems to contradict itself: 'none of the rest dared to join in, but the people held them in high honour,' etc. The narratives of Acts give no more positive picture of the people than do some of the *pericopes* in the Gospels; but it is the writer of Acts who particularly stresses the church's popularity among the people. This is presumably bound up with the 'innocence theme' that appears so prominently in the account of Paul throughout all his legal trials, not least in the last trial at Jerusalem. The Christians are innocent, but wicked individuals rise against them.[4]

[1]This is an allusion to Agrippa's intention to bring Peter 'out to the people' after the Passover (12.4).

[2]Baur, *Paul* I, p. 30, rightly remarks on this, 'It is self-evident how little the persecution of the Christians, which broke out so soon afterwards, confirms this account.'

[3]R. Söder, *Die apokryphen Apostelgeschichten und die romanhafte Literatur der Antike* (Würzburger Studien zur Altertumswissenschaft 3), 1932, p. 160, compares Acts 4.21 and 5.26 with the mention of the multitude in the apocryphal Acts. Both texts of Acts speak of the high priests' having regard to the people; but such passionate partisanship and such counter-measures against the authorities and demonstrations in favour of the persecuted, as in the apocryphal Acts, are not in the canonical Acts. H. J. Cadbury, in *The Making of Luke-Acts*, 1927, p. 306, writes about Luke, 'From the favor of the Lord to the favor of the people is for the author no difficult transition. Vox populi, vox dei; and for this writer "having favor with all the people" is one of the credentials of his heroes.'

[4]Cf. Cadbury, *op. cit.*, p. 306.

V

The Hellenists and Stephen. One of the ways that have been chosen to make light of the persecutions of the church in Jerusalem is the attempt to separate sharply the Hebrews and the Hellenists. It is not the church as such that is persecuted, but only the Hellenists.

According to the traditional view the Hebrews are Aramaic-speaking Jews and the Hellenists Greek-speaking Jews. Archaeological material containing the word 'Hebrew' as a description of individual Jews or members of a single synagogue has brought another view of the 'Hebrews', according to which they are Jews who have emigrated from Palestine. It is supposed that Aramaic is still their native language, and that they may have some knowledge of Hebrew; but the essential thing is their Palestinian origin.[1] Galling has rightly criticized this view in 'Die jüdischen Katakomben in Rom als ein Beitrag zur jüdischen Konfessionskunde',[2] where he writes (p. 354), 'An argument against it is that this characteristic was displaced in the second generation born in Rome, and latterly the majority of all Roman Jews somehow came "from Palestine", so that there was no real distinguishing sign. I should prefer to think that the oldest community of Jews was so called when it was founded, because the terms "Jews" and "Hebrews" were then used indifferently for each other.' Whichever of these two views one adopts, the New Testament gives little help towards understanding the expressions 'Hebrews' and 'Hellenists', as it is not natural in Palestine to apply either the term for Palestinian Jews or the old name of the Jews to a single group of Jewish Christians in Jerusalem.

In Acts 6.1 we meet within the Jerusalem church a distinction between the Hellenists and the Hebrews in the matter of the support of widows. Paul describes himself as a Hebrew in Phil. 3.5 and II Cor. 11.22. In the latter passage he says that he is just as good a Hebrew as are certain Jewish apostles who have come to Corinth. Hellenists are also mentioned in Acts 9.29, where Paul spoke and disputed against the Hellenists, and they tried to kill him. If we assume that those Hellenists

---

[1]Thus Deissmann in Nicolaus Müller and N. A. Bees, *Die Inschriften der jüdischen Katakombe am Monteverde zu Rom*, 1919, p. 24; cf. p. 58; and J.-B. Frey, *Corpus Inscriptionum Judaicarum*, Vol. I, 1936, pp. lxxvi f. Müller and Bees assume (p. 24) that the community of the Hebrews was not a local but a personal one, i.e., 'that its members were scattered and lived all over Rome and the surrounding district. In that way it could easily be explained that two daughters of a πατήρ Ἑβρέων were buried in Porto.' On this, see now H. J. Leon, 'The Jewish Community of Ancient Porto', *Harvard Theological Review* 45, 1952, pp. 165–75: the Jewish inscriptions from Porto in Frey's *Corpus*, Vol. 1, are in part not Jewish, and those that are Jewish are not from Porto but from Rome. There is therefore no proof that Jews lived in Porto.

[2]*TSK* 103, 1931, pp. 352–60.

are the same as Stephen's opponents in 6.9—'Then some of those who belonged to the synagogue of the Freedmen (as it was called), and of the Cyrenians, and of the Alexandrians, and of those from Cilicia and Asia, arose and disputed with Stephen'—then we may suppose that 'Hellenists', like 'Hebrews' (Phil. 3.5), is a Jewish term for Jews, and not a name given by Christians to a faction. As has been said, the difference might be in the language, but also in Palestinian origin. However, Paul was not born in Palestine but in Tarsus, if we are willing to trust Acts on this point; and the supposition that he came from Gischala is as uncertain as everything that we learn from Jerome about the earliest times of Christianity.[1] The choice of language in Phil. 3.5 and II Cor. 11.22 is therefore remarkable if it is to be maintained that 'Hebrew' is used to denote a Palestinian Jew. The same uncertainty seems to me to exist with regard to the Hellenists, who in that case are supposed to be Jews of the Diaspora who have moved into Palestine. But we have nothing to indicate that that is the right explanation—we learn only about the proselyte Nicolaus that he is from Antioch (6.5)—but the possibility exists that the name denotes Jews of a particular kind, so that some of them may indeed have been born in Palestine[2] but be distinct from the Jews who are called Hebrews. As they have their own synagogues,[3] which would presumably be attended by people who came from abroad (e.g., Paul in 9.29), the language in which they worshipped was probably Greek; and it is perhaps most natural to keep to the traditional linguistic explanation for the New Testament, as long as no material is suggested along other lines for a better understanding of the two names.[4]

[1]Both in his *Commentary on Philemon*, on v. 23 (*PL* 26, 617BC) and in *De Viris Illustribus* 5 (*PL* 23, 616A) Jerome relates that Paul was born in Gischala and reached Tarsus from there as a prisoner of war with his parents (as Epaphras reached Colossae). This cannot be reconciled with Acts, according to which Paul was born in Tarsus (Acts 22.3; cf. 9.11; 21.39). The point of view seems to be the one that Jerome happens to mention in what follows in the commentary on Philemon: 'quae illum Judaeum magis indicant quam Tharsensem.' The tradition about Gischala is rightly rejected by Mommsen in 'Die Rechtsverhältnisse des Apostels Paulus', *ZNW* 2, 1901, p. 82 n. 4.

[2]Just as the 'Hebrews' in Rome may possibly have been born there of parents who had immigrated. In any case, some of the Hebrew children mentioned in Frey's *Corpus*, Vol. I, Nos. 291, 502, 510, and 535 could have been born in Rome, and that may also hold good for those who are called Ἑβραῖος, Nos. 354 and 379, and for the exarchon of the Hebrews, No. 317.

[3]This inference may be possible from 6.9.

[4]It is not advisable to regard the Hellenists as Gentiles, as has been attempted, e.g., by H. J. Cadbury, 'The Hellenists', in *Beginnings* 5, pp. 59–74; Windisch in *TWNT* II, pp. 508.26–509.39; and W. Grundmann, 'Das Problem des hellenistischen Christentums innerhalb der Jerusalemer Urgemeinde', *ZNW* 38, 1939, pp. 54 ff. (here so obscure that Hellenists include 'non-Jews, proselytes, Hellenistic Diaspora Jews', p. 58); the narratives in Acts, and not merely Luke's framework, assume that here we are in a Jewish *milieu*. In Acts 11.20 the best manuscripts read ἐλάλουν καὶ πρὸς τοὺς Ἑλληνιστὰς κτλ. (not Ἕλληνας); and this might be an indication that

Of course, people have been interested in looking into the internal circumstances of the very early Church, with the help of the dispute between Hellenists and Hebrews. As, according to the traditional view, everything in Acts is related to the observance of the Law and the preaching of the Gospel to the Gentiles, this matter too is supposed to enlighten us about the differing points of view in those respects. People look away from the Hellenists' widows who were neglected in the daily distribution, and scent in this controversy the beginning of the mission to the Gentiles and of the Pauline freedom from the Law. But neither Luke nor his narrative helps us to take any such view, provided that the mere interpretation of the names does not lead to such far-reaching conclusions as those that we have just refuted. It really is, as it says, a question of the daily distribution and of the Hellenistic widows who felt themselves badly treated. We do not know whether they were really neglected by the Jerusalem church, but in any case modern research has made a point of ignoring their distress.

In this connexion we must mention that the narrative in chs. 6–7 confronts us with many problems. The dispute about the distribution to the widows makes the apostles resolve to give up their personal direction of it and transfer it to seven members chosen by the church. V. 7 is a summary, inserted by Luke, perhaps to separate 6.1–6 from what follows. Here we are told of Stephen, who like Philip, another of the seven, became prominent as a preacher. This sounds strange, since the apostles were giving up the management of the distribution with the very purpose of not neglecting the preaching of the word. The account of Stephen, and particularly the close of ch. 7, is difficult to understand; and it is wise to keep these difficulties in mind when we consider the problems in the text with which we are now occupied.

It has often been thought that the Hellenistic Jews were an outside body of people who were removed from Jerusalem by the persecution after Stephen's death, only the Hellenists being hit by the persecution.[1]

'Hellenists' means 'Gentiles'. This is the case at a later time, if we may trust E. A. Sophocles, *Greek Lexicon of the Roman and Byzantine Period*, 1888, s.v.; see also Liddell and Scott, s.v. But the use of Ἑλληνισταί in Acts 6.1 and 9.29 rests rather on a local linguistic usage which was of rather short duration and which Luke found in his sources. As long as the meaning of 'Hebrews' is uncertain, it is also difficult to get closer to the meaning of 'Hellenists'. There is, of course, no point at all in applying the name 'Hebrews' to Palestinian Jews living in Palestine. In that case the contrast in the name 'Hellenists' would simply mean either that they were Palestinian but not Jews, or more probably that they were Jews but not Palestinian. This latter distinction might certainly be maintained of a family living in Jerusalem and already in the second generation, if it were distinct from the native population in language and certain customs.

[1]Baur, *Paul* I, p. 39; Lietzmann, *The Beginnings of the Christian Church*, p. 71; Nock, *St Paul*, pp. 61 ff., cf. pp. 168 ff.; Goguel, *Les Premiers Temps de l'Église*, pp. 52, 56 f.

But it is wrong to draw a distinction between the Hellenists and Stephen on the one hand and the rest of the church in Jerusalem on the other. We know that the Hellenists grumbled at the Hebrews because of the daily distribution to the widows, but we know nothing of any dogmatic or ethical differences between the two groups. If we have the writer of Acts to thank for Stephen's speech, we have only his opponents' words to judge by, and their accusations against Stephen (6.11, 13 f.) are in no way different from the accusation against Jesus.[1]

It is difficult to decide whether Stephen's speech was composed by Luke, or whether it goes back to old traditions that merely owe their present form to the writer of Acts. The usual leaning has been towards the latter supposition,[2] and clearly it is only thanks to this assumption that we can learn anything at all about the Hellenists and thereby get some impression of their attitude to the temple and the Law—an attitude that can take its place in a development from Jesus to Paul. Of course, it is open to question whether Luke imagined the very early Church as a development, or whether, except for certain specially important accounts, he did not put together a record from individual narratives, as pearls are threaded on a string. It is not likely that tradition gave him much enlightenment about dates, and he hardly knew anything about antagonisms within the early Church, except those that he reports. Nor is it certain that they played such a part as nineteenth-century research attributed to them. Luke is indeed an edifying writer—in the classical meaning of the word—who speaks about God and not about men, even when he is talking about men. His aim is to write a biblical narrative; his very language shows his efforts to express himself in biblical terms.[3]

---

[1]Acts 6.11: 'We have heard him speak blasphemous words against Moses and God', cf. Matt. 26.65; and Acts 6.13 f.: 'This man never ceases to speak words against this holy place and the law; for we have heard him say that this Jesus of Nazareth will destroy this place and will change the customs which Moses delivered to us.' This latter accusation is made against Jesus in Matt. 26.61 and par. Jesus' attitude to the Law could be so described in the Gospels (though not specially so during the trial) as to indicate that he wanted to change the customs that went back to the time of Moses. The sneering words directed against Moses may easily correspond, if it is Stephen's opponents who are speaking about them here, to what Jesus had said about the Law. This accusation of his opponents is contradicted by the fact that Stephen's speech in 7.20–44 gives the highest appreciation of Moses that we meet in the New Testament, the language about him in other passages generally being controversial; see my *Petrus und Paulus*, pp. 119 f. Baur already (*Paul* I, pp. 58 f.) points out that the accusation against Stephen is simply a repetition of the accusation against Jesus.

[2]Thus Knox, *St Paul*, p. 33; cf. his *St Paul and the Church of Jerusalem*, 1925, pp. 39 ff.; Nock, p. 62; Goguel, pp. 81 f. Cadbury is of a different opinion, 'The Speeches in Acts', *Beginnings* 5, pp. 402–27; so are Dibelius and Kümmel, p. 46; cf. Dibelius, 'The Speeches in Acts', *Studies in the Acts of the Apostles*, pp. 138–91.

[3]See A. Wifstrand, 'Lucas och Septuaginta', *STK* 16, 1940, pp. 243–62, and 'Lucas och den grekiska klassicismen', *SEA* 5, 1940, pp. 139–51.

But whether the speech comes from Stephen or from Luke—and it would be unjustified to regard the dilemma as non-existent, and thus suppose that it is always Luke who has composed the speeches with no sources to refer to—its importance in the string of pearls to which we have compared the narratives in Acts must be more strongly underlined than it has hitherto been. We might say that its content is a statement of a Diaspora Jew's attitude to the Old Testament. The speech deals with Israel in exile. It begins with the call of Abraham, who is to leave his kindred and go into the land that God will show him (7.2–4). When he comes into the promised land, God gives him no inheritance in it, not even a foot's length; but he promises to give it to him and his posterity in possession after the exile in Egypt (7.5–7). Stephen tells how Joseph and Jacob went into Egypt, and of the sufferings that Pharaoh brought on the people of Israel as the time approached when God intended to give the people the promised land. Moses has to leave his people and live in Midian for forty years as a stranger, till God reveals himself to him in the burning bush and sends him to Egypt to rescue Israel. It is not till v. 45 that the speaker comes to the immigration into Palestine and of the building of Solomon's temple, and then it is to prove from Scripture that the Almighty does not live in temples built by men's hands (7.45–50); and even before this, in the quotation from Amos (v. 43), he has announced the new exile with the words, 'and I will remove you beyond Babylon.'[1]

In Stephen's speech we see Israel as a fugitive nation to whom God reveals himself outside Palestine; and it is important that this theme

[1]In 'Saint Stephen and the Jerusalem Temple', *Journal of Ecclesiastical History* 2, 1951, pp. 127–42, Marcel Simon has discussed Stephen's speech, and has given an exposition that differs greatly from the above. Thus he regards the quotation from Amos 5.25–7 in vv. 42 f. as a rejection of sacrificial worship; but in the context of the rest of Stephen's speech these words can surely only mean that because the Israelites were idolators, they did not sacrifice to God while they were wandering in the desert. So Lake and Cadbury *ad loc*. Wendt understands Stephen's original meaning in the same way as Simon, but in such a way, be it noted, that the writer of Acts has altered the speech by editing it, so that Amos' words have become a reproach. And Isa. 66.1 f., the quotation in vv. 49 f., which Simon regards as an attack on the temple, is in fact in its original context part of a denunciatory sermon against the ungodly, and fits well with v. 51, where Stephen speaks of the Israelites as always having been stiff-necked and always having resisted the Holy Spirit. If Isa. 66.1 f. is interpreted in modern Old Testament research to mean that no building of temples is to be allowed (see Volz, *Jesaia II*, Kommentar zum Alten Testament 9.2, 1932, pp. 288 ff.), we have to ask whether such an interpretation was possible outside or within the very early Church, or whether it seemed natural (see Billerbeck I, p. 333). The transition from v. 50 to v. 51 can best be understood if we take into account Isa. 66.2b–4 (which is not quoted) where God looks to the man who is humble and contrite in spirit, but will punish one who arouses his displeasure. Simon argues on p. 133 from the use of χειροποίητον in the LXX and among the Greek-speaking Jews when he explains v. 48, ἀλλ' οὐχ ὁ Ὕψιστος ἐν χειροποιήτοις κατοικεῖ, but the sentence does not bear out the validity of these arguments; see also Moulton and Milligan and Arndt and Gingrich s.v.

dominates the speech that concludes the account of the church in Jerusalem. In the following chapters we are told of events that take place outside that city. It is true that Jerusalem is their centre, but they take place further and further away; and we come back to Jerusalem only when these events in Samaria, Caesarea, Antioch, and the Gentile Christian churches make it necessary. That is the case when the news that Samaria has received God's word reaches the apostles in Jerusalem, and they send Peter and John to Samaria (8.14, cf. v. 25). The incident of the Ethiopian treasurer takes place on the road between Jerusalem and Gaza, and might possibly mean that Philip was sent on a mission from Jerusalem (8.26?), but as Luke has it, the only thing it has to do with the city is that the treasurer has been there on a pilgrimage. The story of Paul's call at Damascus mentions first his participation in the persecution in Jerusalem (9.1 f.; cf. vv. 13 f.), and then ends with the account of his going to Jerusalem (9.26-30). In 9.32-43 Peter is in Lydda and Joppa. His baptism of Cornelius in Caesarea (ch. 10) involves an explanation of the matter on his arrival in Jerusalem (11.1-18).[1] Then follows the story of the origin of the church at Antioch; and the collection in that church for the brethren in Judaea results in the sending of Paul and Barnabas, which takes us back in ch. 12 to Jerusalem. 15.2 also deals with events in Antioch, which result in the journey of Paul and Barnabas to Jerusalem and the Apostolic Council there. The detailed description of events in Jerusalem and Caesarea in chs. 21-26 is also occasioned by Paul's journey from Ephesus to Jerusalem (19.21, but here there is no mention of the collection which, according to Paul's letters, is an essential motive) and it concentrates so heavily on Paul's experiences that the Jerusalem church is mentioned only in 21.17 f. In this way Stephen's speech about fugitive Israel serving God in a strange land receives a certain force, as it forms the transition from the description of the church in Jerusalem to the description of the mission in 'all Judaea and Samaria and to the end of the earth' (1.8).

If there are real reminiscences of Stephen's point of view in the speech in ch. 7, it does not mean that the speech at once becomes an

[1]We should again notice the strong expressions (11.1): 'Now the apostles and the brethren who were in Judaea heard ὅτι καὶ τὰ ἔθνη ἐδέξαντο τὸν λόγον τοῦ Θεοῦ. And in 11.18, 'When they heard this they were silenced. And they glorified God, saying, "Then to the Gentiles also God has granted repentance unto life." ' Cf. 15.7, 'that by my mouth the Gentiles should hear the word of the gospel and believe', and 19.10, 'so that all the residents of Asia heard the word of the Lord, both Jews and Greeks', and 21.19, 'After greeting them, he [Paul] related one by one the things that God had done among the Gentiles through his ministry'; cf. 15.4. These expressions in Luke's writings remind us of Paul's mention of the mission to the Jews in Rom. 10.14-21, and of the mission to the Gentiles in Rom. 15.15-23.

expression of the Hellenists' views and so of a radical break with the views of the church. There is still no proof that such ideas were anything unusual in the Jerusalem church at that time. If we think that the church as a whole held to a fully Jewish point of view, then, of course, the speech denotes something new and radical pointing to a coming separation from the religion of the temple. But the idea of Israel's disobedience from the very beginning till the time of Jesus is one that we have already met in the Gospels, e.g., in the parable of the vineyard and the wicked tenants (Matt. 21.33–41 and par.), and references to the rejection of the earthly temple and the expectation of the coming Messianic temple are also found in the words of Jesus (Matt. 21.42–44 and par., and in other passages where the temple is mentioned in the Gospels).[1] With regard, therefore, to Stephen's views on this matter, the speech contains nothing that he could not have learnt from Jesus, just as the unsparing criticism of Israel may be an echo of the speeches of Moses and the prophets to their own people, as is suggested by the quotations that are interwoven.[2]

An important question with regard to Stephen's speech is whether those themes are used in a speech proclaiming the Gospel before the seat of justice, or whether it is merely a proclamation of judgment. In the former case the speech is an accused Christian witness's confession before the authorities, his opponents' accusations being met with a confession of the Gospel instead of with a defence. But in the latter case it is of some importance whether the speech expresses, as a proclamation of judgment, what Stephen may have said or thought, or whether in any case this purpose of the speech is to be attributed to Luke, who indeed alludes repeatedly to Israel's rejection. As it is hardly possible to find objective criteria for deciding between the two possibilities, we shall suppose that here as elsewhere Luke has it that Israel is rejected, but that we cannot be sure that Stephen could say that himself. Perhaps it is more likely that, like Paul, he stressed the people's hard-heartedness, but presumably added, again like him, that God was constantly trying to save his own wandering people.[3]

It has been thought that the persecution of the church in Jerusalem

---

[1]See, e.g., Joachim Jeremias, *Jesus als Weltvollender*, 1930; see the index, p. 88, under Tempel.

[2]Thus also Peake, in 'Paul and the Jewish Christians', *BJRL* 13, 1929, p. 34, rightly remarks, 'The Law is scarcely touched upon; no hostility is expressed towards it nor any anticipation of its abolition.'

[3]The speech certainly mentions the many people whom God has sent to Israel, although they are mentioned to show that Israel has always been disobedient. From the fact that the speech is broken off (7.54 ff.) we cannot infer that its intention was to be supplemented by the ending that we have lost; for it is quite usual for speeches in Acts to be broken off, being nevertheless complete; see Cadbury in *Beginnings* 5, pp. 425 f., and M. Dibelius, *Studies in the Acts*, pp. 160 f.

after Stephen's death was directed solely against the Hellenists. In this way it appears plain that the primitive Church's point of view was entirely Jewish, as the only people persecuted were those who were beginning to detach the Church from Judaism. Goguel writes[1] that the writer of Acts made the persecution of the Hellenists relate to all the Christians, so that the latter, with the exception of the apostles, were scattered in Judaea and Samaria. He rightly remarks that the apostles cannot have remained in Jerusalem without being molested; but that consideration, though sound, is no argument for leaving the text of Acts completely out of account. Lietzmann takes the same view as Goguel, and goes on, 'That probably means that the persecution was directed only against the Hellenists, who were hostile to the Mosaic law, whereas the true Palestinian Jews remained unmolested.'[2] We can see how a quite definite interpretation, with no additional reasons, is given to the words 'they were all scattered . . . except the apostles.' Luke must mean that the Christians had to leave Jerusalem for a time. The single exception that he admits is the apostles, about whom he is either told by his sources or led to believe by his own way of thinking that they did not leave the holy city (Acts 1.4, cf. pp. 210–12). The dispersion of the Christians need not have lasted long; nor is it certain that Peter's departure during King Agrippa's persecution (12.17) means the beginning of a continued absence from Jerusalem. In cases where the authorities exiled a section of the population, we see that the latter generally comes back after a certain time, often without any official repeal of the ban.[3] There is, indeed, no reason for the presumption that in these rather different circumstances the fugitives should not have returned to Jerusalem, like Peter after the death of King Agrippa, and the fugitive members of the church, including the Hellenists, as soon as the persecution had ceased. But as we possess only these few disconnected narratives, we lack the connecting links that might help us to a complete understanding of the story.[4]

We have tried to show above that nothing is related by Luke about Stephen (and the Hellenists) that has not already been related about Jesus; and we thus have to suppose that there was, according to Luke's sources and his own conception of the facts, no contrast between Jesus, Stephen, and the original Church as such. Baur tried to prove

---

[1]*Les Premiers Temps de l'Église*, p. 57.
[2]*The Beginnings of the Christian Church*, p. 71.
[3]See F. H. Cramer, 'Expulsion of Astrologers from Ancient Rome', *Classica et Mediaevalia* 12, 1951, pp. 9–50.
[4]This is opposed to Baur, *Paul* I, p. 39: 'Had all the Christians in Jerusalem left the city with the exception of the Apostles, something more would certainly have been said of the return of the fugitives to the Church, which still continued to exist in Jerusalem.'

(*Paul* I, p. 39) that the Hebrews, together with the apostles, attached themselves more closely to the worship in the temple and were therefore not regarded as enemies of the Jews. He refers to Luke 24.53 (about the disciples after the Ascension, 'and were continually in the temple blessing God'); Acts 3.1, 'Now Peter and John were going up to the temple at the hour of prayer, the ninth hour.'; 3.11; 4.1; 5.25, 'And some one came and told them, "The men whom you put in prison are standing in the temple and teaching the people." ' The passages referred to but not quoted are in my opinion quite superfluous. Baur did not, however, name all the passages that might support his view; one might add Acts 2.46, 'And day by day, attending the temple together and breaking bread in their homes. . . .'; 5.42, 'And every day in the temple and at home they did not cease teaching and preaching Jesus as the Christ.' These two passages are probably general descriptions coming from the writer of Acts, like Luke 24.53. The other passages show us Peter and John on the way to the temple at the time of prayer (3.1), and the apostles preaching in the temple (5.25). Just as Jesus spoke and discussed in the temple while he was staying in Jerusalem, his disciples also used it to spread their message. If they also, as is shown in 3.1, 2.46, and 5.42, took part in the services in the temple, there is no need to infer from that that their point of view was a purely Jewish one. It is also related of Paul that he took part in religious ceremonies in the temple, e.g. in a purification connected with a Nazirite vow (Acts 21.26), and that he did everything possible to reach Jerusalem by Pentecost (Acts 20.16). This is certainly one of the points on which the letters do not directly support the narrative of Acts; but Paul's behaviour here agrees with his attitude to Judaism elsewhere (see pp. 42–49). In any case, Luke can hardly have told this about Paul with the intention of showing that he was nearer than the early Church to the worship in the temple. He may very well have assumed, even in the primitive Christian period, a freer attitude to the temple services; and therefore no sort of weight can be attached to the passages that are supposed to prove that the Jerusalem church as a whole, or in any case the Hebrews, kept to the temple or to the Jewish religion at all. For Jesus' disciples, both as Jewish Christians and as missionaries to the Jews who were making pilgrimages from all over the world to Jerusalem, the temple and the meetings for prayer to which the crowd flocked were a natural objective.

Finally we come once more to the list of the seven guardians of the poor, the most important being Stephen (Acts 6.5). The result of the Hellenists' complaint that their widows were overlooked in the daily distribution was that the twelve called a church meeting and proposed that seven men of good repute, full of the Spirit and of wisdom, should be chosen; and the twelve would appoint them to the service of the daily distribution. Thereupon the seven men were elected (6.5). They seem to have been elected by the whole church, and it might therefore be imagined that they would come from the Hebrews as well as from the Hellenists; but it is usually assumed that, except for Nicolaus who was a proselyte from Antioch, they were Jews of the Diaspora. It is true, Lake and Cadbury write on 6.5, that the Palestinian Jews often had Greek names, but it is unlikely that in a group of six or seven Palestinians all without exception had Greek names. Among the twelve apostles there are only two with Greek names.

It may not be right to draw conclusions from the twelve apostles about conditions in Jerusalem, as they probably all came from Galilee, where the custom about names may have been different from that in the capital. It is not easy to get enlightenment on the Jewish custom about names in Jerusalem through the graves found in that city, as inscriptions with Greek and Semitic names are often found there in the same burial-ground, while neither the kinship of the buried nor the dates of the burials can be determined with certainty.[1]

It seems very unlikely that the problem was solved by electing from the dissatisfied section of the church all the members of the new committee that was to arrange matters in the future; a more likely supposition is that at any rate some of the seven were Palestinian Jews. If that is the case, Stephen or Philip for instance may be Palestinian Jews, while the others, about whom we have no information beyond their names, apart from late information dating from the second century, may have been Diaspora Jews. If that is the case—and it is not less likely than that they were all Jews of the Greek-speaking Diaspora—then Stephen's behaviour was in no way an expression of Hellenist-Jewish views, and the persecution that broke out after his death was not directed specially against the Hellenists. We again see an example of interpreting from a general assumption a detail that is not clear; and the interpretation has led to a series of assumptions that come to have the status of established facts. We can only say for certain that it is unlikely that all seven guardians of the poor were Hellenists. In any case, Stephen may quite well have been a Hebrew and therefore a representative of the Jerusalem church as such, and not merely a representative of a temporary Hellenistic minority which the next persecution is said to have removed for ever from the church in

---

[1]As far as I know, no attempt at a comprehensive survey of Jewish names has been made since Zunz, *Namen der Juden*, 1836, republished 'corrected and enlarged' in Dr. Zunz' *Gesammelte Schriften*, Vol. II, 1876, pp. 1–82.

Jerusalem—a church that, in the main and apart from that minority, was, according to such a view, entirely Jewish in its outlook.

VI

Peter and Cornelius. If it is correct, as has been assumed above, that Peter and the other Hebrews have the same point of view as the Hellenists (as none of the groups has a purely Jewish point of view), and regard themselves as the preachers of a new message, the narrative in Acts about the first baptism of Gentiles takes on a special interest. We are used to thinking of the demand for circumcision and the observance of the Law as arising as soon as there is any talk of missionary work among the Gentiles; but the narrative of Cornelius disillusions us at once on this, as it contains nothing from start to finish about those two fundamental points; on the contrary, it is concerned with the question how far one is justified, as a Jew, in going into a Gentile's house. The firm rejection of the thought that presents itself to Peter during the vision in Joppa (10.10–16), and the visions that precede his visit (10.3–7; cf. vv. 22 and 30–33, and 10–16), are evidence that so far he has not only not gone in to any Gentile, but that he has not even regarded as a duty the preaching of the Gospel to the Gentiles. That is stressed in Peter's speech in Cornelius' house, as he asserts, with a plainness that must in such a place be unmistakable, that the Gospel is for Israel alone: v. 36, 'the word which he sent to Israel,' and v. 42, 'and he commanded us to preach to th^ people.' Only the outpouring of the Holy Spirit on the Gentiles who are gathered there shows him and the other Jewish Christians what in fact the speech already implied, namely that they are to venture to baptize Gentiles.[1]

In his 'The Conversion of Cornelius'[2] Martin Dibelius has tried to distinguish between the original harmless 'legend' about Cornelius' baptism by the apostle Peter, and its editing by Luke, who lifts the story into the realm of principles. Dibelius separates Peter's vision of the sheet that is let down from heaven (10.9–16), his speech in Cornelius' house (10.34–43), and the justification in Jerusalem of his association with Gentiles (11.1–18), together with a few details of his arrival at Cornelius' house (10.27–29), and the references to the Christians from Joppa who went with him and became witnesses of what took place (10.23b, 45; cf. 11.12). There remains an original narrative describing

---

[1]The verses in question are 34–5: 'Truly I perceive that God shows no partiality, but in every nation any one who fears him and does what is right is acceptable to him', and v. 43: 'To him all the prophets bear witness that every one who believes in him receives forgiveness of sins through his name.'
[2]*Studies in the Acts*, pp. 109–22.

the God-fearing Gentile Cornelius, to whom an angel manifests himself, bidding him send for Peter from Joppa. The Holy Spirit moves Peter to follow the messengers to Caesarea, and in Cornelius' house the Holy Spirit falls on the Gentiles who are there, so that they speak in tongues, and thus it becomes clear to Peter that he is to baptize them.

There is no room for doubt that Luke worked on the story of Cornelius, and that he has given it its present form, in which certain parts are repeated for the sake of special emphasis. But the features that Dibelius wants to remove as being superimposed on the original 'harmless legend' are not to be distinguished fundamentally from the details that he allows to remain. In 10.34–43, for instance, the speech emphasizes, as we have already mentioned, that the Gospel is meant for Israel only, while on the other hand vv. 34 f., 43 express the new truth revealed by what has happened; and Peter's vision of the sheet and the clean and unclean animals underlines the fact that he was not prepared for the Gentiles' request. And the command that Peter received from the Spirit, and the outpouring of the Spirit on the Gentiles gathered in Cornelius' house, show likewise that without those signs from above Peter would have neither gone there nor baptized.

Dibelius prefers to interpret the vision differently. He thinks it is a matter here of clean and unclean foods, and of how far the latter were allowed to Christians. Another Petrine tradition about a vision of this kind has been worked by Luke into the originally simple legend, which, like the narrative of the Ethiopian treasurer (8.26–40), contained only the story of a conversion. It would be possible to criticize Dibelius' separation of sources on details, but it is more important to emphasize that the separated legend is not at all 'harmless'. It will not eliminate the point of the narrative—even the narrative that has been thus separated—namely that Peter goes to a Gentile because the Holy Spirit tells him to, and that when the Spirit makes the Gentiles who are gathered there speak in tongues, he baptizes them. It is, and remains, a striking story, which cannot lose its epoch-making character by having parts here and there removed from it. It is presumably correct that the allusion to unclean foods in 11.3 is due to Luke, who knew about the narrative that follows about the Council at Jerusalem and the food laws for the Gentile Christians; but it is incorrect to make that a reason for relating the vision (10.10–16) to foods and not to people.[1]

---

[1]The sheet from heaven, containing all kinds of animals, reminds one of Noah and the ark; but the patriarch kills and sacrifices only clean animals (καθαρός twice in Gen. 8.20) after the flood had ceased. God commands that from now on all animals are to be food for man (9.3), while, however, prohibiting the eating of meat with blood in it (cf. Acts 15.20). An interpretation that can leave out of account the separation of clean and unclean animals sees particularly in 9.10 a confirmation of the words to Peter, 'What God has cleansed, you must not call common' (Acts

As a rule people wish to stress that it was Peter who received here a call to the Gentiles, and they are right if we think of Luke; that is how he must have regarded the narrative. As we read in 8.14 that Samaria had received God's word, so we read here that the Gentiles had received it (11.1; cf. 11.18 and 15.7). But Dibelius is thus far right, that we have to distinguish between the original legend and its editing by Luke. The original legend certainly tells how Peter goes to the Gentiles at the command of the Spirit, but it is not the story of a call. It is a question of an episode without any decision based on principle, maintained on the. basis of Jewish Christianity's interest in the Gentiles, and becoming significant with the successful launching of the mission to the Gentiles. It reminds us of the narratives that were preserved in the Gospels about Jesus. Peter was not sent to the Gentiles any more than Jesus was, but it came about that when the Gentiles were in distress they turned to Jesus, and the narratives of that were preserved and played a part in tradition, because the relation of the very early Church to the Gentiles underwent a rapid development. In ch. 9 we shall examine these texts more closely (see pp. 260–64).

For the present we must confine ourselves to describing the original Cornelius story as a narrative about a Gentile whose baptism was due to special circumstances. It was not a question here of something self-evident, as would have been the case if the narrative came from circles that took an active and favourable attitude towards the mission to the Gentiles. No, it existed as a tradition in places where one's attitude towards the Gentiles was a problem. It is full of tensions, as, for instance, in the speech (10.34–43) where it is said at the same time that the Gospel is destined only for Israel and that the forgiveness of sins in the name of Christ is for everyone who believes in Christ. The same tension lies over Peter's behaviour when he has seen the vision; he makes objections, and has to be ordered to do what God wants him to.[1] In these tensions we recognize the conflicting points of view that are found in the story of the Canaanite woman (Matt. 15.22–28 and par.).

Now at last we can come to the most important thing in this narrative. Both in its original form, as a story about Peter's helping a certain Gentile, and in its fundamental application, which we already supposed had led to its preservation and took shape with it, long before Luke adopted

---

10.15). It is more natural to apply to men the account of the flood with the covenant that follows it (Gen. 9.1 f. and v. 8 f.). God indeed makes a covenant here with Noah and his three sons, from whom the population of the whole earth is descended (Gen. 9.18 f.). Thus the words of Acts 10.15 can be applied without any difficulty to men.

[1]Compare here Ananias' objections in 9.13 f., though they do not sound as sharp as Peter's words.

it, it dispenses with the features that the tradition of research would lead us to expect. We hear nothing of what the Jewish Christian church both may and must require from the Gentiles. The problem simply is: Can I and may I go to the Gentiles? On this point too the narrative of Cornelius is like the *pericope* of the Canaanite woman. Peter has only received the command to preach to Israel, just as Jesus was sent only to the lost sheep of the house of Israel; but the Holy Spirit determines nevertheless—and confirms it with the sign of speaking in tongues—that Peter is to baptize those Gentiles.

We read nothing about these Gentiles' having to be circumcised or about their being ordered to observe the Jewish Law; nor are any rules laid down even about eating clean and unclean foods—only Luke just touches that problem in 11.3. Thus those who first related this 'harmless legend' had no clear-cut Jewish point of view; they did not at once react as Jews and say that a Gentile must first become a proselyte and could then be received into the Church through baptism. They knew that God could introduce a new dispensation by an angel or the Holy Spirit,[1] just as they themselves, as former Jews and present Jewish Christians, were living under a new dispensation, the New Covenant.

VII

The Council at Jerusalem. The kind of thing that has been shown by an examination of the Cornelius narrative can also be said about the narrative of the meeting that is usually called the Council at Jerusalem. It is interesting to see what does not happen, but certainly would have happened if the Jerusalem church had had a clear-cut Jewish point of view.

The church and its leaders, the apostle Peter and James the Lord's brother, do not represent a Jewish point of view. There are only two smaller groups that represent what in Paul's letters we call Judaizing, namely the demand that the Gentiles who become Christians shall be circumcised and be bound to keep the Law. We have already remarked above that the narratives of Acts do not give a clear and complete picture of the primitive Church. In spite of that, we will pause here to point out that it is on the occasion of the Council at Jerusalem in ch. 15 that we first meet Judaizing in Jerusalem; and very characteristically it is neither the leaders nor the church, but two smaller groups, that appear as Judaizers. It is also, by the way, the last time that we hear

---

[1] Cf. Gal. 2.7–9, 'But on the contrary, when they saw that I had been entrusted with the gospel to the uncircumcised. . . . James and Cephas and John. . . . gave to me and Barnabas the right hand of fellowship.'

of Judaizing in Acts, either in Jerusalem or elsewhere, apart from the text 21.17–25, which we shall discuss later.

The first of the two groups consists of Christians who came down from Judaea to Antioch, and taught the brethren there, 'Unless you are circumcised according to the custom of Moses, you cannot be saved.' Here we have the same demands that the Judaizers made in the Galatian churches. In dealing with Paul's letters we saw that Judaizing is a Gentile Christian heresy which the Gentile Christians did not take over from Jerusalem or the Jewish Christians. It is therefore probable that those itinerant Judaizers among the Gentile Christians are transferred by Luke from the Pauline mission field to Jerusalem, as he makes everything, as far as possible, gather round the Christian centres.[1] Thus Jerusalem is the starting-point of the persecution in 9.1 ff. and of the Judaizing mentioned here, just as the fugitive members of the church take the Gospel from Jerusalem to the Gentiles, and from there too the decisions of the Council at Jerusalem make a final end of Judaizing.

If, as would be the natural thing grammatically, we regard τινὲς κατελθόντες ἀπὸ τῆς Ἰουδαίας (15.1) as the subject of ἔταξαν (in v. 2),[2] then these opponents appear as visiting overseers from Jerusalem, and we have here, as so often before, a description of the behaviour of such emissaries (cf. 8.14 ff.; 9.32–43; 11.22–30). But in this case it is shown that the church in Jerusalem did not send them out. We owe to Acts the picture of the mother church wielding authority over the new churches that arise, even when the latter do not owe their origin to the work of Jerusalem Christians. But that is not the only point of view from which Acts looks at the mission to the Gentiles. In 15.3 Paul and Barnabas, on their way up to Jerusalem, give an account of the conversion of the Gentiles, and the churches in Phoenicia and Samaria are delighted about it. They are received with greater reserve in Jerusalem,[3] where they relate everything that God has accomplished through them. It is noted here, as in 15.12 and 21.19, that Paul and his fellow-workers are carrying on the mission to the Gentiles at a distance, and that the church in Jerusalem has nothing to do with it. The agreement that Paul mentions in Gal. 2.7–9 is therefore assumed here, that Peter is to go to the circumcised, and he himself to the Gentiles.

---

[1]On Luke's presentation of the history of the early Church as a history of Christian centres, see p. 104.

[2]The Western Text says outright that these Jerusalem people determine that Paul, Barnabas, and some others are to go up to Jerusalem to be judged by the apostles and elders (ed. Ropes in *Beginnings* 3, p. 139). Cf. ἀπολυθέντες in 15.30; this may mean 'acquitted'—cf. Lake and Cadbury *ad loc*.

[3]This reception is at the same time more reserved than in 21.20. Goguel has no good grounds for holding that the reception was more cordial in the year 44 than in the year 58 (*Les Premiers Temps de l'Église*, pp. 66 f.).

In 15.5 Luke seems to give another explanation of the Council at Jerusalem. Here it is not the brethren from Jerusalem who went to the Gentile Christian churches; but former Pharisees in Jerusalem say that it is necessary to circumcise 'them' and to charge them to keep the Law.[1] We have not heard much about the Pharisees elsewhere in Acts. Gamaliel, through whose influence the Sanhedrin adopted a temporizing policy towards the church in Jerusalem, is a Pharisee (5.34). Later, in 23.6–9, we hear of the Pharisees in the Sanhedrin and of their reaction to Paul's behaviour during the hearing there. Paul mentions elsewhere (26.5) that as a Pharisee he has lived in conformity with the strictest views on Jewish religious practice. It should be added here that according to Luke Jesus goes to Pharisees and eats with them (Luke 7.36 and 14.1).

The meeting that follows does not realize the expectations that the preliminaries aroused. There is not one word about the group of former Pharisees above-mentioned. Paul and Barnabas are certainly mentioned, but they are given so modest a place that this is rightly emphasized by Dibelius[2] as being a literary touch. The narrative of the two apostles about God's great deeds among the Gentiles is only briefly mentioned in 15.12 (cf. v. 3), and we hear nothing about the narrative's content, because, of course, the readers of the book know it already from Acts. In fact, the account of the Council at Jerusalem in Acts 15 is a literary performance, and its aim is not the understanding of historical events.[3]

The essential thing in the Council is what is said by Peter and James, in speeches recognizing the preaching of the Gospel to the Gentiles. Both Peter and James appeal to the Cornelius story as the decisive event that revealed God's will in this matter (15.7–9, 14). This confirms the above interpretation of ch. 10, the essential content of Peter's speech being Luke's view of the Cornelius episode as a settlement of the question on basic principles, James agreeing with that interpretation at the beginning of his speech. Here Peter adds a rejection of the demand that Gentile Christians must keep the Law, taking his stand on the point that neither the Jewish Christians themselves nor their fathers were able to bear such a yoke. But the Jewish Christians believe that they, like the Gentile Christians, are saved by the grace of the Lord Jesus. It has been thought that Peter here expresses a Pauline thought that Luke wrongly puts into his mouth; but that is not the case.[4]

[1]On αὐτούς see Lake and Cadbury *ad loc.*
[2]*Studies in the Acts*, p. 96.
[3]Dibelius, *loc. cit.*
[4]Dibelius is of the opinion that what we have here is not Pauline, but an expression of Luke's theology (*op. cit.*, p. 95). We have seen above (pp. 125–29) that what Peter is supposed to have said here is either Petrine or at any rate Jewish Christian.

If we consider Peter's attitude to the Law, as we see it in Acts, we have to collect those passages in the first twelve chapters, where circumcision, observance of the Law, and so on, which are important for this question, are mentioned. The Law was mentioned in the accusation against Stephen (6.13) and in his speech (7.53). In Paul's speech in Pisidian Antioch he says that through Jesus 'forgiveness of sins is proclaimed to you, and by him every one that believes is freed from everything from which you could not be freed by the law of Moses' (13.38 f.). The expression ἔθος is used (6.14) in the accusation against Stephen, and again with regard to the Jerusalem people's demands in Antioch (15.1). Nor are 'the Gentiles' mentioned very often in what goes before. In 9.15 Paul is called to carry Christ's name before the Gentiles and kings and the sons of Israel. In the Cornelius narrative we meet both ἀλλόφυλος (10.28) and τὰ ἔθνη (10.45; 11.1, 18). Nor do we hear anything about the Gentiles indirectly. Further back we have mentioned 2.39, 'For the promise is to you and to your children and to all that are far off . . .,' but we have made that relate to the Jews in Palestine and of the Diaspora (see p. 213 n. 1). In 3.26 Peter says, 'God, having raised up his servant, sent him to you first. . . .'[1] In 4.27 it is said that the kings of the earth (as in Ps. 2.1 f.) were gathered together in Jerusalem against Jesus, namely Herod and Pontius Pilate, with the Gentiles and the peoples of Israel. In 10.28 and 11.19 f. Jews and Gentiles are contrasted with each other.

There is therefore nothing to be learnt from other texts in Acts about Peter's attitude to circumcision and the observance of the Law. We can see that it is only through God's deliberate intervention that he goes to Cornelius' house, preaches, and baptizes Gentiles. The attitude that he adopts to the Law must therefore, if it is to be historically probable, be based on a development within Jewish Christianity under the influence of Jesus and the events after Pentecost. We shall see later (pp. 247–55) that his words fit in quite well with the rest of what we know about the primitive Church.

James in his speech agrees with Peter's view of the Cornelius episode and points out that God has spoken in the Old Testament about a mission to the Gentiles. This occurs in Amos 9.11 f., quoted loosely from the LXX, which deviates considerably here from the M.T. This seems remarkable in a speech by James the Lord's brother, in the church at Jerusalem, and it would therefore be natural to attribute the speech to Luke. But what is even more striking is that its content agrees, not with Luke's views on redemptive history, but with those of the primitive Church. According to the quotation, God will first rebuild the fallen

[1]See p. 261.

dwelling of David (i.e., Israel), and when that has been done, it will have an effect on the Gentiles (ὅπως in v. 17). In God's plan of salvation, the salvation of Israel is not only the decisive event, but also the first. The line of thought here is the same as in Romans, 'to the Jew first and also to the Greek' (Rom. 1.16; 2.9 f.).

This view is repeated and stressed at the end of James' speech. Because of God's plan of salvation for the Gentiles, which is proclaimed in the quotation from Amos, they are not to be burdened with the Law; they are to be saved by God as Gentiles, not as Jews. It will be adequate to make a few modest requirements, namely the prohibitions contained in the apostles' decree that they 'abstain from the pollutions of idols and from unchastity and from what is strangled and from blood'. But these prohibitions are necessary, because 'from early generations Moses has had in every city those who preach him, for he is read every sabbath in the synagogues.' The last verse (v. 21) of this speech has understandably given rise to difficulties. We explain it in the sense that, owing to his way of regarding man's salvation, James assumes that Israel will convert the Gentiles some day,[1] and that therefore these particular prohibitions are necessary in order to make the synagogues all over the world missionary centres for Christ's Gospel. James' optimistic view here can be contrasted with Paul's words about the mission to the Jews (Rom. 10.14–21), 'Lord, who has believed what he has heard from us?'

These speeches might be called the Transactions of the Council. The two leaders speak, and the matter at issue is clear. Then on James' proposal it is resolved to announce these rules in a letter from the apostles and elders in Jerusalem to the churches in Antioch, Syria, and Cilicia, instead of requiring circumcision and the observance of the Law. At the same time it is noted that the people from Jerusalem who confused the churches were not sent out by the apostles and elders.

The Council at Jerusalem occupies an important place in the structure of Acts; it is foreshadowed by the Cornelius narrative, and is mentioned later on Paul's last visit to Jerusalem (21.25). The questions that occasion the Council have no connexion with the Jerusalem church as we know it from Acts 1–12. In Palestine there are churches composed of Jewish Christians who are doing missionary work among the Jews, but who have no missionary duty towards the Gentiles. As

[1]Cf. Paul in Rom. 11.12, 'Now if their trespass means riches for the world, and if their failure means riches for the Gentiles, how much more will their fullness mean!' And in 11.15, 'For if their rejection means the reconciliation of the world, what will their acceptance mean but life from the dead?' Cf. Jewish pronouncements about Israel's significance for the Gentiles, e.g., Test. Levi 14.3 f., 'And you are the lights of heaven like the sun and moon. What will all the Gentiles do if you delude yourselves in ungodliness?'

far as James' speech reflects the missionary views of the primitive Church, Israel is to be won for Christ first, and thereby the Gentiles are also to be won. An incident like Peter's visit to Cornelius is an exception which becomes important later. It is not till the mission to the Gentiles begins with Paul's first missionary journey that the demand for circumcision and observance of the Law becomes vocal. As soon as this demand is raised, it is rejected by the apostles and elders and the church at Jerusalem. As we have said, it is only two groups, in Antioch and Jerusalem respectively, that insist on it.

The question is now whether the description in Acts corresponds to the historical facts. As usual, Jerusalem makes the decision and sends the right delegates in place of the false emissaries, who are not acknowledged. It may be that it was necessary, for Luke's account of the history of the primitive Church as a history of Christian centres, to transfer to Jerusalem from the Pauline mission-field, where according to Galatians they belonged, the opponents who were demanding circumcision and observance of the Law. In that way those who raised the question in Antioch (and might be Judaizers of the same kind as those in Galatians), as well as the converted Pharisees who speak at the Council at Jerusalem, will belong to Jerusalem. The actual negotiations at the Council (15.6 ff.) seem to have no place for these Pharisaic opponents.

In Luke's editing of the Cornelius narrative we meet the accusation against Peter, 'Why did you go to uncircumcised men and eat with them?', and the apostle's explanation that the Lord had commanded him to do so. Now we know from Gal. 2.11 ff. that Peter ate with uncircumcised men at Antioch, and Luke's words here may be an actual reminder that Peter had taken the initiative. We know indeed from Galatians that, even if he temporarily regretted his freer point of view, he came to see, through Paul's energetic protest, that this later behaviour of his was wrong. Paul's agreement with 'those who were of repute' in Jerusalem, about which he tells in Gal. 2.1–10 and about which he no doubt often spoke, may have given occasion for people to know of a meeting at which an agreement had been reached.

Luke seems to string together quite diverse elements so as to be able to give his account of such a council. He puts into the mouth of some members of the Jerusalem church the demands of the Judaizers inside the Pauline churches. The two most important leaders of Jewish Christianity, Peter and James—John is mentioned for the last time in Acts 8.14, but is named by Paul in connexion with the Jerusalem meeting on which he comments—dominate the Council, which is so completely controlled by Jerusalem that it contradicts Paul's description of the meeting in Gal. 2.1–10. But if we disregard the use made of the Cornelius episode in the speeches, the rest, viz., Peter's mention of the Law, and James' account of the scheme of salvation, may quite well express the views of the primitive Church. It is difficult to reconcile the universal foundation that James gives to the decisons of the apostles' decree ('in every city', v. 21) with its geographical demarcation (v. 23). It is certainly possible that Luke may be on historical ground in relation to the decisions of the apostles' decree. The Noachic rules have been referred to[1] as a parallel to James' rules. But in the latter case we have a Jewish Christian attitude showing an eagerness for missionary work among the Gentiles that is in very marked contrast to what one could expect according to the traditional attitude. It cannot be unquestioningly assumed that it was Jerusalem that laid down these regulations for Syria and Cilicia, even if it is not quite clear where the dividing line was drawn between Peter's mission field and Paul's. It is not a matter of a separation between Jews and Gentiles, one person carrying on his work among the Jews and the other among the Gentiles of the same city; it is a matter of geographical demarcation. Peter preached to the Jews in Palestine and the great eastern Diaspora,[2] while Paul went out into the Diaspora of the Greeks. It seems reasonable to trust the account of Paul's missionary activity in Acts, according to which he begins in the synagogue, and afterwards goes to the Gentiles. Peter's missionary work, on the other hand, certainly begins in the synagogue, but it hardly reached further than the God-fearing Gentiles within the orbit of the Jewish community. We have to assume that the separation of the two mission fields must have existed as long as Peter and the other leaders of the mission to the Jews, even though they acknowledged the mission to the Gentiles, believed that they must now concentrate on the salvation of Israel, so as to bring about through it the salvation of the Gentiles too. That separation continued till the apostles' death.

Luke transferred to Jerusalem the decision about the authorizing of the mission to the Gentiles, and made Peter and James its advocates, but he has not yet ventured to take the decisive step of regarding them as apostles to the Gentiles—that does not come till later, during the sub-apostolic age, when the twelve earliest disciples of Jesus are regarded, not only as the highest authorities of the Church, but also as the apostles to the Gentiles.

In this there is a decisive contrast between the description in Acts and Paul's account in Gal. 2.1–10, because Paul, with everything still fresh

---

[1]Lake, *Beginnings* 5, p. 208; cf. Wendt, p. 234.
[2]Most of the Jews lived in Palestine, Egypt, Syria, and Mesopotamia.

in his memory, tells of his connexion with Jerusalem and Jesus' first disciples up to about the middle of the first century. Luke, on the other hand, composed his narratives in Acts at a time when by the death of the apostles what was apostolic had become something authoritative alongside Jesus. It was then that the Gospels and the whole written tradition (the sub-apostolic letters) were written down. But it is also the period during which Paul was overshadowed in his own churches, or at least in his own mission field, by the twelve disciples in Jerusalem who had taken into their care the mission to Israel; for now, as Israel has receded into the background in the Church's thought, they are beginning to change, after the likeness of Paul, into apostles to the Gentiles.

VIII

Paul's visit to James. On Paul's arrival in Jerusalem (Acts 21.17–25), he is received by James the Lord's brother together with the elders. He has a friendly reception (v. 20 and the whole context); but later James expresses his apprehension that there may be an unpleasant reception awaiting him in Jerusalem. The text that follows[1] is generally understood to mean that the Jewish Christians as such have quite a different idea of Paul from the one that James and the elders have. The latter are anxious as to how he will fare, as the others regard him as an apostate and an enemy of the people. Finally James informs Paul of the regulations for the Gentile Christians (21.25) which have been drawn up in Jerusalem in Paul's absence and which are in the apostles' decree in Acts 15.28 f.

The latter is, of course, a construction that is incompatible with the text of Acts 15, where those regulations represented the result of a meeting of Paul and Barnabas on one side and Peter, James, and the Jerusalem church on the other. But by interpreting this text critically in view of Gal. 2.6, in which Paul knows nothing of any additions by 'those who were of repute', people construct two meetings, namely the one mentioned in Gal. 2.1–10 and another where, in contradiction to the text of Acts, the people of the mission to the Jews make regulations on their own authority about the mission to the Gentiles. From that it is supposed that James' reference to these Jerusalem regulations comes as a complete surprise to Paul. It is clear that this theory does not fit in with the text, which indicates a harmonious relation between the two; and the reference to the apostles' decree must therefore be meant in the same sense. There is no difficulty in interpreting the text in completely the opposite way, namely as indicating that Jerusalem is

[1]See above pp. 72–76.

solidly with Paul in his attitude to the Gentiles, as the apostles' decree provides that the Gentiles are not to be circumcised or to observe the Law, but that they can confine themselves to these simple commands.[1]

If James is described here as a friend of the mission to the Gentiles, that is true, not only for Acts, but also for the whole of the New Testament. In the account of the Council at Jerusalem (Acts 15) James makes a speech protesting against any obligation on the Gentiles to be circumcised, and expressing what seems to have been the missionary view held in Jerusalem, namely that first the Jews and then the Gentiles are to hear the Gospel. We meet the same positive attitude in Paul's account of a meeting in Jerusalem in Gal. 2.1–10; and this is not weakened by the mention of 'certain men from James' in Gal. 2.12 (see pp. 100 ff.). In ch. 4 we considered in more detail the picture of James as it is drawn in the New Testament and in the primitive Church, and we saw that what the New Testament says has been interpreted through late and unreliable information, and that on that basis a Jewish James has been drawn who fits in with the Tübingen School, but not with our sources or with a sound historical method.

But if here, as elsewhere in the New Testament, James has taken up a favourable attitude towards the mission to the Gentiles, is that true at the same time only of the elders in Jerusalem, and not of the whole church there? James and the elders say to Paul (21.20 f.), 'You see, brother, how many thousands there are among the Jews of those who have believed; they are all zealous for the law, and they have been told about you that you teach all the Jews who are among the Gentiles to forsake Moses, telling them not to circumcise their children or observe the customs.' This remark is surprising, because the church in Jerusalem is described in Acts 15 and Gal. 2.1–10 (cf. 1.24) as well disposed and understanding towards the mission to the Gentiles; and Luke has just said in 21.17, about the friendly reception that Paul received from the Jerusalem Christians, γενομένων δὲ ἡμῶν εἰς Ἱεροσόλυμα ἀσμένως ἀπεδέξαντο ἡμᾶς οἱ ἀδελφοί. Wendt writes on this, 'The brethren who gave Paul and his Gentile Christian companions a friendly reception cannot be the Jerusalem Christians in general of whose distrust of Paul we read in v. 21, and of whom we are told in v. 22 that they will hear of his arrival; nor can they be the heads of the church, whom Paul did not meet till the next day (vv. 18 f.). They were therefore individual Christians, who probably belonged to Mnason's family or were among his friends and neighbours.' Wendt interprets οἱ ἀδελφοί in v. 17 in relation to vv. 21 f., so that the contradiction disappears; but in Acts

[1]So Lake and Cadbury *ad loc.*

οἱ ἀδελφοί is a constantly recurring expression for the whole body of Christians in a place, for the church (or churches).[1] While, therefore, v. 17 agrees with Acts as such, vv. 21 f. do not fit the context.

But the text of Acts 21 is very difficult in many respects. It is already remarkable that the church members in Jerusalem seem to have no suspicion that James and the elders have quite a different view of Paul from their own. But if that were the case, James could surely say that he and the elders would now disabuse the members, so that the latter should realize that everything that they had heard was wrong, and should adopt a favourable attitude towards the Gentile mission and Paul. Nothing of the kind is said; on the contrary, the responsible leaders of the church propose something quite different. As they dare not tell the truth—James' attitude to Paul is here just as hazy and equivocal as his attitude to Christ according to Hegesippus (Eusebius, *h.e.* II, 23.4–18)—they resort to a trick. Paul is to act a play before the eyes of the church—he is to take part in a Jewish purifying ceremony in the temple in connexion with a Nazarite vow, and in that way dissipate all the church's wrong ideas.

This certainly sounds remarkable. Responsible leaders have a different point of view from that of the main body of people whom they are supposed to lead, but to whom in the everyday course of things they accommodate themselves; and they therefore induce another Christian leader, who is visiting them at an inopportune moment, to make an effective demonstration to correct the church members' wrong ideas which those responsible leaders have made no effort to rectify. If we keep to the text that we read, James the Lord's brother is revealed as an equivocal person, a cowardly leader of the church, and a bad Christian.

By merely deleting two words we can not only save James' good reputation, but also obtain a much clearer text. In v. 20, BAC read ἐν τοῖς 'Ιουδαίοις (the words are missing in ℵ), and D reads ἐν τῇ 'Ιουδαίᾳ; this is later changed in the *koine* text to 'Ιουδαίων. We have already drawn attention to the unreasonable aspect of James' behaviour, which is in contrast to what is related elsewhere in Acts about him and the Jerusalem church. But the context too is evidence that what we read cannot be correct, as the words to Paul can refer only to the Jews and foreshadow his arrest. Where the text is wrong is in regarding these Jews as Jewish Christians; and all difficulties disappear if the text is slightly altered to make it clear that James and the elders are speaking of the Jews. Without any authority in the manuscript, I propose as the

[1]Thus Acts 9.30; 10.23; 11.1, 29; 12.17; 14.2; 15.1, 3, 22 f., 32 f., 36, 40; 16.2, 40; 17.10, 14; 18.18, 27; 21.7; 28.15 (cf. 22.5 about the Jews in a similar meaning).

original text πόσαι μυριάδες εἰσὶν ἐν τῇ Ἰουδαίᾳ, καὶ πάντες ζηλωταὶ τοῦ νόμου ὑπάρχουσιν.[1]

In favour of this alteration, which it will be seen consists in deleting τῶν πεπιστευκότων, we may bring forward the following points: (1) there are not many thousands of Jewish Christians in 'Judaea', whether that means Judaea or Palestine. In Jesus' time Jerusalem had about 25,000–30,000 inhabitants,[2] and Palestine about 500,000.[3] As πόσαι μυριάδες must probably mean at least 5 times 10,000—that is 50,000,[4] the Jewish Christians in Palestine at that time would make up about a tenth of the whole population. That is unlikely. The whole of the New Testament testifies that the spreading of the Gospel among the Jews was not crowned with success. In the Synoptic tradition many of Jesus' sayings indicate that the Jews will not accept the Gospel. In Paul's writings we see it clearly recognized (Rom. 9–11) that the Jews have rejected the Gospel. But it is not only historically that we have to reject the text, but also from literary considerations—Luke, in fact, wishes to show through Acts how the Jews reject the Gospel.[5]

(2) The text does not make sense if it is a question of the Christian church members, and not of a danger that threatens from the Jews outside the church. The responsible leaders of those who are named in vv. 20 f. will, of course, not say about them, 'And they have been told about you that you teach all the Jews who are among the Gentiles' etc. On the other hand, the Christian leaders may speak like that of the non-Christian Jews.

---

[1]Baur himself proposed the deletion of τῶν πεπιστευκότων (*Paul* I, p. 211): 'We must ask, how did all these thousands of believing Jews come into a church, which, according to all accounts, could not have been very important. The Jewish inhabitants of Jerusalem in general might perhaps be correctly spoken of as consisting of "many thousands," and the supposition seems very clear that the words τῶν πεπιστευκότων, added on to Ἰουδαίων, are spurious.' See also E. Schwartz, 'Die Chronologie des Paulus', *Nachrichten von der Gesellschaft der Wissenschaften zu Göttingen, Philos.-hist. Klasse*, 1907, No. 3, pp. 289 f., with reference to a correct criticism of the text. Nock writes (p. 136), 'We may well be somewhat sceptical about this reference to the multitude (literally 'myriads') of Jewish Christians: the danger was from ordinary Jews.'
[2]J. Jeremias, 'Die Einwohnerzahl Jerusalems zur Zeit Jesu', *Zeitschrift des Deutschen Palästina-Vereins* 66, 1943, pp. 24–31.
[3]Thus Harnack, *Mission*, p. 12.
[4]μυριάδες is often used of a large, innumerable quantity, and that meaning would fit the text quite well here. Quite often, too, there is no word after μυριάδες to indicate what is being counted (this would be the case if τῶν πεπιστευκότων in the text were deleted); see Liddell and Scott, H. van Herwerden, *Lexicon supple-torium et dialecticum*[2], 1910, Moulton and Milligan, and Stephanus' *Thesaurus* s.v. τῶν πεπιστευκότων may have come into Acts 21.20 from v. 25, the first words of which are περὶ δὲ τῶν πεπιστευκότων ἐθνῶν, a copyist with a later view of Jewish Christianity having made the Gentile Christians and the Jews in v. 20 parallel parts of the church, and so introduced a permanent misunderstanding of the earliest Jewish Christianity.
[5]Cf. H.-W. Surkau, *Martyrien in jüdischer und frühchristlicher Zeit*, 1938. p. 115.

(3) Nor does v. 22 make sense if it is a question of the Jewish Christians whom Paul has come to visit. The text here reads, 'What then is to be done? They will certainly hear that you have come.'

(4) The accusation in these people's mouths (21.21) is the same as in what follows, when the Jews accuse Paul. Already in 21.28 when there is a tumult in the temple, we hear the accusation, 'This is the man who is teaching men everywhere against the people and the law and this place.' Except for Paul's teaching 'against the people' they are the same accusations as were levelled at Stephen. If the temple is not expressly mentioned in 21.20 f., it is presumably because Luke likes to introduce variety, and the temple is already included in the proposal about taking part in the ceremony of purification in the temple.

If we agree to this alteration of the text, the account of Paul's reception by James and the elders in Jerusalem becomes a text showing that the church welcomes his visit gladly, but that the Jews are ready to pounce on him. His participation in the Jewish ceremony proposed to him by the Jerusalem leaders out of consideration for the intractable Jews, and in which he participated whole-heartedly in accordance with his views about Israel after the flesh, did not allow him to escape their persecution.

IX

After these exegetical considerations it is now possible to answer the question that was raised at the beginning of this chapter: Does Acts justify us in maintaining that the primitive Church's point of view was entirely Jewish, apart from its belief that the crucified Jesus was identical with the coming Messiah? We have already seen, in passing, that the participation of the primitive Church in the ceremonial prayers, and its repeated visits to the temple, do not mean that it kept to an entirely Jewish point of view. The participation in the temple service and in the mission to the numerous people from the city, and to the pilgrims who came together in great numbers from the Jewish colonies throughout the world, must have seemed quite natural from a purely Christian point of view. Paul always felt that he was a Jew as well as a Christian, and there is nothing to indicate that the account in Acts of his participation in the ceremony of purification relating to a Nazirite vow, and his subsequently bringing into a Jewish context his preaching of the Resurrection, does not correspond to historical facts.

Circumcision and the observance of the Law are very seldom mentioned in the texts quoted. That may be because those rules of Jewish piety were taken for granted and therefore did not need to be mentioned; but the reason may also be that the rules did not lay down preconditions that were taken as a matter of course in the life of the primitive Church. Luke does not like describing quarrels and disunity within the Church. For him there are external antagonisms, e.g., antagonisms between the Church and the Jews; but the new community generally appears with closed ranks. Any antagonisms that may exist between Hebrews and Hellenists, or between Jerusalem Christians on the one hand and Paul and Barnabas on the other, are dissolved without difficulty at a meeting, and so disposed of for good. And in Luke's work, with its simple but vigorous lines, a more complicated attitude towards the Law than a clear Yes or No would be out of place.

In occasional passages we do hear of circumcision and the observance of the Law. If we disregard the Old Testament contexts where the allusion has no topical significance (as περιτομή in 7.8), we read of circumcision in 15.1, 5, where the Jerusalem Christians in Antioch, or alternatively the former Pharisees in the Jerusalem church, demand that the Gentile Christians be circumcised. Besides that, we hear that the Jews reproach Paul with teaching the Jews of the Diaspora not to let their children be circumcised (21.21).[1] Jewish Christians from Caesarea and Jerusalem are referred to (10.45 and 11.2) as οἱ ἐκ περιτομῆς, but each time it is clearly in contrast to the Gentiles.[2]

The same holds good for νόμος as for περιτομή. Apart from passages where the word is used in an Old Testament context (7.53 is uncertain, but in 13.15 there is no topical application), it is used in 6.13 in the Jewish accusation against Stephen, 'This man never ceases to speak words against this holy place and the law.' In 6.14 he is accused of saying that Jesus 'will destroy this place, and will change the customs which Moses delivered to us.' The word ἔθος, which is used here, recurs in 15.1 in the demands that the Jerusalem Christians make of the Gentile Christians in Antioch, 'Unless you are circumcised according to the custom of Moses. . . .', as does νόμος in 15.5, where the one-time Pharisees demand of the Gentile Christians the observance of the Law as well as circumcision. If we disregard here Paul's words (13.39) and the Jewish accusations against him outside Jerusalem (18.13), nothing more is said about circumcision and the observance of the Law till we come to James' speech in 21.20 ff. (21.20, 24, 28; ἔθος in v. 21). In the following chapters Paul's attitude to the Law and the customs are mentioned several times. Paul was educated according to the strict manner of the Law of the fathers (22.3), he has not offended against the Law (25.8), nor against the customs (28.17)—as he was accused of doing (23.29; 24.6). And he catches the august High Priest

[1] Timothy's circumcision is mentioned in 16.3.
[2] τὰ ἔθνη in 10.45 and ἄνδρας ἀκροβυστίαν ἔχοντες in 11.3.

himself (who is supposed to judge him according to the Law) acting illegally (παρανομῶν, 23.3).

Disregarding here the legal proceedings against Paul, which will occupy us later (see ch. 11), it is important to keep in mind that circumcision is mentioned only in the less essential sections of the Cornelius narrative, and was not originally a part of it. Circumcision is in no way demanded here for Gentile Christians. On the contrary, the problem is, How can a Jew enter a Gentile's house? At the Council at Jerusalem in ch. 15 circumcision and the observance of the Law belong to previous history, which in Luke's account is joined to what follows (v. 10 refers back to vv. 1–2 and v. 5). The demands for circumcision and the observance of the Law are made in Antioch by Christians who have come from Jerusalem but were not sent out by the Jerusalem church, and later in Jerusalem by a group consisting of converted Pharisees. Otherwise we meet these characteristic expressions of Jewish piety only in the accusations of Jews against Christians, namely against Stephen and Paul.

Now is Luke right in thinking that the demand for circumcision and the observance of the Law within the Jerusalem church was enforced in respect of the Gentile Christians? According to his account, the two groups that made the demand were of little or no importance. They presumably brought forward their demand in the more loyal form of a wish to see it authorized as a command by the Jerusalem church. Have we a credible tradition here, or has Luke, by joining together the various elements of which the narrative of the Council at Jerusalem consists, and by small additions and alterations, transferred the concern of the Gentile Christian Judaizers from the Pauline churches to Jerusalem, because everything will take place and be decided in the original Christian centres?

It is, of course, possible that the demand may have been raised in Jerusalem by Jewish Christians, but it is unlikely, because the aim that Jewish Christianity saw before it was to convert Israel and thereby to lead the Gentiles to the Church. The mission to the Gentiles, which Paul and others have begun, can therefore hardly arouse interest among the Jewish Christians, and it must appear to them a tiresome and superfluous roundabout way. In their opinion the Gospel is to be preached to Israel, and then the Gentiles will be ready, like fruit ripe for the harvest. So the demand for circumcision and observance of the Law, which was made to the Gentiles, is possible and probable among Gentile Christians, but improbable within Jewish Christianity.

Thus the narratives are clear. They show us a Christian church in Jerusalem, outwardly conforming to Judaism, but in fact clearly distinct from it, so that relations are strained between Jewish Christians and other Jews; and this repeatedly leads to a persecution of the Church.

Much has been said about the theological tendency of Acts, the starting-point generally being that in that work Luke allows himself more freedom in relation to his sources than he did when working out his Gospel. That, however, is by no means certain. His dependence on the relation to the we-source and the Jerusalem narratives at the beginning of Acts may quite well be of nearly the same kind as it was in the case of the sources of Luke's Gospel. In any case, any tendency that he shows in Acts does not appear so consistently that people can easily agree about it. This may be simply because he depends more on tradition, and is less independent as an author, than is generally assumed.

There are certain features which meet one's eye and which seem repeatedly to have led to the hypothesis that Acts was written in defence of Paul at his trial.[1] This hypothesis, though attractive in itself, must be rejected, because the writer cannot have been one of Paul's pupils writing during the apostle's lifetime. The document, in fact, gives the impression of having been written in the sub-apostolic age, and of bearing traces of the changed attitude of that age to the time of the apostle.

Baur too claimed to see a theological tendency in Acts (introduction to *Paul*), and of course the writer actually had a tendency or a theology, but as there was no contrast such as the Tübingen School supposed between Jewish and Gentile Christianity, what Luke was doing did not consist in getting rid of that contrast and making the two opposing points of view agree. It was something quite different, which in fact would also be very well suited to a plea for the defence before the imperial seat of justice after the proceedings in Jerusalem and Caesarea in the account in Acts. Luke describes in his two-volume work, the Gospel and Acts, the origin of Christianity within Judaism, and its subsequent separation from it because of the Jews' unbelief. That separation is no human work—God guides and determines the Christian leaders' decisions step by step; and therefore nothing happens without the leading of the Spirit or a revelation. Groping and resisting, the disciples and apostles let themselves be brought to go to the Gentiles or to seek out new mission fields.

The Jews are disobedient, and will not accept the Gospel; that is

[1] See G. S. Duncan, *St Paul's Ephesian Ministry*, 1929, pp. 96–100, and H. Sahlin, 'Der Messias und das Gottesvolk', *Acta Seminarii Neotestamentici Upsaliensis* 12, 1945, pp. 30–51.

emphasized in three different contexts, and the result of their refusal is that the mission turns instead to the Gentiles (13.46; 18.6; 28.25–28); but we also hear of the Jews' unbelief on various other occasions. That is how the sub-apostolic age regards the Jews—they would not hear the Gospel, so it is now being preached to the Gentiles. We meet the idea with Paul in Rom. 9–11; but for him the Jews are not excluded, as the salvation of the Gentiles leads to that of the Jews. In the sub-apostolic age the situation is different—then the Jews are abandoned as unbelieving, and the emissaries shake off the dust from their feet as a testimony against them, and go on to take the Gospel to others, who are willing to hear it.

If therefore we have in Acts a view of the Jews that corresponds to the sub-apostolic age, we may well suppose that the view of the Jewish Christians in Acts 15.1, 5 rests on the writer's addition or interpretation from the point of view of that later period. In the Gentile church of his own time the Jewish Christians were regarded as people who demanded circumcision and observance of the Law from all who went over to Christianity; and even if that did not characterize without qualification every kind of Jewish Christianity in the second half of the first century, it may be assumed that the writer is not here talking at random. But when he attributes such demands to the Jerusalem Christians of the earliest period, he does an injustice to the earlier Jewish Christianity, and the primitive church in Jerusalem, which Paul knew and of which he spoke. It is true that the church confined itself to preaching to Israel; but in doing so it cherished the hope that the conversion of the chosen people would lead to the salvation of the Gentiles. It is true that the Jewish Christians had their children circumcised and observed the Law in their own way; but they believed that they were justified, not by works of the Law, but by faith in Christ Jesus.

9

ISRAEL AND THE GENTILES

IN this chapter we intend to summarize the results of the exegetical
inquiries of the previous chapters, and to add a few other inquiries
and reflections. We hope thereby to give the first sketch of the earliest
history of primitive Christianity as it will appear when we have freed
ourselves from the traditional picture that the Tübingen School draws
of Paul and primitive Christianity as a whole. The new picture can only
be a sketch, which the discussion that is to be expected is sure to
modify.

I

Before we begin the task, we must submit another source that has
to be brought into the investigation. In the earlier chapters we have
used partly (in chs. 4 to 7) Paul's letters, and partly (in ch. 8) Acts as a
source for Jewish Christianity. In doing so we took the path that research
has commonly chosen, though it can hardly be maintained that the
results are the usual ones. But there is a third important source for
Jewish Christianity; research has neglected it, but we intend to deal
with it briefly here in conjunction with the other two that have already
been used. We refer to the Gospels. Our four Gentile Christian Gospels
contain the traditions of Jewish Christianity. Or, to put it more clearly,
the traditions of the Palestine churches were taken over by the Gentile
Christian churches outside Palestine, where they were written down in
the form that we know as the four Gospels.

If in what follows we disregard John's Gospel, it is not because we
think that the Johannine tradition is any less significant than the Synoptic.[1] But we are concerned here, as elsewhere, to discuss the central
problems of Pauline research, and not to allow ourselves to be enticed
into secondary questions, however alluring they may seem, for the new
view of Paul needs no support from outside. The Tübingen School's

[1]See particularly a number of important articles by Fridrichsen on John's Gospel:
'La pensée missionnaire dans le Quatrième Évangile', *AMNSU* 6, 1937, pp. 39–45;
'Missionstanken i Fjärde evangeliet', *SEA* 2, 1937, pp. 137–48; 'Jesu avskedstal i
fjärde evangeliet, En introduktion till den johanneiska frågan', *SEA* 3, 1938, pp.
1–16; 'Kyrkan i fjärde evengeliet', *STK* 16, 1940, pp. 227–42. Unfortunately we have
no Fridrichsen bibliography to help us to find the many inspiring articles that have
come from his lavish hand. The titles enumerated above will certainly prove to
represent only a part of his contributions to the Johannine question.

traditional interpretation does not do justice to the real central Pauline problems; the new interpretation, on the other hand, allows the texts to come into their own. We therefore keep to the usual distinction between the first three Gospels and John's Gospel, and we use only the material of the former.

The Jewish Christian tradition that is found in the Synoptic Gospels was not appreciably remodelled by the transition from the Jewish Christian to the Gentile Christian churches. At the time when the transition took place, the material had assumed such a definite shape that no considerable changes could be made. The changes in the traditional material on Jewish Christian ground may have been of greater extent; but it is assumed here that in its main features the tradition goes back to Jesus, while the framework round the *pericopes*, and with it sometimes the understanding of individual words and narratives, was shaped by those who transmitted the tradition. Besides that, changes and additions of a more radical kind may have occurred. As, however, in the Church's view Jesus' words were always of present validity, it is true in general that that present validity was firmly maintained by slight changes at a time when the Church was in the midst of a far-reaching development and remodelling.

The Gospels are therefore not only collections of the transmitted sayings of Jesus; they are at the same time sources of the Palestinian Jewish Christianity that has transmitted those collections. It is hardly conceivable that those individual sayings of Jesus would have been preserved unless they had been believed to have an importance beyond the situation in which they were first uttered. When Jesus talked with Jewish opponents about questions of the Law and expressed a different view of it from the scribes of his time, for instance, such sayings would not have been handed down if the primitive Church had had an entirely Jewish point of view. So from the fact that those sayings of Jesus were preserved we may infer that questions about the validity and exposition of the Law were of immediate moment to the earliest Jewish Christianity in Palestine.

In dealing with contexts of that kind it will soon be discovered that different sayings of Jesus, and therefore different cycles of problems and different solutions, were joined together by a process of editing that may go back to the evangelist or have been undertaken before him. The various solutions that were possible within Jewish Christianity, and have been joined together here in an apparent mutual connexion, can be regarded either as stages in a development, or as contrasts contending with each other within the church in Palestine.[1]

[1]Thus, e.g., the various sayings in the context of Matt. 15.1–20 and Mark 7.1–23.

Just as in the preceding pages we have consulted Paul's letters and Acts about the earliest Jewish Christianity, in order to find out whether it is true that it took a purely Jewish point of view (apart from its belief that the crucified Jesus was identical with the coming Messiah), so we will once more ask the same question here: Is it true that that picture of the primitive Church is to be found in the Synoptic tradition?

There is no doubt that the answer must be No. According to the testimony of Paul and also of Acts, Jewish Christianity is quite different from what it is assumed to be by New Testament research as a whole, guided by the tradition of the Tübingen School. And the witness of the Synoptic tradition agrees with our primary source, Paul, as well as with Acts, whose witness, like the material of the Gospels, has undergone various editings, and therefore cannot compare with Paul's letters in value.

In the story of the temple tax (Matt. 17.24–27) we have evidence of a clear distinction between Jewish Christianity and Judaism. The collectors of the temple tax ask Peter whether 'your' teacher pays this tax, and gets the answer Yes. In the house later Jesus asks Peter the question, 'What do you think, Simon? From whom do kings of the earth take toll or tribute? From their sons or from others?' And when he said, 'From others,' Jesus said to him, 'Then the sons are free.'

The general view is that this story is old and Palestinian.[1] In his conversations with Peter, Jesus gives two solutions to the problem of the temple tax, one that is feasible in practice, and one that is the right way of acting on principle. In order not to give offence in the Jewish *milieu* where they work, Jesus and Peter are to pay the tax to the temple. But the correct solution of the question lies in the introductory words of the conversation, which contrast kings' sons and strangers with each other, and lead to the conclusion, 'Then the sons are free.'

The contrast between the sons, who are free, and the strangers, who have to pay a tax to God whose temple is in Jerusalem, is applied here by Jesus to the Christians and Jews. The former are God's sons, but the Jews are strangers to him, and are therefore rightly compelled to pay a tax to his temple in Jerusalem. In these words of Jesus we meet early

[1]Thus E. Klostermann, *Das Matthäusevangelium* (HNT 4)², 1927, pp. 145 ff. When Bultmann, in his *Geschichte der synoptischen Tradition*², 1931, pp. 34 f., speaks of an Antioch or Damascus origin beside this possibility of a Palestinian origin, with reference to B. H. Streeter, *The Four Gospels*, 1926, p. 504, it must be remarked that the weight of the stater in Antioch and Damascus is not the only thing that makes Streeter think that Matthew's Gospel originated in the first of the two cities mentioned. But, as may be seen on the same page of Streeter's book, it is the traditional view of the Antioch church as a *via media* between the Judaizers and the antinomianism of some of Paul's followers, that suggests such an interpretation. In this way the *a priori* ideas of the Tübingen School cause a Palestinian text to be transferred to Antioch.

evidence of the attitude of the original Jewish Christianity to Judaism—the Christians are sons, and for God the other Jews are strangers. Here we already have the view that the Church, the new people of God, takes of itself as a people that, as the true Israel, is distinct from the Jews.

But this self-assessment of the new people of God lies behind the whole Synoptic tradition's view of the Jews and their Law. Jesus, and after him the Church, take an independent attitude to the questions that have become of immediate concern through the coming of the Messiah and the dawning of the time of salvation; and we see in every way that the questions and their treatment have no connexion with the Jewish traditions. The Messiah and the new Israel see the Old Testament in the light of the mighty acts of God in their generation, and therefore cannot associate themselves with the Jewish conceptions and interpretations.

The new people of God therefore stands outside the scope of customs of Jewish piety. There is a question, for instance, of a fast that is observed by the Pharisees and also by the disciples of John the Baptist, while Jesus' disciples do not observe it (Matt. 9.14–17 and par.). Jesus is asked why his disciples do not fast. The answer is that Jesus himself is the norm for his disciples' fasting. As long as he is with them they cannot fast, but a time will come later when he will no longer be with them, and then they are to fast. Klostermann[1] sees a contradiction in the two answers—Mark 2.19 f., 'My disciples shall fast later'; and v. 21 f., 'My disciples shall have nothing more to do with the old customs.' In our rendering of Jesus' words we have shown that there is no such contradiction between the two answers, but that everything that is said has its meaning in the fact that Jesus is the norm for what his disciples are to do and are not to do, including their fasting. Therefore they cannot follow the old customs, but are to rejoice while Jesus is with them, and are to fast when he is taken from them.

People have claimed to see the remark about the disciples' future fasting as a foundation of the Church's later adoption of the practice of fasting,[2] but it seems to me right not to lay as much weight on the disciples' present non-observance of fasting and their future observance of it, as the commentators like to do, but to put the emphasis on the difference between the present, when Jesus is with his disciples, and the future, when he will leave them alone for a time. Whereas his life on earth with his disciples is as festive as a wedding-feast, the time between

---

[1] *Das Markusevangelium*[2], 1926, p. 31.
[2] Thus, e.g., Klostermann, *op. cit.*, p. 32; Dibelius, *From Tradition to Gospel*, ET 1934, p. 65; and Bultmann, *op. cit.*, pp. 17 f.

his death and his return will be one of mourning, when his disciples will mourn and fast as a matter of course, just as now during his life on earth they are in no position to do so. These are indeed not the only passages in the Gospels where the time of tribulation is spoken of when Jesus is taken from them and he has left his disciples alone, and it will be difficult for them to be faithful and to stand firm in the temptations and distress that will come over the earth before Jesus' return.[1]

The Jewish custom which Jesus most frequently criticizes in defining his attitude to it is the observance of the Sabbath. In Matt. 12.9–14 and par. (the healing of the man with the withered hand), Luke 13.10–17 (the healing of the infirm woman), and Luke 14.1–6 (the healing of the dropsical man) we have three violations of the Sabbath where, after effecting a cure on the day of rest, Jesus has to defend his action against his opponents' attacks. It is only in Luke 13.14 that the attack is instigated directly by the ruler of the synagogue, and there it is directed, not against Jesus, but against the people. In Matt. 12.10, on the occasion of the healing of the man with the withered hand, Jesus is asked whether it is allowed to heal on the Sabbath. In the parallel passages in Mark and Luke a careful watch is kept to see whether Jesus will heal on the Sabbath, so that he can then be accused; and Luke adds specially that Jesus knew their thoughts. Jesus expresses himself variously in the three versions of this story of healing. In Matthew his reply consists in pointing out that everyone would pull a sheep out of a pit into which it had fallen on a Sabbath, and that a man is worth much more than a sheep. In Mark and Luke the answer consists in a counter-question that goes down to first principles: 'Is it lawful on the sabbath to do good or to do harm, to save life or to kill?' (ἀπολέσαι in Luke).

In Luke 14.5 we have a parallel to Jesus' answer in Matt. 12.11 f., but the point is different. It is a question here, not of a sheep that has fallen into a pit (the example stressing the greater worth of a human being), but of the obvious fact that everyone would at once pull out his son or ox that had fallen into a well on a Sabbath. Luke 13.15 f. is not about such an unfortunate event on the Sabbath, but about something that is necessary every day, including the day of rest—untying an ox or an ass from the manger and leading it away to water it. How much more ought that daughter of Abraham, whom Satan had bound for eighteen years, to be freed on the Sabbath? In spite of their apparent agreement, therefore, there is no absolute agreement between the

[1] J. Jeremias, *The Parables of Jesus*, ET 1954, p. 42 n. 82 (cf. *TWNT* IV, p. 1095. 38 ff.), regards these words as a later modification of Jesus' original words about the judgment.

individual narratives in their line of argument, just as there is real agreement in the outward events only in Matt. 12.9–14, Mark 3.1–6, and Luke 6.6–11.

Another violation of the Sabbath, the plucking of the ears of grain by the disciples on a Sabbath (Matt. 12.1–8; Mark 2.23–28; Luke 6.1–5) is distinguished from those just mentioned by the fact that it is not Jesus but his disciples who break the Law.[1] In the course of the conversation Jesus uses scriptural evidence (in Matthew several pieces of evidence) in support of his point of view; and here again the conflict about pious practices is taken back to the question of the time of salvation and the Son of Man—'the Son of man is lord of the sabbath.'

In these clashes between Jesus and his opponents, which make clear to us the lasting differences between Jewish Christianity and its Jewish surroundings, we see that the Christian church in Palestine paid the temple tax, but refused to keep the commandment about the Sabbath according to strict rules or to share in the fasting habits of specially pious people. Behind these—if you like—small deviations there is the fundamental law that Jesus, living on earth and afterwards ruling from heaven, was the highest authority and therefore stood above the Law. The saying that the Son of Man is Lord of the Sabbath (Matt. 12.8 and par.) also means that the Son of Man is Lord of the Law.

Jesus, and after him the primitive Church, interpreted the Old Testament according to God's great saving acts in the midst of which they stood. Therefore the Jewish interpretation of the Law and of the rest of the Old Testament was declared to be invalid. That interpretation had striven to keep the Jew in obedience towards the God of the Law, and to unite him with God's demands in the details of everyday life. Now that was all invalid, because the time of salvation was dawning, and because God's demands were shown to be stricter, and his love richer. Jesus can show how the Jews make void the word of God by their human tradition (Matt. 15.3–9; Mark 7.6–13).

But the lordship of the Son of Man over the Law is shown much more clearly in his treatment of the Law itself. In the *pericope* about marriage and divorce (Matt. 19.1–12; Mark 10.1–12) Jesus criticizes Moses and his Law. When Moses allowed the Jews to write a certificate of divorce and become divorced, it was because of the people's hardness of heart. But God's will for man and wife is revealed in the creation

---

[1] It is doubtful whether, like Bultmann (*op. cit.*, p. 14), we are justified in inferring from this distinction between the Master who has to make his position in the matter clear, and the disciples whose practical keeping of the commandment relating to the Sabbath is in question, that we have here the practice of the later Church which receives its divine authorization from Jesus in the course of a dispute. It is difficult to maintain such a distinction on the strength of the conversations about the Sabbath.

and in the words that were then spoken; and Jesus renews God's demands on men by giving to his disciples as a guiding principle the order of things which was established at creation, and which Moses had for a time declared invalid.[1] This *pericope* is important, because it shows not only that Jesus puts aside the Jewish interpretation that blunted the Law's demands, but that he radically criticizes Moses as an interpreter of God's will in the Law, and condemns that interpretation as being in opposition to the plain words of the earliest times. If we confine ourselves to looking at the examples quoted, where Jesus dissociates himself from pious customs and criticizes them, it may seem as if he were modifying or repealing individual commands. But the declarations of principle help us to understand the meaning of Jesus' individual sayings, and it becomes clear to us that Jesus does not put aside individual commands, but makes the Law stricter.

We see the same thing in the Sermon on the Mount, where there are examples of all the views that we have already met. Jesus criticizes the practice of Jewish pious observances (Matt. 6.1–18), and gives a different interpretation of the Law from the usual Jewish one (Matt. 5.21–48) with the words, which are characteristic of the new point of view, 'You have heard that it was said . . . but I say to you. . . .' (5.21 f., 27 f., 31 f., 33 f., 38 f., 43 f.). While some of these interpretations may be regarded as new expositions of the words of the Bible, others are undoubtedly critical of the Law itself, for instance, 5.38–42. Not even in the Sermon on the Mount can there be any doubt that through his exposition of the Law Jesus makes God's demands more exacting.

The earliest Jewish Christianity therefore followed Jesus in his radical criticism of the Jewish view and observance of the Law, as it made him the Church's norm for the interpretation of the Law and the fulfilling of God's commands. What we found in Paul's letters, which was confirmed by Acts, also emerges from the Synoptic Gospels as sources of the earliest Jewish Christianity, which holds a special point of view, independent of Judaism.

There are certainly individual texts that have been produced as proofs of Jewish fulfilment of the Law within the primitive Church. In the section about Jesus' attitude to the Law (Matt. 5.17–20) for instance, it has been felt impossible to attribute to Jesus words like those in v. 18: 'Till heaven and earth pass away, not an iota, not a dot, will pass from the law until all is accomplished', or v. 19: 'Whoever then relaxes one of the least of these commandments and teaches men so, shall be called least in the kingdom of heaven; but he who does them and teaches them shall be called great in the kingdom of heaven.' People therefore

[1] Cf. Gal. 3.17 f.

imagine that these words originated within the Church. It cannot be a matter here of polemics against Jewish teachers of the Law—the words must be directed against the Hellenists.[1] Verses 17–19 show the attitude of the conservative Palestinian church as against that of the Hellenistic church.

It is, however, unlikely that Jewish Christians who kept the Law could use declarations like those of Matt. 5.18 f. towards Christians who did not keep the Law at all. These sentences can find their application only between Christians who observed, or thought they observed, the whole Law, in controversy regarding other Christians who omitted to observe certain parts of it. The sentences would therefore be meaningless in relation to Gentile Christians who did not keep the Law in the Jewish sense. We could find a *Sitz im Leben* for such words in a situation like that described by Luke concerning the Jerusalem church in Acts 15, where a small minority of former Pharisees demand of the church that the Gentile Christians must be circumcised and keep the Law.

But not only is Luke's account very improbable. Even if it were accurate, a temporary minority could hardly gain lasting influence over the tradition of Jesus. These words must therefore rather be regarded as spoken by Jesus in conjunction with his general efforts to lead the Jews back to God's demands in his Law. The two declarations quoted about the iota and dot and the abolition of the least commandment and the teaching of men according to this changed Law, fit in fact into Jesus' polemics against the all too negligent conception and observance of the holy God's demands on his creatures.

In Matt. 23.2 f. there is a remarkable reference to the scribes and Pharisees: 'The scribes and the Pharisees sit on Moses' seat; so practise and observe whatever they tell you, but not what they do; for they preach, but do not practise.' That is a strange remark, because Jesus criticizes, both in ch. 23 and in other contexts, what the scribes and Pharisees say, and not merely what they do. It has been supposed that his approval is limited to what they rightly teach as Moses' words,[2] or that his remark should be regarded as requiring people to hear without implying approval. Thus Merx[3] prefers to read ἀκούετε as the oldest text where Nestle reads ποιήσατε καὶ τηρεῖτε, and to regard the text as follows (p. 321): 'The scribes and Pharisees have usurped

[1]Bultmann, *op. cit.*, pp. 146 f.; Klostermann, *Das Matthäusevangelium*, pp. 40 f. Bultmann's use of the words 'Hellenists' and 'Hellenistic' is not clear (see the passages quoted in the index, especially pp. 330 ff.). On pp. 146 f., for example, 'Hellenists' means Christians outside Palestine, presumably of Gentile origin.
[2]B. Weiss, *Das Matthäus-Evangelium* (Meyer 1)⁸, 1890, *ad loc.*
[3]Adalbert Merx, *Die vier kanonischen Evangelien nach ihrem ältesten bekannten Texte* etc., Part 2, first half, 'Das Evangelium Matthaeus', 1902, pp. 319–22.

Moses' authority; hear whatever they may say to you, but do not act as they do, for they themselves do not do what they say.' Finally, Klostermann regards this beginning of v. 3 as a concessive introduction which does not express Jesus' real opinion. None of these expositions is completely convincing, even if we must agree with their common starting-point, that neither Jesus nor the earliest Christian Church can have required conformity to the teaching of the scribes and Pharisees. Either the text cannot be right, or we have not yet understood its real meaning. It is, in fact, not the only passage in Matt. 23 where we find difficulties, and the problems that it presents deserve to be discussed in a monograph.

It may be said in conclusion that the attitude taken by Jesus and Jewish Christianity to the Law is independent of the legal discussions of Judaism. In spite of parallels on details, there are fundamental differences. Jesus and his disciples break out of the Jewish tradition, and seek to gain a new understanding of the Old Testament, which is the common starting-point for them and the Jews. God makes his demands on men, and we must therefore understand the Law as coming from the living God, whose Messiah is Jesus. But such an interpretation, which uses as its norm not human gifts and possibilities, but God's holy nature and will, is more critical and re-creative in its results than any criticism from outside could be.

II

What is valid for the attitude towards the Law is also valid for the attitude towards the Gentiles. If we start from the tradition of the Tübingen School in modern Pauline research, we should have to expect the Gospels to testify that the early Church held firmly to the Law on Jewish principles, and that it was interested in winning the Gentiles over to a point of view that combined the Jewish attitude to the Law with a belief in the crucified Jesus as the coming Messiah. But just as we have seen above that Jewish Christianity had its own attitude towards the Law which deviated markedly from that of the Jews, so we shall see in the following pages that within the early Church there was no interest in winning the Gentiles for Judaism.

As we shall see, the fact that Jewish Christianity does not carry on a mission to the Gentiles is no conclusive evidence of a distinction between Jewish Christianity and Judaism, as the latter too had no interest in any mission to the Gentiles. But Jewish Christianity is different from Judaism in that on the one hand it had no wish whatever to make prose-lytes, while on the other hand it regarded the Gentiles as an object of future missionary activity which would put the Gentiles on the same level as the Jews. In both cases belief in the Gospel is required.

In the first three Gospels there are sayings of Jesus that indicate clearly that the new message is to be taken only to Israel, and not to the Gentiles. In his charge in Matt. 10.5, when he sends out the twelve, Jesus says to them, 'Go nowhere among the Gentiles, and enter no town of the Samaritans'; and those who are sent out are told that they will not have gone through all the towns of Israel before the Son of man comes (10.23).[1] Matthew's Gospel, from which these two passages are taken, ends by telling how the risen Christ commands his disciples now to leave the Jews and Palestine and to go and make disciples of all the Gentiles (28.19). In the same Gospel the Jewish colouring is preserved, so that Jesus can say, 'And if you salute only your brethren, what more are you doing than others? Do not even the Gentiles do the same?' (5.47), or 'And in praying do not heap up empty phrases as the Gentiles do' etc. (6.7), or, about anxieties, 'For the Gentiles seek all these things' (6.32). We read later (18.17) about the church member who will not repent of his faults, 'Let him be to you as a Gentile and a tax collector.' In the eschatological teaching too in ch. 24 everything is seen from a Jewish point of view, e.g., in v. 9, 'you will be hated by all the Gentiles for my name's sake', and in v. 14, where the preaching of the Gospel to the Gentiles is thought of as the last of the eschatological events, 'And this gospel of the kingdom will be preached throughout the whole world, as a testimony to all the Gentiles; and then the end will come.'

The Gospel is therefore destined solely for Israel, but the chosen people is unbelieving. By following Matthew's Gospel here we learn that Israel is hard-hearted, and that in consideration of this impenitence in Jesus' generation, Moses allowed divorce through a certificate of divorce (19.8). Again and again Jesus characterizes this generation as evil and adulterous (12.39; 16.4), faithless and perverse (17.17); therefore no sign shall be given to it except the sign of the prophet Jonah (12.39; 16.1–4). Jesus' generation is a brood of vipers, which can say nothing good, because it is evil (12.34); cf. 7.11, 'you, who are evil.' This generation, Jesus says, is like children who are sitting in the market place and will play neither at weddings nor at funerals (11.16–19). Well did Isaiah prophesy of this generation, when he said, 'This people honours me with their lips, but their heart is far from me', etc. (15.8 f.). The temple, which was intended as a house of prayer, they have

[1]This is an utterance on which the mission to the Jews seems to have acted very faithfully in its fruitless preaching to Israel (cf. Rom. 10.14–21), though it was thought later that the towns of Israel included the Jewish Diaspora in the east.

made a den of robbers (21.13), and they interpret the Law in such a way that Jesus cannot help grieving over its teachers (ch. 23). We must add to this that Jesus sends his disciples out as sheep among wolves (10.16).

Because of Israel's unbelief and hardness of heart Jesus is compelled to lament over the cities where he worked, and to prophesy their downfall. As he commands his disciples (10.14 f.), so he himself has to shake the dust from his feet as a testimony against the unbelieving cities of Chorazin and Bethsaida, and especially Capernaum (11.20–24). Indeed, Jerusalem itself will be devastated (23.37–39; 24.15–22). There has even been handed down to us a saying of Jesus that utters a curse over the withered fig-tree, 'May no fruit ever come from you again!' (21.19). The saying probably refers to Israel and contains a threat (cf. Matt. 8.11 f.); but if it is meant to contain a final judgment on Israel it is no saying of Jesus, but must have originated in the generation from which our Gospels in their present form come. In Matthew's chapter of parables we hear that God's intention with Jesus' parables is that he should speak to deaf ears in Israel (13.10–17).

Jesus' native town of Nazareth does not receive him (13.53 f.), and this draws from him a saying that applies to the whole people and country: 'A prophet is not without honour except in his own country and in his own house' (13.57). In the story of the Passion we see the Sanhedrin and the people reject Jesus as Messiah and condemn him to be crucified (chs. 26–27). In the parable of the vineyard that is let to faithless tenants (21.33–41), and with the added words about the stone that the builders rejected (21.42–44), Jesus stigmatizes the responsible authorities, and with them the people, who reject him as the Messiah. The same thing happens in the parable of the royal wedding feast (22.1–14), where the guests decline the king's invitation, and some of them assault his servants.

There has been a tendency to believe that this picture of Israel as the unbelieving and hard-hearted people was formed only gradually either during Jesus' life and work among his people, or rather perhaps by his disciples after his crucifixion and in view of the Jews' permanent disbelief of the Gospel. But that opinion is hardly correct. Jesus is described as not ceasing, in spite of his rejection, to preach to his unbelieving people; and we know from Acts what is confirmed by the Synoptic Gospels through the picture that has just been drawn of Jesus—that Jewish Christianity did not cease to preach to Israel, in spite of the latter's unbelief. The historical accuracy of this can be seen from Rom. 10.14–21, where we learn that the apostles who were sent out to the Jews continued their work faithfully, in spite of the Jews' unbelief and hardness of heart.

This procedure of the primitive Church can be most easily explained as a faithful following of Jesus' preaching to his unbelieving people. The background in Jewish Christianity is that the Gospel will be preached to Israel, and that, thanks to Israel's acceptance of salvation, the Gentiles will share in its blessings. Preaching to Israel is therefore the necessary task which the people's unbelief and hard-heartedness cannot cancel. This view of Israel's part in the salvation of mankind in spite of its permanent unbelief shows that there is a close tie with Israel and that it must presumably go back to Jesus. All his life Jesus was subject to the same destiny as Isaiah—he is to follow with regard to Israel the way that God has commanded, but the result will only be unbelief and hardness of heart. After Jesus, Jewish Christianity held to that close tie with Israel, and in practice acted accordingly, although the mission to the Jews remained fruitless. The disciples fared as the Master had fared.

In this account of the preaching of Jesus, and later of his disciples, to Israel, the Gentiles seem to have no place. That, however, is not quite correct. Although they occupy only a modest place in the tradition of the earliest Jewish Christianity, they have a place, and we shall see that it is not a very small one. The Gentiles are not to be preached to now, as we heard in the passage from Jesus' mission charge, but they will nevertheless share in salvation when it is being completed.

In 1937 B. Sundkler published, together with Fridrichsen, 'Contributions a l'étude de la pensée missionnaire dans le Nouveau Testament'.[1] He discusses 'Jésus et les païens' (pp. 1–38), and shows there how the traditional presentation of the problem—particularism or universalism—is inapplicable to our sources and the time in which they originated. In the idea of Jerusalem as the navel of the world, with the temple as the very central and highest point on the earth, he finds the explanation of Jesus' attitude to the mission. In Jerusalem, the centre of the world, Jesus carries out a work that is of importance for the whole world and so for the Gentiles. He cleanses the temple and thereby renews the world, for the temple is the world's centre, and the mission that he has put before himself as his aim is the world's rebirth.

This weighty article helps us to a new presentation of the problem, without our having to suffer, as the earlier generation did, any interference of modern ideas in our work on the New Testament. But its interest in Jesus' attitude to the Gentiles makes his relation to the Jews recede into the background. In what sense, we have to ask, can we speak

[1]In *AMNSU* 6, ed. A. Fridrichsen, 1937. Sundkler's article also appeared in *RHPR* 16, 1936, pp. 462–99.

of a mission to the Jews, or is Jesus' work to be regarded solely as a series of actions of a cosmic and soteriological kind?

Similar considerations apply to Jeremias' article, 'The Gentile World in the Thought of Jesus'.[1] Here we are told how Jesus himself did not evangelize among the Gentiles, and forbade his disciples to do so. But such an attitude is contradicted by his promise to the Gentiles that they should share in God's kingdom, and indeed should reach it alone. Jeremias explains the contradiction by regarding Jesus' work in Israel as only a preparation for what is essential, the salvation of the Gentiles. On the last day, when Israel is to be judged, the Gentiles are to flock to Zion's holy hill from all the ends of the earth. He writes (p. 28), 'The calling of Israel by Jesus is preparatory work; it is the presupposition for the coming of the gentiles to Zion. The gathering of the gentiles itself is God's powerful eschatological action, the last great revelation of the unbound grace of God.'

Jeremias' explanation of this contradiction is in my opinion not the right explanation of the many details that he gathers and interprets with his usual mastery. It was only the sub-apostolic Church that regarded Jesus in such a way as to suppose that Israel, after its 'No' to the preaching of the Gospel, now proves, after the death of the apostles and the destruction of Jerusalem, to be rejected by God because of its unbelief and hardness of heart. Jesus, the earliest Christianity, and Paul know no limits to God's love of the chosen people. For God the salvation of the Gentiles is bound up with the salvation of Israel, just as Israel's salvation is of importance to all the Gentiles.

The texts that used to be quoted as evidence of Jesus' interest in the Gentiles[2] must for the most part be regarded as inappropriate if we want to prove from them what used to be read out of them. And yet there remains something that needs explaining. When Jesus, in sending out his twelve disciples, says to them, 'Go nowhere among the Gentiles, and enter no town of the Samaritans, but go rather to the lost sheep of the house of Israel' (Matt. 10.5 f.), his words surprise us. Was it necessary to say that? Especially with the background of what follows, that Judaism was no evangelizing religion, it is remarkable that Jesus needed to say, 'Not to the Gentiles, not to the Samaritans'. Even if we delete 'rather' in 10.6 as a later addition, it is clear that it had to be pointed out that the new message was to be taken to Israel, but not to Gentiles and Samaritans. The view must therefore have existed from the first that the Gospel concerned everyone; and so it had to be laid down that the sending of the twelve disciples concerned no one but the Jews.

[1] *SNTS Bulletin* 3, 1952, pp. 18–28.
[2] See, e.g., Harnack, *Mission*, ch. 4, pp. 39 ff. (*ET*, pp. 36 ff.).

This is confirmed by the narratives about Gentiles whom Jesus helped, and by the account of Peter's going to Cornelius' house.[1] These narratives were handed down by circles that carried on an exclusively Jewish mission, and they testify that the Gentiles' place in the plan of salvation occupied the thoughts of the Jewish Christian churches, whose work was concerned only with Israel. If that had not been the case, the narratives would not have been preserved till the time when the mission to the Gentiles had become a reality and a recognized factor in the life of the Church.

We have seen in ch. 4 that the leading men in the mission to the Jews come into touch, at a meeting in Jerusalem, with the mission to the Gentiles (pp. 119–29), but that this does not mean that they themselves begin missionary work among the Gentiles, or ask other people from their own circle to undertake such work. Thus the editing of these narratives[2] makes clear to us the trend of ideas and problems within Jewish Christianity.

It is clear, therefore, that the Jewish Christian churches in Palestine, like Jesus and his first disciples, were greatly concerned with the place that the Gentiles were to have in the plan of salvation. In the period after Jesus' earthly life and up to the meeting in Jerusalem Jewish Christianity carefully preserved these narratives about Gentiles, and found in them the solution of the question about the Gentiles' part in that salvation. But after the mission to the Gentiles had become a general concern of the Church, although the Church was divided into the mission to the Jews and the mission to the Gentiles, people went more deeply into questions about the salvation of the Gentiles. We can find traces of the churches' work on the problems in those narratives, as in the later editing of the tradition in the writings of the evangelists and in Luke's Acts. It is now emphasized that Jesus and Peter have already introduced the mission to the Gentiles, although it was true for both of them that the time was not yet ripe for it.

Just as we pointed out in ch. 8 how much the narrative of Cornelius was edited by earlier transmitters of tradition as well as by Luke, so we have in the Gospels a narrative in which Jesus helps a Gentile; and in its present form it plainly shows traces of an editing which for its part testifies to the keen interest in it, and the problem it presented in the circles concerned with its preservation. It is the story of the Canaanite woman, which is handed down in Matt. 15.21–28 and Mark 7.24–30. In both forms it begins with a negative reply by Jesus to the woman

---

[1]On the Cornelius narrative see pp. 228–31.

[2]It is important that it is the Gentiles who seek out Jesus and later Peter (cf. Sundkler, p. 31). It is a question of a centripetal movement.

who asks for help, but the conversation leads to his granting her request and healing her daughter.

In Matt. 15.24 Jesus says, 'I was sent only to the lost sheep of the house of Israel', and this reminds us of 10.5 f., 'Go nowhere among the Gentiles, and enter no town of the Samaritans, but go rather to the lost sheep of the house of Israel.' When, in spite of this refusal, the woman persists in asking for help, Jesus expresses his refusal figuratively: 'It is not fair to take the children's bread and throw it to the dogs.' But when the woman answers, 'Do it, Lord, please;[1] even the dogs eat the crumbs that fall from their masters' table,' Jesus refuses his help no longer, and answers, 'O woman, great is your faith! Be it done for you as you desire.'

In Mark the story is given a different form. The remark that Jesus is sent only to Israel is not there. Jesus' discouraging words (7.27) are similar to the second refusal in Matthew (15.26), as they too speak of the children's bread and the dogs. Mark's wording of this is the same as Matthew's, but with an introduction that gives the words quite a different meaning: 'Let the children first be fed.' Whereas in Matthew Jesus' words mean that we cannot take bread from the children and give it to the dogs, in Mark they mean that the dogs shall not get their food till the children have had their meal.[2] That sequence—to the Jew first and also to the Greek—we know from Rom. 1.16; 2.9 f.; it is also indicated in Acts 3.26: 'God, having raised up his servant, sent him to you first. . . .'; cf. the preceding v. 25: 'You are the sons of the prophets and of the covenant which God gave to your fathers, saying to Abraham, "And in your posterity shall all the families of the earth be blessed." ' Here we have, just as in Mark 7.24–30, what we called the missionary conception of the earliest Jewish Christianity (see above, p. 112). A Pauline modification of that conception appears in Acts 13.46, where πρῶτον is also used. Here Paul and Barnabas say to the Jews in Pisidian Antioch, 'It was necessary that the word of God should be spoken first to you. Since you thrust it from you, and judge yourselves unworthy of eternal life, behold, we turn to the Gentiles.'

Thus in Mark's version of the story of the Canaanite woman the point is different from that in Matthew's. It is a matter of course that the dogs shall have bread too, but only after the children. The question,

---

[1]On ναί see Fridrichsen, pp. 10–13 in *Coniectanea Neotestamentica* 1, 1936 (*AMNSU* 2).

[2]My exposition differs somewhat from Cerfaux's in his studies of Mark 7.27 f., 'L'aveuglement d'esprit', *Le Muséon* 59, 1946, pp. 267–79, especially p. 275. I owe to Cerfaux's acute observation the comparison between πρῶτον in v. 27 and πρῶτον in Rom. 1.16; 2.9 f. I have tried to expand this comparison with the passages quoted from Acts.

in fact, is how far the time has come for the Gentiles to be helped, and not, as in Matthew, how far Jesus is to help them at all. With Matthew the starting-point is—though in quite a different way—just such a refusal as in the Cornelius narrative, where Peter says, 'You yourselves know how unlawful it is for a Jew to associate with or visit any one of another nation' (Acts 10.28). It is probably because of this difference between Matthew's version and Mark's that the latter does not emphasize the woman's faith as the decisive point on which Jesus' granting of her request is based in Matthew; for in Mark the introductory words of the refusal, presupposing the Gentiles' later sharing in salvation, start from the assumption that Gentiles and Jews will hear and believe and be saved in the same way. That is Peter's point of view in Gal. 2.15 ff. and Acts 15.7–11. When in Matthew the Canaanite woman is helped by Jesus because of her faith, that also shows that it was expected that the Gentiles would attain salvation in the same way as the Jews; but the sharper contrast between them indicates a wish to stress that the Gentiles believed, but that the Jews did not (cf. Matt. 8.10).

Thus Mark's version starts from the assumption that the Gentiles are to hear the Gospel after the Jews; and it is left open to debate whether that sequence can be departed from. Can the Gentiles hear the Gospel before it has been preached to all the Jews? The answer is Yes; it is possible to carry on a mission to the Gentiles while the mission to the Jews continues its more important work towards Israel. Matthew's account takes a more dramatic shape. Jesus is at first silent at the Canaanite woman's request (v. 23a), and it is the disciples who turn to him and thereby evoke the first refusal, which seems to be addressed only to them and not to the woman (vv. 23 f.; cf. v. 25). Not till the woman asks Jesus a second time does she receive his discouraging answer (v. 26) in words which coincide with those in Mark (7.27), but which have a different meaning: what belongs to Israel cannot be given to the Gentiles. The woman's last words[1] have a different significance in Mark and Matthew because of the different content of Jesus' previous remark. In Mark, where it is too soon to give the dogs bread, the woman's remark gives us to understand that even while the children are eating, the dogs are already beginning their meal under the table. In Matthew, on the other hand, the woman's words indicate that, even if

---

[1]Is this saying a common proverb? See its use in Philostratus, *The Life of Apollonius of Tyana* I, 19 (ed. F. C. Conybeare, Loeb Classical Library, 1912, Vol. I, pp. 52 f.): . . . καὶ τὰ μὲν ἄλλα ὀρθῶς ἀναγράφειν . . . , ὁπόσαι γνῶμαί τέ εἰσι καὶ δόξαι τοῦ ἀνδρός, ταυτὶ δὲ τὰ οὕτω μικρὰ ξυλλεγόμενον παραπλήσιόν που τοῖς κυσὶ πράττειν τοῖς σιτουμένοις τὰ ἐκπίπτοντα τῆς δαιτός, ὑπολαβὼν ὁ Δάμις «εἰ δαῖτες», ἔφη, «θεῶν εἰσι καὶ σιτοῦνται θεοί, πάντως που καὶ θεράποντες αὐτοῖς εἰσιν, οἷς μέλει τοῦ μηδὲ τὰ πίπτοντα τῆς ἀμβροσίας ἀπόλλυσθαι.»

the bread rightly belongs to the children, the dogs get their share of it all the same. In Matthew it is expressed more clearly than in Mark that the right of the Jews has to give way to the humble faith of the Gentiles. The Canaanite woman has realized that she has no claim on Jesus' help, but for that very reason it is granted to her. The Jew's right to salvation—by hearing the Gospel—is shown to be invalid by the help that Jesus gives the woman. Out of her distress and unworthiness she calls for his help and receives it. It is therefore quite clear that the problem behind Matthew's version is the authorizing of the mission to the Gentiles, not, as in Mark, the time of its beginning. Matthew's version seems to have been shaped early in the history of that mission, and was to prove that it had been authorized by a narrative about Jesus' healing the daughter of a Canaanite woman. The mission to the Gentiles, and Jesus' attitude to it, are a real problem in Matthew, whereas Mark's version assumes that it is to take place, though not just yet.

It still remains to inquire whether Jesus' introductory discouraging answer in Matthew (vv. 24 and 26) represents a point of view which exists in Jewish Christianity and which the *pericope* is to refute. As the salvation of Israel is presumably always regarded as the way that is to lead the Gentiles to share in the salvation that is to come in the last days,[1] the introductory words in Matthew's version cannot exclude the Gentiles from the salvation of mankind; but they may possibly mean that no mission was to be carried on among them, as they were to receive their share in salvation by other means.[2] It is possible that within the mission to the Jews people felt that they would not finish their work in all the towns of Israel (Matt. 10.23), and that a mission to the Gentiles was therefore out of the question. Perhaps that is expressed in the words about children and dogs in Matt. 15.26, which in that case mean that it would not be right to break off the mission to the Jews in order to carry on a mission to the Gentiles, as there is not enough time for both before Christ's return. The hard saying about the dogs and the children may have been chosen so as to elicit the woman's answer; but it may also express the Jews' view of the Gentiles, which is rejected by the *pericope*.

The *pericope* of the Canaanite woman shows that Jewish Christianity did not carry on a mission to the Gentiles, but that it recognized that

---

[1]Thus, e.g., Paul in Rom. 11.12, 15, James in Acts 15.14–21; John 4.22.
[2]Jeremias (*SNTS Bulletin* 3, pp. 25–28) has tried to show that the Gentiles are to be gathered together by the angels only at the end of the world (Matt. 8.11 and par.; 25.31 f.; Mark 11.17; Matt. 5.14; Mark 4.32; Matt. 12.41 f.; 11.21–24; Mark 14.9; Matt. 5.35); but it seems to me that none of these passages is convincing or excludes the existence of a mission to the Gentiles.

such a mission was authorized. In Mark's version there appears the usual point of view—possibly the later one—within Jewish Christianity, that the Gentiles are to be saved at a later time in the same way as the Jews. Because the Gentiles believe (the centurion at Capernaum, Matt. 8.5–13 and par., and the Canaanite woman, Matt. 15.21–28), and because they receive the Holy Spirit and speak with tongues (Acts 10.47) like the Jews, they receive Jesus' help and are baptized. In fact, the Gentiles believe, but Israel does not. In the very last days, when Jewish Christianity is being persecuted and only a few stand firm, the Gospel is to be preached to the Gentiles (Matt. 24.14).

These ideas are those of Jewish Christians. The only thing that they have in common with Paul is the point on which he agrees with Jewish Christianity—that the Gospel is the power of God for salvation to every one who has faith, to the Jew first and also to the Greek (Rom. 1.16). On the other hand, they lack what is peculiar to Paul's missionary conception, that the Jews' unbelief leads to the preaching of the Gospel to the Gentiles, and that the latter's faith will again be a means for God to convert his own people. Where elements of this Pauline missionary conception appear, combined with the demand for circumcision and observance of the Law, we are met, not with Jewish Christianity, but with Judaizing.

III

It seems remarkable that missionary zeal towards the Gentiles is not greater in the earliest Jewish Christianity, as it is generally believed that in Jesus' time Judaism underwent a development with regard to its views of the Gentiles, and so carried on an extensive missionary activity among them.[1] It is granted that in earlier times the Jews separated themselves from the neighbouring peoples, and kept scrupulously aloof from the Gentiles among whom they lived outside Palestine. But in the Hellenistic period even they were stirred by the spirit of the time and felt called to evangelize among the Gentiles. This was particularly true of the Jews in the Greek Diaspora, who had more liberal views than the Jews in Palestine; and that Jewish mission is regarded as one of the features that prepare the way for the coming of Christianity, Paul and other missionaries to the Gentiles being influenced by that work and its basic ideas.

That view, however, is incorrect. Judaism is not an evangelizing religion, even in New Testament times. It was possible then, as always,

[1] In spite of his later arguments in the article 'The Gentile World in the Thought of Jesus', Jeremias begins with the words (p. 18), 'When Jesus began his ministry, Israel had a missionary age as she had never had before and never has had since.'

for non-Jews to be received into the Jewish community, and with the general interest in oriental religions there was an accession of non-Jews to the synagogues too, greater, perhaps, than either before or afterwards; but that was not the result of a mission. Judaism neither possessed any missionary theory nor felt any call to receive the Gentiles into the chosen people;[1] and it cannot be proved that the Diaspora Jews felt differently on this point and were more eager for a mission than were the Jews in Palestine. It is with Christianity that a mission to the Gentiles begins, because Christianity has a message that concerns the Gentiles as well as Israel.

Of the pieces of evidence on which has been built up the idea of Judaism as a religion that evangelized among the Gentiles in Jesus' time, the first, according to Schürer,[2] is the overcoming of Jewish particularism with the help of the prophetic idea of God. According to Deutero-Isaiah, Israel is to be a light to the Gentiles, its religion is to become the world's religion, and the Gentiles too are then to be accepted by God. Schürer certainly admits that this universalism did not become generally accepted within Judaism. In theory the particularist idea no doubt predominated, especially in Palestinian Judaism, but in practice it was different. Even the Pharisees in Palestine developed a zeal for conversion, as we can see in Matt. 23.15: '. . . for you traverse sea and land to make a single proselyte.'

These observations by Schürer are in no way convincing. Deutero-Isaiah's utterances were not understood correctly, and have not played the part that Schürer assumes them to have played.[3] As regards what Jesus said about the eagerness of the scribes and Pharisees to make a single proselyte, we must admit that this passage is one of the obscure ones in Matt. 23.

If we respect the traditional view that the Jews of that time carried on a widespread mission, it is strange, not merely that it is supposed in Matt. 23.15 to proceed from Palestinian Judaism, but also that Judaism performs such labours to gain only one individual. If that individual is to form a contrast to the immense efforts of the scribes

---

[1] See Sverre Aalen, *Die Begriffe 'Licht' und 'Finsternis' im Alten Testament, im Spätjüdentum und im Rabbinismus* (Skrifter utgitt av Det Norske Videnskaps-Akademi i Oslo II. Hist.-Filos. Klasse 1), 1951, pp. 202–32.

[2] Schürer III, pp. 162 ff.

[3] Schürer on p. 163 quotes Isa. 42.1–4, 6; 49.1–6; and 56.1–8. I content myself here with quoting Billerbeck on Isa. 42.1–4 (I, p. 630): 'Moreover, the use of these prophetic sayings is in rabbinical literature somewhat rare and uninformative.' In Vol. II, p. 139, Billerbeck writes, 'The basic passages Isa. 42.6 and 49.6 are hardly mentioned in rabbinic literature', etc. The other passages quoted in Billerbeck, where verses from these sections of Isaiah are used or interpreted, show that the point of view with regard to the Gentiles is not universalist. (The use of Isa. 56.7, quoted in Vol. I, pp. 852 f., is characteristic.) See Aalen, *op. cit.*, p. 205.

and Pharisees, such a modest result seems to be necessarily bound up with the content of the saying.

For one who thinks, like the author of the present book, that even in Jesus' time Judaism was not an evangelizing religion, this saying sounds strange in Jesus' mouth. It can be more easily imagined that the Church later criticized Jewish proselytizing in view of its own great results achieved in the Gentile world. While the Gospel wins great numbers of Gentiles over, immense efforts are needed to gain even one single proselyte for Judaism, and when that is achieved, the man's last state is worse than the first. With this meaning the saying comes from the period after the beginning of the mission to the Gentiles; and the Church which carries out this work rejects the wholly unsuccessful attempts by Judaism to proselytize the Gentiles.

It would be possible for the Church to be thinking here of the Jewish proselytizing that went on in connexion with the matrimonial alliances and political intrigues of the Herod family. In the year 43 Herod Agrippa I held a conference in Tiberias of kings from the Near East. That meeting seemed to the Romans so dangerous that the governor of Syria interrupted it and told the participants to go home (Josephus, *Ant*. XIX. 8.1, §§ 338–41). Present were Agrippa's brother Herod of Chalcis, who was married to Agrippa's daughter Bernice (*Ant*. XIX. 5.1, § 277), Antiochus of Commagene, whose son was to marry Drusilla, another of Agrippa's daughters (*Ant*. XIX. 9.1, § 355), Polemon of Pontus, later also of Western Cilicia, who later married Bernice (*Ant*. XX. 7.3, §§ 145 f.), Polemon's brother Cotys, king of Armenia Minor, later of Bosphorus, and Sampsiceramus of Emesa, whose daughter Iotape was married to Agrippa's brother Aristobulus, and whose successor Azizus later married Drusilla.

About the connexion between politics and religion in these royal marriages we learn in Josephus, who tells us that Epiphanes, the son of Antiochus IV, did not after all marry Drusilla, as he refused to be circumcised (*Ant*. XX. 7.1, § 139). Instead of that, Azizus married her, as he was willing to be circumcised (*loc. cit.*). In the same way, Polemon was circumcised to be able to marry Bernice; but when she left him, he ceased to observe Jewish customs (XX. 7.3, §§ 145 f.).

Here it really was necessary for the scribes and Pharisees to traverse sea and land to gain a single proselyte, as theological collaborators in the matrimonial alliances of the Herod family; and it must have been agreeable to the participating scribes and Pharisees that the demands came entirely from the Jewish side. For the Church it may have been a natural comment that the result of such a conversion to Judaism was that the proselyte become twice as much a child of hell as the travelling

Pharisees, especially when the kings concerned took over with the Jewish religion the persecution of the Christians, as Agrippa did. But this last remark can be interpreted in various ways.[1]

If, on the other hand, the words were spoken by Jesus, they may refer only to the *Pharisaic* proselytes within the Jewish connexion, i.e., the Jews who are won for Pharisaism by the work of the Pharisaic scribes.[2] While the Pharisees shut off God's kingdom from the great mass of the Jews (23.13, the previous verse), they hunt for pupils and do their utmost to win individual people over; but the result of their efforts is that the proselytes become worse than their Pharisaic teachers.

In Schürer's view, conditions in the Diaspora were quite different. Here theory was already more tolerant than among the Pharisees in Palestine. To use an expression from Harnack,[3] there was some tendency towards an 'accommodation of Judaism' ('Entschränkung des Judentums'), as the meeting with Greek religiosity caused Judaism to put general religious and ethical ideas into the foreground, and to give a less prominent place to what was specifically Jewish, that is, to matters of form and ceremony. The Jews of the Diaspora felt it their duty, in conformity with the thought of Deutero-Isaiah, to make Israel a light for the Gentiles.

The proof of this is the extensive Jewish literature that aimed at convincing the Gentiles of the stupidity of idolatry, and by pointing to the coming judgment, to win them over to faith in one true God and to a more sober and moral way of life.[4] This Jewish literature, however, can in no way prove that the Jews wanted to win the Gentiles. As was the case later with the greater part of the corresponding Christian literature, this Jewish literature was aimed at a target within its own religious community. What is expressed here is the continual contrast and conflict between Judaism and the Gentile *milieu* in which the Jews lived their own lives; it was a matter of protecting the believing Jew against the strong influence of paganism that surrounded him in language

---

[1]On the above section see *The Cambridge Ancient History* X, 1934, pp. 680 f. (M. P. Charlesworth) *et passim*, Schürer I, pp. 556 ff. (ET, I. 2, pp. 159 ff.) *et passim*, and the articles on the Herod family and the kings connected with it by marriage, in Pauly-Wissowa.

[2]Thus W. C. Allen, *St Matthew* (ICC)³, 1922, *ad loc*. Allen, however, gives a different interpretation from that given here. As to a possible use of προσήλυτος within the Isis religion, see Arndt and Gingrich s.v. with reference to Reitzenstein. Josephus uses τοὺς προσιόντας of the Essenes' 'proselytes' (*Bellum* II. 8.7, § 142). In the Qumran Manual of Discipline (DSD) in 5.6 נלוים is used of those who seek admission to the sect (Niph. of לוה, 'to join someone').

[3]*Mission*, ch. 1, pp. 5 ff. (ET, pp. 1 ff.).

[4]It is emphasized at the same time that efforts were not always made to get the Gentiles to embrace the Law in its entirety and become members of the Jewish communities. As a rule the aim was merely to convince them on the general fundamental ideas of Judaism. Cf. Harnack, *op. cit.*, pp. 14 ff. (ET, pp. 9 ff.).

and *milieu*. It was likewise necessary to protect Judaism in the face of the cultural and philosophical ideals of the time, so that the educated Jews should not give up their religion as a primitive worship which was impossible in the Hellenistic civilization.

This Jewish literature in the Greek language, therefore, has its public among the educated Jews, and its object is to confirm them in the religion of the fathers. Like Christianity later, Judaism associates itself with the learned exegesis of the time in the form of allegorical interpretation, and with certain aspects of the philosophy of the time; and it clothes its own religious and ethical content in a philosophical language which greatly influences and changes the religious standpoint that is to be represented. But whereas Christian literature, which in Alexandria represents in large measure a continuation of the Jewish literature of that city, applies itself with missionary aims to the surrounding Gentile world, all the Jewish literature in the Greek language is an internal concern, and it cannot be used as proof that Judaism is a missionary religion.

Evidence that Judaism regarded itself as the teacher of the Gentile world is found by Schürer (III, p. 164) in Justin's *Dialogue with Trypho*, 121 f. (it would be more accurate to include part of 123.1 f. with this), where Isa. 49.6 is regarded in this way. Aalen is right in rejecting this view of the passage in Justin.[1] Justin distinguishes between proselytes and Gentiles, and the Old Testament promises that concerned the Gentiles cannot have found their fulfilment, as the Jews suppose, in the proselytes who joined Israel by circumcision, but in the Christians who, although they were found worthy to be called God's people, remain uncircumcised Gentiles. According to Justin, then, in view of this passage from Isaiah, the Diaspora Judaism as well as the Palestine Judaism[2] thought only of proselytes, and did not consider that it had any obligation towards the Gentile nations as a whole.

Schürer speaks later of the results of those efforts (pp. 164 ff.).[3] In his opinion Josephus and Acts are our most important sources. In *Contra Apionem* II.10, § 123, Josephus says that many Greeks have accepted the Jewish laws; and he says so in a connexion where it is a question of proving that the converted Greeks who had later renounced Judaism could tell nothing of any oath to show no goodwill to a stranger, particularly to the Greeks—Apion had attributed such an

---

[1] *Die Begriffe 'Licht' und 'Finsternis'*, pp. 223 f.

[2] Cf. the above-mentioned interpretations of Isa. 56.7 in Billerbeck I, pp. 852 f.

[3] If we, like, e.g., Moore, *Judaism* I, 1932, pp. 348 ff., try to establish the supposed great results of Jewish propaganda on the basis of the Jews' large population caused by an increase of proselytes, and quote Harnack, *Mission*, pp. 13 ff. (ET, pp. 8 ff.), we must not disregard Harnack's cautious words (p. 13; ET, p. 8), 'Either our calculation is wrong—mistakes are almost inevitable in a matter like this—or', etc.

oath to the Jews. This passage, of course, has no value as evidence that the Greeks went over to Judaism in large numbers—especially in a controversial context directed against anti-Semitic attacks; and still more especially when the author is Josephus.

Josephus mentions later in the same work—II.39, §§ 280 f.—that the grandeur of Moses and his laws is shown by the fact that the latter have been imitated by the whole world. The first to imitate them were the Greek philosophers; but the masses too had for a long time shown a keen interest in the Jewish worship of God, so that there was no town among the Greeks or barbarians where the Sabbath was unknown, and where fasting, lighting of lamps, and many of the Jewish customs as to food were not observed. The last passage speaks of imitation, and not of any Gentile adoption of Jewish customs. If we take into account that Josephus is concerned here with ideas ranging over the antiquity of the Mosaic Law and its adoption by the Greeks in their philosophy and in all the good things of their culture, as we know them from Jewish, and later from Christian literature, this passage from his writings is of no importance as evidence of the great results of Jewish propaganda. It is clear that this bias shows us Judaism on the defensive; and the priority of the Law in relation to all the Greek achievements allows fancy a free rein.[1]

Of greater interest is Schürer's third passage, in which Josephus tells that the Jews in Antioch attracted a great number of Greeks to their services, and had to a certain extent received those Greeks among them (*Bell. Jud.* VII. 3.3, § 45). Various passages in Acts agree with this statement. Schürer mentions the beginning of Paul's address to the congregation in the synagogue at Pisidian Antioch (13.16): 'Men of Israel, and you that fear God', and again in 13.26: 'Brethren, sons of the family of Abraham, and those among you that fear God' (cf. 13.43, 50). In Thessalonica Paul gains a great many of the devout Greeks (17.4), and in Athens he preaches in the synagogue to the Jews and the devout persons (17.17). And as a special triumph of the Jewish zeal for conversion Josephus produces the conversion to Judaism of the royal house of Adiabene.[2]

The flaw in this argument in Schürer and many others consists in arguing backwards from an effect to a quite definite cause, and in thus overlooking the possibility that the effect might be caused by something quite different. Such an accession of 'Greeks' to Judaism (presumably not understated by Josephus and Luke) need presuppose no mission on the Jews' part, any more than a zeal for proselytizing. The

---

[1]Against Schürer, III, p. 166 n. 49 (ET II. 2, p. 306 n. 271).
[2]*Ant.* XX. 2–4, §§ 17–96.

influx may be due to the general interest in oriental religions, an interest which induced the Gentiles to seek salvation sometimes in the eastern mystery cults, and sometimes in the synagogue. The early missionary history of Christianity proves in no small degree that the Gentiles were receptive to new religions.

It is important to distinguish, with modern research, between the missionary idea and interest in proselytizing. In 'Två missionsföredrag'[1] Fridrichsen has written of Jewish propaganda that it was mainly trying to make proselytes, and was not a real mission for the kingdom of God.[2] Aalen, in his above-mentioned book, gives a firm foundation to that difference between mission and trying to make proselytes; he does this with the help of inquiries into the *kabod* idea in the Old Testament, Judaism and rabbinism. He says here about the Jewish writings of the period we are considering (p. 205), 'There is no real missionary conception in these writings, if we understand by mission a message or missionary initiative going out from the centre, striving to reach the Gentiles where they are, and meeting them just as they are, for their own sake. The *doxa* is inseparably bound up with Israel and Jerusalem. No one can share it without "coming to it", becoming a proselyte, i.e., without becoming a Jew.'

Aalen admits on p. 206 that even if the Jews carried on no mission, they did make a far-reaching and effective attempt to proselytize, and he refers to passages in Acts and in Josephus, and also in the Apocalypse of Baruch 1.4; 41.4; 42.4; 48.19.[3] Nevertheless his inquiry as to missionary work and proselytizing in Judaism ends with the following judgment (p. 228): 'We can therefore say with certainty that the Jews regarded neither as a possibility nor as a task any change in the religious state of the Gentiles in that period.'

In our opinion, that judgment denies not only that Judaism was a missionary religion but also that the Jews were concerned to proselytize. There is no theoretical basis for supposing that Judaism had more interest in proselytizing just then than before and since. The 'accommodation of Judaism' ('Entschränkung des Judentums') of which Harnack spoke really denotes an accommodation between the civilization and philosophy of the time and persistence in the Jewish faith and the Jewish religious community, just as the later philosophizing Church Fathers were firmly anchored in the Church. It was not Judaism that

---

[1]*Ny kyrklig tidsskrift* 11, 1942, p. 76.

[2]Cf. Fridrichsen, 'Missionens bibliska grund', *Svenska kyrkans missionsstyrelses årsbok*, 1946 (pp. 10–19), p. 14: 'A Jewish drive towards expansion, a piece of synagogue imperialism.'

[3]In my opinion these passages from the Apocalypse of Baruch do not deal with proselytes.

prepared the Christian mission and at the same time provided an explanation of it. It was something quite new, which certainly has its presuppositions in the Old Testament, but which cannot be explained as coming from Judaism.[1]

IV

Jesus and the very early Church denote something quite new in relation to Judaism.

Jesus came forward in Israel as the Messiah whom the Jews awaited. He did not turn to others besides the Jews, and he forbade his disciples to go to Samaritans and Gentiles. This apparent particularism is an expression of his universalism—it is because his mission concerns the whole world that he comes to Israel. It is a question of a representative universalism of the same kind as that which we shall later find in Paul (see pp. 276–79).

Jesus lived under the Law, but he had his own view of how the Law was to be fulfilled; and when he was reproached with breaking it, he explained his deviation by reference to principles. The difference consisted, not in his neglecting to observe the whole of the Jewish rules and commandments, but in his view of God's will, and therefore his interpretation of the Law, both of which were different from those common to the Jews. For him God's requirements were much stricter than the Law and the Jewish interpretations; but God's love was much stronger than the Jews had realized.

From the very beginning Jesus' work as preacher and healer was condemned to failure. That fact rests, not on differences in detail, which are emphasized by his disputations with his opponents, nor even in his breaking the rules of correct religious observance in his care for the suffering—rules which the Jews felt obliged to observe in all circumstances. For behind those differences was the heart of the matter—that the kingdom of God was dawning, and that the Son of man was in their midst. The choosing of Israel was not something on which the Jews can count, for God, by his own sovereign will, determines who is chosen.

Therefore Jesus is bound to fare like the prophets before him. As always, Israel is unbelieving and stubborn, and this generation, which experiences greater things than all previous generations, is unbelieving and disloyal to a quite exceptional degree. Jesus must therefore go the

[1] On the difference between the Jewish 'apostles' and the Christian apostles see my remark in 'Paul, the Apostles, and the Twelve', *ST* 3, p. 100.

way of suffering, and drain the cup as the Father wills it. From his death salvation will break forth, both for Israel which crucified him and for the Gentiles.

Only in Israel, God's chosen people, can Jesus speak and act for the whole world; and only in Jerusalem, the holy city and the centre of the world, can he be rejected as the Messiah and suffer for the whole world.[1] The Old Testament and Judaism presuppose that the coming of salvation will be decided in Jerusalem by the meeting of the Messiah and his people. The whole world is to enjoy the blessed fruits of that event. In the same way, Jesus believes, it is to Israel that he and his disciples are to bring the good news.

Jesus' work ended in Jerusalem by his being rejected by the Jews as Messiah, condemned to death, and crucified. His first disciples, who had lived with him but had left him in the lurch in his sufferings, now settled in Jerusalem and began to preach the Gospel there. The Messiah had now come, but the Jews had killed him. But as God had raised him from the dead, there was now salvation in the risen Messiah for all who would believe in him. At that time 'all' still meant only the Jews. It was certainly known that salvation was also for the Gentiles; but that lay in the future, and the preaching to Israel was to bear fruit first. It may have been thought at first that that preaching to Israel was to last till Christ's return, and so bring about the salvation of the Gentiles at the final judgment; but from a very early time it was accepted that the Gentiles too were to hear and believe. It was therefore a matter of winning Israel for the Gospel; and then Israel, believing, would become a light to the nations.

In their preaching of the Gospel the first disciples are confronted by the same task as Jesus—that of preaching salvation to the Jews. For them Jerusalem is the world's centre, where the whole world's salvation will be decided. The Gospel is therefore to be preached to the Jews, from the same apparently particularist, but really universalist, point of view, from which Jesus had turned to Israel. And part of the Gospel is that the Jews have rejected Jesus and crucified him, but that it is now

[1]Although Jeremias, and after him Sundkler, so strongly emphasize Jesus' work in Jerusalem, the Synoptic tradition, with its record of speeches and deeds in places outside Jerusalem, especially in Galilee, can show conclusively that people have gone too far in tying Jesus' work to Jerusalem. Tradition shows a preference for a village *milieu*, preferably in Galilee, which is always apt to surprise us when we come from Acts to the Gospels. I have not found it possible to be convinced by the interesting points of view in E. Lohmeyer, *Galiläa und Jerusalem*, 1936, and R. H. Lightfoot, *Locality and Doctrine in the Gospels*, 1938. But when the Galilean disciples moved to Jerusalem after the Resurrection, the Synoptic tradition does not seem to have been affected by it. The temple presumably plays a smaller part in that tradition than in Jesus' life. The false witnesses' words about the temple and the account in John's Gospel of several visits by Jesus to Jerusalem may indicate this.

offered to them if they will only believe in it and confess Jesus, the crucified.

We can see this from the passages in Acts that speak of Jesus' death
and resurrection. His death is described in Acts 2.22 ff.; 3.13 ff.;
10.37 ff.; and 13.23 ff., and it is stressed that 'you' or 'the Jews' in
Jerusalem or Palestine denied and killed him, but that God raised him
from the dead. And through that, by God's will, there is good news for
Israel, if their children will change their ideas and be converted, so
that their sins may be blotted out. That is the Gospel of the earliest
disciples to the Jews in Jerusalem, Palestine, and the Diaspora.[1]

But the apostles' preaching too was met by the Jews with unbelief.
Just as they had refused to believe Jesus and had killed him, so they
rejected the apostles' preaching and persecuted them. The primitive
church in Jerusalem and in the rest of Palestine kept the tradition that
Jesus had left. The preaching to Israel went on, although the chosen
people persistently refused to believe and sought to take the preachers'
lives.

There is no distinction between Hebrews and Hellenists. However
we regard these two groups within the very early Church, they are
agreed on preaching the Gospel to Israel. And at the same time both
differ unmistakably from the remaining Jews, who persecute the early
Church on the ground of those differences. From the Synoptic tradition
that Jewish Christianity has handed on, we know that the latter acknowledges the Law, but in quite a different way from the Jews. Outwardly,
of course, all Jewish Christians followed, in the main, the Law's
instructions, which were observed by all Jews. That they did not, however, follow all the instructions we may infer from the fact that they
were persecuted. Dibelius and Kümmel rightly remark (*Paul*, pp. 23 f.),
'In purely legalistic religions offences of ritual or ethics are always
regarded as worse than deviations from dogmatic doctrines.'[2] Here
again, Jewish Christianity is the true guardian of the tradition that goes
back to Jesus.

After Jerusalem has for some time been the settled domicile of the
earliest disciples and of the first church of any considerable size, they

[1]We can see in Rom. 10 that we have here the earliest Christian teaching. Paul
speaks here of Israel's obduracy. In 9.30–33 we hear only of Jesus' earthly life in
Palestine, his rejection by the Jews, and his crucifixion. Immediately after Paul has
made this terrible pronouncement, that the Jews have crucified the Messiah, he
prays for their salvation (10.1 f.). In 10.4 he emphasizes that Christ is the end of the
Law, namely by his death on the cross (already referred to in 9.32 f.). Later in ch. 10
there follows the account of the Jews' rejection of the Gospel when the apostles
took it to them.

[2]Stephen (Acts 6.13 f.) and Paul (21.28 ff.) are accused of speaking against the
temple and the Law. James, the Lord's brother, was stoned, according to Josephus
(see pp. 113 ff.), because he transgressed the Law.

begin their work among the Jews of the eastern Diaspora. This change presumably goes back to Paul.[1] When, after a short activity in Syria and Cilicia, he makes the whole of the Roman empire his mission field, he visits the churches of Judaea (being impelled by a revelation) to arrange for further work in Syria and Cilicia, which he must now leave behind him. He succeeds in inducing James, Peter, and John to take over the mission on that predominantly Jewish territory. And it is still more important that those three send him and Barnabas to the Gentiles, just as the two missionaries have a share in sending Peter to the Jews in the eastern Diaspora.

This change does not mean that the first disciples cease to evangelize only among the Jews; it means that they cease to be tied to Jerusalem, to which Christ will return. As long as they remained in the holy city, their message was bound to reach the Jews of the whole world through the innumerable pilgrims and other visiting Jews. But from now on, Jewish apostles go to the Jewish Diaspora in the east, to take the Gospel to the ends of the earth (Rom. 10.18).

It is quite natural that we are not told in detail about this later mission to the Jews. The ruin of the Jewish nation, and with it of the Jewish Christian churches, has blotted out the tracks of the missionaries who went to the Jews. But the little that has been preserved shows us what we should have learnt if the sources had been preserved. We hear from Paul (Rom. 10.14 ff.) about the apostles who were sent out to the Jews, about their preaching and its complete fiasco. They were both heard and understood by the Jews; but they fared as Isaiah said: 'All day long I have held out my hands to a disobedient and contrary people' (Rom. 10.21).

The Synoptic tradition too has preserved words and narratives that have been repeated to illustrate the mission's speaking to deaf ears. In the story of Peter's catch of fish (Luke 5.1–11) we trace in Peter's words the inevitable weariness of the missionaries who had gone out to the Jews: 'Master, we toiled all night and took nothing'; and in what follows we trace their unshakable willingness to continue: 'But at your word I will let down the nets.' And of the hope of those tired and disappointed toilers we are told, 'And when they had done this, they enclosed a great shoal of fish; and as their nets were breaking, they beckoned to their partners in the other boat to come and help them. And they came and filled both the boats, so that they began to sink.' Indeed, Peter and those who were with him were overcome with alarm at the catch that they had made. In the story of a wonderful catch of fish in John 21.1–14 we hear first that the disciples go out with Peter

[1]See pp. 120–22.

to fish, but that 'that night they caught nothing.' 'Then Jesus said to them, "Cast the net on the right side of the boat, and you will find some." They cast their net, and now they were not able to haul it in, for the quantity of fish. . . . Simon Peter went aboard and hauled the net ashore, full of large fish, a hundred and fifty-three of them; and although there were so many, the net was not torn.' In spite of the differences between the two accounts, this one too is about Peter, the apostle to the Jews, who has fished unsuccessfully all night, but whose net is filled to overflowing through Jesus' intervention.

One single piece of evidence as to Peter's mission field in the eastern Diaspora is preserved in I Peter, where he is elsewhere described as an apostle to the Gentiles. Here, however, there is still a greeting to the readers from the church where he is staying, namely 'she who is at Babylon, who is likewise chosen' (5.13).[1]

V

The earliest churches preserved the traditions of the manifestations of the risen Lord, and knew exactly where they had taken place—by the grave, inside Jerusalem, in Emmaus, or on a hill in Galilee or at Lake Tiberias. The first disciples had seen the Lord in those places, and had been called to preach the message about him to Israel. But when Christ revealed himself near Damascus to Paul, who was born at Tarsus in Cilicia, something momentous in the Church's history happened. Not only was he not a Palestinian; he was even a persecutor of the Church. And it was to him that Christ revealed himself as both the suffering and the glorified Christ, as he was walking along the caravan route near Damascus. That event did not fail to have consequences.

Paul is in many respects at one with the first disciples. For him too Israel and Jerusalem are the centre of the world; and Israel's salvation is therefore the most important aim in the short interval between Resurrection and return. But the way is not, as the first disciples thought, by preaching to Jews only. Where that remains fruitless, the missionaries are to turn to the Gentiles, for whom God has also destined his salvation.[2] And where Paul and the other missionaries do this, great results follow; the Gentiles believe in Christ and are baptized, while the Jews persist in unbelief.

[1] As to Peter's sphere of work, see my *Petrus und Paulus*, pp. 69 f.
[2] See especially the passage I Thess. 1.4 f. (important in religious history), where Paul asserts that God has made the Gentiles the object of his election. V. 5 shows how God's choice is made known by outward signs. Paul's preaching of the Gospel to the Gentiles consisted not only in words (as in the Jewish synagogues; here the problem of unbelief is touched on), but also in power and in the Holy Spirit (cf. I Thess. 2.13).

These experiences bear out Paul's missionary theory that because of the Jews' unbelief and hardness of heart God has decided to have the Gospel preached to the Gentiles, and that the result of that missionary work will in turn react on the Jews through their jealousy of the believing Gentiles, because the latter obtain what was promised to Israel. With a confidence which we know neither from the Gospel tradition nor from Acts in their present form, Paul proclaims that the full salvation of the Gentiles is to usher in the full salvation of Israel.

We can set out the different points of view in a table showing the agreement and the essential differences. In the view of Jewish Christianity, the Gospel was destined first for the Jews and afterwards for the Gentiles. Paul realizes that the Gospel in the preaching of Jesus, and later of the apostles (including himself) had been rejected by the Jews, and that therefore the great thing was to take it to the Gentiles, whose acceptance of it would lead again to the salvation of the Jews. Finally, we have the view of the later Gentile Church, which knows that the Jews have said No to the Gospel, and that God is therefore sending his message out to the Gentiles, but which has no idea that the salvation of the Gentiles is connected with the salvation of Israel before Christ's coming in glory. The Jews' 'No', which is irrevocable, is followed by the Gentiles' 'Yes'; and it is therefore right that the Church is a Gentile Church.

Missionary ideas in early Christianity

	Jews	*Gentiles*	*Jews*
Jewish Christianity	Yes	Yes	
Paul	No	Yes	Yes
The sub-apostolic Church	No	Yes	

In that sequence we see the vital difference between Paul and the first disciples. Has the moment now come, or has it not, for evangelizing among the Gentiles, so that what is most important for both groups, namely Israel's salvation, can be achieved? That difference in missionary outlook is expressed outwardly by dividing the work into the mission to the Jews under Peter and the mission to the Gentiles under Paul.

As we saw in ch. 2, Paul's view is that Christ will return soon, and that before that happens the Gospel must be taken to the Gentiles, and so to Israel. He has thus no thought of the Gospel's being preached for centuries the world over; on the contrary, he calculates only in decades. As long as the Gospel has not reached the Gentiles, Christ's return cannot take place, nor can Israel be saved before this fullness of the Gentiles. The apostle's call consists in his taking the Gospel to the Gentiles over the whole world, and it is a matter of urgency. We see in Rom. 15.23 that he thinks he has completed the task for the eastern territory. He no longer has 'room' there, and he intends, after a short stay in Rome, to begin west of Italy, and so to complete his mission to the Gentile world.

We might be surprised at this line of thought, as it accords so ill with modern missionary theory. But two examples may throw light on it. We know from Gal. 2.7–10 that the missionary work was divided between Peter and Paul, the former being the apostle to the circumcised, and the latter to the Gentiles. Now we have in Romans two passages in which Paul speaks of the mission to the Jews and the Gentiles respectively. The first is in Rom. 10.14–21. This is about the apostles who are sent to Israel, and their complete failure—'Lord, who has believed what he has heard from us?' When Paul quotes Ps. 19, 'Their voice has gone out to all the earth, and their words to the ends of the world', most modern commentators agree with Sanday and Headlam, who say, 'As a matter of fact the Gospel had not been preached everywhere. . . . But all that St Paul means to imply is that it is universal in its character.' On the other hand, if we take the words literally, they mean that the apostles who were sent to the Jews have now finished their work. Although they have not been everywhere or preached the Gospel to every single Jew, yet they have finished the work as far as Israel as a whole is concerned. The parts to which they have preached may be taken as the whole, the Jewish people; and Paul may therefore assert, as he does in what follows, that Israel is unbelieving and hardened.

The second example, this time about the mission to the Gentiles, is in Rom. 15.17–24. Paul is speaking here of the fullness of the Gentiles, which is to end Israel's unbelief and lead to all Israel's salvation. It is above all on the shoulders of Paul, the apostle to the Gentiles, that the task is laid of bringing about the fullness of the Gentiles, and of thereby preparing the salvation of Israel; and here, in Rom. 15.23, we have the weighty announcement that he has completed a large part of this preparatory work, as he has hitherto worked from Jerusalem to Illyria, but has now no longer any room in those parts. Having made it a point of honour to preach the Gospel where Christ has not been heard of, he now proposes to visit Rome, which already has a church, on his way through, so that he can use it as a missionary base for his work in Spain. Thus at the time of the letter to the Romans Paul has finished in the east, and intends, after visiting Jerusalem, to begin the mission in the west. But just as we may ask whether the apostles who were sent to the Jews have already finished with the whole of Israel, so it may equally well be asked whether at that moment Paul has really finished with the east. If we count the churches that he has founded and the other churches of which we hear in his letters, and if we assume a similar number of such churches founded by other missionaries who were sent out by Christ, we get a modest number of churches in the east, with a membership reckoned rather in thousands that in tens of thousands. And yet Paul asserts that he has finished in the east. His line of thought must be that he has never imagined that every single person should hear the Gospel and come to a decision about it, but that all the Gentile nations should do so, and that by the fact that people in, e.g., Corinth, Ephesus, or Philippi came to a decision about the Gospel, the nation in that region had to decide for or against Christ. For the whole of the east, therefore, there has been a representative acceptance of the Gospel by the various nations, and that is why the apostle has no longer any room in that sphere of activity, and is to go on to the Spaniards, Gauls, and Britons.

This Pauline train of thought, which we may describe as representative universalism, is Semitic. It assumes that a part takes the place of the whole. It does not anxiously ask whether all have now had the opportunity of giving their answer to the Gospel; it asks what answer that part that has been approached has given. That answer is regarded as the answer of the whole to the offer of salvation.

On his way through the Gentile world Paul met with no resistance from Jewish Christianity, or from competing pagan currents such as gnosticism, as the latter is generally regarded. His difficulties were the usual problems that confront the missionary to the pagans when he has to preach the Gospel with no kind of preparation. Pagan elements may then remain in the converts' faith, or features of the Christian message may have been understood one-sidedly and therefore incorrectly.

Thus the Gentile world of that time—in the quite general meaning of the word—and the Pauline gospel give occasion for the conditions and problems of which we are told in Paul's four great letters. In spite of all the difficulties, there is no doubt that the apostle's work is successful, and that it grows about him, not only where he himself has been, but also where his fellow-workers or the Christians of his churches have taken the Gospel.

But behind that work there are sufferings. As Christ suffered, so his apostle suffers. His tribulations are many, but he bears them willingly for the sake of the churches, if that is the only way they can be spared. And as he expects his imprisonment in Rome to end in his execution, he considers dispassionately whether it is not necessary for him to remain alive for the sake of Philippi and other churches, and so he becomes assured that he is not to die and be with Christ, although he would much rather do so (Phil. 1.23 f.).

VI

No conflict existed between Jewish Christianity and Paul. The latter felt that he himself was a Jew, that Christianity was the true Judaism, and that the Church was the true Israel. He also regarded Jerusalem as the centre of the world, and Israel's conversion as the most important event in the short time before Christ's return. He could therefore understand the other point of view of the earliest disciples; but the latter were also in a position to understand the mission to the Gentiles.

The earliest Jewish Christianity was distinct from Judaism, because Christ represented the norm for the former's view of the Old Testament. The Son of Man was Lord over the Law. It observed, indeed, part of the Law and customs, but it did not believe that salvation depended on the works of the Law. It realized in a new way that salvation was a matter, not only for Israel, but for all the Gentile nations; only the time had not yet come for carrying on a mission to the Gentiles. If only Israel could be won over, the Gentile world too would have its share in salvation; and therefore the mission had to concentrate on Israel as the most important thing in the plan of salvation and as forming the strategic point from which the destiny of the Gentiles too was to be decided.

To the meeting in Jerusalem (Gal. 2.1–10) comes Paul from the far-off mission to the Gentiles. The agreement that is made here confirms the distinction that already existed between the mission to the Jews, which the earliest disciples were carrying on, and the mission to the Gentiles, which Paul and certain other missionaries had begun. The agreement is kept. Jerusalem does not interfere with Paul's missionary sphere, for example by sending emissaries or levying taxes there.

But among the Gentile Christians of Asia Minor there arises a heresy, that of Judaizing, which has no connexion with Jewish Christianity. We see this most clearly in the fact that it presupposes Paul's view of missions. The Gospel is preached to Gentiles as well as to Jews; but Paul's strong emphasis on Jerusalem as the centre of the world has been misunderstood, and there is a longing to be like the Jewish Christians there, who are imagined to be real Jews and Christians at the same time, and who preach circumcision and the observance of the Law. Paul and his preaching are in no circumstances repudiated, but he is reproached with having left out those important parts of the message that the apostles in Jerusalem sent him out to preach. Paul can reject this Gentile Christian heresy, which we meet only within the

Galatian churches,[1] by pointing out that he is in full agreement with Jerusalem.

The agreement reached at the Jerusalem meeting remained in force till the apostles' death. When the first Christian generation, with the leaders who were called by the risen Lord, had gone, events took place which marked a decisive change in the course of the Church's history. The destruction of Jerusalem, following soon afterwards, and the expulsion of the Jews from Palestine, put an end to Jewish Christianity. The mission to the Jews, which was of equal status with the mission to the Gentiles, recedes from that position. Has not Israel already said No to the Gospel? Is it not therefore now simply a matter of taking the message to the Gentiles?

Palestinian Christians emigrate to the Gentile Christian churches and take the Palestinian tradition with them. The writing of the Gospels is an important result of that emigration. At the same time Peter, and in general the twelve apostles whom Jesus had sent to Israel, attain a constantly increasing importance in the Gentile Church, while Paul, who did not belong to the twelve, becomes overshadowed. When the Gentiles take over the twelve apostles, the important change comes that they are no longer regarded as apostles to the Jews, but as apostles to the Gentiles. Christ has sent them to the Gentiles (Matt. 28.18–20), and more and more is known of their missionary work there. Peter has worked in Asia Minor, and has written I Peter to the Christians there. Later tradition makes the twelve apostles divide the world among themselves, each going to his own part of it. It has been forgotten that these disciples were to stay in Jerusalem till Israel was converted.

In this sub-apostolic period Judaizing appears in a new and greatly modified form as a tendency among the Gentile Christians to lay an exaggerated stress on the Old Testament and its characteristic features. It is no longer a question of circumcision and observance of the Law after the Jewish manner, but of a nomistic Christianity, whose Bible is, in essentials, the Old Testament. In *I Clement* we have an example of the Church's regarding Old Testament figures as Christians of the very earliest period of the Church; and in the *Epistle of Barnabas* we read remarks like this (13.1): 'Let us now see whether this people (the Church) or the first (the Jews) are the heirs, and whether the covenant is meant for us or for them.'

From Ignatius, who has quite a different point of view, we hear in the *Epistle to the Philadelphians* (8.2) about how the relation between the two Testaments was regarded among the opponents whom he met

---

[1]Cf. chs. 5–8. The opponents in Philippi (Phil. 3.2 ff.) are not Judaizers but Jews. See E. Lohmeyer and M. Dibelius *ad loc.*

on the way: 'For I heard certain people saying, "If I find it not in the charters,[1] I believe it not in the Gospel." And when I said to them, "It is written," they answered me, "That is the question." '

Thus we have here again in the Gentile church a mixture of things Jewish and Christian. That kind of Jewish interpretation of Christianity has nothing to do with the contemporary Judaism or Jewish Christianity of this later time. People no longer seek out the Jews to preach the Gospel to them; and the Jewish Christians, in the oldest meaning of the term, have perished with the destruction of Jerusalem and the ruin of the nation. The writings quoted, and other writings from the first and second centuries, therefore tell us of discussions of these matters within the Church. People are concerned with Israel after the Spirit and with the Church's right to identify itself with it and to inherit its promises.

The solicitude shown by Jesus, the disciples, and Paul for Israel after the flesh, and the missionary work by which they risked their lives in Jerusalem, have been forgotten.

[1]'The charters' is a vague expression which is open to various interpretations; but it seems likely that it refers to the Old Testament.

IO

PAUL AND JERUSALEM

PAUL'S relation to Jerusalem has generally been wrongly judged. People have imagined that he stood between Jerusalem and Rome, with his back turned to the one and his eyes looking towards the other. It is he, in fact, who accomplishes Jesus' words to the disciples in Acts 1.8: '. . . You shall be my witnesses in Jerusalem and in all Judaea and Samaria and to the ends of the earth.' After a few tentative efforts in Damascus and Jerusalem Paul turns to the Gentile world. He thinks in Roman terms, and he soon directs his gaze to the capital of the empire as the goal of his journeys. From the point of view of later Church history, where Rome and its Christian church play an ever larger part, such a view is natural. But it will be the aim of this chapter to show that the goal that Paul keeps before his eyes on all his journeys and in all his apostolic activities is Jerusalem, and that up to his last journey Rome played no decisive part in his plans. Only in the trial at Jerusalem (to be discussed in the next chapter) does it become clear to him that his call as apostle to the Gentiles now compels him to give his testimony before the emperor in Rome.

We have taken over from an older generation the view that Paul is the great missionary strategist. He follows the important trade routes through the Roman world, and establishes his churches in the great centres, so that they may serve as mission bases for the neighbouring provinces (see p. 65). If that had been Paul's missionary outlook, he would have been certain very soon to turn his gaze westward, towards Rome, which was bound to be the ideal radiating centre, both geographically and because of its importance to the whole empire. He certainly has a missionary strategy, but it has nothing to do with this modern point of view. Moreover as we have seen, he is not the opponent of Jerusalem and the apostate detested by the Jewish Christian mission, any more than he is the Roman citizen who enjoys for his preaching the advantages of the *pax Romana*, the security at law enforced by the Romans.

The supposed opposition between Paul and Jerusalem was intensified to a very marked degree by Ferdinand Christian Baur and his pupils, the Tübingen School; and if we assume that school's view of a conflict

282

between Paulinism and Jewish Christianity, we can understand how Paul has come to be regarded as standing between Jerusalem and Rome, and so having his back towards Jerusalem and his eyes towards Rome.

If that is the case, Paul turns away from Jerusalem, full of the new message that he is to preach, the specially Pauline gospel, Paulinism. But however much he would like to do so, he cannot turn his back for ever on the Jerusalem church and with it the Jewish Christian Church as a whole. He repeatedly has to turn round to ward off the constant attacks that come from the first disciples and the Jewish Christians. As soon as they can, they fall on him, and they force themselves on his churches when he thinks that those churches can exist without him and that he himself can go on to new tasks among the Gentiles.

Paul's situation is therefore supposed to be as follows: the great work in the Roman world, with its extraordinary results and advances, falls to pieces more and more behind him, as the Jewish Christian opponents press in and try to sow discord between the Gentile Christian churches and their apostle. So he is resorting to self-defence when he continually tries to call Jerusalem to account and reach an agreement covering him in the rear and enabling him to go on to new tasks. In his eyes Jerusalem is the tiresome mother church which he would like to give up, but with which he must be continually treating, struggling, and pleading, while at the same time he has to struggle desperately in his own Corinthian and Galatian churches.

But could Paul give up Jerusalem? That would be easy to suppose if he were as he is often supposed to be. If he were the originator of Pauline theology, Paulinism, as he is generally represented, or if he were the religious genius whose rich and lively religiosity we see in his letters, then it would have been natural for him to want to cut the connexion in the rear and build up something new and independent. In that way he would have been free of all the weariness and conflicts to which he was permanently exposed by the hostile Jewish Christian church with its totally different point of view.

Those for whom the apostle is the man who builds up his own work, and in spite of that does not break with the first disciples and the mission to the Jews, generally explain this inconsistency to themselves by the fact that he could not make the break, because in spite of everything he was not independent, but felt himself for his own part dependent on Jerusalem, besides not being in a position to do without Jerusalem and the authority of the first disciples in his work.[1]

Thus Paul, who was at first so consistently regarded as the fearless

[1]See above, p. 76 n. 3.

champion of Paulinism, or as the independent proclaimer of his own religious experiences, can now be characterized as a remarkably contradictory person, who professes freedom from the Law and from the authority of Jerusalem, and is at the same time a calculating ecclesiastical politician, not quite irreproachable morally, whose fate it has become to appeal to a freedom that he does not possess, and to give the impression that he has an independence which the actual conditions invariably deny.

We have shown in the preceding pages that Paul is not an opponent of Jerusalem, and that the earliest disciples there are not opponents of Paul. He is, in fact, no such independent phenomenon, hovering, as one might say, free in mid air and with no traditions, as people have tried to suppose. Not that he lacked independence, but even with his unique call and his very personal views, he is yet within the tradition of the primitive Church. When we are dealing with Paul, it is always worth while to follow out his ideas in the other New Testament writings. Even when we have thought that his views were all his own, it will often be found that he is an independent exponent of an early Christian discussion of the very same problem. Sometimes it will be found that his outlook is more like that of primitive Christianity, and therefore more Jewish, than is the rest of the New Testament debate. That is connected with the fact that his letters are older than the other New Testament writings and have undergone no editing by the later Church.

As Paul stands within the tradition of the primitive Church, and does not merely pretend to do so, it would be quite unnecessary for him to pursue in his letters any lines of ecclesiastical policy that would land him in hypocrisy and untruthfulness; and it is most unlikely that he did so. This view of Baur and the Tübingen School, who have forced New Testament research into all these conclusions, is, in fact, a modern hypothesis about the development of the primitive Church. This hypothesis has thus led to the erroneous interpretation of Paul as the modern liberal protagonist of freedom, who, however, has to make concessions because of the power of those with orthodox views, and who, in fact, does so beyond the limits of what is right and proper. In the present chapter we shall come across a fresh example of a revival of the theme associated with Baur, which has led to a crude distortion of Paul's behaviour in connexion with the collection for the poor of Jerusalem.

In ch. 2 we touched on the fact that Paul's journeys and their objects are a part of his theology. He subjected both Jerusalem and Rome to the theological consideration: What do they mean in the history of salvation? How can they be approached with the Gospel? What is the work that he is called on to carry out particularly in these cities? Such theological problems find their solution, not in a connected theory, but in the working programme of a missionary. Those are the questions that matter, and that are to be investigated in relation to the two cities in this and the following chapter. We first consider Paul's relation to Jerusalem.

II

Paul had grown up at Tarsus in Cilicia as the son of Jewish parents whose religious outlook was that of the Pharisees.[1] From his childhood Jerusalem was probably the centre of the world for him, where in the temple of the only true God the feasts were celebrated to which all Jews, and not least those of the Dispersion, wished to go up. As a young man he was granted the opportunity of staying in the holy city, and he is said to have studied under the Pharisee and scribe Gamaliel (Acts 5.34; 22.3).[2] But he exchanges that studious life for the active one—and this is typical of Paul—by taking part in the persecution of the Christians, till the call on the road to Damascus leads him to a new existence and a new kind of activity.

For Paul as a Christian and an apostle the significance of Jerusalem was only increased. Not only had the great saving actions of the Old Covenant taken place in the holy city; but there Jesus had been delivered up and crucified, and had risen again on the third day. There in the centre of the chosen people Jesus' first disciples were now living, and were trying to convert Israel to Christ. Paul thought, as they did, that the conversion of Israel was the decisive event in the plan of salvation; and there in Jerusalem the last events in the history of the world and of salvation were to take place. There Antichrist was to manifest himself, take his seat in the temple on Sion, and proclaim himself to be God (II Thess. 2.3 f.). But then Christ, by his second coming, would end the lordship of Antichrist, and from Jerusalem would bring in the age of the kingdom of God (II Thess. 2.8–10; cf. the quotation from Isaiah in Rom. 11.26 f.).

Of his connexion with the Jerusalem church we have different accounts in Acts and in his letters. In Acts he goes back to Jerusalem soon after the Damascus experience (9.23–26),[3] and is introduced by Barnabas to the apostles (9.27); but persecution forces him out of Jerusalem, so that he has to seek refuge in his native town of Tarsus (9.29 f.). From there Barnabas fetches him later to work in Antioch (11.25). After working together in that city for a year, they go up to

[1] On his Tarsus origin, see p. 80 and p. 219 with n. 1. Of his parents' piety as Pharisees we know only from Acts 23.6.
[2] See p. 80.
[3] But see p.80 n. 1.

Jerusalem with a gift of money that has been collected for the relief of a famine (11.26–30), and that journey comes at the time when Peter is arrested and Herod Agrippa dies (11.30; 12.1, 25). Then, after Paul's first missionary journey, there follow the dispute over the necessity of Jewish Law for the Gentile Christians in Antioch, and the submission of that question in Jerusalem (ch. 15). The apostles decide in favour of Paul's missionary practice, at the same time asking the Gentile Christians to keep certain specified rules. Paul's second journey too ends with a visit to Jerusalem; this is merely indicated in 18.22, so that some have assumed it to refer only to a visit to the church at Caesarea. Finally there comes the last visit to Jerusalem (21.15 ff.), taking place at the end of the third journey, when Paul is nearly murdered in the temple, but is rescued by Roman soldiers. That rescue, however, is the prelude to an imprisonment lasting for years in Jerusalem, Caesarea, and Rome.

The picture that Paul's letters give us of his connexion with Jerusalem looks rather different. After a lapse of three years he went back from Damascus to Jerusalem, not to seek advice from the earliest disciples, but to get to know Peter (Gal. 1.18); and the visit lasted only a fortnight. After a lapse of fourteen years he went to Jerusalem again, now in company with Barnabas and Titus, and here, with the full recognition of Paul, an agreement is reached on the division of the one Church into the mission to the Jews and the mission to the Gentiles (Gal. 2.1–10).

Thus the accounts in Acts and in Paul's letters of his visits to Jerusalem do not agree; and the description of the first visit in Gal. 1.18 f. is incompatible with Acts 9.26–30.[1] The same is true of the description of a meeting in Jerusalem between Paul and Barnabas on the one side and the leading disciples within the mission to the Jews on the other, in Gal. 2.1–10 and Acts 15.[2] But in spite of the great differences, which make it impossible to bring the accounts of Acts and of Paul into harmony, what they have in common is that the relation between the two groups is good, and that the earliest disciples and the church in Jerusalem have declared their solidarity with Paul and the mission to the Gentiles.

The result of the Tübingen School's view of the marked contrast between the primitive Church and Paul has been that people have searched in the texts for evidence of the disunity of the two groups. In ch. 4 we dealt at some length with Gal. 2.1–10, but we postponed the discussion of one detail—that the apostle to the Gentiles was to remember the poor. It has been supposed that the remark was a

[1]See pp. 80 f.
[2]See ch. 4.

euphemistic mention of a compulsory levy on the Gentile churches for the 'mother church' in Jerusalem, and that it was imposed on Paul in return for the far-reaching concessions to which the apostles very reluctantly consented. If that view were right, Paul's account of the apparently harmonious meeting in Jerusalem would be evidence of the ill-will that the mission to the Jews cherished towards the mission to the Gentiles, and of Paul's dependence on the original disciples of Jesus.[1] That interpretation has the closest connexion with the question of Paul's attitude to Jerusalem, and will therefore best be discussed in this chapter.

The apostle to the Gentiles is to remember the poor, 'which very thing', Paul writes, 'I was eager to do' (Gal. 2.10). It is natural to understand 'the poor' as the poor of the Jerusalem church, and not, as some have preferred, as the whole Jerusalem church, which they suppose to have had the additional name of 'the poor' as an honourable epithet. In any case the other letters show that Paul is thinking of the poor in the literal sense (II Cor. 8.13 f.; 9.12; Rom. 15.26). We do not know why the saints in Jerusalem have so many poor among them, whom they themselves cannot help, nor do we know what Paul is referring to when he says that he was eager to help them. He might be supposed to be referring to some such previous relief as that mentioned in Acts 11.27–30; 12.25, or—as is more likely—to be alluding to something that took place after the meeting in Jerusalem, and of which the Galatians knew something, namely the beginning of the collection that is repeatedly discussed in the four great letters. In so far as the letter to the Galatians was written at a late stage of the third journey, it is clear that the passage indicates the collection during this journey.

This solicitude for the poor who were among the Jewish Christians in Jerusalem has recently received in Karl Holl's well-known treatise, 'Der Kirchenbegriff des Paulus in seinem Verhältnis zu dem der Urgemeinde',[2] an interpretation that revives the Tübingen School's conceptions. Holl points out (pp. 58 ff.) that we read of 'the poor' in Gal. 2.10, and of 'the poor among the saints' in Rom. 15.26, as if the collection concerned only part of the Jerusalem church, namely the needy members. Paul speaks differently when he asks for contributions to the collection, speaking here only of 'the saints' or 'the saints in Jerusalem' as the recipients. The passages are I Cor. 16.1; II Cor. 8.4; 9.1, 12; Rom. 15.25, 31. Now we must not suppose, so Holl argues, that the complete expression is 'the poor among the saints', which,

---

[1] So Lietzmann, *The Beginnings of the Christian Church*, pp. 73 f.; Knox, *St Paul*, pp. 111 ff.; Goguel, *Les Premiers Temps de l'Église*, p. 100; cf. Dibelius and Kümmel, *Paul*, pp. 125 ff. and 155 f.
[2] *Gesammelte Aufsätze zur Kirchengeschichte* II, pp. 44–67.

because the readers already knew about it, was shortened to 'the saints'. For in the very passage where the longer expression is used (Rom. 15.26), the Gentile churches' duty of giving is based on their having received spiritual gifts from Jerusalem—i.e., from the whole church there—and not on the existence of distress in the Jerusalem church. 'The saints' is therefore a name for the Jerusalem church, which may also be called 'the poor'; and those 'saints' or 'poor' have requested a contribution from the Gentile Christians. However much Paul may stress that everyone's gift is voluntary, and that the size of the gift is left to everyone's individual judgment, it is nevertheless a case of a tax that the Gentile churches have to pay.

Holl was an outstanding historian, but not a good exegete. He denies that 'the saints' is an abbreviation of 'the poor among the saints' by producing a list of six passages where only 'the saints' is written; but he overlooks the fact that of those six passages three are from II Cor. 8–9, which speak expressly of the recipients' need, while the last two are taken from Rom. 15, which actually speaks in v. 26 of 'the poor among the saints'. There remains only one passage that speaks of 'the saints' without any specific explanation, viz., I Cor. 16.1, where everything is said concisely, and where it is natural to understand the expressions with the help of the other letters with their more ample phraseology.

Thus we cannot persuade ourselves that either 'the saints' or 'the poor' should designate the church in Jerusalem. And finally, it is impossible to hold to the assertion that the help for the poor of that church was a contribution that it forced on the Gentile churches at the meeting mentioned in Gal. 2.1–10. In such a case we should have to take into account that whenever Paul mentions the collection and emphasizes its voluntary character, he is guilty of an untruth; and it seems to me more probable that Holl is mistaken in his assumption. In the case not only of an apostle, but of any person of past times, it is easy, but not fair, without sound and massive evidence to put up a theory that can be maintained only by assuming that he was guilty of persistent, conscious, and gross untruthfulness.

But apart altogether from the apostle's attitude to truth, it is unlikely that Holl can be right in his assumption. He thinks, in fact, that the mother church supervised the Gentile churches, but that at the same time the apostle could mislead the latter into thinking that their contribution to Jerusalem was purely voluntary. He overlooks the fact that the Pauline churches were well informed about conditions in the Jewish Christian part of the Church, and that no such important regulation as one that made the Gentile Christian churches liable to pay taxes to

Jerusalem could in any circumstances have been unknown to them.[1] Paul would never have had much luck with an untruth about conditions on which the churches may have been as well informed as he himself.

We may therefore assume that what Paul says about the collection for the poor in Jerusalem—a collection that was taken during his third journey and is reflected in the four great letters—is entirely credible. We are dealing here with a gift from the Gentile Christian churches to the church in Jerusalem; it was organized by Paul as a voluntary gift, and he himself undertook the work of his own free will and without any kind of compulsion. What is the significance of such a gift? We can answer that question by inquiring how Paul speaks about it in the texts where he is asking his churches for it. But we must, of course, also ask whether there are other motives hidden behind his eagerness for this collection and appearing in other contexts in his letters.

Whereas the brief mention of the collection in I Cor. 16.1–4 does not enlighten us about the apostle's motives, the detailed explanation in II Cor. 8–9 is of the greatest value. We learn here that the collection is voluntary. In ch. 8 Paul says, after the request in v. 7, 'I say this not as a command, but to prove by the earnestness of others that your love also is genuine.' And in 9.7 he says, 'Each one must do as he has made up his mind, not reluctantly or under compulsion, for God loves a cheerful giver.' After that we hear that the proceeds of the collection are to help to relieve want among the saints; we read in 8.13–15, 'I do not mean that others should be eased and you burdened, but that as a matter of equality your abundance at the present time should supply their want, so that their abundance may supply your want, that there may be equality.' Paul points to Ex. 16.18, where it is said that the Israelites who gathered manna in the desert all had enough to eat; and he says in 9.12, 'For the rendering of this service not only supplies the wants of the saints but also overflows in many thanksgivings to God.'

Besides these two important pieces of information, that the collection is voluntary and that it is to relieve the saints' want, we learn that the Gentile Christians' help will have further effects on the church in Jerusalem. This is said in 9.12 (which we have already quoted) and in the two verses following, which must be quoted in the context: 'For the rendering of this service not only supplies the wants of the saints but

---

[1]For those who assume, like Holl, that Jerusalem regularly undertook visits of inspection to the Gentile churches, those churches' ignorance of any liability to pay taxes to Jerusalem is quite untenable. My own view (see pp. 109 f. and 129–32) that Paul is the source of the Galatians' information about Jerusalem, and (pp. 104 f.) that no emissaries come from Jerusalem or the other Jewish Christian churches to the Gentile churches, might seem to support the assumption of such ignorance. But such supposed ignorance always breaks down on Paul's personal integrity, and also on the Gentile Christian churches' interest in conditions in Palestine.

S.M.–K

also overflows in many thanksgivings to God. Under the test of this service, they [viz., the saints in Jerusalem] will glorify God by your obedience in acknowledging the gospel of Christ, and by the generosity of your contribution for them and for all others; while they long for you and pray for you, because of the surpassing grace of God in you.' We see here, so to speak, an ecumenical aim in the collection among the Gentile Christians for the church in Jerusalem.

If the Tübingen School's views about the opposition and conflict between Paul and the first disciples in Jerusalem are warranted, and the latter caused the difficulties in Corinth, this voluntary collection for his relentless opponents becomes quite improbable. He could in the same breath describe his opponents as servants of Satan and address to the church that they are afflicting a request for generous help for them and their accomplices. If the Jerusalem church is in such want as we are told here, but is at the same time indefatigable in sending out apostles and emissaries to work against Paul in his own churches and so try to win those churches over to Jerusalem and the Jewish Christian doctrine, we see a further peculiarity—Paul collects voluntarily for Jerusalem, although the church there, in spite of its poverty, uses its modest means to pay the travelling expenses of people who are to oppose the apostle in the Gentile Christian churches. Paul is therefore supposed to have collected money voluntarily for the benefit of the Jerusalem Judaizing mission in his own churches. Let anyone believe that who can. These untenable assertions must, of course, be rejected. The ecumenical effect is a weighty concern of the apostle, because he wishes to bring about a close connexion between the new churches among the Gentiles and the mission to the Jews.

In Rom. 15.30–32 we feel how anxious the apostle is as to whether the collection will achieve its object: 'I appeal to you, brethren, by our Lord Jesus Christ and by the love of the Spirit, to strive together with me in your prayers to God on my behalf, that I may be delivered from the unbelievers in Judaea, and that my service for Jerusalem may be acceptable to the saints. . . '

We can understand these words better if we realize what work the collection involved, and how much time it cost Paul to organize it and to induce the churches to make a generous contribution during his ceaseless work for the fullness of the Gentiles. A large part of his third missionary journey must have been devoted to organizing and winding up the collection. At the same time the struggle with the church at Corinth and the difficulties in the Galatian churches were in progress. It is obvious that those happenings were bound to cripple the collection and endanger its successful completion.

We see this particularly clearly in the apostle's relation to the church at Corinth, where the two letters to the Corinthians give us some information about the course of things. The opposition between him and his church became so accentuated in the period between the two letters that he was compelled to offer it the choice between submitting to him as Christ's apostle and being thrust out of Christ's fellowship. That terrible quarrel, which threatened to annihilate the missionary work in the whole of Achaia, meant not only the possibility of painful loss which would bring Paul before Christ's judgment seat without the Corinthian church, so that one of the Gentile nations had heard the Gospel without accepting it. As long as the quarrel raged, it meant at the same time that the mission in the east was far from finished, that Paul could therefore not go on to the west, that the fullness of the Gentiles was thereby postponed to a distant future, and that the hope of Christ's early coming vanished.

Nevertheless Paul shows no inclination to give way to the Corinthians; but after the event he feels an unspeakable relief at their submission. He can now come to them and start them on their return to Christ's Church, besides which he wants to put before them the thoughts to which the mission to the Gentiles and the conflict with the Judaizers have given rise. What happened in the Galatian churches we do not know. Here we have only one letter, written at the beginning of the struggle, and so we do not know whether the events there were like those at Corinth, and whether Paul finally won them back too into the Gentile churches' fold. There is something that might suggest that the struggle was much more devastating than at Corinth. We shall learn more about it when we examine those texts in Paul's letters and in Acts, which inform us about the collection and the journey on which he took the proceeds of the collection to Jerusalem.

III

We have in Gal. 2.10 what is presumably the oldest text about the collection: 'Only they would have us remember the poor, which very thing I was eager to do.' This text may have been written either before or after the Galatians had been asked to take part in the great collection. Of course, we also have to ask whether this solicitude for the poor in Jerusalem is expressed in regular collections or in one big collection. In I Cor. 16.2–4, as well as in II Cor. 9.4, it is planned as one collection which Paul will arrange during a visit, and which in the first text and in Rom. 15.25–27 is mentioned in connexion with his journey to Jerusalem with the collection (in I Corinthians, however, only on certain conditions). It is therefore more probable that it is a question of one big collection in the Pauline churches, the proceeds being taken to Jerusalem on one single occasion.

The next question will be what churches took part in the collection; and here the different letters show interesting variations. In I Cor. 16.1 Paul says, 'Now concerning the contribution for the saints: as I directed the churches of Galatia, so you also are to do.' Possibly this stressing of the Galatians is a parallel to Paul's repeated appeal to the other churches in I Corinthians (see above, pp. 181 f.), for in II Cor. 8.10 he says, 'It is best for you now to complete what a year ago *you began* not only to do but to desire.' But in any case we know as early as this that the churches in Corinth (Achaia) and among the Galatians are taking part in the collection.

The next time that we hear of the collection is in II Cor. 8–9. This text speaks only of the churches in Macedonia and of the Corinthians and the other Christians in Achaia. The Macedonians are mentioned in 8.1–6, where their cheerful generosity is stressed as being exemplary, and again in 9.2–4, where we hear of the impending arrival of the Macedonian messengers. 8.4 seems to indicate that the Macedonians did not originally take part in the collection, but that by much persuasion they induced Paul to allow them to do so. If we combine this with 9.2— 'For I know your readiness, of which I boast about you to the people of Macedonia, saying that Achaia has been ready since last year; and your zeal has stirred up most of them'—we get the following picture of the collection: the Corinthians have from the first shown keenness and initiative for it. Their willingness has stimulated others, including the Macedonians, so that the latter have asked Paul to allow them to take part in the collection. Presumably their extreme poverty, which is mentioned in 8.2, was the reason why Paul would not bring them into the work from the beginning.[1]

In the period between the two letters to the Corinthians conditions have changed—the Macedonians have gone on with the collection, while with the Corinthians it has come to a standstill; and now it is a question of proving with renewed strength that the original zeal of which Paul had boasted is a reality. This interpretation seems to confirm the view that the Macedonians were not at first included, but only the Galatians, Corinth, and the rest of Achaia. Now the Galatians are out of it, and we might get the impression that no collection was being made anywhere except in Macedonia and Achaia.

What we infer from the text in II Corinthians seems to emerge still more clearly from Rom. 15.26, where we read, 'For Macedonia and

---

[1] If it was a question of a tax, were the Macedonians not liable?

Achaia have been pleased to make some contribution for the poor among the saints at Jerusalem.' The Galatian churches are not mentioned at all here, but the assumption is justified that Paul is counting all the participating churches, or at any rate the important ones; and the Galatians must have been among the latter if they, in conjunction with Corinth, were the first to support the collection.[1]

Besides Paul's letters we have Acts as a source. As we know, the collection is not mentioned in Acts, but there is no doubt that the journey to Jerusalem at the end of Paul's third missionary journey is identical with the journey of which he speaks in Rom. 15.25–27. The list of his companions on this journey to Jerusalem in Acts 20.4 f. is therefore of special interest to us, as we should like to learn what churches took part in the collection, and we know that those churches were to send envoys with him to Jerusalem. Paul indicates this, as we can see, in I Cor. 16.3 f.: 'And when I arrive, I will send those whom you accredit by letter to carry your gift to Jerusalem. If it seems advisable that I should go also, they will accompany me.' In II Cor. 9.3–5 he has sent on ahead the brethren mentioned in 8.17–23 'lest if some Macedonians come with me and find that you are not ready, we be humiliated —to say nothing of you—for being so confident. So I thought it necessary to urge the brethren to go on to you before me, and arrange in advance for this gift you have promised, so that it may be ready not as an exaction but as a willing gift.' Paul will therefore arrive with the envoys of the Macedonian churches, who are to accompany him on the journey to Jerusalem. According to Acts 20.3 he originally intended to go direct from Corinth to Syria, and that assumes that when he arrives in Corinth he has with him all the representatives of the churches. So it is incumbent on the Corinthians to finish the collection and produce a handsome gift, so that their former good reputation, which Paul had apparently not wanted to injure during the dispute with the church, should not suffer. He therefore sends Titus and the two brethren on ahead, to give the church the chance to make good all that it had neglected to do during the struggle against Paul.

Churches taking part in the collection

I Cor. 16.1	GALATIA	Corinth (*Achaia*)	
II Cor. 8.1 ff.		Corinth (*Achaia*)	Macedonia
Rom. 15.26		*Achaia*	Macedonia
Acts 20.4 f.	DERBE?		Beroea, Thessalonica, Doberos?
			Asia

[1]Goguel, *Les Premiers Temps de l'Église*, p. 109, mentions, among other things, the possibility that the Galatians' contribution had been taken to Jerusalem earlier.

We must therefore presume that Paul's uncommonly large group of travelling-companions in Acts 20.4 f. is composed of representatives of the churches that have taken part in the collection for Jerusalem. Besides the writer of the we-passages there belong to it Pyrrhus' son Sopater of Beroea, the Thessalonians Aristarchus and Secundus, also Gaius of Derbe, and Timothy, and from Asia Tychicus and Trophimus. How many the following 'we' in v. 5 includes, whether it is only Paul and the writer of the we-passages, or whether more are meant, we cannot say with certainty. That makes it difficult to speak with greater certainty about the representation of the different churches, but there are other difficulties too. Sopater comes from Beroea, and Aristarchus and Secundus come from Thessalonica. That means a numerically strong representation of the Macedonian churches, according well with their zeal for the collection, about which we hear from Paul in II Cor. 8.1–5. It has even been suggested that the Macedonian delegation should be increased by one, namely by Gaius, who is mentioned directly afterwards. Lake and Cadbury remark (*ad loc.*) that Acts 19.29 mentions Gaius and Aristarchus together as Macedonians. That suggests that $\Delta\epsilon\rho\beta\alpha\hat{\imath}os$ belongs to Timothy, or at any rate is originally meant for Timothy, who follows directly afterwards. 'Thessalonians' and 'Asians' are before the names of people in the list; and Acts 16.1 mentions, though rather vaguely, regarding Derbe and Lystra, that Timothy is there. That may mean that Timothy came from Derbe. Thus Gaius too will be a Thessalonian, whereas Timothy will be from Derbe.

Clark, in his edition of Acts, has a note on 20.4[1] where he regards the $\Delta ov\beta[\,?\,]\rho\iota os$ that is read in D (d reads *douerius*, gig *doberius*) as a name of an inhabitant of a Macedonian town. The reading in D stands for $\Delta ov\beta\acute{\eta}\rho\iota os$, a man from the town of Doberos; and this again makes Gaius a Macedonian.

It is possible to include another of the travelling-companions among the representatives of Macedonia. If we regard Luke as the author of the we-passages, and if we further suppose that he stayed at Philippi between Paul's first visit to that city on the second journey (16.11 ff.) and his leaving Philippi after Easter on the third journey (20.6), we may suppose him to be an envoy from the church at Philippi.

If we agree with Lake and Cadbury in making $\Delta\epsilon\rho\beta\alpha\hat{\imath}os$ relate to Timothy, we get—as was the case with Luke—a representative of a church, as in both cases one of Paul's fellow-workers represents the church concerned. And if we also agree with the South Galatian theory, according to which the Galatian churches also included the towns in which Paul preached on his first missionary journey, we have thus an

---

[1]*Op. cit.*, pp. xlix f.; cf. pp. 374 f.

envoy of the Galatian churches; but in that case the latter is not a representative sent by those churches; and that might indicate that the collection was seriously hindered by the dispute.[1] If, on the other hand, we read the text that most of the manuscripts contain, Γάϊος Δερβαῖος, we have in Gaius, on the same suppositions as before, a representative —presumably an authorized representative—of the Galatian churches, who was travelling with the apostle. If we are right here, these churches too seemed to have remained with Paul in spite of the dispute, so that they too took part in the collection and sent an envoy to Jerusalem with the rest. But this assumption rests only on many unsafe suppositions about the text of Acts and its interpretation, and therefore cannot be maintained in opposition to II Cor. 8–9 and Rom. 15.26.

These considerations for and against the Galatian churches' participation in the collection lose much of their force when we discover that, according to Acts, neither Corinth nor Achaia had any representative among Paul's travelling-companions. II Cor. 8–9 gives us information about his plans and preparations to put the collection through at the last moment. Acts 20.2 f. tells us of his spending three months in Greece; it is not expressly said that he stayed in Corinth, but it is generally assumed that he did so. The possible absence of a Galatian envoy in Acts is therefore not so serious if there was also none from Corinth among the travelling-companions. In spite of Acts' silence on this point, the Galatians may have taken part in the collection and sent representatives to Jerusalem with Paul; and these may be included in the 'we' in Acts 20.5, or Acts' list of the participants may have been incomplete. But we cannot thus get round the fact that II Corinthians and Romans are silent about any participation by the Galatian churches in the collection. As we shall very soon see, the first of those two texts does not mean that the Galatians cannot possibly have taken part in it.

We meet with further difficulties in Tychicus and Trophimus, who come from Asia, Trophimus being described in 21.29 as an Ephesian. We are told here that Jews from Asia, who had seen Trophimus with Paul in Jerusalem, thought that Paul had taken him into the temple. Does the presence of these two brethren from Asia in the travelling-suite mean that the churches there took part in the collection? In the texts discussed above, taken from Paul's letters, we do not hear of any participation; in neither I Cor. 16.1, II Cor. 8.1 ff., nor Rom. 15.26 are the churches of Asia named among those taking part in the collection. Of those texts Rom. 15.26 is the most important.

In I Cor. 16.1 Paul tells the Corinthians at that early stage that they

---

[1]This cannot be said in the case of Luke if he is to be regarded as representing Philippi, as there are already representatives of the Macedonian churches here.

are to do as the Galatians are doing; and it is not certain that all the participants in the collection are mentioned there. In II Cor. 8.1 ff. the Macedonians' zeal is mentioned to the Corinthians as an example, and we could infer from that text that those churches—and not the Galatian churches any longer—are now collecting for Jerusalem.

But it is in II Cor. 8–9 that we find remarks that might indicate that more than these two groups of churches are taking part in the collection. In fact, before the emissaries come from Macedonia, Titus is to look after the collection in Corinth, in conjunction with two brethren, who are mentioned in 8.18–24 (cf. 9.3). About these two brethren we are told, 'With him we are sending the brother who is famous among all the churches for his preaching of the gospel; and not only that, but he has been appointed by the churches to travel with us in this gracious work which we are carrying on, for the glory of the Lord and to show our good will. We intend that no one should blame us about this liberal gift which we are administering, for we aim at what is honourable not only in the Lord's sight but also in the sight of men. And with them we are sending our brother whom we have often tested and found earnest in many matters, but who is now more earnest than ever because of his great confidence in you. As for Titus, he is my partner and fellow worker in your service; and as for our brethren, they are messengers of the churches, the glory of Christ. So give proof, before the churches, of your love and of our boasting about you to these men.' This text shows us that both the brethren mentioned are emissaries of the churches—unfortunately we are not told which churches—and about the first Paul says that he has been chosen by the churches to go to Jerusalem with the gift in Paul's company. Of course, the churches that have chosen this man are neither in Achaia nor in Macedonia; it is most natural to suppose that churches outside those two provinces are meant.

There are therefore two possibilities, one being that the Galatian churches are involved, in which case the first of the brethren mentioned might be Gaius of Derbe, who, according to Acts 20.4, is among Paul's travelling-companions.[1] But those who are with Paul after he has left Ephesus, and who are sent on ahead to Corinth from a place in Macedonia before Paul himself arrives there with the Macedonian envoys, may of course, on the other hand, be envoys from Asia, and possibly

---

[1] It can hardly be Luke who is meant. It is possible that II Corinthians was written after Paul had gone on from Philippi, so that Luke could be one of his party and be identical with the brother who is not only sent on ahead with Titus, but is also to accompany Paul to Jerusalem (cf. Acts 20.4). But because of his lengthy stay in Philippi the writer of the we-passages does not seem to have been particularly suitable for organizing the collection in Corinth before the Macedonian envoys arrive with Paul.

the same as the two companions from there (Acts 20.4), Tychicus and Trophimus.

These two interpretations, which put Gaius of Derbe, or alternatively Tychicus and Trophimus of Asia, among Paul's travelling-companions as envoys of churches that are taking part in the collection, are made difficult by Rom. 15.26, where Paul says of this whole affair that Macedonia and Achaia have been pleased to make some contribution for the poor among the saints at Jerusalem. At that moment, when the collection is closed and Paul is waiting for the winter to pass and the sea journey to be resumed, so that he can take to Jerusalem the money collected and a group representing the churches concerned, a mention of Macedonia and Achaia leads one to suppose that all the participating churches are mentioned. In that case the people from Asia and Gaius— if he should be from Derbe—must be travelling-companions whose churches did not take part in the collection. But from II Cor. 8–9 it may be supposed that there are envoys from other churches than those in Macedonia and Achaia, so that one Pauline text does not accord with the other.

Unfortunately we must now call a halt to these reflections without having reached any certainty on whether the Galatian churches and Asia took part in the collection. But it is certain in any case that the collection is now closed, and that the churches' representatives are gathered round Paul.

IV

With that the preparations for the journey to Jerusalem are concluded. For years Paul has worked hard with the preparation and carrying out of a collection for the church at Jerusalem. Heavy storms have swept the mission fields where the collection began, and things have happened that might have overshadowed that ecumenical work; but the apostle stood firm. He set the work in motion and carried it through with an energy with which he would like to inspire his churches. Now he is ready to travel; and it only remains now for us to review the situation at the beginning of the journey.

By means of the letter to the Romans it is possible for us to judge of the situation immediately before Paul's journey to Jerusalem with the gift that had been collected. The letter, in fact, was written while he was in Greece, just before he left (Acts 20.3). This is where we hear for the first time about the church in Rome, a church which in many people's imagination played a great part in Paul's life. People usually judge of his relation to it by the introductory part of the letter and the section that follows in Rom. 1 about his eagerness to go to Rome, and in doing so overlook chapter 15 with its qualifications of the first strong expressions.

In the introductory passage Paul includes the church at Rome in all the Gentiles whose obedience to the faith he is to bring about, for which he has received grace and apostleship (1.5). In the next section he calls on God as witness when he wants to stress how he thinks of them unceasingly and asks that somehow by God's will he may now at last succeed in coming to them (1.9 f.). For he longs to see them, so that he may impart some spiritual gift to them (1.11). The Roman Christians are to know that he has often intended to come to them, but has so far been prevented—we need only think of the difficulties in Corinth and the Galatian churches, which have put off the completion of his missionary work among the Gentiles in the east. The purpose of his coming is to be that he may reap some harvest among them as well as among the rest of the Gentiles. He is under obligation to all the Gentile nations, and is therefore eager to preach the Gospel to the church at Rome too (1.13–15).

In ch. 15 we have important explanations which may make clear to us what Paul means by this preaching of the Gospel at Rome. It is not a matter of missionary activity, but of a visit that is to strengthen the existing church, for he says in 15.20 that he makes it his ambition not to preach the Gospel where Christ has already been named, lest he build on another man's foundation. His task, as we know from I Cor. 3.10 ff., is to lay a foundation on which another man can build. Because that pioneering work has been delayed, he has often been hindered (he continues in 15.22 f.) from coming to Rome. But now, as he no longer has room for work in those eastern lands, and has been longing for years to visit the church at Rome, he will come to them on his journey to Spain, for, he writes in 15.24, 'I hope to see you in passing, and to be sped on my journey by you, once I have enjoyed your company for a little.'

Thus the Gospel preaching of which Paul speaks in ch. 1 is no missionary preaching, but preaching for the strengthening of a church already there, and the visit is to be of short duration and only a breaking of the journey. For Rome is not the journey's goal; he is on his way to Spain, now that the missionary work in the east has been completed— he wants to go 'not where Christ has already been named' (v. 20). Rome, on the contrary, is an intermediate station on the way to the new mission field, and he is allotting the church the honourable task of supporting his further journey westward—he writes, 'to be sped on my journey there by you' (v. 24), i.e., to Spain. Rome seems to become a mission base, as Philippi was on the second missionary journey, his loyal friends, who gave him economic support when his own manual work could not provide the necessary means for his missionary work in the front line.

The letter to the Romans was therefore sent to the church at Rome to ask it to co-operate in the new advance in the west; but it is not like the other Pauline letters. It does not, in fact, as we saw in ch. 7, take into account conditions in Rome, but takes a more general line, as Paul, during his stay in Corinth after the end of the struggle with his churches in Asia Minor and Achaia, gathers the conclusions of the innumerable discussions and controversies into which he has been forced by Judaizers, Jews, and Gentile Christians during his third journey. Romans is a balance-sheet that he draws up during his winter stay in Corinth towards the end of the third missionary journey. That balance-sheet is destined, either in writing or orally, for his own churches and those in Palestine, and is written down in the form of the letter to the Romans, to prepare the church in Rome for his coming and for their important task of being a missionary base for his work in the west.

It is not possible here to give a detailed account of how the various lines of thought in Romans are to be interpreted on this view of the letter's origin. I must content myself with a reference to the observations on the subject in Manson's article which states the case, and whose arguments I have set out on pp. 198 f.

I propose to show only in respect of chs. 9–11 the consequences that such a point of view has for the exposition of the text. There is perhaps no better example of how the strong dogmatic interest that has attached itself to the content of Romans—right through the history of the Christian Church, especially with the Reformers and the Reformed Churches—has given that exposition a dogmatic bias. We see how New Testament exegetes have conformed to systematic theology and believed that the ideas that Paul expressed about God's election and the Jewish people relate to God's predestination of individuals and the Jews' destiny in world history to come, or even concern the Jews' destiny in a period which even for us lies in the future. Here the fact has been disregarded that in these chapters Paul is speaking as a missionary about the immediate problems of the Gentile and Jewish missions of his own day, and that the aims that he sees before him do not lie hidden in the distant future, but are already close to their realization, as Israel's conversion and Christ's coming in glory will soon be accomplished facts.

Modern exegetes too have found it difficult to realize what a central part the problem of the Jewish people's destiny plays, or at any rate has played, in Christian theology. The question really was whether God's promises became null and void if the chosen people did not attain salvation. Could the Gentile Christians then rely on God's promises of salvation when the chosen people had become vessels given over to perdition?

If ch. 9 lays down that God has sovereign power over salvation and perdition, ch. 10 shows how God demands only the belief of the heart and the confession of the mouth; and the Jews of the whole world have heard this from the apostles, but they have hardened their hearts. Israel, however, has not been rejected by God, Paul explains in ch. 11; but as the salvation of the Gentiles is the first result of the Jews' fall, God's plan is that the fullness of the Gentiles shall bring about the salvation of all Israel. God's way of salvation is expressed in mercy to the disobedient, and so he saves all.

If this account represents a balance-sheet that Paul drew up in Corinth immediately before he left for Jerusalem, we can find here some of the distinctive marks of the Christian mission of those years. The mission to the Jews faces complete bankruptcy. To bring it about that people invoke Christ and are thereby saved, it is necessary for Christ to send out apostles, as Paul shows in 10.14 f.: 'But how are men to call upon him in whom they have not believed? And how are they to believe in him of whom they have never heard? And how are they to hear without a preacher? And how can men preach unless they are sent *(ἀποσταλῶσιν)*?' And after Paul has thus shown what is necessary to bring about the invoking and salvation, he finds that all the conditions are fulfilled—the apostles *have* gone out and preached: 'As it is written, "How beautiful are the feet of those who preach good news!" But not all have heeded the gospel ['not all' means not all the Jews]; for Isaiah says, "Lord, who has believed what he has heard from us?" So faith comes from what is heard, and what is heard comes by the word of Christ' (10.15–17). In the next passage Paul refutes various objections: 'But I ask, have they not heard? Indeed they have; for "Their voice has gone out to all the earth, and their words to the end of the world" ' (10.18). In other words, Christ's emissaries have gone out to the Jews of the whole world, preached to them, and everywhere met the same impenitence among the chosen people. As is quoted a few verses later from the prophet Isaiah, 'All day long I have held out my hands to a disobedient and contrary people' (10.21).

The apostle Peter and the others who were sent out by Christ to preach had thus returned with no results. But among the Gentiles things had gone quite differently. Here salvation had been attained as a result of Israel's rejection of the Gospel; and Paul looked forward to the fullness of the Gentiles which was to give the signal for the conversion of Israel.

However strange it may sound, the way to the salvation of Israel is by the mission to the Gentiles. The faithful and zealous apostles to the Jews have achieved nothing, while Paul, the apostle to the Gentiles, is through his work among the Gentiles the essential motive force for the salvation of all Israel. The method is expressed by Moses in Deut. 32.21: 'I will stir them to jealousy with those who are no people; I will provoke them with a foolish nation' (quoted in Rom. 10.19). It is here that Paul gets the word παραζηλόω, 'to make eager or jealous'. And his method is as he puts it in 11.13 ff., 'Now I am speaking to you Gentiles. Inasmuch then as I am an apostle to the Gentiles, I magnify my ministry in order to make my fellow Jews jealous *(παραζηλῶσαι)*, and thus save some of them.' The present situation with the streaming in of the Gentiles may provoke the Jews to jealousy, so that a certain number of them accept the Gospel and are saved; and the fullness of the Gentiles will bring with it the salvation of all Israel. We infer from the context: all Israel is saved in an exactly similar way, namely through jealousy.

We have already observed above (pp. 47–52) that Paul uses, besides the noun 'fullness', πλήρωμα, the cognate verb πληρόω in a connexion that no doubt denotes the same fact as is expressed by the fullness of the Gentiles. In Rom. 15.19 Paul says that he has fully preached the Gospel of Christ from Jerusalem and as far round as Illyricum, πεπληρωκέναι τὸ εὐαγγέλιον τοῦ Χριστοῦ. From a purely territorial point of view, therefore, we can say that for the east the fullness of the Gentiles has been achieved, but that it still remains to Paul to preach Christ's Gospel fully in the lands westward of Rome and Italy. But if it is true that the present influx of Gentiles is already arousing jealousy, it is of course difficult to separate sharply what is happening from what is coming, from the moment of time when the fullness of the Gentiles is reached and all Israel is converted.

V

Against the background of that existing situation at the beginning of the journey we have to keep before us the aims that Paul had set himself for his journey to Jerusalem. The first aim to be mentioned is, of course, connected with the gift that was collected in the Gentile churches, thanks to work extending over many years. As Paul expresses it in Rom. 15.31, the church at Rome is to pray for him so that his service that takes him to Jerusalem may be acceptable to the saints. Of course, it is very near his heart that his ecumenical task in relation to the Jerusalem church may be successful, so that the Jewish Christians may praise God for the faith of the Gentile Christians, and may pray and long for them, as Paul wrote in II Cor. 9.13 f. Paul always attached a special importance to Jerusalem in the plan of salvation, and it is easy to understand how important the gift was, not only from a material point of view, but at the same time as an encouragement to the harassed Christian church in Jerusalem, situated in the midst of Judaism, whose mission to its fellow-countrymen, as Paul says, has led only to a realization of Israel's complete impenitence. It must also have been near to Paul's heart that the balance-sheet that he had drawn up after the struggles during the third missionary journey with the optimistic expectation that all Israel would be saved (Rom. 9–11) might be taken to the apostles to the Jews, who had at last exclaimed despairingly, 'Lord, who has believed what he has heard from us?'

But apart from this self-evident ecumenical task, as we have called it—that of handing over the money gift, giving encouragement, and discussing the points on which he had become clear during the conflicts from which he had just successfully emerged, Paul must have had other reasons for going to Jerusalem. We can infer this from two circumstances that are worth considering: (1) The journey to Jerusalem meant that he ran a serious risk which could not be justified merely by the ecumenical task, because it would have been possible to send the money gift, and the balance-sheet in the form of the letter to the Romans, without exposing him to the serious risk of his life. (2) There travels with him a large body of church representatives, a fact which suggests that they had to carry out another task besides that of handing over the money gift.

As to the great risk that Paul incurred by going to Jerusalem, Romans and Acts are at one. We read in Rom. 15.30 f. that the church at Rome is to strive together with Paul in its prayers that he may be delivered from the unbelievers in Judaea. In Acts we meet one announcement after another of Paul's death or threatened death awaiting him in Jerusalem. It begins with the Jews' plotting against his life (20.3), on which account he changes his plans for the journey. In his speech to the elders at Miletus the apostle says that they will not see him again; the Holy Spirit compels him to travel to Jerusalem, but in every city the Holy Spirit testifies to him that imprisonment and afflictions await him (20.22–25). What happens in every city is told us directly in connexion with Caesarea, where the prophet Agabus binds himself with Paul's girdle, and says, 'Thus says the Holy Spirit, "So shall the Jews at Jerusalem bind the man who owns this girdle and deliver him into the hands of the Gentiles" ' (21.11). The last expression is similar, as we shall see later (p. 320) to the one applied to Jesus in the third announcement of the Passion. In spite of these clear prophecies of danger and death, Paul goes on to Jerusalem. It cannot have been only the 'ecumenical' task that compelled him to risk his life, for it could have been performed without his personal participation.

The second circumstance that claims our notice and reveals the apostle's special interest in the Jerusalem journey is the uncommonly large number of travelling-companions that accompany him. We have already seen that it is a matter of representatives of various Gentile churches. According to Acts 20.4 f. there are at least eight men travelling with him to take the money gift. I Cor. 16.3 f., II Cor. 8.16–24 and 9.3–4 indicate that there were more delegates than Luke mentions; and so we ask ourselves how large a sum had been collected, and whether it could easily defray the expenses of a journey for at least ten men. Those travelling-companions must have had a considerable significance, for otherwise, the gift would hardly have been reduced by a considerable sum for travelling expenses. Of course it was important for members of the churches among the Gentiles to go to Jerusalem and make personal contact with the church there;[1] and such representatives were a pledge that everything in connexion with the transfer of the gift was done properly, as Paul indicated in II Cor. 8.18–21. But in spite of everything, it is difficult to see why so many are travelling.

Now is there any explanation of these two circumstances—that Paul goes up personally with the gift at the serious risk of his life, and that on that journey he is accompanied by such a large group consisting of representatives of the Gentile churches? There is such an explanation, and it lies in Paul's view, expressed in Rom. 11, of the connexion between the mission to the Gentiles and the mission to the Jews. It is his intention to save the Jews by making them jealous of the Gentiles, who are accepting the Gospel in great numbers; and now he is going up to the stronghold of Israel, to the disobedient, as he calls them, with a representative company of believing Gentiles.

They go up to Jerusalem with gifts, as it had been prophesied that the Gentiles would when the last days had come. As is written in Isa. 2.2 f. and Micah 4.1 f., 'It shall come to pass in the latter days that the mountain of the house of the Lord shall be established as the highest of the mountains, and shall be raised above the hills; and all the nations shall flow to it, and many peoples shall come, and say: "Come, let us go up to the mountain of the Lord, to the house of the God of Jacob; that he may teach us his ways and that we may walk in his paths." For out of Zion shall go forth the law, and the word of the

---

[1]The Jerusalem Christians' longing for the brethren in Corinth is mentioned in II Cor. 9.14.

Lord from Jerusalem. . . .'[1] And we read concerning Jerusalem (Isa. 60.5 f.), 'Because the abundance of the sea shall be turned to you, the wealth of the nations shall come to you', and in the lines that follow we are given a picture of how all kinds of animals and gold, silver and frankincense are taken over land and sea to the holy city.

This assumption, that the emissaries of the Gentile churches and their gifts represent a fulfilment of Old Testament prophecies, is confirmed by Paul's declarations during the subsequent trial, according to Acts. He says in his speech before King Agrippa, 'And now I stand here on trial for hope in the promise made by God to our fathers, to which our twelve tribes hope to attain, as they earnestly worship night and day. And for this hope I am accused by the Jews, O king!' (26.6 f.). And in the speech to the Jews in Rome he says, 'It is because of the hope of Israel that I am bound with this chain' (28.20). Paul's words show that the object of that journey, which involved his imprisonment, is the fulfilment of God's promise that the nation shall be saved.[2]

We might try to reject this assumption by pointing out that this delegation of the believing Gentiles cannot be τὸ πλήρωμα τῶν ἐθνῶν. The fullness of the Gentiles cannot have come about as long as the apostle has not reached the west. This might look tempting, but the argument will not hold water, because all eschatological points of time are uncertain, and it is difficult for anyone living and taking part in the last days to know exactly at what eschatological point of time he is. Nor is a conception like 'the fullness of the Gentiles' quite clear. It does not mean that every Gentile has heard the Gospel, but only that the various Gentile nations have heard it. And that idea of a representative reception could apply, not only to a single nation, but to the Gentile nations as a whole. Here too a representative selection of the peoples would justify a missionary advance to Israel. Such a delegation from the eastern nations would perhaps not be without effect on the chosen people.

Moreover, there is the possibility that Paul imagined that the salvation of the Jewish people would be of decisive importance for the mission to the Gentiles. He writes in Rom. 11.15 about the Jews, 'For if their rejection means the reconciliation of the world, what will their acceptance mean but life from the dead?' It is, indeed, an ordinary idea among the Jews that Israel's salvation will be of immense import for

[1] Cf. Isa. 60; 25.6–8 (twice quoted by Paul); Jer. 16.19; Zech. 14.16; Ps. 22.27–29 (important because of Paul's use of this Psalm—see pp. 332 f.), etc. See Joachim Jeremias, 'The Gentile World in the Thought of Jesus', *SNTS Bulletin* 3, 1952, pp. 25 f.

[2] This applies particularly to 26.6 f., if, with Wendt, we read v. 8 immediately before v. 23. In that case it is not necessary to regard vv. 6 f. in the same way as 24.21 and possibly to interpret 23.6 in the same way. ἐπαγγελία may refer here, as elsewhere in Acts, to the coming of salvation to Israel (cf. p. 314 and p. 211 with n. 1).

the rest of the world, consisting of Gentiles, so that Paul would be saying nothing new here if the context in which the words stand were not so completely different from all the ordinary Jewish spheres of thought. The observation is meant to point out to Gentile Christian readers that Israel's conversion, which was not generally expected by the Gentile Christians, is certain to come about and will be of the greatest significance.

Some have thought that the strong expression 'life from the dead' refers to the life that begins with the awakening from the dead in the coming aeon.[1] Sanday and Headlam consider another possibility, namely that it denotes the spreading of the Gospel and a strong spiritual awakening.[2] But this interpretation has the drawback that the eschatological events that are soon to come do not leave time for such a sudden increase in the spreading of the Gospel. We should in that case have to imagine that after the salvation of the Jews there would be a short space of time in which the mission to the Gentiles, united with Israel, would experience the great things that are promised in the Old Testament.

In any case, Paul goes on his way to Jerusalem to meet death, faithful to his call, filled with the task that he sees before him as the central one in all his missionary work, namely the mission to Israel. In that service he risks his life; and although rescued from the Jews' attempt to lynch him in the temple, he now becomes involved in the Roman legal machinery, which takes him slowly, all too slowly, to his death.

VI

If we adopt this interpretation of the object of Paul's journey to Jerusalem, a number of details in Rom. 9–11 take on life and colour. We see how the apostle can say at first (9.1–5) that he wishes that he himself were accursed and cut off from Christ for the sake of his brethren, 'my kinsmen by race'. Lietzmann thinks that Paul is using here a rabbinical expression for strong love, expressing the speaker's wish to take over the torments of retribution in the life to come for the person concerned. This expression of a wish in the case of one or more people who are ready to make expiation for a single deceased person seems in some examples in Billerbeck (III, p. 261) to be a purely conventional turn of speech. And Lietzmann has overlooked the fact that

[1]Thus B. Weiss, who stresses the fact that Paul does not say ἀνάστασις ἐκ νεκρῶν, because the apostle's gaze already reaches out beyond this event to the blessed things that follow. Thus too Lietzmann.
[2]Thus too O. Bardenhewer, *ad loc.*: 'A mighty upsurge of Christian faith and Christian life on the whole earth.' Zahn holds a similar view.

a big gap has to be covered between on the one hand using the expression for the individual's expiation for the individual, and on the other hand the individual's wish to be an expiation for Israel.[1]

To understand Paul's words, we must turn to the examples quoted in Billerbeck II, pp. 280 f. (note i.), which deal with the vicarious suffering undergone on behalf of the nation by great figures of redemptive history. Although there is no verbal agreement, there is in Rom. 9.3 a parallel between Paul and Moses. We read in Ex. 32.31 f., 'So Moses returned to the Lord and said, "Alas, this people have sinned a great sin; they have made for themselves gods of gold. But now, if thou wilt forgive their sin—and if not, blot me, I pray thee, out of thy book which thou hast written." ' The similarity between this passage and the one in Paul's letter is in the seriousness with which the person concerned wishes to sacrifice himself vicariously.

In both these situations, in fact, nothing is said of expiating the people's sins in general, but in Moses' case and in Paul's there is the wish to atone vicariously for the nation in respect of a situation in which it has sinned without the possibility of forgiveness. In Exodus, after the conclusion of the Covenant on Mount Sinai, the people had not the patience to wait for Moses to come back with the tables of the testimony, but had a calf made, and sacrificed to it. Similarly the coming of the Messiah and the conclusion of the New Covenant indicate the moment when Israel again shows its disobedience in the very hour of grace. What punishment, indeed, had Israel deserved for its disobedience, except to be annihilated? But in both cases a great figure of redemptive history intercedes and declares himself ready to suffer vicariously the punishment that the nation has deserved.

The next passage to have immediate importance in this way is 9.26. In the last line of the quotation from Hosea 1.10 there is an ἐκεῖ, which may be an addition by Paul to the LXX text.[2] If that is the case, we must consider with Sanday and Headlam whether Paul has Palestine in mind when he uses this ἐκεῖ, just as the text of Hosea originally alluded to the Holy Land. If Paul does the same, he is presumably suggesting with the quotation and his addition that the Gentile nations are to gather in Jerusalem, where the Messianic kingdom is to be established—cf. 11.26. Sanday and Headlam mention this possible interpretation, pointing out that Paul is often strongly influenced by the language and even the conceptions of Jewish eschatology, although

---

[1] We meet this wish as a conventional remark in R. Ishmael in Neg. 2.1 (Billerbeck III, p. 261).

[2] Rahlfs has this ἐκεῖ in the text of his short edition of the Septuagint, Stuttgart, 1935, whereas it is absent from Ziegler's edition of the *Duodecim Prophetae* (*Septuaginta* etc., XIII), Göttingen, 1943; see the apparatus.

in his more spiritual utterances he seems to be fully independent of them. Here, for all their reserve, Sanday and Headlam have probably grasped Paul's view correctly that in Jerusalem the Gentiles are to be proclaimed sons of God, in conformity with the role that Paul in fact ascribes to Jerusalem.[1] Thus we may make the passage in the quotation refer to Jerusalem, to which place Paul is now on his way with the delegates of the Gentile churches. The words thereby take on a meaning of immediate importance: 'Those who were not my people I will call "my people", and her who was not beloved I will call "my beloved". And in the very place where it was said to them, "You are not my people", they will be called "sons of the living God." ' Israel will realize that God has by his grace accepted the Gentiles as his people, and will thereby be filled with jealousy which in Paul's eyes opens the way destined by God for salvation.

Another passage which has caused the exegetes difficulty, but which can be explained by Paul's situation, is 10.10: 'For man believes with his heart and so is justified, and he confesses with his lips and so is saved.' Why is anything said here about confessing? Is it because of the quotation in v. 8,[2] or are faith and confession, justification and life only rhetorical parallels?[3] Pallis thinks that confession mean here confession before the authorities; and presumably that view is correct. It must again be said here that the idea of confessing before the authorities must have been very much in Paul's mind just then; he was thinking of the journey that he was about to make to Jerusalem, and so of the confession that he was about to make before his own people, perhaps before the Sanhedrin.

Lastly, there is in ch. 11 an Old Testament example that shows a parallel with Paul's situation as it then was, and at the same time reveals the great difference. Elijah comes before God with the words against Israel, 'Lord, they have killed thy prophets, they have demolished thy altars, and I alone am left, and they seek my life' (11.3). Bloody persecutions had gone over the Church at the Jews' instigation; and the last words from the quotation, about the Jews' seeking his life, were only too applicable to Paul's person (see pp. 309 f.). As the prophet he stands alone against the people's superior numbers, and finds himself in danger of losing his life. And as Elijah comes back from his stay among the Gentiles to force a decision between Baal and Jehovah by

---

[1] Sanday and Headlam suggest another interpretation, according to which ἐχεῖ refers to the whole world. But whereas the first-mentioned interpretation explains the strong emphasis on the 'place' in the quotation, the latter interpretation cannot explain such emphasis, and is therefore not a likely one.

[2] Dodd on 10.6–9.

[3] Althaus *ad loc.*

the trial of strength on Mount Carmel, Paul is now on his way from the
Gentile world to show stubborn Israel the obedience of faith as it had
become reality in the believing Gentiles. It is important that, unlike
Elijah, Paul does not appear before God against Israel, but that his
heart's desire and concern before God is the salvation of the Jews (10.1).
It is Moses, not Elijah, whom Paul resembles.

VII

We have accompanied Paul on his last journey to Jerusalem. He
went up in the service of his people, Israel, with the Gentile churches'
gift and the new thoughts that had grown out of the missionary work
and out of the conflicts during the third missionary journey, filled above
all with the great hope of Israel's salvation. The emissaries of the
Gentile churches who went with him were to take their gifts to the poor
of the holy city and thereby fulfil the prophets' promises of the last days.

The destination was Jerusalem, but the journey took him to Rome,
and Paul gradually realized that he was to go to Rome, and that by
sending him there God was pursuing a definite purpose. That will be
discussed in the next chapter.

II

PAUL BEFORE THE EMPEROR

I

WE saw in the previous chapter how Paul went up to Jerusalem, full of anxiety, but also full of hope that the conversion of the Gentiles, which was clearly shown in their gifts and in the large number of the churches' representatives, might arouse the jealousy of the Jews and so bring about the salvation of all Israel. That hope was not realized. The Jews certainly showed ζῆλος, an ambiguous term that expresses an idea ranging from zeal to jealousy. But their zeal and jealousy only led to an attempt, first to lynch Paul in the temple, and later to murder him treacherously during the trial. The great turning-point in his nation's destiny, which he had desired with all his heart, God's acceptance of Israel, which was to be like life from the dead (Rom. 11.15), did not come.

Roman soldiers snatch him, still alive, from the mob in the forecourt of the temple, and take him to safety; but now he is a prisoner waiting to be judged.

We infer from the account in Acts of Paul's activities up to then that the Jews attacked him in two ways—partly by doing their best to murder him, and partly by trying to get him sentenced to death by a Roman court.

Even in Lystra on the first journey, according to Acts 14.19, the Jews tried to kill him: 'But Jews came there from Antioch and Iconium; and having persuaded the people, they stoned Paul and dragged him out of the city, supposing that he was dead'; and in Acts 20.3 we are told of a plot against him which he frustrated by changing his plans for the journey. The Western Text of this passage speaks of a conspiracy which was made by Jews in Greece, and which makes him propose to go to Syria; but the Spirit commands him to go back through Macedonia. The Egyptian text, on the other hand, makes him intend to go to Syria in any circumstances, but he changes his route in view of the Jews' conspiracy. If we take into account his wish, on the following journey through Macedonia and Asia Minor to Syria and Palestine, to be in Jerusalem for Pentecost, we can interpret the Egyptian text as

309

follows: Paul would have liked to go direct from Corinth to Palestine, but gives that route up because he would fall a victim to the conspiracy on the way. He and his companions were probably to be taken to Palestine by the Jewish pilgrim ships used in connexion with the Easter festival in Jerusalem. But as these spell danger for him, he chooses a longer overland route, which causes a delay of so many weeks that he can now hope to reach the temple in time for Pentecost only by pressing on urgently.

These conspiracies and plots seem to be directed spontaneously against Paul's life; but the Jews go still more frequently to the legal authorities as a means of getting the better of their formidable opponent. We might recollect here that, according to II Cor. 11.24 he received five times at the hands of the Jews forty lashes less one. Such trial and punishment in the synagogue are not mentioned in Acts. On the other hand, it gives examples of Jewish accusations against Paul before the authorities, as in Thessalonica in Acts 17.6 f., where Jews look for him and Silas, and then drag Jason and some of the brethren before the city authorities, crying, 'These men who have turned the world upside down have come here also, and Jason has received them; and they are all acting against the decrees of Caesar, saying that there is another king, Jesus.' In contrasting the emperor with Jesus Basileus, this passage reads almost like John 19.15, where Pilate says to the Jews, 'Shall I crucify your king?', and the chief priests answer, 'We have no king but Caesar.' There is a very Jewish ring in the accusation against Paul in Corinth, where the Jews say to Gallio, 'This man is persuading men to worship God contrary to the law' (18.13). But the proconsul refuses to deal with this purely Jewish question.

During Paul's last stay in Jerusalem an attempt was made, both to murder him and to sentence him to death. Whether the Jews who choose the first way have supporters in the Sanhedrin and other official Jewish circles is uncertain. Only in the latter case do the Jews who want to liquidate Paul seek the co-operation of the chief priests and elders, because an inquiry in the Sanhedrin must be arranged if he should come out of the Romans' hands, in which he is safe (23.14 f.). Many things suggest that the first scene in the temple, involving the riot and ending with his arrest, was improvised. The people involved are Jews from the province of Asia, who seize him and thereby set the whole legal machinery in motion, as they do not manage to kill him (21.27 ff.).

In this connexion we must now draw attention to something that is important in dealing with Paul's life in the period after the great letters. While as regards his earlier life certain statements in Acts can be checked with the help of his letters, that is not possible for the period of his long imprisonment. Of three letters written during that time (i.e., the period of his imprisonment in Rome), namely Philippians, Colossians, and Philemon, only Philippians can give us any enlightenment about his personal affairs and the legal proceedings in which he was involved. In Colossians we are only told (4.7), 'Tychicus will tell you all about my affairs; he is a beloved brother and faithful minister and fellow servant in the Lord.' So that letter gives us no information about what we should like to hear.

Acts, on the other hand, can apparently provide a complete and connected account of these years of Paul's life, as it contains a great deal of information about the legal proceedings. Further, these sections are presumably from the we-source, to which we can attach a special value among all the reports about Paul. Unfortunately a closer examination of these texts shows that they leave us very ignorant as to certain important questions, most of all with regard to the trial and the course that it took.

II

It would greatly help us to understand Paul's thoughts and actions during the trial if we could understand it from the Roman point of view. How had the Roman authorities in Palestine dealt with it, and what was the charge against Paul? What does the appeal to the emperor mean, and according to what formalities does a legal trial take its course before an imperial court? Further, what was the Roman authorities' opinion of Paul personally and of his mission to the Gentiles? If we could know something about all this, we should be on firmer ground when we investigate Acts' and Paul's views about the trial.

We consider the trial first from the Roman point of view. In an article frequently quoted, the distinguished ancient historian, Theodor Mommsen, has dealt with 'Die Rechtsverhältnisse des Apostels Paulus',[1] and so with Paul's trial in Palestine and his appeal to the emperor; and H. J. Cadbury has written about 'Roman Law and the Trial of Paul'.[2]

Mommsen's article is written essentially for theologians, and can scarcely produce anything not already known to jurists (p. 81). It discusses the course of the trial according to Acts, and, apart from some quite small retouches, he thinks that the course of events in the early empire was as recorded, and that Acts' account of the trial is historically correct in all its main points.

Cadbury's article, which was written about thirty years later, begins

[1] *ZNW* 2, 1901, pp. 81–96.
[2] *Beginnings* 5, pp. 297–338.

by acknowledging a fact that is already clear to the reader of Mommsen's article, namely that our knowledge of Roman law and administration of justice at the time of Paul's trial is uncertain (p. 299). The codification of Roman law belongs to a later period, and even that can give no clear information on the questions that arise in the account given in Acts; and this is in spite of the new material that we owe to the discoveries of Egyptian papyri since Mommsen's time.

Mommsen and Cadbury agree that the writer of Acts does not draw a clear picture of the trial and of the appeal to the emperor in Rome. Luke is not, as has sometimes been assumed, well versed in legal matters. But whereas Mommsen constantly works from the assumption that Paul is within Roman jurisdiction from his arrest till his appeal to the emperor, Cadbury steadily pursues the problem whether he should not have been judged by the Sanhedrin. If Claudius Lysias had not interfered in the tumult in the temple court, Paul would have been brought before the Sanhedrin—if he had escaped alive from the angry mob—and judged there. The hearing of his case before the Sanhedrin in ch. 23 might have led to decisive action by the court if its internal dispute had not made any real settlement of the case impossible. Finally, Festus' proposal that Paul should take his case to Jerusalem means not only that the court is to meet in Jerusalem, but that Paul is to be judged there by the Sanhedrin, and not by Festus; and so Paul decides to appeal to the emperor in Rome. These possibilities which Cadbury points out (though only as possibilities) must be considered in dealing with the layman's account of Paul's case in Acts.

Moreover, Cadbury assumes that in these cases of appeal the emperor himself pronounced the verdict; and in view of our ignorance of the procedure before the imperial court, he thinks we may assume that they were decided, not through witnesses, existing law, or precedent, but by the free judgment of the court of appeal. This assumption does not seem unreasonable, as a supreme court often serves as a source of law and often decides individual cases more according to its own judgment than according to existing law.

Unfortunately, as may be inferred from these articles, it is impossible to say anything definite about Paul's case from the Roman point of view. We know very little about appeals to the emperor, and the juridical material does not help us to make any real progress in understanding the account of the legal proceedings in Acts.

III

Our only course, therefore, is to investigate Acts thoroughly so as to understand Luke's picture of the case. It has, indeed, already become clear to us that Luke did not understand much about law, and that he describes the juridical problems in these complicated proceedings very incompletely;[1] but his account, besides being our only source, will in spite of its inadequacy in other respects give us valuable insight into what people thought of Paul's conduct during his case, and possibly into what Paul himself thought about the trial.

According to the account in Acts, Paul comes to Jerusalem with a considerable number of Gentile Christians, and is given a friendly reception by James and the elders. They ask him to participate in the Nazirite vow of four men, so as to lay the rumours, which are circulating about him, that he is teaching the Diaspora Jews to forsake Moses. But before the time-limit of the Nazirite vow has expired, Paul is attacked in the temple. It is interesting here that the Jews from the province of Asia, who are the originators of the tumult in the temple, shout something that might serve to indicate the nature of the whole of the following proceedings: 'This is the man who is teaching men everywhere against the people and the law and this place; moreover he has also brought Greeks into the temple, and he has defiled this holy place' (21.28). The charge is therefore directed against Paul not only because he is said to have violated the prohibition of the entry of Gentiles into the temple; it is also concerned with his activities in the whole world.

This outcry sets the whole town in confusion, but the tribune and his soldiers come to Paul's aid. The next day the tribune sends him to the Sanhedrin, 'desiring to know the real reason why the Jews accused him' (22.30). This remark seems to assume a Jewish *démarche* to the tribune, as it is difficult to see otherwise why the commandant in Jerusalem, who had just saved a Roman citizen of Tarsus from being lynched in the temple, should apply to the council for information. In 22.30–23.10 there follows the scene with Paul before the Sanhedrin, where he says that he has lived before God in all good conscience up to that day (23.1). Paul means this quite generally, without thinking of a concrete charge of violating the temple; and the same is true of his exclamation that brings the Pharisees into conflict with the Sadducees in the council, 'Brethren, I am a Pharisee, a son of Pharisees; with respect to the hope

---

[1]At the same time it is important to realize with F. J. Foakes Jackson (*Josephus and the Jews*, 1930, p. 169) 'that the very brief record in Acts gives an amazingly correct picture of the state of affairs in Palestine, considering that the ruin of the Jewish nation in torrents of blood must have made events before the war a dim memory to the generation which followed. Of these the Jews have preserved scarcely any Hebrew or Aramaic tradition. One cannot but be struck with astonishment that the obscure sect of the Christians of the first century should have produced a record which, if it seems unsatisfactory to us by its brevity and absence of information on certain points, should have been as accurate in its general features as that found in the last chapters of the Book of the Acts of the Apostles.'

and the resurrection of the dead I am on trial' (23.6). In this text the two expressions 'hope' and 'resurrection of the dead' may be combined to give 'hope of the resurrection of the dead', as is suggested in 24.21, which reads, 'except this one thing which I cried out while standing among them, "With respect to the resurrection of the dead I am on trial before you this day." ' If we keep in mind Luke's gift and liking for variation by repetition and reference to previous passages, the hope may be thought of as an independent item beside the resurrection of the dead, as is the case in Paul's speech in ch. 26, where the hope is in the promise of the Messiah's coming or the salvation of the nation (26.6), and the resurrection of the dead is mentioned by itself. Of course, in the first case the close connexion is in the fact that the Messiah has indeed risen from the dead. In the latter case ἐπαγγελία is used, as it commonly is in Acts, of the salvation that will come to Israel (cf. p. 211 with n. 1).

As Paul's life is threatened by a conspiracy of Jews, the commandant in Jerusalem sends him to Caesarea, and writes to the governor that he took him down to the council and found there that he was accused about questions of their law but charged with nothing deserving death or imprisonment (23.12–35).

When the matter is then brought before the governor Felix in Caesarea, the charges against Paul, as presented by the spokesman Tertullus, read as follows: 'We have found this man a pestilent fellow, an agitator among all the Jews throughout the world, and a ringleader of the sect of the Nazarenes. He even tried to profane the temple. . . .' (24.5 f.). Paul defends himself against this charge, asserting that he has given no cause for disturbance in Jerusalem 'as . . . it is not more than twelve days since I went up to worship at Jerusalem; and they did not find me disputing with any one or stirring up a crowd, either in the temple or in the synagogues, or in the city' (24.11 f.); and again, they found him bringing alms and offerings, 'purified in the temple, without any crowd or tumult' (24.18). It is probably in answer to the charge of profaning the temple that he says (v. 13), 'Neither can they prove to you what they now bring up against me.' His activities in the whole world are referred to in the following words (vv. 14–16); 'But this I admit to you, that according to the Way, which they call a sect, I worship the God of our fathers, believing everything laid down by the law or written in the prophets, having a hope in God which these themselves accept, that there will be a resurrection of both the just and the unjust. So I always take pains to have a clear conscience toward God and toward men' (cf. the wording in 23.1, quoted above). And here follows the above-mentioned reference to the proceedings in the Sanhedrin: 'Or else let these men themselves say what wrongdoing they found when I stood before the council, except this one thing which I cried out while standing among them, "With respect to the resurrection of the dead I am on trial before you this day" ' (24.20 f.).

When after two years Festus takes the matter up again, 'the Jews who had gone down from Jerusalem stood about him, bringing against him many serious charges which they could not prove.' The content of the accusations can be inferred from Paul's answer: 'Neither against the law of the Jews, nor against the temple, nor against Caesar have I offended at all' (25.7 f.). There follows Festus' proposal to open the case in Jerusalem, whereupon Paul appeals to the imperial judgment seat, and with that the matter is at an end for the governor. We notice Paul's remark, 'To the Jews I have done no wrong, as you know very well' (25.10). Then we hear of the visit of King Agrippa, who is introduced by a conversation with Festus; the latter tells him what has happened, and reports the Jews' charges as follows: 'When the accusers stood up, they brought no charge in his case of such evils as I had supposed; but they had certain points of dispute with him about their own superstition, and about one Jesus, who was dead, but whom Paul asserted to be alive' (25.18 f.).

When Paul defends himself before King Agrippa, Festus puts a few words in first which show that the defence is taking place so as to provide him with material for his report on Paul to the emperor (25.26). Paul's speech, which tells of his Jewish past, his call, and his missionary activities, serves, according to the introductory words, as a defence against everything of which the Jews accuse him (26.2). First he mentions how he has lived as a Pharisee from his youth up. Now he is standing before the court on trial 'for hope in the promise made by God to our fathers, to which our twelve tribes hope to attain, as they earnestly worship night and day. And for this hope I am accused by the Jews, O king! Why is it thought incredible by any of you that God raises the dead?' (26.6–8). After that Paul describes himself as a persecutor of the Christian Church up to the moment when Christ met him outside Damascus and called him to be a servant and witness. He was not disobedient to the heavenly vision, 'but,' he says, 'declared first to those at Damascus, then at Jerusalem and throughout all the country of Judaea, and also to the Gentiles, that they should repent and turn to God and perform deeds worthy of their repentance' (26.20). A little later in the speech we hear, 'To this day I have had the help that comes from God, and so I stand here testifying both to small and great, saying nothing but what the prophets and Moses said would come to pass: that the Christ must suffer, and that, by being the first to rise from the dead, he would proclaim light both to the people and to the Gentiles' (26.22 f.). And Paul enumerates Old Testament texts as proof of this, till Festus interrupts him by exclaiming, 'Your great learning is turning you mad' (26.24). Of the impression that the speech had made we learn in the last two verses of the chapter: 'And when they had withdrawn, they said to one another, "This man is doing nothing to deserve death or imprisonment." And Agrippa said to Festus, "This man could have been set free if he had not appealed to Caesar" ' (26.31 f.).

Lastly, Paul's words to the leaders of the Jews in Rome should be mentioned: 'Brethren, though I had done nothing against the people or the customs of our fathers, yet I was delivered prisoner from Jerusalem into the hands of the Romans. When they had examined me, they wished to set me at liberty, because there was no reason for the death penalty in my case. But when the Jews objected, I was compelled to appeal to Caesar—though I had no charge to bring against my nation. For this reason therefore I have asked to see you and speak with you, since it is because of the hope of Israel that I am bound with this chain' (28.17–20).

From these charges against Paul, which, though repeated, are not always quite the same, we can pick out two points that seem naturally to provide a legal accusation against him. The first is that he took Gentiles with him into the temple. Except for his access to the outer forecourt (the court of the Gentiles), the Gentile who ventured into the sanctuary was punished by death; and anyone who provided the occasion of such profanation of the temple was presumably liable to a similar fate. The second point in the charges is that Paul stirred up unrest and sedition among the Jews of the whole world. That probably meant that the offence was directed against the emperor, so that the express mention of an offence against Caesar (25.8) refers to both these points in the accusation.[1] Meanwhile the last point relating to the apostle's activities among the Jews of the whole world leads to a new question that plays the most important part in the trial, namely to Paul's attitude to the Jewish religion; and here his attitude cannot be sharply separated from the second point—that his activities are said to cause unrest among the Jews of the whole world.

The cry with which some Jews from Asia attack Paul in the temple (21.28) already contains both the points mentioned; 'This is the man who is teaching men everywhere against the people and the law and this place; moreover he also brought Greeks into the temple, and he has defiled this holy place.' The same thing is said by Tertullus, the

---

[1]Lake and Cadbury, *ad loc.*, regard the offence against the emperor as identical with Paul's preaching of Jesus as Messiah, Mommsen, *op. cit.*, p. 91, as identical with both points in the indictment.

Jewish authorities' lawyer, when the case comes before Felix (24.5 f.);
'For we have found this man a pestilent fellow, an agitator among all
the Jews throughout the world, and a ringleader of the sect of the
Nazarenes. He even tried to profane the temple. . . .' Paul probably
has this in mind when he says, speaking in his own defence before
Felix, 'Neither can they prove to you what they now bring up against
me' (24.13). In the same speech Paul also takes up the second point, as
to the unrest that he is said to have caused among the Jews of the whole
world, maintaining that he gave no sort of cause for tumult or sedition
during his stay in Jerusalem (24.11 f., 18). Again in Paul's speech before
Festus in ch. 25, where the Jews' charges are not specified, we may
conclude that the same two points were involved, as he answers,
'Neither against the law of the Jews, nor against the temple, nor against
Caesar have I offended at all' (25.8); and a little later, 'To the Jews I
have done no wrong, as you know very well' (25.10).

We have already described Paul's attitude to the Jewish religion as
an important factor in the legal proceedings; and this factor cannot
always be clearly separated from point 2 which concerns his activities
among the Jews of the whole world. We hear, for instance, in the
hearing before the Sanhedrin, how he exclaims, 'I am a Pharisee, a son
of Pharisees; with respect to the hope and the resurrection of the dead
I am on trial' (23.6); and from the report that follows we may take it
that the Sanhedrin seriously discussed his Damascus experience, for
we read that some of the Pharisees took the view, 'We find nothing
wrong in this man. What if a spirit or an angel spoke to him?' (23.9).

When he is taken before Felix, Paul makes his profession 'But this
I admit to you, that according to the Way, which they call a sect, I
worship the God of our fathers, believing everything laid down by the
law or written in the prophets, having a hope in God which these
themselves accept, that there will be a resurrection of both the just and
the unjust' (24.14 f.). Just as he insists in his speech before Festus (as
mentioned above) that he has done no wrong to the Jews, so in his
speech before King Agrippa he not only gives a clear account of his
Jewish youth as a Pharisee, which was interrupted by a heavenly revelation to which he has since been obedient; he also emphasizes that what
he believes and hopes is Jewish (26.6 f.); 'And now I stand here on trial
for hope in the promise made by God to our fathers, to which our
twelve tribes hope to attain, as they earnestly worship night and day.
And for this hope I am accused by the Jews, O king!' And later (vv.
22 f.): 'To this day I have had the help that comes from God, and so I
stand here testifying both to small and great, saying nothing but what
the prophets and Moses said would come to pass: that the Christ must

suffer, and that, by being the first to rise from the dead, he would proclaim light both to the people and to the Gentiles.' With that he goes over to the series of scriptural proofs from the Old Testament, and is interrupted by Festus' remark, 'Your great learning is turning you mad.' Finally, we might mention the passage that was quoted above (p. 316): 'But when the Jews objected, I was compelled to appeal to Caesar—though I had no charge to bring against my nation, for this reason therefore I have asked to see you and speak with you, since it is because of the hope of Israel that I am bound with this chain' (28.19 f.).

To anyone who makes Paul represent a radical Paulinism, this account of the apostle in Acts during the legal proceedings seems completely misleading. Paul cannot adjust himself to Judaism in the way that he does here. But to anyone who has read and understood Romans, especially chs. 9–11, the account seems historically possible.[1] Paul makes no distinction between Judaism and Christianity, as we do. He himself is a Jew, and through Christ he is a Jew or Israelite in the full sense of the word. The Church's most important task is the conversion of Israel; it is the culminating point in the short history of the Church between Christ's ascension and return, and from that point life and salvation radiate to the whole world. The separation between Judaism and Christianity—a separation which seems to us a matter of course, and which has been carried so far in modern theology that the connexion with the Old Testament is often quite severed—was not at that time a reality.

Christianity was regarded as a Jewish sect, and it felt, as we can see in Paul, that it was a continuation of Israel, and that it was the real Israel. But the Jews had no such ideas, and were not satisfied with the official view that the Church was a Jewish sect. Judaism, in fact, was a recognized religion, a *religio licita*; and a sect within that religion had the benefits of such recognition. It would be quite a different matter if it could be established that Christianity was a new religion. The Romans distrusted new religions, and especially new oriental religions; a number of those that had obtained legal recognition in Rome and the Roman empire had at first been forbidden and passed through a time of persecution, though none of them had a history of such bloody persecution as the Christian Church before it was finally recognized by Constantine.

[1]This does not exclude the possibility that Luke may have compiled his account of Paul so consistently that it takes us beyond anything that can be fitted in with the letters. On this, see the critical remarks on Acts 21 in P. Vielhauer, 'Zum "Paulinismus" der Apostelgeschichte', *EvTh* 10, 1950–1, p. 7, though the author, relying on Baur, misunderstands Paul.

It was therefore in the interest of Judaism that the clear separation of the Christians which it had undertaken within its own sphere should be recognized by the Roman authorities; but so far that had not come about. We see in Acts 18.12–15 that the Jews at Corinth complain to Gallio, 'This man is persuading men to worship God contrary to the law.' That was true in two respects. If Christianity was in opposition to the law of the Jews and therefore did not belong to the recognized Jewish religion, it was also at the same time in opposition to the law of the Romans, as it was a new and unsanctioned oriental religion that was to be subjected to careful and critical supervision. But the Jews' attempt fails. The Roman Gallio is not interested, and rejects the matter as a purely Jewish concern of which a Roman judge takes no cognisance and with which he ought not to be troubled: 'If it were a matter of wrongdoing or vicious crime, I should have reason to bear with you, O Jews; but since it is a matter of questions about words and names and your own law, see to it yourselves; I refuse to be a judge of these things.'

We see that this unsuccessful local action in Corinth is now resumed by the Jews' supreme authorities in Jerusalem in much more favourable conditions. One of the leaders of the new movement had profaned the temple—or so it was asserted—and had been sowing discord in Jewish colonies all over the world by speaking against the temple and the Law. It was now time for it to be officially laid down that this new movement was not Jewish, but was outside that *religio licita*, whose protection it did not deserve at all. Paul's vigorous vindication of his claim to belong to the Jewish religion does not merely consist therefore of statements whose probability we can recognize on the basis of his letters; to us they are entirely convincing in a court case that aims at separating Christianity from Judaism. Both before the Jewish and before the Roman seat of justice in Palestine Paul makes good his claim that he is being prosecuted for something in which he believed even as a Pharisee, namely the resurrection of the dead. In these proceedings the Resurrection of Christ has come into the foreground in a peculiar way.

Another important feature is the emphasis on Paul's innocence. As in all the earlier legal cases or religious conversations—and Acts is a book that reports a surprisingly large number of proceedings of that kind before the authorities[1]—it is constantly clear that the accused is innocent. He has neither profaned the temple nor caused unrest anywhere in the world, and he professes with a good conscience the faith of his fathers as it is set forth in the Old Testament.

The last feature to which we would draw attention is the similarity

[1]See below, p. 331.

of the apostle and the accused Christ. We may emphasize, for instance, that Paul's trial occupies the same place in Acts as the Passion in the Gospels—the great coherent narrative, which concludes the work and is regarded as its culmination. Just as there are messages that foretell the Passion, so Paul's trial and sufferings are foretold in what precedes them. Even at the time of the call, Christ says to Ananias (9.15 f.), 'Go, for he is a chosen instrument of mine to carry my name before the Gentiles and kings and the sons of Israel; for I will show him how much he must suffer for the sake of my name.' The journey to Jerusalem on the third journey is accompanied by clear prophecies of the apostle's coming sufferings. Paul says in Miletus in his speech to the elders of Ephesus (20.22–25), 'And now, behold, I am going to Jerusalem, bound in the Spirit, not knowing what shall befall me there; except that the Holy Spirit testifies to me in every city that imprisonment and afflictions await me. But I do not account my life of any value nor as precious to myself, if only I may accomplish my course and the ministry which I received from the Lord Jesus, to testify to the gospel of the grace of God. And now, behold, I know that all you among whom I have gone about preaching the kingdom will see my face no more.' The elders weep as they go with Paul to the ship (20.37 f.).

An example of the testimony of the Holy Spirit 'in every city' is contained in ch. 21, where we are told that a prophet named Agabus came down from Judaea while Paul was staying at the house of Philip the Evangelist at Caesarea. The prophet took Paul's girdle, bound his own feet and hands, and said, 'Thus says the Holy Spirit, "So shall the Jews at Jerusalem bind the man who owns this girdle and deliver him into the hands of the Gentiles" ' (21.11). And Luke continues, 'When we heard this, we and the people there begged him not to go up to Jerusalem. Then Paul answered, "What are you doing, weeping and breaking my heart? For I am ready not only to be imprisoned but even to die at Jerusalem for the name of the Lord Jesus." And when he would not be persuaded, we ceased and said, "The will of the Lord be done" ' (21.12–14). The arrival in Jerusalem follows directly afterwards, and a week later Paul is arrested.

The passage quoted above, Acts 21.11, in which Agabus says that the Jews will bind Paul in Jerusalem and deliver him into the hands of the Gentiles (παραδώσουσιν εἰς χεῖρας ἐθνῶν) reminds us of the predictions of the Passion in the Gospels (Matt. 16.21; 17.22 f.; and 20.17–19 with par.). Not only have we παραδίδοσθαι εἰς χεῖρας ἀνθρώπων in Matt. 17.22; Mark 9.31; Luke 9.44, but it is said of the Jews that they παραδώσουσιν αὐτὸν (i.e., Jesus) τοῖς ἔθνεσιν in Matt. 20.19 and Mark 10.33 (the parallel is lacking in Luke). This is fulfilled during the legal proceedings.[1] As in Jesus' trial, Jews and Gentiles, the governor and the Herodians, all work together. It is the Jews who do their best to get the prisoner sentenced, and it is the Romans who do not want to be used by them and who try to delay matters, but who will nevertheless finally serve the Jewish interests.

Paul, like Jesus, is first accused of a crime against the temple. According to the evidence of false witnesses, Jesus is said to have spoken of destroying the temple and rebuilding it (Matt. 26.60 f.; Mark 14.57 f.; not in Luke, but see Acts 6.14); and Paul is accused of taking a Gentile into the temple (Acts 21.28 ff.). If we are right in the explanation that we suggested of Paul's intention as to the collection (see ch. 10, pp. 301–5), Jews from Ephesus may have misunderstood the idea that the Gentiles should take gifts to Jerusalem. They may have thought that the Christians of Gentile origin were themselves to take their gifts up to the temple. That misunderstanding is concealed behind their accusation, but of course, it has no sort of connexion with what actually happened.

Another point of resemblance between the cases of Jesus and Paul is that during the trials both have a scene with the High Priest. In Jesus' case it is the well-known scene in John's Gospel, where one standing by strikes Jesus in the face and says, 'Is that how you answer the high priest?', whereupon Jesus answers, 'If I have spoken wrongly, bear witness to the wrong; but if I have spoken rightly, why do you strike me?' (John 18.22 f.). In Paul's case it is while the trial is being conducted by the Sanhedrin that the High Priest Ananias orders those who stood by him to strike him on the mouth. We then read, 'Then Paul said to him, "God shall strike you, you whitewashed wall. Are you sitting to judge me according to the law, and yet contrary to the law you order me to be struck?" Those who stood by said, "Would you revile God's high priest?" And Paul said, "I did not know, brethren, that he was the high priest; for it is written, "You shall not speak evil of a ruler of your people" ' (Acts 23.3–5).

After the introductory charge of committing an offence against the temple, the final and crucial accusation is brought against both Jesus and Paul on the ground of their calling—against Jesus, because he declared himself to be the Messiah, and against Paul, because as Christ's apostle he preached throughout the world that the Messiah had risen from the dead.

We could quote several other features of this kind. For example, we see the people rising against Paul, just as they turned against Jesus

[1] On the other hand, this does not happen with Paul; and this strengthens the evidence of the apostle's similarity to Christ in the account of the trial in Acts. We hear of it in Paul's speech in Acts 28.17: δέσμιος ἐξ Ἱεροσολύμων παρεδόθην εἰς τὰς χεῖρας τῶν Ῥωμαίων.

in the Gospels' story of the Passion. The scene in which Paul speaks from the steps leading to the fortress of Antonia shows us the hostile mob like the one that had gathered outside Pilate's judgment hall.[1] One small linguistic observation may show how far-reaching the agreement was felt to be. In John's Gospel οἱ 'Ιουδαῖοι is used sometimes of a popular commotion (e.g., 6.41), sometimes of the authorities in Jerusalem (e.g., 18.14), sometimes possibly of the Pharisees (e.g., 5.10 f.), etc. This peculiar use of language is paralleled in Acts 22.30; 23.12, 20, 27; 24.9; cf. 25.7, 24; 28.19. In Paul's reply (25.10 f.), and in his speech before King Agrippa in ch. 26, 'Ιουδαῖοι is used without an article (25.10; 26.2, 4, 7, 21).[2]

Thus there are many points of resemblance between Christ and his apostle, both of whom are innocent and are condemned in spite of that. Certainly the view has been held that Paul was released after the lapse of two years at Rome, either on the ground of a technical peculiarity concerning cases of appeal,[3] or because the utterances of the Roman officials as to the outcome of the proceedings have such a positive ring.[4] But the clear predictions of his arrest and imprisonment, and his own words, that the Ephesian elders will see him no more (20.25, cf. v. 38), can in Luke's present context only prepare the readers for Paul's death.

IV

We may now ask what the apostle himself thought about these legal proceedings and his appeal to the emperor's court. We have already mentioned that, of the letters written during his imprisonment, Philippians is the only one that enlightens us about his personal affairs and the trial.

[1] In Acts 21.36 the mob shouts after Paul, αἶρε αὐτόν, and in 22.22, αἶρε ἀπὸ τῆς γῆς τὸν τοιοῦτον· οὐ γὰρ καθῆκεν αὐτὸν ζῆν, cf. an alternative reading of 28.19: καὶ ἐπικραζόντων· αἶρε τὸν ἐχθρὸν ἡμῶν. In the story of Jesus' Passion the crowd shouts (Luke 23.18), αἶρε τοῦτον, κτλ., and in John 19.15, ἆρον ἆρον, σταύρωσον αὐτόν. See further material in Lake and Cadbury on Acts 21.36.

[2] Blass-Debrunner, § 262: 'As with the name of the opponent in speeches in Attic courts.' The remarks in § 262.1 f on the article missing from "Ελληνες and 'Ιουδαῖοι seem to be incorrect, as Paul often uses these names of peoples in contrast to one another, e.g., εἴτε 'Ιουδαῖοι εἴτε "Ελληνες (I Cor. 12.13, etc.). If we separate these contrasting pairs from the rest of the examples, there is no clear difference in the use of the article among the New Testament writers.

[3] If the defendant had waited two years in Rome, and the prosecutors had not come forward with their charge, he was to be released. Such is Lake's hypothesis; see Cadbury in *Beginnings* 5, pp. 326–32.

[4] The Roman officials express themselves as to Paul's innocence, in relation to the Jewish accusations, in 23.29; 25.18 f.; 26.31 f. But it is not certain that his innocence, which these passages show, rules out his condemnation and execution. For example, the last passage, Acts 26.31 f., has been held to mean that Festus might have acquitted him; but the result of Paul's appeal to the emperor is that the case must now take its course to the bitter end (Ed. Meyer, *Ursprung und Anfänge des Christentums* III, 1923, pp. 55–57).

Acts 28 gives us some information about the apostle's outward affairs (vv. 16, 30 f.) and his attempts to enter into relations with the Jews in Rome (vv. 17–20 and 23 f.). From what he says of his situation in Phil. 1.12 f., and of Timothy and Epaphroditus in Phil. 2.19–30, we may conclude that he had the same freedom that is described in Acts, namely to receive visitors, and, in spite of his imprisonment, to carry on missionary work and to look after the distant churches. But as to any effect that the time he spent as a prisoner in Rome had on the church there we hear nothing in Acts. Here in Philippians we learn that the apostle's imprisonment filled most of the brethren with greater confidence to speak the word of God without fear (1.14).

The next verses, 15–17, where a distinction made between 'some' and 'others' (τινὲς μέν and τινὲς δέ in v. 15, οἱ μέν and οἱ δέ in vv. 16 f.), have been interpreted in the most varied ways. Dibelius and Barth think that vv. 15–17 are an excursus. In v. 14 Paul speaks of the influence of his imprisonment on the preaching of the Gospel; through this it occurs to him from how many different motives Christ is preached. But as not only v. 14, but also vv. 16 f. refer directly to Paul's situation as a prisoner, this interpretation is not probable. Others have thought that the church at Rome is divided into a majority, τοὺς πλείονας, which is taken up again in the τινὲς δέ, and a minority, τινὲς μέν.[1] But it would be most natural to regard τινὲς μέν and τινὲς δέ etc. in vv. 15–17 as two subdivisions of τοὺς πλείονας—Paul's stay as a prisoner in Rome has inspired most of the brethren there with greater confidence to preach the word of God fearlessly. Some perhaps do so from envy and rivalry and self-seeking, intending to add affliction to the apostle's chains, while other do it from love, because they know that he is put there to defend the Gospel. And Paul is great enough to be pleased that Christ is preached in all kinds of ways, whether in pretence or in truth.

If one divides the church at Rome into a Pauline majority and a minority, one is inclined to suppose that there are Judaizers behind this smaller group. That is a supposition into which we are always misled when we are thinking of people who are ill-disposed towards Paul, or who are merely different from him—they are simply Judaizers. But we have no solid ground for thinking that the different groups have different doctrines. We know that Paul's imprisonment gave them all in common greater courage for preaching, and that he rejoices in their zeal. There is a distinction between the two groups in their view of Paul's case. Some people know that in that affair he has the task of

---

[1] So M. R. Vincent, J. B. Lightfoot and E. Lohmeyer interpret the phrases as subdivisions of the majority of the brethren. See the important contribution of O. Linton, 'Zur Situation des Philipperbriefes', *AMNSU* 4, 1936, pp. 9–21.

defending the Gospel, while others do not think so. By being transferred to Rome and by his imprisonment and trial he has brought unrest into the church there, and divided people into different camps according to their views. Indeed, the effect of his presence was always great, wherever he went; and now in Rome the decisive question was: Is it really Paul's task to defend the Gospel?

As we cannot learn any more about it from Paul's writings, the obvious course is to look up Acts and see whether the explanations that we get there fit in with the picture in Philippians. For Acts the main question in Paul's trial is whether Christianity is Judaism or not. Before both Jewish and Roman courts in Palestine Paul stresses his claim that he is being reproached with believing what he had already believed as a Pharisee—that there is a resurrection of the dead. We have the impression that the Jewish accusers wanted to prove that Christianity is not Judaism, so that the Roman authorities should lay it down that Christianity, not being a Jewish sect, was outside Judaism, and therefore did not share the rights of that *religio licita*.

It was scarcely these questions that caused the different attitudes to the apostle within the church at Rome. But a charge against a well-known Christian leader of transgressing a penal law has always had the effect of isolating him in relation to his Church. It stands to reason that it is then simpler to sacrifice such a person for the sake of the Gospel or the Church, so that the charge is merely a personal one. If the accused had had the task of defending the Gospel, it would be a different matter. But as it is a personal charge, the existence of the whole Church is at stake because of the accused leader; and Paul's case involves something so irrelevant as the profanation of the temple in Jerusalem, and his not unassailable conduct during his journeys in the east. Church history, even the most recent, shows us how the Church is tempted to leave its leaders in the lurch when they are accused of criminal offences and not for the Gospel's sake.

Paul had to experience this too. Only a certain number of the numerous zealous preachers of Christ were convinced that he was held prisoner and accused for the Gospel's sake. Others did not refrain, in their preaching of Christ, from dissociating themselves from Paul and his personal fate, their argument being that, though such a scandal in the Church was indeed a painful affair, the Gospel was not identical with that particular leader, who was soon to receive his sentence for his own personal crime. The Gospel and Paul were two quite different things, and the task was now so to separate them from each other that no confusion was possible for anyone. In that way they thought to afflict the apostle in his imprisonment (Phil. 1.17).

But they can do him no serious harm, for his cause is so bound up with the Gospel that no preaching for Christ comes amiss to him. And the upshot of the trial can only be for good—for the honour of Christ and the service of the churches. Paul knows that there are many in Rome and Philippi, and elsewhere too, who are convinced that he is destined to defend the Gospel in his trial at Rome; and he himself is clear that he is the one whom God has called to fight for it in Rome— that he has to defend and establish it firmly, not by his missionary activity or his immediate activity there, but by the trial itself, which brings the apostle before the emperor.[1]

This new outlook is distinct from his former ideas, and must have matured in his mind during his long imprisonment. We know from Rom. 15 that he was considering plans of what he should undertake when the difficult visit to Jerusalem was successfully accomplished. He was to travel to Spain to introduce the missionary work in the west, after he had at last completed the preaching of the Gospel to the Gentiles in the east. He knew, of course, that he was called to preach Christ's Gospel to all Gentile peoples, so as to prepare for the coming of the Lord in glory. And now he remained a prisoner, and the Gentiles had to wait—indeed, Christ had to wait, because his messenger was in prison. God's salvation could not become a reality.

Paul was like a captured eagle. He was not of a weak constitution. He suffered neither from chronic illness nor from weak nerves. That has been found out by Pauline investigators of our own time through texts that have been misunderstood.[2] On the contrary, he possessed a consuming energy and in general a dynamic temperament, which we can still feel today as we read his letters. The heavy storm thunders over our frail constitution and our weak nerves.

Prison was a torment to that active, indefatigable man, the more so

[1]It is Lohmeyer's merit to have drawn attention to this in his commentary; see, e.g., his treatment of Phil. 1.7.

[2]There are signs that this misunderstanding is now losing ground. J. Knox, *Chapters in a Life of Paul*, pp. 90 f., asserts that Paul was not ill, and comes to the conclusion (p. 91), 'The evidence on the whole supports at this point the statement of the author of the Acts of Paul—"of vigorous physique".' Cerfaux, in 'L'anti-nomie paulinienne de la vie apostolique', *Recherches de Science Religieuse* 39 (Mé-langes J. Lebreton), 1951, pp. 229 f., is not fully convinced that the words 'messenger of Satan' in II Cor. 12 refer to illness. P. Menoud, in *L'Église naissante et le Judaïsme* (Études théologiques et religieuses, 27.1), 1952, p. 14, says: 'In the same way, according to II Corinthians, it is a "messenger of Satan" that prompts the Jewish opposition to the Gospel, both by the obstacles which they put in Paul's path, and by their own unbelief (II Cor. 12.7). Indeed, it is in this circle of ideas that the obscure passage in II Corinthians about the "thorn in the flesh" and the "messenger of Satan" to "harass" the apostle becomes explicable.' This interesting interpreta-tion, however, is less convincing than that of Koch (pp. 433–48), who agrees with Theodoret (*PG* 82, 449A) that the 'messenger of Satan' refers to acts of violence, annoyances, and popular tumults. Paul refers here to the apostle's incessant persecu-tions, the 'sufferings of Christ'.

in his case because he knew that he was called to take the Gospel to the Gentiles and that he was now cut off from all possibility of carrying his service through to the end. No words are strong enough to describe the torments that the apostle must have had to endure in prison in Jerusalem and Caesarea.

In that darkness he received comfort from God, as Acts tells us. In the night after the hearing by the Sanhedrin (23.11) the Lord came to him and said, 'Take courage, for as you have testified about me at Jerusalem, so you must bear witness also at Rome.' These words can be regarded in two ways. If we view them in the context of everything that we are told about Paul in Acts, they will mean that he is to preach in Rome, as he formerly (9.29) preached in Jerusalem. This would fit in well with the plan that Luke had for the whole book. But if this vision by night is part of the we-source, it seems most reasonable to relate it to the present stay in Jerusalem, and in that case what is referred to must be Paul's testimony before the Jerusalem authorities. In that case we hear only of the testimony before the authorities, both in Jerusalem and in Rome; and the promise means that Paul shall testify before the authorities in Rome too.[1]

On the latter interpretation this passage agrees with the revelation that Paul has on the voyage to Rome. After a storm lasting many days, when everyone has given up hope of being saved, he goes to his travel-ling-companions (27.21–24) and encourages them by saying, 'For this very night there stood by me an angel of the God to whom I belong and whom I worship, and he said, "Do not be afraid, Paul; you must stand before Caesar; and lo, God has granted you all those who sail with you." ' God therefore intends to save his apostle and take him to Rome, so that he can stand before the emperor. And then the angel adds, 'and lo, God has granted you all those who sail with you.' Here there appears a gradation, which must not be overlooked, in the story of salvation. God intends to take his apostle before the emperor; that is the crucial point. And besides that, God grants to that apostle 275 human lives on board the ship, so that they shall live too.

This revelation, which emphasizes the fundamental importance of Paul's witness before the emperor in Rome, confronts us with the question of the significance for the apostle of the appeal, which enables him to bear witness before the emperor. We are therefore asking here a

---

[1]The repetition of the account of the apostle's call (chs. 9, 22, and 26) is a problem that is still waiting for a satisfactory solution. W. L. Knox, in *The Acts of the Apostles*, p. 27, thinks that the repetition in chs. 22 and 26 is to show that Christ is to be preached to the Gentiles as well as to the Jews. But these repetitions while the trial is actually going on might be meant to stress that even during his trial Paul is the apostle to the Gentiles—now, in fact, more than ever, as he is on his way to the emperor to testify before kings and nations.

theological question, and so we reject from the outset the idea that the appeal to the emperor was a last expedient, used by a Roman citizen who was condemned to death by the highest provincial court or saw death confronting him as the certain end of his trial. This detail too, like the whole of Paul's life and work, is to be understood as proceeding from his call and his apostolic work.

V

We wish to submit here some material which we could have already produced for investigating in more detail the procedure in a legal action before the imperial court, but which is more in place in this context. It is the so-called Pagan Acts of the Martyrs.[1] The name is badly chosen;

[1]These Acts were made available by U. Wilcken in 'Zum alexandrinischen Antisemitismus', *Abhandlungen der philos.-hist. Klasse der Sächsischen Gesellschaft der Wissenschaften* 27, 1909, Abh. 23, pp. 783–839. Here are, according to Wilcken's classification; (A) the Acts of Isidore and Lampon, namely BGU II, 511 and P. Cairo 10448 (Wilcken pp. 800–6). New texts of these Acts have been published later: P. Oxy. VIII, 1089; Papyrus in Berlin, P. 8877, ed. Woldemar Graf Uxkull-Gyllenband: 'Ein neues Bruchstück aus den sogenannten heidnischen Märtyrerakten', *Sitzungsberichte der Preussischen Akademie*, 1930, No. 28, pp. 664–79; and Brit. Mus. Inv. 2785, ed. H. I. Bell: 'A New Fragment of the Acta Isidori', *Archiv für Papyrusforschung*, 10, 1932, pp. 5–16. (B) the Acts of Paul and Antoninus, namely P. Par. 68, P. Lond. I, pp. 227 ff. and BGU I, 341 (Wilcken, pp. 807–22). (C) the Acts of Appian: P. Oxy. I, 33 (Wilcken, pp. 822–5), to which has been added later P. Yale Inv. 1536, ed. C. Bradford Welles: 'A Yale Fragment of the Acts of Appian', *Transactions and Proceedings of the American Philological Association*, 67, 1936, pp. 7–23. (D) A Berlin Fragment, BGU II, 588 (Wilcken, pp. 825 f.). Other texts also counted in this literature are: P.Oxy. X, 1242, which has been called 'the Acts of Hermaiskos', an unimportant fragment (P. Fay. 217, *Fayûm Towns and their Papyri*, 1900, Egypt Exploration Fund, Graeco-Roman Branch, Vol. III, p. 302), and P. Oxy. III, 471, a speech for the prosecution by Trajan, probably directed against the former prefect C. Vibius Maximus, which may possibly have been counted erroneously among the Acts. (Regarding the older literature, see A. von Premerstein, 'Zu den sogenannten alexandrinischen Märtyrerakten', *Philologus*, Supplementary Vol. XVI, No. II, 1923, pp. 1–3, and C. Bradford Welles' above-named article, pp. 9–15.) As far as I know, the following texts have been added later: P. Bibl. Univ. Giss. 46, ed. A. von Premerstein: *Alexandrinische Geronten vor Kaiser Gaius. Ein neues Bruchstück der sogenannten Alexandrinischen Märtyrerakten*, Giessen, 1939 (Mitteilungen aus der Papyrussammlung der Giessener Universitätsbibliothek, V, = Schriften der Ludwigs-Universität zu Giessen, 1936). This papyrus is so incomplete that it cannot be read, and Premerstein's 'Umschrift mit Ergänzungen' is in my opinion useless guesswork. In 1941 there appeared P. Oxy. XVIII, 2177, called by the editors 'Acta Alexandrinorum'. Athenodorus may be the same here as the person of the same name in the Acts of Hermaiskos; the emperor is presumably Hadrian. The text's connexion with Alexandria seems uncertain. The editors' argument that the place is Rome (p. 97: 'but the presence of the Emperor accompanied by senators leaves us in little doubt that the action took place in Rome') is not convincing, especially in the case of Hadrian, who is known as 'the travelling emperor'. Lastly, there appeared in 1948 'Caracalla et les troubles d'Alexandrie en 215 après Jésus-Christ' by P. Benoit and J. Schwartz, *Société Fouad Ier de Papyrologie, Études de papyrologie* VII, 1948 (Cairo), pp. 17–33, papyrus published without more detailed description or inventory number (dating on p. 32, but without discussing reasons). It reports a legal case before Caracalla while he was in Alexandria.

it could more rightly be called the Acts of Alexandrian Independence.[1] In a number of papyri, reports have been found of cases against Alexandrian citizens, as a rule high officials, which take place in Alexandria or before the emperor in Rome. The background is generally provided by disputes between Jews and Greeks in Alexandria, and the documents are about cases of this kind and the deaths of Alexandrian citizens.[2] Special attention has been given to the vigorous remarks made by the Alexandrian defendants about the emperor who is sitting in judgment over them.[3] Lake and Cadbury have drawn attention to a parallel between the Acts of Appian and Acts 26.24 f., where Festus says to Paul that his great learning is turning him mad, to which the apostle replies, 'I am not mad, most excellent Festus, but I am speaking the sober truth.'[4] Unfortunately these texts throw no definite light on the form of legal cases before the emperor. Possibly the texts, taken together, make up a novel about the difference between the Alexandrians and the emperors who sided with the Jews.[5]

[1] The similarity to the Christian Acts of the Martyrs consists only in the formal matter that it is an entry of a legal case; but it is by no means certain that the accused are condemned to death in all instances, or even that, if they are executed, they die solely on account of their 'case'. Are they condemned, on the analogy of the Christian martyrs, on account of the name only, or on account of the *flagitia cohaerentia nomini?* It would be better to call these Acts the Acts of Alexandrian Independence, because in fact they are concerned with the Alexandrians' rights and their attempts to assert them in relation to the emperors and the Egyptian prefects, often in opposition to the Jews in Alexandria, who enjoy imperial protection.

[2] Legal cases involving Alexandrian citizens are narrated in the Acts of Isidore and Lampon, of Paul and Antoninus, of Appian, and in the Caracalla papyrus, edited by Benoit and Schwartz. In the Acts of Hermaiskos an Alexandrian and a Jewish embassy from Alexandria stand before the emperor Trajan. Of the other papyri that can be interpreted, P. Oxy. XVIII, 2177 and P. Oxy. III, 471 contain no cases against Alexandrian citizens. According to the Acts of Appian, Theon, Isidore, and Lampon were executed, and Appion is sent to the place of execution. Bradford Welles, p. 13 n. 32, is inclined to assume that the defendants were generally condemned and executed—an assumption which, in view of the fragmentary character of the texts, is possible but by no means certain.

[3] In P. Oxy. X, 1242, col. 3, lines 41, 44, 45 f., there is a clear expression for the behaviour of the citizens before the emperor in several of the Acts: αὐθάδως ἀποκρίνεσθαι.

[4] P. Oxy. I, 33, col. 4, lines 9 ff.: Αὐτοκράτωρ· Ἀππιανέ, (ε)ἰώθαμεν καὶ ἡμεῖς μαινομένους καὶ ἀπονενοημένους σωφρονίζειν· λαλεῖς ἐφ' ὅσον ἐγώ σε θέλω λαλεῖν. Ἀππιανός· νὴ τὴν σὴν τύχην, οὔτε μαίνομαι οὔτε ἀπονενόημαι κτλ. We may here make comparisons with the Acts of Carpus, Papylus, and Agathonike, in the Greek version § 21, ὁ ἀνθύπατος εἶπεν· Πολλὰ ἐάσας σε φλυαρῆσαι κτλ. (Ausgewählte Märtyrerakten, ed. R. Knopf, 3rd ed. by G. Krüger, 1929, p. 12, lines 11 ff.).

[5] The theory that these Acts together represent a novel about the matters at issue between the Alexandrians and the emperors does not gain probability through the last published pieces (see on P. Oxy. III, 471 and XVIII, 2177, p. 327 n. 1 and n. 2 above). If people continue to combine under these Acts all the legal proceedings and speeches that deal in any way with the Alexandrians and the emperors, it will be difficult to support the assumption that they form a unity. But we could also go about it the other way and try to separate the texts that may represent a novel, and at the same time refuse to accept some of the more recent texts, e.g., P. Oxy. XVIII, 2177, because they resemble only in a limited degree the Acts first found.

In another novel we might allow ourselves the hope of getting an authentic picture of the emperor's tribunal, the more so as the author was in touch with court circles. We refer to Philostratus' novel about Apollonius of Tyana. Books VII and VIII tell of Apollonius' prosecution before the emperor Domitian. Unfortunately the novel is as vague here as are the so-called Pagan Acts of the Martyrs, so that we can learn nothing of the course that such a prosecution took. It would be of interest for New Testament studies if we could ascertain more accurately the legal meaning of the words ἀπολογία and ἀπολογεῖσθαι. In Phil. 1.7 Paul speaks of the defence and confirmation of the Gospel,[1] and in II Tim. 4.16 he says, 'At my first defence (ἀπολογία)[2] no one took my part; all deserted me.' In about twenty passages in Philostratus the noun ἀπολογία or the verb ἀπολογεῖσθαι is used in a legal sense about defence before a court.[3] It looks as if Philostratus may have given us the material for understanding Paul's speech at his first defence, the whole legal action consisting of first a private interrogation before the emperor, and then the trial itself, which ended with the verdict. It is, in fact, not clear whether this first hearing gave opportunity for a defence or not, and it is equally uncertain whether the trial itself assumed further legal proceedings or only the private interrogation already mentioned.[4]

[1]Lohmeyer maintains (p. 24 with n. 2) that ἀπολογία and βεβαίωσις are well established technical expressions, and Dibelius agrees; but he writes (p. 63), 'Of course, the expressions ἀπολογία and βεβαίωσις are not used in their technical sense here, and therefore do not relate to speech or interrogation or guarantees . . ., but suggest association of a legal kind. It is meant that the procedure in arrest and prosecution serves the Gospel.' Dibelius' view is supported by several commentators, e.g., J. B. Lightfoot and E. Haupt (in the 6th edition). A less certain view of these two possibilities is taken by M. R. Vincent, K. Barth, G. Heinzelmann and P. Bonnard. P. Ewald relates both expressions to Paul's trial.

[2]The usual interpretation here has been that the first defence took place during Paul's first trial in Rome at the end of the fourth journey (see Dibelius and C. Spicq), but in any case it was a defence before a court.

[3]The references are to his *Life of Apollonius of Tyana;* ἀπολογία: VII, 33 (ed. Conybeare, Loeb II, p. 244, lines 6, 10); 35 (246.7); 40 (260.14); 41 (262.2); VIII, 7 (292.21; 324.18; 338.3); 11 (358.5); 12 (360.15, 21; 362.6). ἀπολογεῖσθαι: VII, 29 (230.13); 32 (240.21 f.); 34 (246.4 f.); 40 (260.14); VIII, 1 (272.2); 7 (306.23; 324.17; 336.29); 12 (360.16, 17, 19).

[4]We are told about the private interrogation in VII, 32–34, and about the crucial trial itself in VIII, 1–10; it is not clear how long the interval between them was. In VIII, 7 (326.16) Apollonius says, λέξω πάλιν, ἃ καὶ πρώην εἶπον, ἡνίκα ᾐτιῶ ταῦτα. Conybeare translates, 'what I said to you the day before yesterday'. πρώην may mean that, but it can equally well mean 'recently'. In the latter case Apollonius is thinking of the first interrogation, which seems to have taken place several days before. This is confirmed by the following considerations. According to VII, 36 (248.1), two days after the private interrogation a Syracusan goes to Apollonius in prison, and in the afternoon of the same day Apollonius exchanges his prison for a less rigorous one (40; 260.8 ff.). The next day he sends Damis to Dicaearchia, where the latter arrives three days later (41; 262.3, 12). On the day following, which must mean a week after the first interrogation, Apollonius meets Damis and Demetrius in a miraculous way, after he has been acquitted on the same day in Rome (VIII, 12; 360.1–5, 19 ff.). As Philostratus' work seems to be badly put together from different sources, Conybeare may be right in his translation; but in that case πρώην

Even if these texts leave us in ignorance about the form of legal proceedings before the emperor, they may suggest a possible explanation of the apostle's trial in Rome. In the so-called Pagan Acts of the Martyrs, and in Philostratus' novel about Apollonius of Tyana, we meet philosophers who defend themselves before the emperor. Apollonius does so with remarkable mildness, almost tameness, although at another time in conversation with Vespasian he has spoken golden words about the wise sovereign.[1] The Alexandrian champions of their city's independence, on the other hand, speak brave words before they die. Appian, for instance, describes the emperor as a tyrant. No, says the emperor, I am a βασιλεύς, 'a true king'; but Appian then says that the emperor's father, Antoninus, was fit to be emperor, being, in fact, a philosopher, but that his son is the direct opposite.[2] Here we see one of antiquity's contrasts, with a long tradition behind it—the philosopher before the ruler, as in the case of Diogenes and Alexander the Great.

But it is easy to see that there is no such contrast in the trial of the apostle before the emperor; we should rather look for parallels in the Old Testament and the Jewish world. We see in the latter how the martyrs of the Maccabean times took a firm stand against Antiochus Epiphanes;[3] and in the Old Testament we at once think of the prophet who goes before the king, and who generally stands there to rebuke and to announce punishment. We can think, for instance, of Elijah before Ahab—Paul, in fact, mentions Elijah in Rom. 11.2–4—or Nathan and David in II Samuel 12.1–14. The man who stands on the

---

must, on the basis of the calculation just made, allude to a new sitting between the two already mentioned. But as the reference to the earlier sitting on p. 326 fits in extremely well with the report of the first sitting in VII, 33 (242), this assumption is improbable, and so I do not think Conybeare's translation can be right.—In connexion with these remarks I readily point out that, besides the examples quoted, there is various source material available for trials before the emperor, not only in historical literature, but also in *belles-lettres*, as the above examples illustrate. Although these passages may not show the finer points of law with any certainty, they may make clear the popular conceptions of such trials, and possibly confirm on certain points what we know in advance or may assume.

[1]Apollonius' speech before the emperor, which he is said to have prepared but not delivered on this occasion, is in VIII, 7 (pp. 286–354). About his being with Vespasian in Egypt we are told in V, 27–38 (Vol. I, 522–62). A parallel to the αὐθάδως ἀποκρίνεσθαι of the Alexandrian Acts is to be found only in IV, 44 (I, 454.24 ff.) in the interrogation before Tigellinus when Apollonius had been arrested in Rome during the reign of Nero.

[2]P. Oxy. I, 33, col. 2, lines 4–13.

[3]Before the death of the seven brothers and their mother in II Macc. 7, the second (v. 9), fifth (vv. 16 f.) and sixth brothers (vv. 18 f.), the mother (vv. 27–29) and the seventh brother (vv. 31, 34–37) address the king bravely and proclaim to him God's punishment. In the corresponding account of Eleazar and the martyrdom of the seven brothers and their mother in IV Macc. 5–17, Antiochus Epiphanes is described as a tyrant, while the Jewish martyrs are philosophers. Both jointly and separately the seven brothers threaten the tyrant with God's punishment.

boundary between the Old Covenant and the New, John the Baptist, goes before Herod Antipas and tells him that the king is guilty of adultery; and that declaration carries with it his execution. But none of these messengers has good news to announce.

There are clearer and better parallels to be found in the New Testament itself. We will first ask what importance the New Testament attaches to testimony before the authorities. Jesus did not proclaim himself publicly as Messiah, but in the night when he was betrayed he acknowledged before the High Priest that he was the Messiah (Matt. 26.64 and par.). Such is the importance of testimony before the authorities. Acts is a book that deals with proceedings in one court of law after another. Peter and John and all the apostles are brought before the council, Stephen is accused, Paul opens a debate on religion before Sergius Paulus in Cyprus. Later he has difficulties with the authorities in Philippi and Thessalonica, he has to defend himself before the tribunal of the Areopagus because of his preaching activities,[1] he is accused before Gallio, and finally stands before the Sanhedrin, Felix, Festus, and King Agrippa. Why is all that so important in missionary history? Why does Pilate play so great a part that he still has a place in the Christian creed?

There is also a saying of Jesus that points to the importance of the testimony before the authorities. It is in Matt. 10.18–20, and reads, 'And you will be dragged before governors and kings for my sake, to bear testimony before them and the Gentiles. When they deliver you up, do not be anxious how you are to speak or what you are to say; for what you are to say will be given to you in that hour; for it is not you who speak, but the Spirit of your Father speaking through you.' These words remind us that the disciples are to be taken before governors and kings to bear testimony to them and to the Gentiles. We must keep this in mind, if we speak here of an apostle to the Gentiles. In Mark 13.9–11 Jesus says the same thing, adding, however, that the Gospel must first be preached to all nations; this gives special emphasis to the first of the two sayings: 'But take heed to yourselves; for they will deliver you up to councils; and you will be beaten in synagogues; and you will stand before governors and kings for my sake, to bear testimony before them. And the gospel must first be preached to all nations. And when they bring you to trial and deliver you up, do not be anxious beforehand what you are to say; but say whatever is given you in that hour, for it is not you who speak, but the Holy Spirit.'

These passages have something in common with the one by Paul that has already been quoted from II Timothy (see p. 329). I am

[1] So Lake and Cadbury *ad loc.*

not of the opinion that that letter was written by Paul; but certain parts
of it are undoubtedly Pauline; and that is true of this important passage,
II Tim. 4.16–18: 'At my first defence no one took my part; all deserted
me. May it not be charged against them! But the Lord stood by me and
gave me strength to proclaim the word fully, so that all the Gentiles
might hear it. So I was rescued from the lion's mouth. The Lord will
rescue me from every evil and save me for his heavenly kingdom. To
him be the glory for ever and ever. Amen.' In this text, as in Mark
13.9–11, we find that preaching the Gospel to all the Gentiles is closely
connected with testifying before the authorities, and in the epistle with
testifying before the emperor.

These two things go together, and, for the dying apostle, testifying
before the emperor during the trial in Rome meant that his call was now
after all no incomplete service, but that it was possible for him, even
as a prisoner, to complete the work that Christ had entrusted to him—
to preach the Gospel to all the Gentiles. When he could no longer
travel to reach the many Gentile nations that Christ had put under him
by his call to be an apostle, there opened to him, through his appeal
to the emperor, a way to carry the Gospel further in spite of his imprisonment. The apostle testified before the emperor and preached the word,
and thus the preaching to the Gentiles was completed, πληροφορέω in
the same sense as πληρόω, which is used for it elsewhere.[1] He had now
fully preached God's word, and all the Gentiles had heard it.

One more point in this text must be emphasized. We have spoken
earlier about the similarity to Christ on which Luke lays stress in relation to Paul during his trial. In this text, II Tim. 4.16–18, it is the apostle
himself who points out the resemblance to Christ in his trial and death.
It is well known that Ps. 21 (EVV 22) is used in describing Christ's
Passion. Now, as Nestle points out, Ps. 21.22 is reproduced in II Tim.
4.17 in the words ἐκ στόματος λέοντος, 'from the mouth of the lion'. But
it is not only in v. 17 that the text leans on this Psalm.[2] Its first nine
verses speak of the writer's having been abandoned by God and all
men. The verb ἐγκαταλείπω from Ps. 21.2 also appears here, in

---

[1]Cf. pp. 48 f.; and cf. τελειόω in Acts 20.24: ὡς τελειώσω τὸν δρόμον μου καὶ
τὴν διακονίαν ἣν ἔλαβον παρὰ τοῦ Κυρίου Ἰησοῦ, διαμαρτύρασθαι τὸ εὐαγγέλιον τῆς
χάριτος τοῦ Θεοῦ.
[2]W. Lock, p. 116, draws attention to the following points of agreement between
Ps. 21 (LXX) and II Tim. 4.16–18 (and v. 10): Ps. 21.2 ἐγκατέλιπες with II Tim.
4.10, 16; Ps. 21.5, 9, 21 ἐρύσω, ῥυσάσθω, ῥῦσαι, with II Tim. 4.17 f.; Ps. 21.12 οὐκ ἔστιν
ὁ βοηθῶν with II Tim. 4.16; Ps. 21.14, 22 σῶσόν με ἐκ στόματος λέοντος with II Tim.
4.17; Ps. 21.17 πονηρευομένων with II Tim. 4.18; Ps. 21.6, 22 ἐσώθησαν, σῶσον with
II Tim. 4.18; Ps. 21.24 δοξάσατε αὐτόν with II Tim. 4.18; Ps. 21.28 πᾶσαι αἱ
πατριαὶ τῶν ἐθνῶν with II Tim. 4.17; Ps. 21.29 τοῦ Κυρίου ἡ βασιλεία with II Tim.
4.18. Lock rightly adds, 'Had St Paul, like his Master, been saying this Psalm in
the hour of desertion?'

v. 16: 'all deserted me.' The words about being rescued from the lion's mouth (v. 17) have several parallels in the Psalm (vv. 5, 9; cf. vv. 14, 17), but they particularly resemble v. 22 already mentioned, 'Save me from the mouth of the lion.' The words immediately before and after this passage in II Timothy, viz., '. . . gave me strength to proclaim the word fully, that all the Gentiles might hear it,' and 'The Lord will rescue me from every evil and save me for his heavenly kingdom,' are matched by Ps. 21.28–30, 'All the ends of the earth shall remember and turn to the Lord; and all the families of the nations shall worship before him. For dominion belongs to the Lord, and he rules over the nations. Yea, to him shall all the proud of the earth bow down. . . .'[1] A detail that is in v. 16, but not in Ps. 22, 'May it not be charged against them!', comes not from the Psalm of passion, but from the Passion itself; it reflects Jesus' words in Luke 23.34: 'Father, forgive them.' Stephen too had said in the hour of his death (Acts 7.60), 'Lord, do not hold this sin against them.' So we see here how, during the trial that is to end in his death and also in the conversion of the Gentiles, Paul finds strength in the Psalm that was uttered about the sufferings of the Lord Jesus. He will follow in his footsteps; like him he will bear witness and die, and in dying conquer.

The apostle's last words show us that he has found a way through the darkness with which his long imprisonment was covering his call and his work. How can Christ's messenger be kept in chains for years —the apostle to the Gentiles, who is to be the means of bringing about their fullness before Israel's conversion can become a reality and Christ returns in glory? We can see from another example how Paul realized that God, when men bar his way, finds a way round or else a shorter way to achieve his aim. It had seemed to many Christians as if God's promises had invalidated by Israel's No to the Gospel. That, however, was a fallacy, for God's promises cannot come to nothing; and Paul knew it. So, when Israel answered No, God had found a way for the promises to be fulfilled, first in a remnant of Israel and in the Gentiles then living; and in a short time they were to be realized in the fullness of the Gentiles, and thereby for all Israel.

The long imprisonment in Caesarea and Rome was another No to God's clear call and promise. By that No the apostle to the Gentiles was eliminated, and a halt called to his ceaseless efforts to secure the west's allegiance to Christ as he had secured that of the east. And yet that halt does not mean that Christ's calling of the apostle to the Gentiles was thereby made void, for even the imprisonment and the

---

[1] This idea, that when kings and princes acknowledge the Lord, the peoples will do so too, appears likewise in Isa. 49.7 ff.; 51.4 f.; cf. 45.23.

trial, sealed by death, open the possibility that the preaching of the word before the emperor will penetrate to all the Gentile nations. Thus the dying apostle will see his work completed, as the fullness of the Gentiles brings about the salvation of all Israel; and that hope was Paul's strongest incentive. Now salvation is near, and Christ's coming is at the door.

Paul had reached Rome on his way to Jerusalem. He had testified before the emperor, and his death was not far off. But the fullness of the Gentiles had become a reality, and the salvation of all Israel was to be expected. Then Christ was to manifest himself in glory, for judgment and for salvation. The apostle could therefore express in his usual matter-of-fact way what he had achieved: 'I have fought the good fight, I have finished the race, I have kept the faith.'

ABBREVIATIONS

For commentaries on the Acts and Pauline Epistles, a fuller reference is given in contexts where the author's name would not be a sufficient guide.

P. Althaus	*Der Brief an die Römer* (NTD 6), 1932
AMNSU	*Arbeiten und Mitteilungen aus dem Neutest-amentlichen Seminar zu Uppsala*
Arndt and Gingrich	*A Greek-English Lexicon of the New Testament* (tr. and ed. W. F. Arndt and F. W. Gingrich from W. Bauer, *Wörterbuch zu den Schriften des NT*[4], 1952), 1957
P. Bachmann	*Der erste Brief an die Korinther* (KNT 7)[2], 1910 *Der zweite Brief an die Korinther* (KNT 8), 1909
O. Bardenhewer	*Der Römerbrief des heiligen Paulus*, 1926
K. Barth	*Erklärung des Philipperbriefes*, 1928
Beginnings	*The Beginnings of Christianity*, ed. F. J. Foakes Jackson and Kirsopp Lake. Part I, The Acts of the Apostles, Vols. 1–5, 1920–33
H. W. Beyer	*Die Apostelgeschichte* (NTD 5)[4], 1947
BFCT	Beiträge zur Förderung christlicher Theologie
Billerbeck	H. L. Strack and P. Billerbeck, *Kommentar zum Neuen Testament aus Talmud und Midrasch* I–IV, 1922–8
BJRL	*Bulletin of the John Rylands Library*
Blass-Debrunner	F. Blass, *Grammatik des neutestamentlichen Grie-chisch*, bearbeitet von A. Debrunner, ed. 7, 1943
P. Bonnard	*L'Épître de Saint Paul aux Philippiens* (CNT 10), 1950
E. de Witt Burton	*Galatians* (ICC), 1921
BZNW	Beihefte zur *Zeitschrift für die neutestamentliche Wissenschaft*
A. C. Clark	*Acts*, 1933
CNT	Commentaire du Nouveau Testament
CSEL	*Corpus Scriptorum Ecclesiasticorum Latinorum*
M. Dibelius	*An die Thessalonicher I–II, An die Philipper* (HNT 11)[3], 1937 *Die Pastoralbriefe* (HNT 13)[2], 1931
C. H. Dodd	*Romans* (MNTC), 1932
G. S. Duncan	*Galatians* (MNTC), 1934

335

ET	English translation
Eusebius, *h.e.*	Eusebius, *historia ecclesiastica*
EvTh	*Evangelische Theologie*
EVV	English versions of the Bible
P. Ewald	*Der Brief des Paulus an die Philipper* (KNT 11), 1908
A. H. Franke	*Die Briefe an die Philipper, an die Kolosser und an Philemon* (Meyer 9)[5], 1886
D. A. Frövig	*Kommentar til Galaterbrevet*, 1950
GCS	*Die Griechischen Christlichen Schriftsteller der ersten drei Jahrhunderte*
Harnack, *Mission*	A. von Harnack, *Die Mission und Ausbreitung des Christentums in den ersten drei Jahrhunderten*[4] I, 1924 (references to ET of 2nd ed., *The Mission and Expansion of Christianity in the First Three Centuries*, 1908, added where appropriate)
E. Haupt	*An die Philipper, an die Kolosser und an Philemon* (Meyer 9)[6,7], 1897, 1902
C. F. G. Heinrici	*Erster Brief an die Korinther* (Meyer 5)[7], 1888 *Der zweite Brief an die Korinther* (Meyer 6)[7], 1890
G. Heinzelmann	*Der Brief an die Philipper* (NTD 8)[4], 1949
J. Héring	*La Première Épître de Saint Paul aux Corinthiens* (CNT 7), 1949
HNT	Handbuch zum Neuen Testament, ed. H. Lietzmann
H. J. Holtzmann	*Die Apostelgeschichte* (Hand-Kommentar zum NT I.2)[3], 1901
ICC	International Critical Commentary
F. J. Foakes Jackson	*Acts* (MNTC), 1931
Josephus, *Ant.*	Josephus, *Antiquities*
A. Jülicher	*Der Brief an die Römer* (Die Schriften des NT 2)[2], 1908
KNT	Kommentar zum Neuen Testament, ed. T. Zahn
L. J. Koch	*Fortolkning til Paulus' andet Brev til Korinthierne*[2], 1927
E. Kühl	*Der Brief des Paulus an die Römer*, 1913
M.-J. Lagrange	*Saint Paul: Épître aux Romains* (Études bibliques)[3], 1922 *Saint Paul: Épître aux Galates*, 1950

K. Lake and H. J. Cadbury	*The Acts of the Apostles: Translation and Commentary* (*Beginnings* 4), 1933
Liddell and Scott	H. G. Liddell and R. Scott, *Greek-English Lexicon*, new (9th) ed. revised by H. Stuart Jones and R. Mackenzie, 1925–40
H. Lietzmann	*An die Römer* (HNT 8)[3], 1928 *An die Korinther I–II* (HNT 9)[3], 1931 *An die Galater* (HNT 10)[3], 1932
J. B. Lightfoot	*Galatians*[10], 1890 *Philippians*[6], 1881
W. Lock	*The Pastoral Epistles* (ICC), 1924
E. Lohmeyer	*An die Philipper, an die Kolosser und an Philemon* (Meyer 9)[8], 1930
Meyer	Kritisch-exegetischer Kommentar über das Neue Testament, begründet von H. A. W. Meyer
MNTC	Moffatt New Testament Commentary
O. Moe	*Brevet til Romerne*[2], 1948
J. Moffatt	*I Corinthians* (MNTC), 1935
H. Mosbech	*Apostlenes Geringer*[2], 1938 *Første Korinterbrev*[2], 1950
Moulton and Milligan	J. H. Moulton and G. Milligan, *The Vocabulary of the Greek Testament*, 1914 ff.
Nestle	E. Nestle, *Novum Testamentum Graece*[20], 1950
n.F.	neue Folge
n.s.	new series
NTD	Das Neue Testament Deutsch
A. Pallis	*Romans*, 1920
par.	parallel(s)
PG	Migne, *Patrologia Graeca*
PL	Migne, *Patrologia Latina*
A. Plummer	*II Corinthians* (ICC), 1915
E. Preuschen	*Die Apostelgeschichte* (HNT 4.1), 1912
RHPR	*Revue d'Histoire et de Philosophie Religieuses*
A. Robertson and A. Plummer	*I Corinthians* (ICC)[2], 1914
W. Sanday and A. C. Headlam	*Romans* (ICC)[5], 1902

A. Schlatter	*Gottes Gerechtigkeit. Ein Kommentar zum Römer-brief*, 1935
H. Schlier	*Der Brief an die Galater* (Meyer 7)[10], 1949
Schürer	E. Schürer, *Geschichte des jüdischen Volkes im Zeitalter Jesu Christi*[4], 1901–11 (references to ET of 2nd ed., *A History of the Jewish People in the Time of Jesus Christ*, 1898–1900, are added where appropriate)
SEA	*Svensk exegetisk årsbok*
F. Sieffert	*Der Brief an die Galater* (Meyer 7)[7], 1886
SNTS	Studiorum Novi Testamenti Societas
C. Spicq	*Saint Paul: Les Épîtres Pastorales*[2], 1947
ST	*Studia Theologica*
StAns	*Studia Anselmiana*
STK	*Svensk teologisk kvartalskrift*
R. H. Strachan	*II Corinthians* (MNTC), 1935
TLZ	*Theologische Literaturzeitung*
TSK	*Theologische Studien und Kritiken*
TU	Texte und Untersuchungen zur Geschichte der altchristlichen Literatur
TWNT	*Theologisches Wörterbuch zum Neuen Testament*
TZ	*Theologische Zeitschrift*
UNT	Untersuchungen zum Neuen Testament
M. R. Vincent	*Philippians and Philemon* (ICC), 1922
B. Weiss	*Der Brief an die Römer*[9], 1899
J. Weiss	*Der erste Korintherbrief* (Meyer 5)[9], 1910
H.-D. Wendland	*Die Briefe an die Korinther* (NTD 7)[5], 1948
H. H. Wendt	*Die Apostelgeschichte* (Meyer 3)[9], 1913
H. Windisch	*Der zweite Korintherbrief* (Meyer 6)[9], 1924
T. Zahn	*Die Apostelgeschichte des Lucas* I–II, 1921 *Der Brief des Paulus an die Römer* (KNT 6), 1910 *Der Brief des Paulus an die Galater* (KNT 9), 1905
ZNW	*Zeitschrift für die neutestamentliche Wissenschaft*
ZRGG	*Zeitschrift für Religions- und Geistesgeschichte*
ZTK	*Zeitschrift für Theologie und Kirche*

INDEX OF REFERENCES

OLD TESTAMENT

APOCRYPHA AND OTHER LATER JEWISH WRITINGS

NEW TESTAMENT

EARLY CHRISTIAN WRITINGS

INDEX OF AUTHORS